# SUPERPLONK 2002

## ABOUT THE AUTHOR

Malcolm Gluck is wine correspondent of the *Guardian* newspaper. He is 104 years old and lives in London which he negotiates almost exclusively by bicycle. He is known to exaggerate – but never about wine.

# SUPERPLONK 2002

## MALCOLM GLUCK

**CORONET BOOKS**
Hodder & Stoughton

Copyright © 2001 by Malcolm Gluck
First published in Great Britain in 2001 by Hodder and Stoughton
A division of Hodder Headline

The right of Malcolm Gluck to be identified as the Author of the Work has been
asserted by him in accordance with the Copyright, Designs and Patents Act 1988.

A Coronet paperback

1 3 5 7 9 10 8 6 4 2

A CIP catalogue record for this title is available from the British Library

ISBN 0 340 82378 X

Typeset by Rowland Phototypesetting Ltd,
Bury St Edmunds, Suffolk
Printed and bound in Great Britain by
Clays Ltd, St Ives plc

Hodder and Stoughton
A division of Hodder Headline
338 Euston Road
London NW1 3BH

To Barrie Gibson, David Stewart, Simon Cooper and Paul Trelford for introducing me, via *superplonk.com*, to the 21st century

'. . . I love corn and wine. They are our chief and our oldest luxuries. Time has brought us substitutes, but how inferior! Man has deified corn and wine but not even the Chinese or the Irish have raised temples to tea and potatoes.'

From *Coningsby*, by Benjamin Disraeli

# CONTENTS

# INTRODUCTION

Ever mindful of Ecclesiastes 2:3 – 'I sought in mine heart to give myself unto wine' – I became a writer on the subject in the late 1980s. The first *Superplonk* column appeared in the *Guardian* thirteen years ago. The wine guides quickly followed.

It occurred to me I might be read; might find appreciative readers. What I never anticipated was how much critical lather my championing of good value wine would cause to bubble out of the pens of the incensed, the entrenched, the green-eyed, the me-too hacked off, and the various noodleheads that collectively form the bulk of the wine media and the wine book reviewing fraternity.

If I gave the matter of my new career path any thought it was that I would quietly and industriously beaver away in my little corner, drinking my way along the nation's wine shelves and reporting on my findings, whilst the rest of humanity, *Guardian* readers and *Superplonk* guide buyers excepted, would cheerfully ignore me, as we do the rarer breeds of flat-worm. But it was not to be.

My very first annual wine guide, in January 1991, was greeted with mild disdain but it was the second, that same year in November, which caused hackles to rise in certain quarters and a certain rural wine merchant wrote to Faber & Faber, my then publisher, announcing his disgust that someone should seek to popularise the wine in supermarkets. He would, he added charmingly, like to shoot the author. His own business, it was revealed, was struggling to survive in the face of the then vicious recession and it was I who was driving him on to the rocks.

The newspaper reviewers began to take notice of the book and generally, as the years rolled by and with each one a fresh edition of the guide appeared, the sound of grinding axes was deafening. One mistake I made, or rather the publishers did, was to permit the book to become top of its category in the Best Sellers charts in *The Sunday Times* year after year. It was also the only wine book to feature annually amongst the One Hundred Top Selling books of the year.

It was not a good way to become popular with the dinosaurs: the stick-in-the-mud wine merchants, the long-established wine scribes, the old boys and girls brigade. And, when I compiled a vast list of all the reviews, stinking and fragrant, I had received over the years since the first *Superplonk* was published and wrote it up as this current book's introduction, it was not a good way to become popular with my publisher. 'It's 17,000 words long!' she expostulated. 'Stick it on the website. Spare your readers so lengthy an introduction.'

And so I did. However, never one to throw good work away, and mindful that it took me many months to compile with the help of Linda Peskin, my assistant, I have done as advised. If you want to trawl through what I put together then please visit *superplonk.com*, access Articles, and go to Brickbats & Bouquets – 12 years of critical response to *Superplonk*.

# HOW I RATE A WINE

Value for money is my single unwavering focus. I drink with my readers' pockets in my mouth. I do not see the necessity of paying a lot for a bottle of everyday drinking wine and only rarely do I consider it worth paying a high price for, say, a wine for a special occasion or because you want to experience what a so-called 'grand' wine may be like. There is more codswallop talked and written about wine, especially the so-called 'grand' stuff, than any subject except sex. The stench of this gobbledygook regularly perfumes wine merchants' catalogues, spices the backs of bottles, and rancidises the writings of those infatuated by or in the pay of producers of a particular wine region. I do taste expensive wines regularly. I do not, regularly, find them worth the money. That said, there are some pricey bottles in these pages. They are here either because I wish to provide an accurate, but low, rating of their worth so that readers will be given pause for thought or because the wine is genuinely worth every penny. A wine of magnificent complexity, thrilling fruit, superb aroma, great depth and finesse is worth drinking. I would not expect it to be an inexpensive bottle. I will rate it highly. I wish all wines which commanded such high prices were so well deserving of an equally high rating. The thing is, of course, that many bottles of wine I taste do have finesse and depth but do not come attached to an absurdly high price tag. These are the bottles I prize most. As, I hope, you will.

**20** Is outstanding and faultless in all departments: smell, taste and finish in the throat. Worth the price, even if you have to take out a second mortgage.

**19** A superb wine. Almost perfect and well worth the expense (if it is an expensive bottle).

**18** An excellent wine but lacking that ineffable sublimity of richness and complexity to achieve the very highest rating. But superb drinking and thundering good value.

17 An exciting, well-made wine at an affordable price which offers real glimpses of multi-layered richness.

16 Very good wine indeed. Good enough for *any* dinner party. Not expensive but terrifically drinkable, satisfying and multi-dimensional – properly balanced.

15 For the money, a good mouthful with real style. Good flavour and fruit without costing a packet.

14 The top end of the everyday drinking wine. Well made and to be seriously recommended at the price.

13 Good wine, true to its grape(s). Not great, but very drinkable.

12 Everyday drinking wine at a sensible price. Not exciting, but worthy.

11 Drinkable, but not a wine to dwell on. You don't wed a wine like this, though you might take it behind the bike shed with a bag of fish and chips.

10 Average wine (at a low price), yet still just about a passable mouthful. Also, wines which are terribly expensive and, though drinkable, cannot justify their high price.

9 Cheap plonk. Just about fit for parties in dustbin-sized dispensers.

8 On the rough side here.

7 Good for pickling onions or cleaning false teeth.

6 Hardly drinkable except on an icy night by a raging bonfire.

5 Wine with more defects than delights.

4 Not good at any price.

3 Barely drinkable.

2  Seriously – did this wine come from grapes?

1  The utter pits. The producer should be slung in prison.

The rating system above can be broken down into six broad sections.

0  to 10 : Avoid – unless entertaining stuffy wine writer.

10 , 11 : Nothing poisonous but, though drinkable, rather dull.

12 , 13 : Above average, interestingly made. Solid rather then sensational.

14 , 15 , 16 : This is the exceptional, hugely drinkable stuff, from the very good to the brilliant.

17 , 18 : Really wonderful wine worth anyone's money: complex, rich, exciting.

19 , 20 : A toweringly brilliant world-class wine of self-evident style and individuality.

## PRICES

It is impossible to guarantee the price of any wine in this guide. This is why instead of printing the exact shop price, each wine is given a price bracket. This attempts to eliminate the problem of printing the wrong price for a wine. This can occur for all the usual boring but understandable reasons: inflation, economic conditions overseas, the narrow margins on some supermarket wines making it difficult to maintain consistent prices and, of course, the existence of those freebooters at the Exchequer who are liable to inflate taxes which the supermarkets cannot help but pass on. But even price bracketing is not foolproof. A wine listed in the book at, say, a lower price bracket might be on sale at a higher bracket. How? Because a wine close to but under, say, £3.50 in spring when I tasted it might sneak across the border in summer. It happens rarely enough not to concern me overmuch, but wine is an agricultural import, a sophisticated liquid food, and that makes it volatile where price is concerned. Frankly, I admire the way in which retailers have kept prices so stable for so many years. We drink cheaper (and healthier) wine now than we did thirty years ago.

## NOTE:

The prices of 3-litre wine boxes have been adjusted to their 75cl bottle equivalent.

## HEALTH WARNING!

Health Warning is an arresting phrase and I have used it for some years now. I hope by employing it I may save you from working yourself up into a state. Let me explain.

I get a few letters a week from readers (both column and book) telling me that a wine which I have said is on sale in a certain supermarket is not there and that the wine has either sold out or the branch claims to have no knowledge of it; I get letters telling me that a wine is a bit dearer than I said it was; and I get the odd note revealing that the vintage of the 16-point wine I have enthused about and which my correspondent desperately wants to buy is different from the one listed.

First of all, let me say that no wine guide in the short and inglorious history of the genre is more exhaustively researched, checked and double-checked than this one. I do not list a wine if I do not have assurances from its retailer that it will be widely on sale when the guide is published. Where a wine is on restricted distribution, or stocks are short and vulnerable to the assault of determined readers (i.e. virtually all high-rating, very cheap bottles), I will always clearly say so. However, large retailers use computer systems which cannot anticipate uncommon demand and which often miss the odd branch off the anticipated stocking list. I cannot check every branch myself (though I do nose around them when I can) and so a wine in this book may well, infuriatingly, be missing at the odd branch of its retailer and may not even be heard of by the branch simply because of inhuman error. Conversely, the same technology often tells a retailer's head office that a wine is out of stock when it has merely been cleared out of the warehouse. It may still be on sale in certain branches. Then there is the fact that not every wine I write about is stocked by every single branch of its listed supermarket. Every store has what are called retail plans and there may be half a dozen of these, and every wine is subject to a different stocking policy according to the dictates of these cold-hearted plans.

I accept a wine as being in healthy distribution if several hundred branches, all over the country not just in selected parts of it, stock the wine. Do not assume, however, that this means every single branch has the wine.

I cannot, equally, guarantee that every wine in this book will still be in the same price bracket as printed. The vast majority will be. But there will always be the odd bottle from a country suddenly subject to a vicious swing in currency rates, or subject to an unprecedented rise in production costs which the supermarket cannot or is not prepared to swallow, and so a few pennies will get added to the price. If it is pounds, then you have cause for legitimate grievance. Please write to me. But don't lose a night's sleep if a wine is 20p more than I said it is. If you must, write to the appropriate supermarket. The department and the address to write to is provided with each supermarket's entry.

Now the puzzle of differing vintages. When I list and rate a wine, I do so only for the vintage stated. Any other vintage is a different wine requiring a new rating. Where vintages do have little difference in fruit quality, and more than a single vintage is on sale, then I say this clearly. If two vintages are on sale, and vary in quality and/or style, then they will be separately rated. However, be aware of one thing.

*Superplonk* is the biggest-selling wine guide in the Queendom. I say this not to brag but, more important, to acquaint you with a reality which may cause you some irritation. When *Superplonk* appears on sale there will be lots of eager drinkers aiming straight for the highest-rating wines as soon as possible after the book is published. Thus the supermarket wine buyer who assures me that she has masses of stock of Domaine Piddlewhatsit and the wine will withstand the most virulent of sieges may find her shelves emptying in a tenth of the time she banked on – not knowing, of course, how well I rate the wine until the book goes on sale. It is entirely possible, therefore, that the vintage of a highly rated wine may sell out so quickly that new stocks of the follow-on vintage may be urgently brought on to the shelf before I have tasted them. This can happen in some instances. I offer a bunch of perishable pansies, not a wreath of immortelles. I can do nothing about this fact of wine writing life, except to give up writing about wine.

Lastly, one thing more:

*'Wine is a hostage to several fortunes (weather being even more uncertain and unpredictable than exchange rates) but the wine writer is hostage to just one: he cannot pour for his readers precisely the same wine as he poured for himself.'*

This holds true for every wine in this book and every wine I will write about in the years to come (for as long as my liver holds out). I am sent wines to taste regularly and I attend wine tastings all the time. If a wine is corked on these occasions, that is to say in poor condition because it has been tainted by the tree bark which is its seal, then it is not a problem for a bottle in decent condition to be quickly supplied for me to taste. This is not, alas, a luxury which can be extended to my readers.

So if you find a wine not to your taste because it seems pretty foul or 'off' in some way, then do not assume that my rating system is up the creek; you may take it that the wine is faulty and must be returned as soon as possible to its retailer. Every retailer in this book is pledged to provide an instant refund for any faulty wine returned – no questions asked. I am not asking readers to share all my tastes in wine, or to agree completely with every rating for every wine. But where a wine I have rated well is obviously and patently foul then it is a duff bottle and you should be compensated by getting a fresh bottle free or by being given a refund.

# ACKNOWLEDGEMENTS

I am responsible for every word in this book and for tasting all its wines. I do not, however, function alone. Linda Peskin, who checks all the wines for vintages, prices and availability for my weekly *Guardian* column, is responsible for data entry and management of the wine entries for this book. In order for me to write the introductions to each retailer I am indebted to Ben Cooper who does the background research. I am also beholden to various bodies (forever busy) at my publishers: Martin Neild (concerned with my contract and performance), Rowena Webb (who is my editor), Sheila Crowley (who directs the sales team), Karen Geary (who directs publicity), Jamie Hodder-Williams (who directs marketing), Emma Heyworth-Dunn who oversaw the copy-editing and Lyn Parry who did it. I am also grateful to the tireless Georgina Moore who directs herself (into my annual tour of the nation's bookshops). Significant in the shadows are my literary agents Felicity Rubinstein, Sarah Lutyens, and Susannah Godman. I am also in debt to Paul Trelford, *superplonk.com*'s website editor, who supervised the Stop Press data entry.

# PART 1

# A TO Z OF COUNTRIES

# ARGENTINA

Could become the greatest organic vineyard in the world.

## ASDA RED

**Argentinian Bonarda 1999, Asda** `14.5` `−£5.00`

**Argentinian Syrah 1999, Asda** `16` `−£5.00`
Not remotely like Aussie Shiraz or Rhône Syrah, this spicy, rich, deeply textured, well-fruited wine is a revelation. Great concentration of elements.

**Casa Latina Shiraz Tempranillo 1999** `16` `−£5.00`
Terrific buzz about this ripe, tannically-rich wine. Has a plump texture which really sticks to the taste buds. Selected stores.

**Far Flung El Montero Shiraz Reserva 2000** `14` `£5–7`
Rather demure for an Argentinian Shiraz, even though it gallops off in fine style but then canters as it gets to the finish . . . and then becomes rather benign when I wanted more danger.

**Far Flung Malbec 2000** `15` `−£5.00`
Very juicy opening then delicious slow-moving tannins evolve.

**La Nature Organic Barbera 2000** `14` `−£5.00`
Sweet and rich. Great with Indian food.

**Nieto Senetiner Bonarda Reserva 2000** `15` `£5–7`
Very busy-as-a-bee richness and spicy tannins with a lingering aftertaste of cocoa. A wine to appal the snob.

**Nieto Senetiner Merlot Reserva 2000** `14` `£5–7`
Very ripe coating to the plums which turns out to be currants. Then tannins strike and grip. Very individual approach to Merlot I've not trodden before.

**Santa Julia Tempranillo Reserva 1999** `16.5` `£5–7`
Delicious! Delicious! Delicious! I'll say it again . . .

## BOOTHS RED

**El Montonero Bonarda Barbera 1999** `15.5` `−£5.00`

**Finca el Retiro Malbec, Mendoza 2000** `16.5` `£5–7`
Terrific textured plums and ripe

blackcurrants. Good tannins and a rousing savoury finish.

**Libertad Malbec** `14.5` `−£5.00`
**Bonarda 2000**
Rich and ready.

**Mission Peak Red NV** `15.5` `−£3.50`

**Terrazas Alto Cabernet** `14.5` `£5−7`
**Sauvignon 1999**

## BUDGENS RED

**Argento Malbec 2000** `17.5` `−£5.00`
Supremely well-textured and aromatic, complex and dusted with finely wrought tannins, this is simply one of the best wines in the world under a fiver. It delivers such style, class and deliciousness for the money that it seems almost unfair to rate it and thus compare it with reds from France, Italy, Spain, Australia, South Africa and Chile.

**Etchart Rio de Plata** `14` `−£5.00`
**Tempranillo/Malbec**
**1999**
Needs a good spicy banger in front of it.

**La Nature Organic** `14` `−£5.00`
**Barbera 2000**
Sweet and rich. Great with Indian food.

## CO-OP RED

**Adiseno Cabernet** `16` `−£5.00`
**Sauvignon Shiraz 1999**
An affront to civilised values this

rumbustiously rich, outspoken wine. It's hugely loveable, ripe, textured, fleshy and deep and it never shuts up. Great stuff. Superstores only.

**Adiseno Shiraz Reserve** `16` `£5−7`
**1999**
Delicious creamy richness and very smooth tannins. An individual approach to the Shiraz conundrum: do you make it dry or jammy? Here, triumphantly, it is both. Superstores only.

**Adiseno Tempranillo** `15.5` `−£5.00`
**2000**
Delicious plums – with aplomb. Better than many a Rioja.

**Argentine Malbec 2000,** `16` `−£5.00`
**Co-op**
Delicious meaty richness and controlled rampancy of attack – fine tannins, fine fruit.

**Argentine Malbec** `15.5` `−£5.00`
**Bonarda 2000, Co-op**
Brilliant value, brilliant wine. The Malbec gives the jammier Bonarda bite and character.

**Argentine Old Vines** `16` `−£5.00`
**Sangiovese 2000, Co-op**
Out-points any Chianti at the same price because of its weight, lovely toasty finish, and exquisite tannins.

**Argento Malbec 1999** `16` `−£5.00`
Steals across the tastebuds with beautifully textured, soft fruit.

**Bianchi Cabernet** `17` `£7−10`
**Sauvignon 1996**

A stunningly well-composed wine of restraint yet full-blooded richness. The acids and tannins supply the guile, the fruit the gentle spice and firm cassis and chocolate edging. A terrific wine for all sorts of roast bird. Superstores only.

**Bin 99 Argentine**  `16`  `£5–7`
**Cabernet Franc Reserve**
**1999, Co-op**
Exotic hints of wild herbs, gravy, gunsmoke and charred fruit (blackcurrants and plums). Is there a hint of chive and coriander? Terrific food wine. Not at Convenience Stores.

**Corte X Syrah**  `13`  `–£5.00`
**Torrontes 2000, Co-op**
Odd blend of red and a little white (grapes).

**Elsa Barbera 1999**  `15.5`  `–£5.00`

**Graffigna Shiraz**  `16`  `–£5.00`
**Cabernet Sauvignon**
**1999**
Such superb tannins – absolutely delicious. And they coat cherries, plums and blackcurrants with great verve.

**Graffigna Shiraz**  `15.5`  `–£5.00`
**Reserve 1999**
Delicious complexity and dry-to-finish styling in this wine, which carries compelling tannins, firm and savoury. Superstores only.

**La Nature Organic**  `14`  `–£5.00`
**Barbera 2000**
Sweet and rich. Great with Indian food.

**Lost Pampas Cabernet**  `14`  `–£5.00`
**Malbec 1999, Co-op**

**Mission Peak Argentine**  `15.5`  `–£3.50`
**Red NV**

**Valentin Bianchi**  `16`  `£7–10`
**Cabernet Sauvignon**
**1997**
Very big and rich and soft and gently spicy with big tannins.

**Weinert Malbec 1994**  `16`  `£7–10`
Again, the superb creamy tannins of Argentina give the wine distinctive richness.

## M & S RED

**Canale Estate Reserve**  `16`  `£7–10`
**Merlot 1999**
Curious celery undertone to the finish which displays great tannic virtuosity. A wonderful food wine: game, rare meats, cheeses (especially ripe cheddar).

**Rio Santos Bonarda**  `14.5`  `–£5.00`
**Barbera 2000**
Cinnamon-edged cherries and plums.

**Rio Santos Cabernet**  `15.5`  `–£5.00`
**Sauvignon Syrah 2000**
Coriander-edged blackberries, plums and some dried raspberry. Delicious approachable Cabernet.

**Rio Santos Malbec 2000**  `16.5`  `–£5.00`
Superbly structured and brilliantly textured. Cassis, hint of chocolate, touch of cappuccino.

**San Pablo Estate NV**  `16`  `£7–10`
Very smooth delivery of
effortlessly produced sensations of
soft fruits coated with ripe
tannins. A superb blend of grapes
offering boldness, dexterity and
brilliant texture.

**Villar Cortes Cabernet**  `15.5`  `£7–10`
**Sauvignon 1999**
A big juicy Cab driven by the
plums rather than the tannins.

## MORRISONS RED

**Balbi Barbaro 1997**  `16`  `£7–10`
A treat for rich game dishes. The
fruit is packed with flavour –
from raspberries to spiced prunes
– and the tannins are electric.

**Balbi Malbec 1999**  `15.5`  `–£5.00`
Gripping softness – how
amazing! What a paradox! What
a puzzle!

**Balbi Shiraz 1999**  `13`  `–£5.00`
Intensely jammy.

**La Nature Organic**  `14`  `–£5.00`
**Barbera 2000**
Sweet and rich. Great with Indian
food.

**Santa Julia Bonarda**  `16`  `–£5.00`
**Sangiovese 1999**
Superb from nose to throat to
brain cells. Enticing savoury
aroma, deep rich berries for the
tongue and brilliant lingering
tannins for the throat.

## SAFEWAY RED

**Adiseno Reserve**  `15`  `£5–7`
**Malbec 1999**

**Argentinian Bonarda**  `15`  `–£5.00`
**2000, Safeway**
Warm, rich, gently spicy fruit
with a touch of jam but also fine
tannins which are wholly wedded
to the texture.

**Argentinian Cabernet**  `14`  `–£5.00`
**Sauvignon 2000,**
**Safeway**
Juicy, jammy, joyous and
injudicious – except with spicy
food.

**Argentinian Syrah 2000,**  `15.5`  `–£5.00`
**Safeway**
Big, exuberant, coffee-edged
berries, soft tannins, and a finish
of pure chutzpah. Offensively
plump and modern.

**Caballo de Plata**  `13`  `–£3.50`
**Bonarda/Barbera 2000**

**Weinert Malbec 1994**  `16`  `£7–10`
Again, the superb creamy tannins
of Argentina give the wine
distinctive richness. 79 stores.

## SAINSBURY'S RED

**Alamos Ridge Cabernet**  `16.5`  `£5–7`
**Sauvignon 1997**
Compellingly soft yet thickly
knitted fruit of huge style and
precision. Incredibly well-tailored
yet has character and bite. Great
class, terrific polish, loads of
richness. Selected stores.

**Bright Brothers Barrica** `16` `£5–7`
**Cabernet Shiraz 1999**
Comes across like an Aussie with
attitude – thanks to the tannins.
Terrific red wine. Classy, bold,
full of character and beguiling
fruit. 100 selected stores.

**Finca el Retiro Bonarda** `14.5` `£5–7`
**2000**
Juicy fruity curry wine – with the
saving grace of some suave
tannins. Selected stores.

**La Nature Organic** `14` `–£5.00`
**Barbera 2000**
Sweet and rich. Great with Indian
food. 180 selected stores.

**Mendoza Cabernet** `15.5` `–£5.00`
**Sauvignon/Malbec NV,**
**Sainsbury's**
Vibrant juicy fruit with tannins
and authority and balance. An
excellent quaffing red and a wine
for roast vegetables and cheese
dishes.

**Mendoza Country Red** `15` `–£3.50`
**NV, Sainsbury's**

**Santa Julia Tempranillo** `16` `–£5.00`
**2000**
Joyously slurpable and worthy (of
food, companionship, reflective
pursuits). It has softness, stealth
and great generosity. Most
stores.

## SOMERFIELD RED

**Argentine Red 2000,** `15` `–£3.50`
**Somerfield**
Brilliant tippling for the money:

dry rich fruit of great charm.

**Argentine Sangiovese** `16.5` `–£5.00`
**2000, Somerfield**
Superb! If only Chianti could be
this thrilling for the money.

**Argentine Tempranillo** `16` `–£5.00`
**2000, Somerfield**
Stunning texture and class of fruit
for the money.

**Argento Malbec 2000** `17.5` `–£5.00`
Supremely well-textured and
aromatic, complex and dusted
with finely wrought tannins, this
is simply one of the best wines in
the world under a fiver. It
delivers such style, class and
deliciousness for the money that
it seems almost unfair to rate it
and thus compare it with reds
from France, Italy, Spain,
Australia, South Africa and Chile.
Most stores.

**Bright Brothers Barrica** `16` `£5–7`
**Cabernet Shiraz 1999**
Comes across like an Aussie with
attitude – thanks to the tannins.
Terrific red wine. Classy, bold,
full of character and beguiling
fruit.

**Bright Brothers Barrica** `15.5` `£5–7`
**Shiraz 1999**
Chewy coconut and cassis fruit of
depth and daring. Selected stores.

**Bright Brothers San** `16` `£5–7`
**Juan Cabernet**
**Sauvignon 2000**
What depth! What chutzpah!!
What fruit!!!

**Santa Julia Oaked Tempranillo 2000**   16.5  −£5.00
Superb tannins, savoury fruit, alert acids, and a wholly integrated performance from nose to throat.

**Trivento Syrah 2000**   16  −£5.00
Very rich with cocoa-coated tannins.

## SPAR RED

**Argentinian Del Sur 1999, Spar**   14  −£5.00
Meaty richness, decent tannins, some breadth to the fruit and a fair finish.

## TESCO RED

**Argento Malbec 2000**   17.5  −£5.00
Supremely well-textured and aromatic, complex and dusted with finely wrought tannins, this is simply one of the best wines in the world under a fiver. It delivers such style, class and deliciousness for the money that it seems almost unfair to rate it and thus compare it with reds from France, Italy, Spain, Australia, South Africa and Chile. Most stores.

**Bright Brothers Barrica Reserve Cabernet Sauvignon/Shiraz 1998**   15  £5–7

**Catena Cabernet Sauvignon 1996**   17  £7–10
A quite compellingly

concentrated amalgam of very comely Cabernet vegetality and subtle spiciness and big tannins. An excellent bottle for festive lunch (or dinner) where its presence at table will be more amusing, and more explosive, than the funniest Christmas cracker. Available at the 25 Wine Advisor Stores only.

**Deep Purple Shiraz 2000**   14  −£5.00
Love the tannins, not sure about the fruit (and the bottle which is distracting). Most stores.

**Monster Spicy Red Syrah NV, Tesco**   16  −£5.00
Rampant, ripe, rich and very ready for anything the spiciest chef can throw at it, this is an affront to the palate of the stuffy connoisseur but for easy drinking, quaffability and for matching with meat and cheese dishes this is a terrific wine.

**Picajuan Peak Bonarda 2000**   15.5  −£5.00
Lovely texture here which properly knits the meaty fruit, the fine acids and the rich tannins so well together.

**Picajuan Peak Malbec 2000, Tesco**   15  −£5.00
Lovely savoury soupiness saved from stupidity by superb tannins and succulent rich fruit. Most stores.

**Picajuan Peak Sangiovese 2000, Tesco**   14.5  −£5.00

Better than many a Chianti with the same grape. Has a fine texture to it and well-integrated fruit and tannins.

**Q Tempranillo 1998**  16.5  £7–10
This is what more Riojas should be like: energetic, rich, tobacco-tinged, deep, jammy but dry, and full of flavoursome layers of surprises.

**Santa Julia Bonarda/**  15  £5–7
**Sangiovese Reserva**
**1999**
Very rich fruit, good for spicy food. Selected stores.

**Santa Julia Merlot Oak**  15.5  −£5.00
**Aged 2000**
Lovely ripe tannins and cherry/plum fruit. Delicious quaffing. Selected stores.

**Santa Julia Oaked**  16.5  −£5.00
**Tempranillo 2000**
Superb tannins, savoury fruit, alert acids, and a wholly integrated performance from nose to throat.

## WAITROSE RED

**Balbi Malbec Reserva,**  14  £5–7
**Mendoza 1999**
Super ripe richness. Good with spicy food.

**Familia Zuccardi Q**  16  £7–10
**Merlot 1998**
Delicious cheeky, classy ripeness and smokey tannins. Mail Order only.

**Finca el Retiro Malbec,**  16.5  £5–7
**Mendoza 2000**
Terrific textured plums and ripe blackcurrants. Good tannins and a rousing savoury finish.

**Santa Julia Bonarda/**  17  −£5.00
**Sangiovese 2000**
Utterly superb. Wondrous richness and tannic tenacity. Fantastic bargain.

**Trivento Sangiovese,**  14  −£5.00
**Mendoza 2000**
Thick as jam.

## ASDA WHITE

**Argentinian White NV,**  14  −£3.50
**Asda**

**Argento Chardonnay**  17  −£5.00
**2000**
More convincing than many a Meursault at five times the price for it parades fruit of great finesse yet determined flavour and poised ripeness. A delicious, high-class wine of charm and distinctiveness.

**Candela Viognier 2000**  15  £5–7
Since I danced under a full moon (in the vineyard) with this wine's maker, do not suppose I am fatally compromised – alas. It has a fine apricot opening, some middling peachy fruit, and a hint of tangy lemon on the finish. It offers more class than my dancing style.

**Far Flung Viognier**  16.5  −£5.00
**2000**

Beautiful dry apricot fruit with a touch of crème brulée on the finish or is it gunsmoke? Well, it's a delicate beauty for all that but a hugely elegant aperitif.

## BOOTHS WHITE

**Libertad Chenin Sauvignon 2000**  `13`  `−£5.00`
Very dry and a touch reluctant.

**Terrazas Alto Chardonnay 2000**  `14.5`  `£5−7`
Touches of cloying melon. Needs spicy food.

## BUDGENS WHITE

**Argento Chardonnay 2001**  `15.5`  `−£5.00`
Not as gripping as the 2000 but still has classy texture and layered fruit. Almost lazy elegance about it.

**Etchart Rio de Plata Torrontes/ Chardonnay 2000**  `12`  `−£5.00`
Bit raw on the finish.

**La Nature Organic Torrontes 2000**  `14`  `−£5.00`
Delicious little aperitif with lemon and pistachio nuts.

## CO-OP WHITE

**Balbi Shiraz Rosé 2000**  `13`  `−£5.00`
Rich and sticky.

**Bright Brothers Viognier Reserve 1999**  `15`  `£5−7`

**Elsa Semillon Chardonnay 2000**  `14.5`  `−£5.00`
Nervously crisp edge of some wit. Good with food. Superstores only.

**Etchart Rio de Plata Torrontes 2000**  `15.5`  `−£5.00`
Utterly delicious grapey aperitif. Really lovely set-up prior to a meal. Superstores only.

**First Ever Chardonnay 2000**  `13.5`  `−£5.00`

**La Nature Organic Torrontes 2000**  `14`  `−£5.00`
Delicious little aperitif with lemon and pistachio nuts.

**Lost Pampas Oaked Chardonnay 1999, Co-op**  `16`  `−£5.00`
Lovely nutty fruit, chewy and fresh, hint of lettuce crispness.

**Mission Peak Argentine White NV**  `15.5`  `−£3.50`

**Y2K Chardonnay, San Juan 1999**  `16`  `−£5.00`
Very fresh – saves its melon richness for the back of the throat.

## M & S WHITE

**Rio Santos Torrontes 2000**  `14`  `−£5.00`
A precise, crisp, aperitif-style, subtle grapey white.

## MORRISONS WHITE

**Etchart Rio de Plata** `12` `−£5.00`
**Torrontes/**
**Chardonnay 2000**
Bit raw on the finish.

**La Nature Organic** `14` `−£5.00`
**Torrontes 2000**
Delicious little aperitif with
lemon and pistachio nuts.

## SAFEWAY WHITE

**Argentinian** `16` `−£5.00`
**Chardonnay 1999,**
**Safeway**
Delightful union of buttery
ripeness, and melon and
pineapple acidity.

**Caballo de Plata** `15.5` `−£5.00`
**Shiraz/Malbec Rosada**
**2000**
Very interesting and unusual rosé
of thickly textured cherries and
plum. Has a jammy tone
mitigated by good acids and
overall dryness.

**Caballo de Plata** `13.5` `−£3.50`
**Torrontes 2000**

## SAINSBURY'S WHITE

**La Nature Organic** `14` `−£5.00`
**Torrontes 2000**
Delicious little aperitif with
lemon and pistachio nuts.

**Mendoza Chardonnay,** `15` `−£5.00`
**Tupungato Region NV,**
**Sainsbury's**

Dry, elegant, restrained,
underripe but with a slightly oily
texture which is fluid on the
finish and reminiscent of nuts and
melon. Most stores.

**Mendoza Country** `14.5` `−£3.50`
**White NV, Sainsbury's**

## SOMERFIELD WHITE

**Argentine Chardonnay** `15.5` `−£5.00`
**2000, Somerfield**
Deliciously textured, slightly
buttery fruit. Very classy and dry.

**Bright Brothers San** `15.5` `£5−7`
**Juan Chardonnay 2000**
Rich creamy consistency without
being cloying.

**Etchart Torrontes** `14` `−£5.00`
**Chardonnay 2000**
Amusing nutty, grapey aperitif
wine.

**La Nature Organic** `14` `−£5.00`
**Torrontes 2000**
Delicious little aperitif with
lemon and pistachio nuts.
Selected stores.

**Q Chardonnay, La** `15.5` `£7−10`
**Agricola 1999**
Bitter almonds, underripe
gooseberry, melon and lemon.
Class act. Selected stores.

**Santa Julia Syrah Rosé** `15` `−£5.00`
**2001**
Lovely dry cherries.

## SPAR WHITE

**Argentinian Del Sur 2000, Spar**  14  −£5.00
Meaty richness and ripeness. Good with chicken dishes. Individual taste as it finishes.

## TESCO WHITE

**Argentinian Torrontes 1999, Tesco**  13  −£3.50

**Argento Chardonnay 2000**  17  −£5.00
More convincing than many a Meursault at five times the price for it parades fruit of great finesse yet determined flavour and poised ripeness. A delicious, high-class wine of charm and distinctiveness.

**La Nature Organic Torrontes 2000**  14  −£5.00
Delicious little aperitif with lemon and pistachio nuts.

**Picajuan Peak Chardonnay 2000, Tesco**  15.5  −£5.00
Lovely balance of elements which strike warmly yet refreshingly showing melon, pear and lemon. Real bargain quaffing here. Most stores.

**Seriously Fruity Rosé NV, Tesco**  14.5  −£5.00
Curiously, not as fruity as it sounds though ideally suited to rich food. Most stores.

## WAITROSE WHITE

**Bodega Lurton Pinot Gris, Mendoza 2000**  15  −£5.00
Delicious edge of peach, cobnut, and lemon and gooseberry on the finish.

**Catena Agrelo Vineyards Chardonnay 1999**  15  £7–10
Very ripe and rich and in need of ripe rich food.

**Chenin Blanc/ Torrontes, Mendoza 2000, Waitrose**  14  −£5.00
Very dry and calm – almost too calm. Unspicy but has some elegance to the texture.

**Santa Julia Viognier Reserve 2000**  16  £5–7
Brilliant apricot dryness and concentrated texture.

**Trivento Chardonnay 2000**  14  −£5.00
Very rich and gooey.

# AUSTRALIA

To the horror of the French, it's breathing down their necks in the race to dominate the UK wine market.

## ASDA RED

**Andrew Peace Cabernet Merlot 1999** 15 £5–7

**Fox River Pinot Noir 1998** 13 £5–7

**Houghtons Shiraz 1998** 15 £5–7

**La Nature Organic Shiraz Cabernet 1999** 13.5 –£5.00
Mingles jammy berries with gravy-edged tannins. Suits game dishes.

**Maglieri Shiraz 1998** 15.5 £7–10

**Normans Estates Lone Gum Cabernet Merlot 2000** 12 –£5.00
Very sweet and adolescent.

**Normans Estates Pinot Noir 1999** 10 £5–7
Almost without varietal expression.

**Normans Estates Yarra Valley Cabernet 1998** 14 £7–10
Very ripe and forward and in need of robust food.

**Secession Xanadu Shiraz/Cabernet 1999** 15 £5–7
Brilliant spicy juice. A textured curry wine.

**Temple Bruer Shiraz/Malbec 1998** 16.5 £5–7
A wonderfully adult blend of rich jammy Shiraz and dry, tannic Malbec. The marriage is harmonious and energetic, food-friendly and deliciously deep.

**The Potts Family Bleasdale Malbec 2000** 13 £5–7
Very juicy and ripe and ultimately fails to clinch more points because of the looseness of the finish which flops over the taste buds rather than gripping them.

**Vine Vale Grenache 1998 (Peter Lehmann)** 15 £5–7

**Wolf Blass Yellow Label Cabernet Sauvignon 1999** 14 £7–10
Big rich curry wine. Joyous, jolly, jammy.

**Wyndham Estate Bin 444 Cabernet Sauvignon 1998** 15 £5–7
Nice compactness and elegance here.

## BOOTHS RED

**Australian Red Shiraz** `14` –£5.00
**Cabernet Sauvignon**
**NV, Booths**

**Brown Brothers** `13` –£5.00
**Tarrango 2000**
Like fruit juice.

**CV Capel Vale Shiraz** `14.5` £7–10
**1998**
Very vivacious, spicy fruit. Huge
fun for non-serious food – pity
about the serious price tag.

**d'Arenberg d'Arrys** `15` £7–10
**Original Shiraz/**
**Grenache 1998**

**Ironstone Shiraz** `15.5` £5–7
**Grenache 1998**
Sweet and jammy and full of fruit
but has some depth and daring to
its tannins. Very delicious
textured richness to the finish.

**Knappstein Cabernet** `15` £7–10
**Franc 1998**

**Marktree Premium Red** `15` –£5.00
**1999**
Lovely energy to the tannins
which stud the ripe chocolate
fruit, giving it backbone.

**Oxford Landing Merlot** `14` £5–7
**1999**
Rich yet sweet – a paradox
achieved by a marriage of tannins
and ripe berries.

**Penfolds Bin 407** `15` £10–13
**Cabernet Sauvignon**
**1996**

**Rosemount Estate** · `14` £5–7
**Shiraz/Cabernet**
**Sauvignon 2000**
Usual soft red gunge from
Rosemount. Has some tannins,
though, this vintage.

**The Seven Surveys** `16` £5–7
**Peter Lehmann 1998**
This Mourvedre, Shiraz,
Grenache blend is strikingly
forward, ripe and ready, with a
grand soupiness mitigated by
gracious tannins resulting in a
lovely warm, soft, yielding
texture.

## BUDGENS RED

**Koonunga Hill Shiraz** `15.5` £5–7
**Cabernet Sauvignon**
**1999**
Classy stuff here, good tannins
dancing excellent and supple
attendance on blackcurrants and
plums.

**Oxford Landing** `14.5` £5–7
**Yalumba Cabernet**
**Sauvignon Shiraz 2000**
Firm texture, adhesive and
hedgerow-fruited. Has a good
surge of flavour on the finish.

**Penfolds Bin 35** `16` £5–7
**Rawsons Retreat**
**Shiraz/Cabernet 1999**
Hints of tobacco and chocolate to
the rich fruit which has attacking
tannins, gripping and stylish.
Decanted and left to breathe for
several hours, this wine will fool
many people into considering it

to be legendary, highly expensive and . . . to live for.

**Wolf Blass Yellow Label Cabernet 2000**   13   £7–10
Not as vibrant as I recall from previous vintages and the tannins are subdued. The price retains its richness, though.

**Wynns Coonawarra Shiraz 1998**   15   £5–7
Classy, minerally fruit, harmonising berries and very soft tannins.

## CO-OP RED

**Andrew Peace Masterpeace Shiraz 2000**   13   £5–7
This bold pun has more chutzpah than rationality for the tannins have gone walkabout. Not at Convenience Stores.

**Australian Cabernet Sauvignon 1999, Co-op**   13   –£5.00
If this is Cabernet I'm a wall-eyed wallaby . . .

**Australian Grenache 2000, Co-op**   13.5   –£5.00
Very juicy and ripe.

**Australian Merlot 2000, Co-op**   14   –£5.00
Ripe plums with a touch of savoury tannin.

**Australian Merlot 2001, Co-op**   15.5   –£5.00
The new vintage is firmer, more resplendently tannic, and has lovely depth.

**Brown Brothers Tarrango 1999**   13.5   £5–7

**Deakin Select Merlot 1999**   14   £5–7
Rather expensive but held together well on the finish by the fleshiness of the plums and the tannins.

**E & E Black Pepper Shiraz 1996**   16   £20+
Complex perfume of tea, chocolate and very subtle cinnamon. The fruit is very tufted and textured but ultimately polished and unturbulent, but £27? It's a lot of money. But this is a lot of wine. It is rugged yet refined. Superstores only.

**Hardys Coonawarra Cabernet Sauvignon 1997**   16   £7–10
Expensive but has a touch of the 'treat' about it with its firm, rich tannins, tightly evolved blackcurrants and delicious cherries and strawbs. Has a classy finish withal. Superstores only.

**Jacaranda Hill Shiraz 2000, Co-op**   13   –£5.00
Very ripe and fruit-juicy.

**Leasingham Cabernet Sauvignon/Malbec 1996**   16.5   £7–10
The marriage of the wood, fruit and tannins is a sensual ménage à trois of guile and gutsiness. Superstores only.

**Lindemans Cawarra Shiraz/Cabernet 1999**   13   –£5.00

15

Bruised juicy fruit. Not at Convenience Stores.

**Little Boomey** `15` `£5–7`
**Cabernet Merlot 2000**
Has some toasted, nutty edges to the fruit, courtesy of the tannins, and the blackberries and plums come through nicely.

**Rosemount Estate** `13` `£5–7`
**Grenache/Shiraz 2000**
So juicy! Superstores only.

**Wolf Blass Yellow** `13` `£7–10`
**Label Cabernet 2000**
Not as vibrant as I recall from previous vintages and the tannins are subdued. The price retains its richness, though. Superstores only.

## KWIK SAVE RED

**Australian Dry Red** `13` `–£5.00`
**2000, Somerfield**
Simple curry red.

**Australian Shiraz** `14` `–£5.00`
**Cabernet 2000,**
**Somerfield**
Good, basic quaffing: plummy and ripe and not too sweet.

**Banrock Station** `15` `–£5.00`
**Shiraz/Mataro 2000**
Tobacco, raspberries and plums. Knock it back.

## M & S RED

**Cabernet/Shiraz 1999** `12` `£5–7`
Too sweet for me. Or six quid.

**Clare Valley Merlot/** `13.5` `£7–10`
**Cabernet Sauvignon/**
**Cabernet Franc/Malbec**
**1998**
More sweet Aussie fruit. The tannins are bright in this specimen, at least, so you get some mild excitement but not eight quids' worth.

**Honey Tree Cabernet** `15.5` `£5–7`
**Merlot 2000**
The tannins are mildly savoury and delicious but the fruit calls the tune – and it makes fine listening (and quaffing).

**Honey Tree Shiraz** `13` `£5–7`
**Cabernet 2000**
Very sweet and fruity in a way which leaves little to the imagination.

**Honey Tree Grenache** `13` `£5–7`
**Shiraz 1999**

**Honey Tree Reserve** `14` `£7–10`
**Pinot Noir 1999**
Good dry style, good dusky tannins, charming ripe cherries.

**Honey Tree Shiraz** `14` `£7–10`
**Reserve 1998**

**Lenbridge Forge Pinot** `12` `£7–10`
**Noir 2000**
Struggles to please me but obviously not M&S. Nine quid? Too juicy on the finish, surely.

**SE Australian Shiraz** `15` `£5–7`
**1999**

**Shiraz Merlot Ruby** `15` `–£5.00`
**Cabernet Bin 312 2000**
An Aussie Beaujolais – but much

tastier. That's the full, rich, jazzy style anyway.

**South East Australian Cabernet 2000** `16.5` `−£5.00`
Has everything: sexy price tag, sensual texture, inviting perfume, lovely body, and terrific conversation. Irresistible stuff here.

**South East Australian Merlot 2000** `15.5` `−£5.00`
Merlots don't come much softer, subtler or better value than this.

**South Eastern Australian Shiraz 2000** `14.5` `−£5.00`
Plummy yet dry and stylish.

**Twin Wells Heathcote Shiraz 1999** `16` `£7–10`
A delicious feminist Shiraz of striking Germaine Greer fruitiness and intellectual ripeness. Yep. You've guessed. I drank the bottle and got so pissed I wrote the first words which came into my head. So: be warned. This wine is too easy to love.

## MORRISONS RED

**Barramundi Shiraz/ Merlot NV** `15.5` `−£5.00`

**Brown Brothers Barbera 1998** `13.5` `£5–7`
Bit expensive for the style.

**Cranswick Cabernet Merlot 1999** `15.5` `−£5.00`
Real depth and vibrancy, spice and lingering fruit.

**Hardys Cabernet Shiraz Merlot 1998** `15` `£5–7`

**Lindemans Bin 45 Cabernet Sauvignon 1999** `15` `£5–7`

**'M' Australian Shiraz Cabernet NV** `10` `−£5.00`

**Nottage Hill Cabernet Sauvignon/Shiraz 1999** `16.5` `£5–7`
Under six quid, one of Aussie's best big red wine bargains. Thrilling tannins and subtle spiciness.

**Tortoiseshell Bay Mourvedre Shiraz 2000** `12` `−£5.00`
What a sweet wine! Needs curry – urgently.

**Wakefield Shiraz Cabernet 2000** `16` `£5–7`
Spice, depth, complexity, savoury tannins – has it all. Plus a layered finish of great tenacity.

**Woolpunda Cabernet Sauvignon 1999** `13.5` `−£5.00`
Soft, chocolate richness here. Very chewy and deep.

**Yellow Tail Shiraz 2000** `15.5` `−£5.00`
Terrific buzzy fruit, hint of spice, lovely warm tannins, and real personality on the finish.

## SAFEWAY RED

**Annies Lane Cabernet/ Merlot 1999** `13.5` `£7–10`
Selected stores.

17

**Australian Oaked Cabernet Sauvignon 1999, Safeway** `14.5` `−£5.00`

**Australian Oaked Shiraz 1999, Safeway** `14` `−£5.00`

**Australian Shiraz 1999, Safeway** `15` `−£5.00`

**Clancy's Shiraz/ Cabernet Sauvignon/ Merlot/Cabernet Franc 1998** `17` `£7–10`
Perfection at its peak – almost. Will it rate higher if cellared and left to mature? How can it? It has wonderfully integrated generous tannins and plum/cherry/ blackberry fruit.

**CV Capel Vale Shiraz 1998** `14.5` `£7–10`
Very vivacious, spicy fruit. Huge fun for non-serious food – pity about the serious price tag.

**Endeavour Cabernet Sauvignon 1999** `12` `£7–10`
Selected stores.

**Evans & Tate Shiraz 1999** `16` `£7–10`
Very classy and deep, lovely soft tannins, good spicy berries and a fine overall texture of style and substance.

**Hardys Stamp Shiraz/ Cabernet 2000** `13` `−£5.00`
Dry and mutely expressive on the finish.

**Hardys Tintara Shiraz 1998** `13` `£7–10`

Overpriced by 300%. Selected stores.

**Haselgrove 'Bentwing' Shiraz, Wrattonbully 1999** `12` `£7–10`
Too jammy for nine quid. Selected stores.

**Haselgrove 'H' Cabernet Sauvignon/ Merlot 1998** `15` `£13–20`
In spite of the tannins, the sweet finish is destined for Indian food. Selected stores.

**Haselgrove Shiraz, McLaren Vale 1999** `13` `£7–10`
More Oz juice. Selected stores.

**Jindalee Merlot 2000** `12` `−£5.00`
Selected stores.

**Jindalee Shiraz 2000** `13` `−£5.00`
Selected stores.

**Masterpiece Shiraz Malbec 2000** `11` `£5–7`
Oh come! A masterpiece? Selected stores.

**Metala Langhorne Creek Shiraz/Cabernet Sauvignon 1998** `15.5` `£7–10`
Interesting complexity involving liquorice and mint, but the sweetness limits the tannins and restricts the wine to spicy foods.

**Ninth Island Pinot Noir, Tasmania 1999** `11` `£7–10`

**Normans Langhorne Creek Cabernet Sauvignon/Cabernet Franc 1996** `14` `£7–10`

Juicy and dry. Give it another year in bottle. Selected stores.

**Penfolds Bin 128** 13.5 £7–10
**Coonawarra Shiraz**
**1998**
Jammy edge doesn't get resolved by the tannins to the extent that ten pounds is wisely spent here. Selected stores.

**Penfolds Organic** 15.5 £7–10
**Merlot Shiraz Cabernet**
**1998**

**Peter Lehmann The** 17 £5–7
**Barossa Shiraz 1998**
Oh, it's so savoury and ripe yet so elegantly purposeful. A quite gorgeous artefact providing rivulets of rich flavours.

**Rosemount Estate** 13 £5–7
**Grenache/Shiraz 2000**
So juicy!

**Rosemount Estate** 15 £7–10
**Merlot 1999**
Very soft and ripe and suited to meats preceded by poppadums and pickles.

**Rosemount 'Hill of** 17.5 £7–10
**Gold' Shiraz, Mudgee**
**1998**
At last! A Rosemount red with world-class tannins. And it's under a tenner. Beautifully well-knit fruit here, totally captivating, and the texture is gripping, grand, and you feel greedy for more.

**Rosemount Shiraz 1999** 14.5 £7–10
Less juicy attack than previous

vintages, it has some gentle tannins to give it bite.

**Tatachilla Breakneck** 13.5 £5–7
**Creek Cabernet**
**Sauvignon 2000**
Selected stores.

**Tatachilla Foundation** 13.5 £13–20
**Shiraz 1998**
Very ripe and a touch over-reaching for sixteen quid.

**Tatachilla Padthaway** 16 £7–10
**Cabernet Sauvignon**
**1999**
Lovely tangy richness underpins the dry blackcurrants and plums and it's all well held together by firm tannins. Selected stores.

**Tatachilla Shiraz 1999** 15 £7–10
Some alertness here to both fruit and tannins. Selected stores.

**Wakefield Promised** 12 £5–7
**Land Shiraz/Cabernet**
**Sauvignon 2000**
Selected stores.

**Wirrega Vineyards** 16 £5–7
**Cabernet Sauvignon/**
**Petit Verdot 1999**
Terrific mineral aroma, jammy fruit, nice simple tannins. An unpretentiously delicious specimen.

**Wirrega Vineyards** 13 £5–7
**Shiraz 1999**
Very juicy.

**Wolf Blass Yellow** 14 £7–10
**Label Cabernet**
**Sauvignon 1999**

Big rich curry wine. Joyous, jolly, jammy.

**Woolshed Cabernet/** `17` `£5–7`
**Shiraz/Merlot,**
**Coonawarra 1998**
Stunning richness and textured, tangy fruit of huge depth and charm. Multi-layered and magnificently mouth-watering. Top 220 stores.

## SAINSBURY'S RED

**Australian Shiraz NV,** `13.5` `–£5.00`
**Sainsbury's**
Middling fruit which struggles to offer a fiver's worth of value.

**Banrock Station Mataro** `15` `–£5.00`
**Shiraz NV, (3 litre box)**
Price band indicates the 75cl equivalent.

**Hardys Stamp Cabernet** `13.5` `–£5.00`
**Merlot 2000**
Soft, ripe, obvious, lush. Alcoholic fruit juice, you might term it.

**Jacobs Creek Reserve** `14` `£7–10`
**Shiraz 1998**
Rather expensive, if displaying some meaty ripeness, and very good for casseroles and cheese dishes. 170 selected stores.

**Nottage Hill Cabernet** `16.5` `£5–7`
**Sauvignon/Shiraz 1999**
Under six quid, one of Aussie's best big red wine bargains. Thrilling tannins and subtle spiciness.

**Petaluma Bridgewater** `16.5` `£7–10`
**Mill Shiraz 1998**
Very chewy, coal-edged texture, deep and rich and softly spicy. Lovely rich plums, blackcurrants and a touch of leather. Delicious tannins, too, so it has backbone and bite. 180 stores.

**Rosemount Estate** `15.5` `£7–10`
**Shiraz 1998**

**Wolf Blass Yellow** `14` `£7–10`
**Label Cabernet**
**Sauvignon 1999**
Big rich curry wine. Joyous, jolly, jammy.

## SOMERFIELD RED

**Australian Shiraz** `14` `–£5.00`
**Cabernet 2000,**
**Somerfield**
Good, basic quaffing: plummy and ripe and not too sweet.

**Banrock Station** `15` `–£5.00`
**Shiraz/Mataro 2000**
Tobacco, raspberries and plums. Knock it back.

**Encounter Bay Merlot** `13` `£5–7`
**1999**
Ribena.

**Encounter Bay Shiraz** `13.5` `£5–7`
**1999**
Ribena with rusticity. Good with Tandoori hedgehog.

**Hardys Nottage Hill** `16.5` `£5–7`
**Cabernet Sauvignon/**
**Shiraz 1999**
Under six quid, one of Aussie's

best big red wine bargains. Thrilling tannins and subtle spiciness.

**Hardys Tintara Cabernet Sauvignon 1998**    15   £7–10
Sweet but tempered by rich tannins into something resembling wine.

**Jacobs Creek Grenache Shiraz 2000**    13.5   –£5.00
Usual sweet young thing. Needs lots of chillies.

**Jacobs Creek Merlot 2000**    13   £5–7
Sweet, and pricey into the bargain (lack of).

**Jindalee Cabernet Sauvignon 2000**    14   –£5.00
Ripe plums, some juicy tannins, a suggestion of backbone to the finish.

**Lindemans Cawarra Shiraz/Cabernet 1999**    13   –£5.00
Bruised juicy fruit.

**Masterpeace Red 2000**    11   –£5.00
Such tannin-forsaken sweetness! Selected stores.

**Normans Estates Lone Gum Cabernet Merlot 2000**    12   –£5.00
Very sweet and adolescent.

**Normans Old Vines Shiraz 1999**    16.5   £5–7
This is how it should be! Bold berried fruit up to its neck in brilliant uncluttered tannins.

**Omrah Plantagenet Shiraz 1999**    14   £7–10
Usual Aussie juice with a touch more earth than normal. Expensive though!

**Penfolds Bin 28 Kalimna Shiraz 1998**    15   £7–10
Spicy, rich, layered, dry yet full of fruit, urgent-edged tannins – this is typical Aussie Shiraz in many respects except the herbs on the finish.

**Penfolds Koonunga Hill Shiraz 1999**    15   £5–7
Good solid branding. That's what we want, isn't it?

**Rosemount Estate Shiraz/Cabernet Sauvignon 2000**    14   £5–7
Usual soft red gunge from Rosemount. Has some tannins, though, this vintage.

**Secession Xanadu Shiraz Cabernet 2000**    14   £5–7
Has some texture and even – so daringly! – tannins. Selected stores.

**Tortoiseshell Bay Mourvedre Shiraz 2000**    12   –£5.00
What a sweet wine! Needs curry – urgently.

**Wakefield Promised Land Shiraz/Cabernet Sauvignon 2000**    12   £5–7
Selected stores.

## SPAR RED

**De Bortoli Australian Dry Red 2000, Spar** `14` `-£5.00`
Most unusual for an Aussie and all the better for it: character, fruit and tannins.

**De Bortoli Shiraz Cabernet 2000, Spar** `12` `-£5.00`
Lot of loot for such straightforward fruit.

**Normans Unfiltered Grenache 1997** `11` `£5-7`
It may be unfiltered but the baked jamminess of the finish is overwhelmingly toast-spreadable rather than throat-luscious.

**Temple Bruer Cabernet Merlot 1996** `16` `£7-10`
Minty rich berries, fine tannins, a touch of spice and a lovely supple texture.

## TESCO RED

**Angove's Lock 9 Carignan/Mataro/ Shiraz 2000** `10` `-£5.00`
Alcoholic fruit juice. Little character, even less excitement. Most stores.

**Angove's Stonegate Barbera 2000** `14` `-£5.00`
A brilliant curry wine. Soft and juicy. Most stores.

**Australian Cabernet/ Merlot NV, Tesco** `15.5` `-£3.50`
Savouriness and fresh fruitiness combine superbly to create bargain richness and food friendliness.

**Australian Red NV, Tesco** `15` `-£3.50`
Jolly simple slurping here. Great texture and soft tannins and some degree of lingering lushness. Terrific barbecue wine (and for BYOB use).

**Australian Shiraz NV, Tesco** `14` `-£3.50`
Cheap, cheerful, very dry.

**Banrock Station Shiraz 2000** `14.5` `-£5.00`
Buzzes with flavour and dry plummy fruit.

**Banrock Station Shiraz/Mataro 2000** `15` `-£5.00`
Tobacco, raspberries and plums. Knock it back.

**Barramundi Shiraz/ Merlot NV** `15.5` `-£5.00`

**Blue Pyrenees Estate Red 1996** `14` `£10-13`

**Buckleys Grenache/ Shiraz/Mourvedre 1998** `14` `£7-10`

**Casella Carramar Estate Merlot 2000** `14` `-£5.00`
Juicy curry wine. Most stores.

**Chapel Hill Cabernet Sauvignon 1997** `14` `£7-10`

**Coonawarra Cabernet Sauvignon 1997, Tesco** `16` `£5-7`
Superb tangy Cabernet, great tannins, and an excellent example of Coonawarra Cab – it motors with great class and confidence

over the taste buds. One of Tesco's so-called 'Finest' range. Most stores.

**Hardys Stamp Shiraz/ Cabernet 2000**   13   −£5.00
Dry and mutely expressive on the finish.

**Image Cabernet/ Merlot 2000**   13.5   −£5.00
Like a fruit salad, so rich is it and all-embracing. Has spice too – great for raunchy Balti dishes.

**Lindemans Bin 50 Shiraz 1999**   16   £5–7
Vibrant yet subtle, dry yet fruitily round, tannic yet softly textured and tellingly tongue-tingling on the finish. Selected stores.

**McLaren Vale Grenache 1999, Tesco**   13.5   £5–7
Very sweet. One of Tesco's so-called 'Finest' range. At most stores.

**McLaren Vale Shiraz 1999, Tesco**   14.5   £5–7
A plump fruity curry red. One of Tesco's so-called 'Finest' range. At most stores.

**Miranda Rovalley Ridge Petit Verdot 2000**   14   £5–7
Love the tannins, not so keen on the juicy fruit. Probably best with Lebanese vegetable dishes. Most stores.

**Oxford Landing Cabernet Sauvignon Shiraz 1999**   15.5   £5–7

**Oxford Landing Merlot 2000**   15   £5–7
Delicious, simple berries, highly gluggable and smooth. Very polished tannins.

**Penfolds Bin 128 Coonawarra Shiraz 1998**   15.5   £7–10
Very elegant tannins here and very toothsome berries beneath. Has classy texture and a ripe savoury finish. Very precise, polished winemaking.

**Penfolds Bin 28 Kalimna Shiraz 1998**   15   £7–10
Spicy, rich, layered, dry yet full of fruit, urgent-edged tannins – this is typical Aussie Shiraz in many respects except the herbs on the finish.

**Penfolds Bin 35 Rawsons Retreat Shiraz/Cabernet 1999**   16   £5–7
Hints of tobacco and chocolate to the rich fruit which has attacking tannins, gripping and stylish. Decanted and left to breathe for several hours, this wine will fool many people into considering it to be legendary, highly expensive and . . . to live for. Most stores.

**Rosemount Estate Cabernet/Merlot 2000**   14   £5–7
Juicy and rich with some compensation from the tannins.

**Rosemount Estate Grenache/Shiraz 2000**   13   £5–7
So juicy!

**Rosemount Estate** 15 £7–10
**Merlot 1999**
Very soft and ripe and suited to
meats preceded by poppadums
and pickles. Most stores.

**Smithbrook Cabernet** 16 £7–10
**Sauvignon/Cabernet**
**Franc/Petit Verdot**
**1998**
Claret given soul, heart and lots
of soft, fleshy fruit with hard
tannic muscles. Claret made on
Mars. Selected stores.

**St Hallett Faith Barossa** 15 £7–10
**Shiraz 1999**
Soft, ripe, berried and highly
drinkable – with food. The
reluctance of the tannins requires
it be paired with oriental meat
and vegetable dishes rather than
roast European meats. Most
stores.

**Sunstone Fresh Spicy** 12 –£5.00
**Red NV**

**Tim Adams Shiraz 1999** 17 £7–10
One of Oz's class acts with its
texture, evolved tannins and
build-up of exciting textures in
the throat. A lovely wine of class
and distinction. Unerringly
delicious and well-balanced. Great
value here considering how
obscenely priced some Aussie
Shirazes have become. Selected
stores.

**Wilkie Estate Organic** 13 £7–10
**Cabernet Merlot 2000**
Too juicy for nine quid. Selected
stores.

**Wolf Blass Green Label** 16 £5–7
**Shiraz 1999**
Lovely life to the wine, full of
itself as well as layers of plums,
spice and blackberries, and it's at
its most assured and entertaining
with rich food and rich company.
Most stores.

**Wolf Blass Yellow** 15.5 £7–10
**Label Cabernet**
**Sauvignon 1999**
Big rich curry wine. Joyous, jolly,
jammy. Most stores.

**Woolpunda Cabernet** 15 –£5.00
**Sauvignon 1998**

**Woolpunda Merlot** 14.5 –£5.00
**1999**
Very warm and generous-
hearted. Soft, dry, rich and
effortlessly rolling. Selected
stores.

**Woolpunda Shiraz 1998** 16 –£5.00
Soft, very cushy fruit of great
style and mannered richness. It is
wholly without pretension but it
does have poise and plummy
depths. Most stores.

## WAITROSE RED

**Brown Brothers** 13 £7–10
**Nebbiolo 1996**
Very juicy.

**Brown Brothers** 13 £5–7
**Tarrango 2000**
Like fruit juice.

**Charleston Pinot Noir** 11 £7–10
**1998**

**Church Block Cabernet** `15.5` `£7–10`
**Shiraz Merlot, Wirra**
**Wirra Vineyards 1998**
Very elegant and polished. Lovely
texture to it.

**Clancy's Red 1998** `15.5` `£7–10`
Unusually European in feel up
front but the sun shines through
on the finish. Stylish and rich, dry,
complete.

**Deakin Estate Merlot,** `15.5` `£5–7`
**Victoria 2000**
Soft leathery fruit, well accoutred
with ripe tannins. Warm and
friendly.

**Eileen Hardy Shiraz** `14` `£20+`
**1997**
Lot of loot, and not very good
value, but very pert acids and
good tannins. Will age for several
years with distinction. But
twenty-eight quid?! What's going
on in the world?

**Fishermans Bend** `13` `–£5.00`
**Cabernet Sauvignon**
**1999**
Very sweet.

**Garry Crittenden** `14` `£7–10`
**Barbera 'i' 1999**
Wonderful Indian food wine. Like
a vinified soft fruit hedgerow.

**Greg Norman Shiraz** `13` `£7–10`
**1999**
Lacks a convincing finish for ten
quid.

**Jindalee Shiraz 2000** `13` `–£5.00`

**Katnook Cabernet** `15.5` `£10–13`
**Sauvignon 1998**
Delicious tangy minerals, fine
tannins, good rich berries with
liquorice, and a superb, high class
texture. Expensive, yes? Too?
Mmm . . .

**Ninth Island Pinot** `12` `£7–10`
**Noir, Tasmania 2000**
I wonder if they should grow
Pinot in Tasmania.

**Penfolds Clare Valley** `14` `£7–10`
**Cabernet Sauvignon/**
**Shiraz 1999 (organic)**
Has some mild excitement.

**Penfolds Grange South** `14` `£20+`
**Australia Shiraz 1995**
The first Grange I've liked. Drink
it now. It won't improve. Worth
£100? Nope. But the sensuality of
the tannins is awesome. Mail
Order only.

**Peter Lehmann The** `16` `£7–10`
**Barossa Shiraz 1999**
Superb compressed fruit of great
class and richness. Lovely texture
to the fruit. One of the Barossa's
most accomplished Shirazes and,
at its price, still a snip.

**Rosemount 'Hill of** `17.5` `£7–10`
**Gold' Cabernet**
**Sauvignon, Mudgee**
**1998**
At last! A Rosemount red with
world-class tannins. And it's
under a tenner. Beautifully well-
knit fruit here, totally captivating,
and the texture is gripping, grand,
and you feel greedy for more.

**Settler's Station** `14` `£5–7`
**Tempranillo 2000**

Unusual style of Tempranillo. There's more cherry in it and less tannin than we are used to.

**Tatachilla Cabernet Sauvignon/Merlot, McLaren Vale 1998**  `14`  `£7–10`
Ripe and ready. Even has some tannins.

**Tatachilla Foundation Shiraz 1998**  `13.5`  `£13–20`
Very ripe and a touch over-reaching for sixteen quid.

**Tatachilla Growers Grenache Mataro 1999**  `14`  `–£5.00`
Very rich and curry friendly.

**Tea Tree Malbec/Ruby Cabernet 2000**  `13`  `–£5.00`
Juicy and very ripe.

**The Angelus Cabernet Sauvignon, Wirra Wirra 1998**  `16`  `£13–20`
Very elegant and well-structured and beautifully textured. Has warmth yet seriousness with solemnity (unlike, say, so many Cabernet-dominated clarets). An impressive wine of great style.

**Yaldara Grenache Reserve, Barossa 1999**  `3`  `£5–7`

**Yellowtail Merlot 2000**  `12`  `–£5.00`
Love the label.

## ASDA WHITE

**Cranswick Nine Pines Vineyard Marsanne 1998**  `16.5`  `–£5.00`
Astonishing value here and

surprising level of mature layers of rich, ripe fruit. Textured and taut.

**Karalta White 1999, Asda**  `14`  `–£3.50`

**La Nature Organic Chardonnay Sauvignon 2000**  `14.5`  `–£5.00`
One of the better of the La Nature range which is very much a curate's egg. Has some plump peachy fruit with good lemon acids.

**Peter Lehmann Eden Valley Riesling 1999**  `16.5`  `£5–7`
Smacks of earth and minerals. Delivers a tangy lemon and gooseberry richness and a lovely, fresh finish. Outstanding.

**Rosemount GTR 2001**  `13.5`  `£5–7`
This is a whacky blend of Gewürztraminer and Riesling, slightly sweet, gently peachy/gooseberryish/pineappley, and in need of a good spread of Chinese food to be at its most agreeable.

**Rosemount 'Hill of Gold' Chardonnay, Mudgee 1999**  `14`  `£7–10`
Not typically Aussie in its subtleties.

**Rymill Sauvignon Blanc 1999**  `15.5`  `£5–7`

**Wyndham Estate Bin 222 Chardonnay 1999**  `16`  `£5–7`
Excellent price for fruit which excels itself in effortlessly providing taste, refinement and

refreshment. Lingering creaminess gives it great food compatibility.

## BOOTHS WHITE

**Capel Vale CV** `14.5` `£7–10`
**Unwooded**
**Chardonnay 1999**
Like a nervous, slightly confused, Chablis.

**Capel Vale Verdelho** `16` `£7–10`
**1999**
Wonderful concentrated vintage for this warmly-coated, subtly spicy wine.

**Château Tahbilk** `17` `£5–7`
**Marsanne 1998**
Young yet beautifully textured, tangy and tremendously minerally yet ripe. Has layers of pineapple, lemon and gooseberry. Will age for eight to ten years.

**Cranswick Botrytis** `15` `£10–13`
**Semillon 1996 (half bottle)**

**d'Arenberg The Olive** `16.5` `£5–7`
**Grove Chardonnay,**
**McLaren Vale 2000**
Does it have a kind of green olive to the lime and melon fruit? Sheer fantasy I think.

**Deakin Estate** `15.5` `–£5.00`
**Chardonnay 2000**
Lovely clash of tangy crispness and soft richness and ripeness.

**Ironstone Semillon** `16` `£5–7`
**Chardonnay 1999**

Lovely tangy richness and versatility with food.

**Marktree White SE** `13.5` `–£5.00`
**Australia 2000**
The most unlike-Oz white I've ever tasted: dry, edgy, numb.

**Ninth Island** `14` `£7–10`
**Chardonnay 2000**
Elegant, expensive, subtly expressive.

**Oxford Landing** `15.5` `–£5.00`
**Chardonnay 2000**
Lovely texture to the melon/lemon fruit with a hint of toffee.

**Oxford Landing** `16` `£5–7`
**Viognier 2000**
Delightful apricot and lemon fruit with a fine texture and finesse as it finishes.

**Penfolds Bin 21** `14` `–£5.00`
**Rawson's Retreat**
**Semillon/Colombard/**
**Chardonnay 2000**
Pleasant Thai food white.

**Shaw & Smith** `15` `£7–10`
**Sauvignon Blanc 1998**

## BUDGENS WHITE

**Hardys Nottage Hill** `16` `£5–7`
**Chardonnay 2000**
Lovely lemon/melon – the usual thing – but with added oomph.

**Hardys Stamp** `11` `–£5.00`
**Grenache Shiraz Rosé**
**2000**
Lies down on the tongue and

dies.

**Jacobs Creek Dry** `15` `£5-7`
**Riesling 2000**
Delicious young fruit (which will
develop more nuances if cellared
for a couple of years). Has really
balanced, highly attractive
charms.

**Oxford Landing** `15.5` `-£5.00`
**Chardonnay 2000**
Lovely texture to the melon/
lemon fruit with a hint of toffee.

**Penfolds Koonunga** `16` `£5-7`
**Hill Chardonnay 2000**
One of Oz's finest brands – pity
it's gone over a fiver.

**Rosemount Semillon/** `15` `£5-7`
**Chardonnay 2000**
Delicious tanginess and melon
ripeness undercut by fresh lemon.

**White Pointer 2000** `13` `-£5.00`

## CO-OP WHITE

**Australian Chardonnay** `15.5` `-£5.00`
**2000, Co-op**
Deliciously lemony. Has great
charm and crisp delivery of fresh
fruit.

**Barramundi Semillon/** `16` `-£5.00`
**Chardonnay NV**
Simply delicious from nose to
throat – lovely, fresh fruit here.

**Bethany Chardonnay** `16` `£5-7`
**1998**
The extra year of maturity has
added layers of interest. It has a
gorgeous aroma of cooking

butter, the fruit is ripe and nutty,
the finish brings in lime, butter
and almonds. Nice lingering
vegetality. Superstores only.

**Bethany Riesling 2001** `16` `£5-7`
Lovely lemons and touches of
apricot and lime – but better if
cellared beyond five or six years
when it will be even more
sensational. Superstores only.

**Brown Brothers Late** `16` `£5-7`
**Harvested Orange**
**Muscat & Flora 2000**
**(half bottle)**
One of Australia's great dessert-
style wines. Has fresh thyme-
honey richness offset by prim
acids of a lemony tonality.
Superstores only.

**Hardys Chardonnay** `15` `£5-7`
**Sauvignon Blanc 1998**

**Jacaranda Hill Semillon** `13` `-£5.00`
**2000, Co-op**

**Oxford Landing** `16` `-£5.00`
**Sauvignon Blanc 2000**
Superbly subtle riches and
striking cleanness of tonality. A
benchmark fiver's worth of New
World Sauvignon: crisp and fresh
and biting without being
remotely tart or too dry.
Superstores only.

**Rosemount Estate GTR** `15` `£5-7`
**2000**
Drink in the context of oriental
food and the sweet perfume of
exotic fruit is well-tempered.
Superstores only.

**Yellow Tail** `14.5` `–£5.00`
**Chardonnay 2000**
Label of the year certainly but
fruit of the year? Well, it's bright
and breezy, the flippant side of
the grape. Not at Convenience
Stores.

## KWIK SAVE WHITE

**Banrock Station** `14` `–£5.00`
**Colombard**
**Chardonnay 2001**
Tangy, nutty, nice.

## M & S WHITE

**Australian** `12` `–£3.50`
**Chardonnay/Semillon/**
**Colombard 2000**
Lacks punch, polish and
pertinacity.

**Chardonnay Bin 109** `15.5` `–£5.00`
**2000**
Lovely gooseberry touches to
underripe melon, hint of radish,
crisp finish. For all that, it's a
subtle wine not to be taken with
spicy food.

**Honey Tree** `15` `£5–7`
**Gewürztraminer**
**Riesling 2000**
Off-dry melon, sweet raspberry
and lemon fruit – a good
candidate for spicy oriental
food.

**Honey Tree Semillon** `15` `£5–7`
**Chardonnay 2000**
Very mildly rich, soft-toned

quaffer with touches of dry
honey, melon and lemon.

**McLean's Farm** `13` `£7–10`
**Riesling, St Hallett 2000**
Interesting potential here (more
achievable if the wine had been
screwcapped instead of relying on
cork). It has some interesting
minerally touches which need
more bottle age. I'd cellar it for
three to seven years more and
achieve 17 points possibly.

**Semillon Bin 381 2000** `16` `–£5.00`
Delicious layered richness
offering dryness, freshness and
soft fruit touches and fine
pineapple acids. Faint smoky
finish.

**South Eastern** `16` `–£5.00`
**Australian Chardonnay**
**2000**
Great under-a-fiver Chardonnay
here; has elegance, bite,
personality and class.

**Tumbarumba** `14.5` `£7–10`
**Chardonnay 1998**
Good for Thai food.

## MORRISONS WHITE

**Barramundi Semillon/** `16` `–£5.00`
**Chardonnay NV**
Simply delicious from nose to
throat – lovely, fresh fruit here.

**Cranswick Estate** `16` `–£5.00`
**Botrytis Semillon 1999**
**(half bottle)**
Considering its age it's amazingly
complex and well-developed. It

has waxy ripe fruit of sweetness and honeyed depth, superb acids (which will enable it to age well for ten years and beyond), and it's a great value dessert wine.

**Jindalee Chardonnay 1998**    16    −£5.00

Compelling richness and lemony elegant buttery fruit. Beautiful balance and precision.

**Lindemans Bin 65 Chardonnay 2000**    16    −£5.00

Touch more fatness to the fruit in this vintage. Still one of Oz's great, and great value, brands.

**Nottage Hill Chardonnay 1999**    16    −£5.00

Almost in the same league as Lindeman's. Perhaps its true score should be sixteen and three quarters.

**Oxford Landing Viognier 2000**    16    £5–7

Delightful apricot and lemon fruit with a fine texture and finesse as it finishes.

**Penfolds Koonunga Hill Chardonnay 2000**    16    £5–7

One of Oz's finest brands – pity it's gone over a fiver.

**Penfolds Rawsons Retreat Semillon/ Chardonnay/ Colombard 1999**    14    −£5.00

A fish stew wine of no subtlety but easygoing, bruised-fruit richness.

**Rosemount Chardonnay 2000**    16    £5–7

Rich yet subtle. Superb class.

**Rosemount Estate GTR 2000**    15    £5–7

Drink in the context of oriental food and the sweet perfume of exotic fruit is well-tempered.

**Rothbury Cowra Chardonnay 2000**    12.5    −£5.00

Fat and fleshy.

**Stamp Grenache Shiraz 2000**    13    −£5.00

Cherries. Dry cherries.

**Tortoiseshell Bay Sauvignon Semillon 2000**    13.5    −£5.00

Subdued on the finish.

**Wakefield Unwooded Chardonnay 2001**    13    £5–7

Very ripe and fulsomely expressive.

**Yellow Tail Chardonnay 2000**    14.5    −£5.00

Label of the year certainly but fruit of the year? Well, it's bright and breezy, the flippant side of the grape.

**Yellow Tail Verdelho 2001**    15.5    −£5.00

Interesting lip-smacking lemon fruit with hints of spice.

## SAFEWAY WHITE

**Alkoomi Riesling, Frankland River 2000**    14.5    £7–10

Curious translation of German –

but will develop in five years. Selected stores.

**Alkoomi Sauvignon Blanc, Frankland River 2000**   14   £7–10
Very dry and hugely cellar-worthy. Wait three or four years for it to be so much more complex and rich. Selected stores.

**Annie's Lane Semillon, Clare Valley 1999**   15.5   £5–7

**Bleasdale Verdelho, Langhorne Creek 2000**   15   £5–7
Touch of warm spice to the perfectly textured richness. Good with mildly spicy Thai food.

**Capel Vale CV Unwooded Chardonnay 1999**   14.5   £7–10
Like a nervous, slightly confused, Chablis.

**CV Chenin Blanc 2000**   16   £5–7
Deliciously richly textured and gently smoky. Perfect for garlic scallops and clams.

**Endeavour Barrel-fermented Chardonnay, Limestone Coast 1999**   14   £7–10
Ripe and ready for Thai food. Selected stores.

**Hardys Tintara Chardonnay 2000**   13   £7–10
Overpriced by pounds. Selected stores.

**Haselgrove 'H' Chardonnay 1999**   14.5   £7–10

Very rich on the finish. Good with spicy food. Selected stores.

**Jindalee Chardonnay 2000**   16   –£5.00
Simply delightful and layered: gooseberries, melons and pears and subtle lemons. A lovely mouthful of assertiveness yet restraint. Good texture, too.

**Leasingham Bin 7 Riesling, Clare Valley 2000**   13.5   £5–7
Wait four or five years for the petrol to flow. It's numb right now. The screwcap ensures freshness and wonderful development in bottle to, perhaps, eighteen points in 2008. Selected stores.

**Loxton Low Alcohol Chardonnay (1.2% vol)**   11   –£3.50

**Mamre Brook Chardonnay 1999**   16   £5–7
Terrific pulsating melon richness. Yet it's balanced and sane.

**Nepenthe Vineyards Sauvignon Blanc 2000**   16   £7–10
Lingers lushly yet freshly and offers great finely-knitted acids.

**Penfolds Bin 21 Rawson's Retreat Semillon/Colombard/ Chardonnay 2000**   14   –£5.00
Pleasant Thai food white.

**Peter Lehmann 'The Barossa' Semillon 1999**   16.5   £5–7
I love the way this Semillon

graduates its fruit, by nuances, and finishes with great wit.

**Peter Lehmann Vine Vale Riesling, Barossa Valley 2000**   `16.5`  `–£5.00`
Magnificent limey, peachy, melony richness with haunting, minerally acids and a brilliant thick texture. Remarkable wine for the money.

**Robertson Barrel Fermented Colombard 1999**   `13`  `–£5.00`

**Rosemount Estate Show Reserve Chardonnay 1999**   `16`  `£7–10`
Gorgeous gentle creamy finish, fine acids, good melon/lemon richness. A very good class of Chard.

**Rosemount Show Reserve Chardonnay 1998**   `15`  `£7–10`

**Tatachilla Breakneck Creek Chardonnay 2000**   `16.5`  `–£5.00`
Superb texture, oily and rich, and a complex finish. This is an amazing white wine for the money.

**Tatachilla Chardonnay Adelaide Hills 1999**   `15.5`  `£7–10`
Very controlled, dry, classy and charming. Has a luxurious, subtle feel to it. Selected stores.

**Tatachilla Padthaway Chardonnay 2000**   `16`  `£5–7`
Lovely strident richness, creamy

and ripe, which stays fat without being over-the-top. Lingering lushness with a dry edge to the rich finish. Selected stores.

**Wakefield Promised Land Unwooded Chardonnay, Clare Valley 2000**   `13`  `£5–7`
Very odd opulence to it. As if confected. Selected stores.

**Wakefield St Andrew Chardonnay, Clare Valley 1998**   `14`  `£13–20`
I'd be inclined to cellar it for three or four years to allow its vegetal side to develop and become like Burgundy. Selected stores.

## SAINSBURY'S WHITE

**Australian Chardonnay NV, Sainsbury's**   `15.5`  `–£5.00`
Very ripe, very rich, very very Ozzie.

**Hardys Stamp of Australia Chardonnay Semillon (3 litre box)**   `15`  `–£5.00`
Delicious plump, ripe fruit with a fresh undertone of lemon. A brilliantly refreshing tipple of some class. Price band indicates the 75cl equivalent.

**Oxford Landing Sauvignon Blanc 2000**   `16`  `–£5.00`
Superbly subtle riches and striking cleanness of tonality. A benchmark fiver's worth of New World Sauvignon: crisp and fresh

and biting without being remotely tart or too dry. Most stores.

**Penfolds Botrytis** `15` `£5–7`
**Semillon 1998 (half bottle)**

**Rosemount Estate GTR** `15` `£5–7`
**2000**
Drink in the context of oriental food and the sweet perfume of exotic fruit is well-tempered. Selected stores.

**Rosemount Estate** `16` `£7–10`
**Show Reserve Chardonnay 1999**
Gorgeous gentle creamy finish, fine acids, good melon/lemon richness. A very good class of Chard. Selected stores.

**Stowells of Chelsea** `15.5` `–£3.50`
**Australian Chardonnay NV (3 litre box)**
Price band indicates the 75cl equivalent.

## SOMERFIELD WHITE

**Banrock Station** `15` `–£5.00`
**Chardonnay 2000**
Brilliant wine for spicy food. Has textured ripeness and depth.

**Banrock Station** `14` `–£5.00`
**Colombard Chardonnay 2001**
Tangy, nutty, nice.

**Cudgee Creek** `16` `–£5.00`
**Chardonnay Colombard 2000**
Brilliant value pear, pineapple, lychee and raspberry.

**Deakin Estate** `15.5` `–£5.00`
**Chardonnay 2000**
Lovely clash of tangy crispness and soft richness and ripeness.

**Hardys Nottage Hill** `16` `£5–7`
**Chardonnay 2000**
Lovely lemon/melon – the usual thing – but with added oomph.

**Hardys Stamp of** `14` `–£5.00`
**Australia Riesling Gewürztraminer 2001**
Good with Thai dishes.

**Hardys Stamp** `14.5` `–£5.00`
**Semillon/Chardonnay 2000**
Good underripe melon and lemon.

**Hardys Tintara** `13` `£7–10`
**Chardonnay 2000**
Overpriced by pounds. Selected stores.

**Jacobs Creek** `15` `–£5.00`
**Chardonnay 2000**
Simple melon and lemon fruit with a nutty undertone of some elegance.

**Jindalee Chardonnay** `16` `–£5.00`
**2000**
Simply delightful and layered: gooseberries, melons and pears and subtle lemons. A lovely mouthful of assertiveness yet restraint. Good texture, too.

**Lindemans Bin 65** `16` `£5–7`
**Chardonnay 2000**

Terrific. Over a fiver? Shame about that.

**Lindemans Botrytis Riesling 1998 (half bottle)** `15` `£5–7`
Young, sweet, pineappley, honey and lime fruit which is five or six years off its peak.

**Lindemans Cawarra Unoaked Chardonnay 2000** `14` `–£5.00`
Shows true quality of rich lemon fruit with no intrusive wood.

**Oxford Landing Sauvignon Blanc 2000** `16` `–£5.00`
Superbly subtle riches and striking cleanness of tonality. A benchmark fiver's worth of New World Sauvignon: crisp and fresh and biting without being remotely tart or too dry.

**Penfolds Bin 21 Rawson's Retreat Semillon/Colombard/ Chardonnay 2000** `14` `–£5.00`
Pleasant Thai food white.

**Penfolds Koonunga Hill Chardonnay 2000** `16` `£5–7`
One of Oz's finest brands – pity it's gone over a fiver.

**Rosemount Chardonnay 2000** `16` `£5–7`
Rich yet subtle. Superb class. Selected stores.

**Rosemount Semillon/ Chardonnay 2000** `15` `£5–7`
Delicious tanginess and melon ripeness undercut by fresh lemon.

**Shadow Ridge Chardonnay Colombard 2000** `15.5` `–£3.50`
Lovely texture to it – and fine dry fruit of the usual recipe.

**Tortoiseshell Bay Sauvignon Semillon 2000** `13.5` `–£5.00`
Subdued on the finish.

## SPAR WHITE

**Bleasdale Verdelho 1999** `13.5` `£5–7`
Rather expensive for the style, which is vaguely fat and spicy, but good with Thai food.

**De Bortoli Australian Dry White 2000, Spar** `13` `–£5.00`
Very tangy and tartaric acidy.

**De Bortoli Australian Semillon Chardonnay 1999, Spar** `13.5` `–£5.00`
Fat, rich fruit of little subtlety but fine with spicy Chinese food.

**Lindemans Bin 65 Chardonnay 1999** `16.5` `–£5.00`
Simply one of the tastiest, classiest examples of grape under-a-fiver in the world.

## TESCO WHITE

**Australian Chardonnay, Tesco** `16` `–£3.50`
Terrific value here, fully represented by the exuberance of the blue rollers on the label as much as by the tidal wave of

flavour in the fruit. Lush, loving, warm, delicious.

**Australian White NV, Tesco** 15.5 −£3.50
Staggeringly good value: dry, subtle, clean and not OTT and indeed, refreshingly untypical of the style of white wine Australia usually turns out at this price.

**Banrock Colombard Chardonnay 2000** 15 −£5.00
Nice flesh to the fruit which has pear and gooseberry with a distant echo of lime (and, dare I add, a hint of raspberry). A glugging masterpiece of direct fruitiness. Most stores.

**Banrock Station Chardonnay 2000** 15 −£5.00
Brilliant wine for spicy food. Has textured ripeness and depth.

**Barramundi Semillon/ Chardonnay NV** 16 −£5.00
Simply delicious from nose to throat – lovely, fresh fruit here.

**Blue Pyrenees Estate Chardonnay 1997** 16.5 £10–13
A big sticky wine where sticky butterscotch fruit offers a fruit custard finish of striking texture and tenacity. Not subtle but not OTT either. It's deeply meaningful and looking for a relationship. Wine Advisor stores only.

**Bonic Estate Chardonnay 2000** 15 −£5.00
Very ripe, rich and food friendly.

**Brown Brothers Dry Muscat 2000** 14 −£5.00
Very dry and the grapey Muscatiness is a little shy but as an aperitif it works fine.

**Great Southern Riesling 2000, Tesco** 16.5 £5–7
A monument of tanginess and textured minerality. Not only utterly delicious now, with its elegant citricity, but capable of developing for ten years in bottle and becoming nigh-perfect. Brilliant specimen of New World Riesling. One of Tesco's so-called 'Finest' range. Most stores.

**Hardys Stamp of Australia Chardonnay Semillon 2000** 15 −£5.00
In rich fettle, this established brand. Has a conventional recipe, melon and lemon with a twist, subtle, on the finish. This reveals a faint herbiness.

**Hunter Valley Semillon 2000, Tesco** 16 £5–7
I love the way the wine takes you one way only to reveal the other side of itself. This is often the way with this grape and here we get lime, gooseberry and melon, and a hint of raspberry, in bewildering array. Delicious bookworm's wine. One of Tesco's so-called 'Finest' range. Most stores.

**Image Chardonnay 2000** 13 −£5.00
'A girly wine' says Tesco. And so it is, although its buyer is a man. What he means is that this is a

'girls'-night-out' wine packed in a neon-green bottle and labelled like a soft drink. The fruit is plump and easy going.

**Jacobs Creek** `15` `—£5.00`
**Chardonnay 2000**
Simple melon and lemon fruit with a nutty undertone of some elegance.

**Jacobs Creek Dry** `15` `—£5.00`
**Riesling 2000**
Delicious young fruit (which will develop more nuances if cellared for a couple of years). Has really balanced, highly attractive charms.

**Langhorne Creek** `15` `£5–7`
**Verdelho 2000, Tesco**

**Lindemans Bin 65** `16` `—£5.00`
**Chardonnay 2000**
Touch more fatness to the fruit in this vintage. Still one of Oz's great, and great value, brands. Most stores.

**Lindemans Cawarra** `15.5` `—£5.00`
**Chardonnay 2000**
Lovely fruit here suggestive of Cox's apples, ripe pears and a touch of Ogen melon. Great quaffing. Not at all stores.

**Miranda White Pointer** `13.5` `—£5.00`
**2000**
Nervous, edgy freshness.

**Mount Pleasant** `15.5` `£7–10`
**Elizabeth Semillon 1994**

**Normans Unwooded** `16.5` `—£5.00`
**Chardonnay 2000**
Quite superb richness and balance

for a fiver. Elegance and finesse, yet fullness and richness. This is a remarkably complete wine which demonstrates its purity of fruit in all ways. It may have added acids but it's finely balanced. Most stores.

**Overtly Aromatic** `15` `—£5.00`
**White NV, Tesco**
More overt lime fruit than hugely aromatic. A superbly cheeky and tangy wine for oriental food. Most stores.

**Oxford Landing** `15.5` `—£5.00`
**Chardonnay 2000**
Lovely texture to the melon/lemon fruit with a hint of toffee.

**Oxford Landing** `16` `—£5.00`
**Sauvignon Blanc 2000**
Superbly subtle riches and striking cleanness of tonality. A benchmark fiver's worth of New World Sauvignon: crisp and fresh and biting without being remotely tart or too dry. Most stores.

**Padthaway** `16` `£5–7`
**Chardonnay 2000,**
**Tesco**
Touch of warm spice, hint of minerals, suggestion of vegetality. A lovely open-hearted wine of charm and style. Most stores.

**Rosemount** `16` `£5–7`
**Chardonnay 2000**
Rich yet subtle. Superb class. Most stores.

Rosemount Sauvignon `15` `£5–7`
Blanc 2000

Rosemount Semillon/ `15` `£5–7`
Chardonnay 2000
Delicious tanginess and melon
ripeness undercut by fresh lemon.

Rosemount Semillon/ `15` `£5–7`
Sauvignon 2000
Has a fatness and sourness from
the Semillon and a tangy
crispness from the Sauvignon –
the result is a successful marriage.

Smithbrook `15` `£7–10`
Chardonnay 1998

Smooth Voluptuous `15` `–£5.00`
White NV, Tesco

Tim Adams Riesling `16` `£7–10`
2000
Beautiful lime/mineral aroma
and fresh fruit – real tangy
apricots/oranges/limes – all very
very subtle – and a clean lemon
finish. Will age for years and
years with distinction. Limited
distribution.

Tim Adams Semillon `16.5` `£7–10`
1998
Pineapple, pear, melon and lime:
enough of a mouthful for you? It
is for me.

Woolpunda Blue Block `15.5` `–£5.00`
Chardonnay 1998

Yendah Vale `12` `–£5.00`
Chardonnay/Merlot
Rosé 2000
Has an odd medicinal tang.

Brown Brothers Late `16.5` `£5–7`
Harvested Orange
Muscat & Flora 1999
(half bottle)
It's the gorgeous honeyed hard-
fruit acids which make it so
exceptional as a pudding wine.
Great with ice cream.

Bushmans Crossing `13` `–£5.00`
Semillon/Chardonnay
2000
Doesn't quite get to the other
side.

Cape Mentelle `17` `£7–10`
Semillon/Sauvignon
2000
Simply one of Oz's greatest white
wines – in this vintage it even
sports tannins to give the
pineapple, lemons and pears real
grip.

Chapel Hill Verdelho `16.5` `£7–10`
1999
Superb tangy tension between the
gently spicy fruit and firm acids.
Terrific stuff – for food or mood.

Charleston Pinot Gris `15` `£5–7`
2000
Very attractive apricot fruit.

Château Tahbilk `17` `£5–7`
Marsanne 1998
Young yet beautifully textured,
tangy and tremendously
minerally yet ripe. Has layers of
pineapple. lemon and gooseberry.
Will age for eight to ten years.

**Currawong Creek** `13` `−£5.00`
**Chardonnay 2000**

**De Bortoli Yarra Valley** `14` `£10–13`
**Chardonnay 1999**
Very expensive lushness.

**Glenara Organic Dry** `16.5` `£7–10`
**Riesling 1996**
Lovely mature fruit, beginning to
thicken and get interesting, with
tangy minerals, pineapples, limes
and a dry, elegant finish.

**Greg Norman Estates** `13` `£7–10`
**Yarra Valley**
**Chardonnay 2000**

**Hardys Stamp of** `13.5` `−£5.00`
**Australia Grenache**
**Shiraz Rosé 1999**

**Houghton Classic Dry** `15.5` `£5–7`
**White 1998**

**Jindalee Chardonnay** `16` `−£5.00`
**2000**
Simply delightful and layered:
gooseberries, melons and pears
and subtle lemons. A lovely
mouthful of assertiveness yet
restraint. Good texture, too.

**Nepenthe Lenswood** `16` `£7–10`
**Riesling 2000**
Beautiful tangy ripeness which
will reach greater heights of oily
citricity if the wine is cellared for
five to ten years.

**Nepenthe Vineyards** `16.5` `£7–10`
**Lenswood Semillon**
**1998**
Wonderful level of rich fruit and
finely wrought acids. A very

elegant and decisive white wine
of great class.

**Nepenthe Vineyards** `16` `£7–10`
**Sauvignon Blanc 2000**
Lingers lushly yet freshly and
offers great finely-knitted acids.

**Oxford Landing** `17` `£5–7`
**Limited Release**
**Viognier 2000**
Superb dry peach, walnut, pear
and melon with very subtle
lemon edging. An outstanding
Viognier.

**Oxford Landing** `16` `−£5.00`
**Sauvignon Blanc 2000**
Superbly subtle riches and
striking cleanness of tonality. A
benchmark fiver's worth of New
World Sauvignon: crisp and fresh
and biting without being
remotely tart or too dry.

**Penfolds Bin 95a** `13.5` `£13–20`
**Chardonnay**

**Penfolds Old Vine** `16` `£5–7`
**Semillon, Barossa 1998**
I love the strident buttery
richness as it impacts on the buds
and then the stream of lush
acidity which strikes the
throat.

**Penfolds Rawson's** `14` `−£5.00`
**Retreat Bin 202**
**Riesling 2000**
Needs a couple more years. Will
rate 16-plus then.

**Rosemount Estate** `16` `£7–10`
**Show Reserve**
**Chardonnay 1999**

Gorgeous gentle creamy finish, fine acids, good melon/lemon richness. A very good class of Chard.

**Roxburgh Chardonnay** `13.5` `£20+`
**1997**
Thirty quid? Why? In heaven's name why?

**Tea Tree Estate** `13.5` `−£5.00`
**Chardonnay/**
**Sauvignon Blanc 2000**
Dry and fresh. Touches of lemon. Good fish food.

**Voyager Estate** `13` `£10–13`
**Chardonnay 1999**

**Wirra Wirra Oaked** `17` `£7–10`
**Chardonnay 1998**
Superb class here really stretches what Chardonnay can do without coming apart. Lovely ripeness yet delicacy and huge immediacy of impact. Drink it young. It's wonderful young. Limited branches.

**Yalumba Eden Valley** `17.5` `£7–10`
**Viognier 1999**
A quite brilliant and impressively assembled woody Viognier of such elegance and class it towers head and shoulders over so many pricey Condrieu wines.

# AUSTRIA

The world's most eccentric wine nation – with some of the
world's greatest wines.

## TESCO RED

Blauer Zweigelt Lenz `14.5` `−£5.00`
Moser 1997

## SAFEWAY WHITE

Cat's Leap Gruner `12` `−£5.00`
Veltliner 1999

## WAITROSE WHITE

Munzenrieder 1997 `13` `£5–7`
(half bottle)
Cellar it for ten more years to
discover what it can truly deliver.

# BULGARIA

Once Thrace, it supplied mercenaries to Troy and wine to the Spartans – how's that for commercial ingenuity?

## BOOTHS RED

Boyar Cabernet Merlot `12.5` `−£3.50` 1998

## CO-OP RED

Bulgarian Cabernet `15` `−£3.50` Sauvignon 2000, Co-op
Fantastic price for such serious fruitiness and hints of class.

Mount Sofia Merlot `14.5` `−£3.50` Pinot Noir NV
Surprisingly successful amalgam of cherries and tannins and a hint of spice. Superstores only.

Oravinifera Cabernet `16` `−£5.00` Sauvignon Reserve 1996
Plum full of tannins, tenacious and taut, and finely throughout are plums and raspberries and blackberries.

Sliven Merlot/Pinot `13.5` `−£3.50` Noir NV

## KWIK SAVE RED

Bulgarian Cabernet `13.5` `−£3.50` Sauvignon 1999. Somerfield

Bulgarian Country Red `13` `−£3.50` 2000, Somerfield
Rather rustic in its texture.

## MORRISONS RED

Boyar Iambol Cabernet `14.5` `−£3.50` Sauvignon 1999

Boyar Premium Oak `13.5` `−£5.00` Merlot 1997

Danube Red 1999 `13.5` `−£3.50`

## SAFEWAY RED

Azbuka Merlot 1996 `15` `£5−7`

Nazdrave Cabernet `15.5` `−£5.00` Sauvignon 1999

Sapphire Cove NV `14.5` `−£3.50`

Young Vatted Cabernet `14` `−£3.50` Sauvignon 2000, Safeway

Juicy, touch sweet, good tannins. Most stores.

**Young Vatted Merlot** `12` −£3.50
**2000, Safeway**
Most stores.

## SAINSBURY'S RED

**Blue Ridge 617 Merlot** `14` −£5.00
**1999**
Tannins, tight and deep, hold the fruit in a rich grip. Most stores.

**Bulgarian Cabernet** `15.5` −£3.50
**Sauvignon, Sainsbury's**
**(3 litre box)**
Price band indicates the 75cl equivalent.

**Bulgarian Merlot NV,** `15.5` −£3.50
**Sainsbury's**

## SOMERFIELD RED

**Bulgarian Cabernet** `13.5` −£3.50
**Sauvignon 1999,**
**Somerfield**

**Bulgarian Country Red** `13` −£3.50
**2000, Somerfield**
Rather rustic in its texture.

## SPAR RED

**Bulgarian Country** `13` −£3.50
**Wine Cabernet**
**Sauvignon & Merlot**
**NV, Spar**

**Suhindol Estate** `12` −£5.00
**Cabernet Sauvignon**
**2000, Spar**

Bit thin as it opens, but gathers some pace, only to finish dustily.

## TESCO RED

**Reka Valley Bulgarian** `14.5` −£3.50
**Cabernet Sauvignon**
**NV, Tesco**

## WAITROSE RED

**Blue Ridge American** `14.5` −£5.00
**Barrel Merlot 1999**
Good leather and subtly spicy plums.

**Domaine Boyar** `15` −£3.50
**Merlot/Gamza, Iambol**
**1999**

## CO-OP WHITE

**Shumen Chardonnay** `14.5` −£3.50
**Sauvignon Blanc 2000**
Very accomplished blend of styles which is totally harmonised and well-ordered.

**Shumen Muskat &** `14` −£3.50
**Ugni Blanc 1999**
A far from charmless one-step non-wonder: has perfume and grapeyness. An excellent aperitif.

**Sliven Valley of the** `13.5` −£3.50
**Roses Rosé 2000**
Sticky edge but it's not OTT and the cherries are nicely perfumed.

## MORRISONS WHITE

Boyar Pomorie    10    −£3.50
Chardonnay 1998

## SAFEWAY WHITE

Valley of the Roses    14    −£3.50
Rosé 2000
Cherryish, dry and treads a fine
line between delicious and tasty.
Selected stores.

## SOMERFIELD WHITE

Blue Ridge Black Rosé    13    −£5.00
2000

Blue Ridge Chardonnay   13.5   −£5.00
2000
Somewhat anonymous 'catch-all'
Chardonnay.

Bulgarian Chardonnay    16    −£3.50
1999, Somerfield
One of the best Chardonnays I've
tasted from this country. There
are, I assure you, far less
appealing and aromatically
adventurous burgundies on sale
at ten times the price.

Spice Trail White 2000   13.5   −£5.00
And spicy it is. Definite coriander
edge to it.

## SPAR WHITE

Bulgarian Country    11    −£3.50
White NV, Spar

Preslav Estate    12    −£5.00
Bulgarian Chardonnay
2000, Spar
Dry, very dry.

43

# CANADA

I hold this country in great affection (I was once married to a Canadian). Its wives, though, do not offer sustaining relationships.

## WAITROSE WHITE

Mission Hill Private
Reserve Pinot Blanc
1999    11    £5–7

Peller Estates Founders    10    −£5.00
Series Vidal 1999
Dull beyond the arctic circle of belief.

# CHILE

Everybody's favourite – thanks to its incredibly
clement climate.

## ASDA RED

**35 South Cabernet Sauvignon 1999**  `17`  `–£5.00`
Remarkably collected (acid, tannins, fruit) for the money. It lingers, it tongue lashes, it throat teases – a superbly well-marshalled assault on the senses.

**Big Chilean Cabernet 2000 (1.5 litres)**  `15`  `–£3.50`
Lots of savoury plum, a hint of raspberry, a suggestion of herbs. Great glugging.

**Casas del Bosque Merlot 1999**  `14`  `£5–7`

**Castillo de Molina Cabernet Sauvignon 1998**  `15.5`  `£5–7`

**Cono Sur Cabernet Sauvignon Reserve, Rapel Valley 1999**  `16.5`  `–£5.00`
Huge deep fruit and chocolate richness. Not as fruity as the 2000 but still remarkable.

**Cono Sur Pinot Noir 1999**  `16.5`  `–£5.00`
The aroma is of wild raspberries and truffles, the fruit has touches of cassis of Morello cherry, the finish recalls the farmyard. Is this a £100 Richeborg? No, it's a Chilean Pinot for under a fiver.

**Terra Mater Cabernet Sauvignon 1999**  `13`  `–£5.00`
Very sweet for a Cab, especially a Chilean one.

**Terra Mater Carmenère Cabernet Sauvignon 1998**  `14`  `–£5.00`
Odd specimen of rich lushness with a bell pepper undertone. Needs robust food to be at its best.

**Terra Mater Zinfandel Shiraz 2000**  `14`  `–£5.00`
Delicious with Indian food – quite quite delicious.

**Valdivieso Single Vineyard Merlot 1998**  `16.5`  `£7–10`
Superb soft leather and chocolate and cassis and unctuous tannins. Lovely wine with exceptional finesse and grace (for such weight). Selected stores.

## BOOTHS RED

**Apaltagua Carmenère** 13.5 £5–7
**2000**
A relaxed curry wine.

**Carmen Grande Vidure** 16.5 £7–10
**Cabernet Sauvignon**
**1998**
Rousingly perfumed, nobly
leathery and cassis fruit, with piles
of fruity texture. A lovely wine.

**Cono Sur Pinot Noir** 16 –£5.00
**2000**
Delicious vegetal Pinot-osity and
terrific tannins. A lovely cherry
and wild raspberry specimen.

**Sierra Cabernet** 13.5 –£5.00
**Sauvignon 2000**

**Subsol Cabernet** 15 –£5.00
**Malbec 1999**
Rich textured rampancy.

## BUDGENS RED

**Paso del Sol Cabernet** 13 –£5.00
**Sauvignon 1999**
Juicy and ripe with some mildly
arousing tannins.

**Stowells of Chelsea** 14.5 –£5.00
**Cabernet Merlot NV**

**Terra Andina Cabernet** 12 –£5.00
**Sauvignon 2000**
Very ripe and jammy.

**Terra Mater Zinfandel** 14 £7–10
**Shiraz 2000**
Delicious with Indian food – quite
quite delicious.

## CO-OP RED

**Antares Merlot 2000** 16 –£5.00
Superb polish to this classy wine.
It really wins on its lovely rich
texture and elongated stylishness.
Not at Convenience Stores.

**Casa Lapostolle Merlot** 18 £10–13
**Cuvee Alexandre 1997**
One of the finest Merlots on the
face of the planet. The balance of
tannins and complex fruit is a
marvel, so classy, and the finish is
composed of subtle chocolate and
cassis. Marvellous stuff.
Superstores only.

**Chilean Cabernet** 15 –£5.00
**Sauvignon NV, Co-op**
Good, dry, deep fruit of gentility
yet character.

**Chilean Fair Trade** 15.5 –£5.00
**Carmenère 2000, Co-op**

**Four Rivers Malbec** 14 –£5.00
**1999**
Bargain fruity tippling. Great with
food.

**Las Lomas Cot Reserva** 15.5 £5–7
**1999**
Classy, intense, tannic, very dry,
food friendly. Made from singed
fruit? Tastes deliciously so.
Superstores only.

**Las Lomas Organic** 15 –£5.00
**Chilean Red 1999**
Juicy but not overwhlemingly so.
It has excellent balance – alcohol
with tannins – and an urgency to
please. The finish is rich and firm.
Not at Convenience Stores.

**Long Slim Cabernet** 16 −£5.00
**Merlot 2000**
Compelling fruit with touches of
pepper, cooked vegetables, fine
tannins and overall rich berries.
Terrific wine for the money.

**Terra Mater Malbec** 15.5 −£5.00
**1999**

**Terra Mater Zinfandel** 14 £7–10
**Shiraz 2000**
Delicious with Indian food – quite
quite delicious. Superstores only.

**Valdivieso Cabernet** 17 £7–10
**Franc Reserve 1997**
Quite remarkable chocolate
richness here with seemingly
undetectable yet delectable acids
and fine tannins providing great
poise. Intensely civilised tippling
here. Superstores only.

**Viña Gracia Cabernet** 15.5 £5–7
**Sauvignon Reserve**
**1999**

**Viña Gracia Carmenère** 16 −£5.00
**Reserve Especial 1999**
Vibrant, sexy, textured,
beautifully harmonised elements
(fruit, tannins, acids) and a real
flurry of delicious acidity on the
finish.

**Chilean Cabernet** 15.5 −£5.00
**Sauvignon Viña La**
**Rosa 2000, Somerfield**
Superb texture.

**Casa Leona Cabernet** 16.5 −£5.00
**Sauvignon 2000**
Has beautifully constructed
textured hint of spice, touch of
cassis, lovely pert tannins which
are mannered and don't intrude,
and the finish is lilting.

**Casa Leona Merlot** 16.5 −£5.00
**2000**
Superb texture to this wine. It has
tannins like corduroy, fruit like
satin, acids like truffled cherries.

**Cuartel 34 Malbec** 16 £7–10
**Reserve 1999**
Reserved? Don't you believe it.
This wine hares out of the bottle
with a rush of gamy spice and
loads of tannins to tease the
drinker into unresolveable debate:
is it chocolate? coffee? tea? cocoa?
Well, it's something delicious.

**Leon de Oro Merlot/** 17 £7–10
**Cabernet Sauvignon**
**1999**
Decant this wine three to four
hours beforehand but keep the
bottle to stick a candle in. This is
a big but elegant wine with
panache and punchiness. It has
layers of ripe fruit interlaced,
deftly, with wonderful tannins.

**Los Claveles Cabernet/** 15 −£5.00
**Carmenère 2000**
Good warmth to tannins and
richness to the blackcurrants. An
excellent wine for roast
vegetables with melted haloumi
cheese.

**Pirque Estate Cabernet** `16.5` `£5–7`
**Sauvignon/Merlot 2000**
Spicy cherries, coffee, chocolate,
and some kind of baked fruit on
the finish. The lingering
chewiness of the wine leaves a
memorable residue of expresso
and black olives. A delicious
experience, not for the faint-
hearted.

**Sierra Los Andes** `16` `£5–7`
**Merlot Cabernet 1999**
A sweet-edged wine, with rich
deep tannins, to go with spicy
food. Loads of personality here
without it being overbearing.

**Sierra Los Andes** `17.5` `£5–7`
**Reserve Cabernet**
**Merlot 1999**
Magnificent depth of class here.
Brilliant tannins back up pepper,
leather, blackcurrants, chives,
touch of pear, and the whole
package is rolled up into a perfect
texture.

**Tolten Syrah/Cabernet** `17` `£7–10`
**Sauvignon 1999**
A massive attack (without being
an overdose) of rich blackberries
and bouncy tannins which
cascade into daringly overripe and
very raunchy richness over the
palate in an extravagance of depth
and flavour. This is not a wine to
take lightly. It treats the palate
shamelessly.

## MORRISONS RED

**Antares Merlot 2000** `16` `–£5.00`
Superb polish to this classy wine.
It really wins on its lovely rich
texture and elongated
stylishness.

**Condor Chilean Merlot** `14.5` `–£5.00`
**2000**
Combines excellent tannins with
cherries and soft berries. Very
good texture.

**'M' Chilean Cabernet** `14.5` `–£5.00`
**Sauvignon 2000**
As quaffable as a dry, rich
Cabernet can get. Most attractive
texture and warmth of finish.

**Undurraga Carmenère** `12` `£5–7`
**2000**
Odd baked fruit of curious gawky
richness and ripeness.

**Villa Montes Cabernet** `15.5` `–£5.00`
**Sauvignon 1999**

## SAFEWAY RED

**35 South Cabernet** `17` `–£5.00`
**Sauvignon 1999**
Remarkably collected (acid,
tannins, fruit) for the money. It
lingers, it tongue lashes, it throat
teases – a superbly well-
marshalled assault on the senses.

**Acacias Estate Merlot,** `14` `–£5.00`
**Maipo Valley 1998,**
**Safeway**

**Casa Lapostolle Cuvée** `18` `£7–10`
**Alexandre Merlot 1999**
Still one of the most beautifully

integrated Merlots on the planet. Has great fruit, outstanding tannins and complex acids.

**Chilean Cabernet Sauvignon 2000, Safeway** `13` `–£5.00`
Sulphur too evident on the specimen I tasted. But tannins are in. Most stores.

**Concha y Toro Casillero del Diablo Cabernet Sauvignon 1999** `16.5` `–£5.00`
Superb lingering richness, dry, herby, plummy and deft, and the tannins are crunchy without being bitter or twisted. Brilliant texture to the whole performance.

**Cono Sur Cabernet Sauvignon, Rapel Valley 2000** `17` `–£5.00`
An amazingly thickly textured, ripe wine of great depth and profundity. Hordes of flavours crowd the palate, or seem to, rather like intruders at the gate: too many to repel.

**El Cadejo Cabernet Sauvignon 2000** `14` `–£5.00`
Simple glugging charm. Has a warm rich texture to very soft tannins and loose berried fruit.

**Errázuriz Syrah Reserva 1999** `15` `£7–10`
An unusual blend of Rhône and Bordeaux with Italian tannins and earthiness. Most entertaining. Selected stores.

**Isla Negra Merlot 2000** `16.5` `£5–7`
Classic battered leather suitcase aroma introduces superbly voluptuous richness and layered levels of ripe hedgerow fruits with superb, balancing tannins.

**Terra Mater Zinfandel Shiraz 2000** `14` `£7–10`
Delicious with Indian food – quite quite delicious.

**Valdivieso Malbec 2000** `15` `–£5.00`
Tangy berries, warm, slightly chewy tannins, and a jammy finish.

**Valdivieso Single Vineyard Cabernet Franc 1998** `16.5` `£7–10`
Very jammy and spicy yet with brilliant textured tannins. Marvellous food wine. Selected stores.

**Valdivieso Single Vineyard Merlot 1998** `16.5` `£7–10`
Superb soft leather and chocolate and cassis and unctuous tannins. Lovely wine with exceptional finesse and grace (for such weight).

**Viña Morande Syrah 2000** `14` `–£5.00`
Very ripe, bright fruit with grand tannins. Selected stores.

## SAINSBURY'S RED

**Caliboro Carignan Old Vine Reserva 2000** `14` `–£5.00`
Juicy and ripe, quaffably berried

and respectable, and fine with spicy food.

**Chilean Cabernet** `16` `–£5.00`
**Merlot NV, Sainsbury's**
**(3 litre box)**
It's the best red in a box. It has oodles of flavour, toffeed and blackcurranty, with good acids and fine tannins. It is both a great food wine and a great quaffer. Price band indicates the 75cl equivalent.

**Chilean Merlot NV,** `16.5` `–£5.00`
**Sainsbury's**
Wonderful dry elegant opening, then the rich leather (soft, luxurious) cuts in, and then a big finish of savoury depth. A stunning quaff for the dosh.

**Concha y Toro** `17` `–£5.00`
**Casillero del Diablo**
**Cabernet Sauvignon**
**2000**
Berried up to its neck in hedgerow offerings, beautifully structured interplay between tannins and a great texture, complex finish and great class. Most stores.

**Cono Sur 20 Barrels** `16.5` `£10–13`
**Merlot 1999**
So immensely sure of itself and richly endowed with complex berries, acids and lovely tannins that it stands comparison with any Merlot in the world. 85 selected stores.

**Cono Sur Reserva** `16.5` `£5–7`
**Merlot 1999**
Incredibly thickly-knitted and chewy. Great tannins!

**Errázuriz Merlot 2000** `16` `£5–7`
Very aromatic, chewy (almost chocolate-biscuity) fruit of immense flavour and urgent-to-please richness. Selected stores.

**Errázuriz Pinot Noir** `17` `£7–10`
**Reserva 1999**
A complete Pinot: from the aromas of truffle and game sauce as it opens up, through the cherries, raspberries and acids of the fruit, to the lovely tannins and hint of farmyard on the finish. The Côte d'Or et Beaune can only gawp and admire. 80 selected stores.

**Isla Negra Syrah 2000** `16` `£5–7`
Gorgeous textured richness, it makes several examples of the same grape (Shiraz) from Oz seem rather spineless. Most stores.

**La Palmeria Merlot** `18.5` `£7–10`
**Gran Reserva 1999**
Totally astonishing maturity yet freshness. Deep tannins, chewy and ripe, wonderfully textured berries and a magically rich, velvet finish.

**MontGras Carmenère** `16` `£5–7`
**Reserva 1999**
Wonderful chewy texture, very sound tannins, and a lovely crunchy berried finish – you can almost feel the pips in the blackberries. Most stores.

**Terra Mater Zinfandel** 14 −£5.00
**Shiraz 2000**
Delicious with Indian food – quite
quite delicious. Most stores.

**Valdivieso Malbec 2000** 15 −£5.00
Tangy berries, warm, slightly
chewy tannins, and a jammy
finish. Most stores.

**Valdivieso Merlot 2000** 16 −£5.00
A leather bound classic. Touch of
Hardy, hint of Conrad, even a
suggestion of Roth. Most stores.

## SOMERFIELD RED

**Canelo Estate Cabernet** 15.5 −£5.00
**Sauvignon 2000**
Delicious. Has a touch of malt
chocolate on the finish.

**Canelo Estate** 15 −£5.00
**Carmenère 2000**
What lovely understated berries
here. Very elegant.

**Chilean Cabernet** 15.5 −£5.00
**Sauvignon Viña La**
**Rosa 2000, Somerfield**
Superb texture.

**Chilean Cabernet/** 16 −£5.00
**Merlot Viña La Rosa**
**2000, Somerfield**
Fantastic price for such high class
tannins and berries.

**Chilean Merlot 2000,** 16 −£5.00
**Somerfield**
Superb. What more can one add?
The price is amazing for such
richness.

**Cono Sur Cabernet** 16 £5–7
**Sauvignon Reserve**
**1998**
Coffee, cassis, tannins – what a
formula for exquisite quaffing.
Selected stores.

**Cono Sur Pinot Noir** 16 −£5.00
**2000**
Delicious vegetal Pinot-osity and
terrific tannins. A lovely cherry
and wild raspberry specimen.

**Errázuriz Cabernet** 16 £5–7
**Sauvignon 2000**
Superb class in a glass – and by
itself. Great subtle chocolate, fruit
and tannins. Selected stores.

**Isla Negra Cabernet** 16 £5–7
**Sauvignon 2000**
Lip smackingly deep and dry and
delicious. Selected stores.

**Isla Negra Merlot 2000** 16.5 £5–7
Classic battered leather suitcase
aroma introduces superbly
voluptuous richness and layered
levels of ripe hedgerow fruits
with superb, balancing tannins.

**Santa Ines Cabernet** 16.5 £5–7
**Sauvignon Reserve**
**1999**
Magnificent texture, polished
tannins, elegant cut to the finish.

**Tarapaca Gran** 16.5 £5–7
**Cabernet Sauvignon**
**Reserve 1999**
Wonderful layered riches here
combining four fruits, five spices,
three herbs and great single-
minded tannins. Selected stores.

**Terrarum Merlot 2000** `16.5` `£5–7`
Rampant yet doesn't overreach
itself with lovely dry berries and
fruits, brilliantly textured and
tight, and superb tannins.

## SPAR RED

**Canepa Merlot 1998,** `15` `–£5.00`
**Spar**

**Chilean Cabernet** `15` `£5–7`
**Sauvignon 2000, Spar**
Rich energetic quaffing here with
blackberries coated in good deep
tannins.

**Chilean Merlot 1999,** `14` `£5–7`
**Spar**
A rich curry-friendly red of
plummy depth and ripe textured
finish.

**Tocornal Red 2000,** `14` `–£5.00`
**Spar**
Sweetness tempered by dry
tannins make for a firm finish and
some lingering lushness.

## TESCO RED

**Caliterra Syrah 1999** `16` `£5–7`
A very leathery, savoury, pliant
Syrah which oozes charm
without oozing OTT fruit. (Yet it
is unashamedly modern.) Not at
all stores.

**Chilean Cabernet** `16` `–£5.00`
**Sauvignon NV, Tesco**
Chocolate with raspberry with a
hint of earth and blackcurrant on
the finish. And that's just the
finish.

**Chilean Cabernet** `15.5` `–£5.00`
**Sauvignon Reserve**
**2000, Tesco**
Very juicy initial approach, then
the tannins bite. Good quaffing
for blackcurrant fans (but this is
dry to finish). One of Tesco's so-
called 'Finest' range. Most
stores.

**Chilean Malbec NV,** `16.5` `–£5.00`
**Tesco**
What a bargain! Has gorgeous
texture to it (thanks largely to the
lovely tannins) and terrific leather
and blackberry fruitiness.
Surprisingly elegant and balanced
for the money. Most stores.

**Chilean Merlot NV,** `16` `–£5.00`
**Tesco**
Odd sort of Merlot. It's delicious
all right, but it has an unusual
vegetal edge of some intrigue.
Where did it come from? Where
will it go? You may drink it with
pleasure, however, without
reflecting on those questions.

**Chilean Merlot Reserve** `15.5` `–£5.00`
**2000, Tesco**
Delicious pacy fruit here of
texture and depth. Most stores.

**Chilean Red NV, Tesco** `15` `–£3.50`

**Cono Sur Pinot Noir** `16` `–£5.00`
**2000**
Delicious vegetal Pinot-osity and
terrific tannins. A lovely cherry
and wild raspberry specimen.

**Cono Sur Pinot Noir**  **Reserve 1999**
Lovely bitter cherry and wild raspberry fruit with wonderful meaty tannins – why, this wine is a meal in itself.

**Errázuriz Cabernet**  **Sauvignon Reserva 1998**
Hints of cigar box, spice, blackcurrants, raisins, liquorice and a very subtle lingering after-tang of coriander. Utterly delicious. Serious yet totally, captivatingly entertaining.

**Errázuriz Don**  **Maximiano 1998**
Very deep and delicious, superb tannins giving the wine personality and backbone. The overall impression is of power and concentration. Worth eighteen quid? When so much wonderful stuff from Chile costs around a fiver? Well, it rates 16. The tannins give it such class.

**Errázuriz Merlot 2000** 16 £5–7
Very aromatic, chewy (almost chocolate-biscuity) fruit of immense flavour and urgent-to-please richness.

**Errázuriz Syrah**  **Reserva 1998**
Beautifully aromatic, smooth, fruity and completely kitted out. Has hints of tobacco and cocoa within the voluptuous texture and the finish is highly cultured.

**Isla Negra Cabernet** 16 –£5.00 **Sauvignon, Rapel 1999**
A very concentrated, compacted wine with cherries, plums and hint of strawberry. The texture is gripping, gently grand and very gracious as it quits the throat.

**Isla Negra Merlot 2000**
Classic battered leather suitcase aroma introduces superbly voluptuous richness and layered levels of ripe hedgerow fruits with superb, balancing tannins.

**Luis Felipe Edwards**  **Cabernet Sauvignon Reserva 1999**
Juicier than previous vintages and less classically old-style Cabernet. But the tannins are alert and don't let the fruit slip away that easily.

**Salsa Cabernet** 14 –£5.00 **Sauvignon 2000**
Ripe plums, good tannins, very food-friendly fruit altogether. Excellent party wine when you wish to spoil your guests.

**Santa Ines Cabernet/** 17 –£5.00 **Merlot 2000**
Utterly remarkable wine for the money which soaks the taste buds in deep tannins, blackcurrants with spice, a touch of cocoa and cashew nut, and a lingering finish of savoury richness. Operates on the eye, nose and throat and the NHS could do worse than prescribe it to all liverish patients.

**Stowells Chilean Cabernet/Merlot NV**  14.5 −£5.00

**Terra Mater Cabernet Sauvignon 2000** 15 −£5.00
Brisk as many a top-notch claret but has sunnier tannins, more softness to the blackcurrants and greater wallop on the finish.

**Two Tribes Red NV** 14.5 −£5.00
Some really attractive savoury fruit here. Good tannins, too.

**Valdivieso Cabernet Franc Reserve 1999** 17 £7−10
Coffee, chocolate, tobacco, herbs, berries and elongated tannins of real class − it has it all. Nine quid yes. But more than nine quid's worth of fruit.

**Valdivieso Cabernet Sauvignon Reserve 1998**  17 £5−7
Coffee, cocoa, herbs, roast meat, tannins − what a liberal assembly of great riches here. Most stores.

**Valdivieso Carignan 1999**  16 −£5.00
Lovely earthy fruit, herby and warm, with a resounding sense of pleasure-seeking demeanour. A terrific quaffing wine − as well as going robustly with food. Selected stores.

**Valdivieso Malbec Reserve 1997** 16.5 £7−10
Gorgeous baked fruit texture which hardens − encrusted with superb tannins. Very rich and deep, full of stylish edges, and hugely elegant overall. Selected stores only.

**Vision Merlot Reserve 2000** 16.5 £7−10
Oh yes, this is more like it: rich, soft, spicy, layered, gorgeously tannic and brilliantly textured. Great tippling here. Selected stores.

## WAITROSE RED

**Caballo Loco No 4 NV** 16.5 £13−20
The best so far of this non-vintage blend. Individual, classy, deep and rich.

**Concha y Toro Merlot 2000**  14 −£5.00
Very smooth and plump.

**Cono Sur Cabernet Sauvignon, Rapel Valley 2000** 17 −£5.00
An amazingly thickly textured, ripe wine of great depth and profundity. Hordes of flavours crowd the palate, or seem to, rather like intruders at the gate: too many to repel.

**Errázuriz Cabernet Sauvignon 1999** 15.5 £5−7
One of the world's most civilised yet smoothly characterful and quaffable Cabs.

**Errázuriz Merlot 1999** 16 £5−7
Goes subtly peppery and tobacco-edged as it finishes. Lots of warmth, texture and richness here.

**Isla Negra Cabernet** `16` `£5–7`
**Sauvignon, Rapel 1999**
A very concentrated, compacted wine with cherries, plums and hint of strawberry. The texture is gripping, gently grand and very gracious as it quits the throat.

**Mont Gras Carmenère** `15.5` `£5–7`
**Reserva 2000**
Sweet plums and loganberries with a hint of chocolate. Fine-grained tannins complete the recipe.

**Valdivieso Barrel** `16.5` `£5–7`
**Selection Cabernet/ Merlot 1997**
Marvellous evolving fruit which takes delicious seconds to go from ripe blackcurrant to spicy plum. Gorgeous texture and lingering finish.

**Valdivieso Cabernet** `17.5` `£7–10`
**Franc Reserve 1998**
A superb wine of such staggering class (evidence: the texture, the swanky tannins and the aromatic fruit) that much more expensive Bordeaux pales into insignificance beside it. It is complex, tight, highly concentrated and very very lingering.

**Valdivieso Pinot Noir** `16` `£5–7`
**Reserve 1997**
Lovely chewy, gently exotic edge to the Pinot riches which include chocolate and spicy cherries.

## ASDA WHITE

**Casas del Bosque** `15` `£5–7`
**Sauvignon Blanc 1999**

**Chardonnay Reserve** `15.5` `£5–7`
**Cono Sur 1999**
Very rich and food-friendly.

**Chilean Sauvignon** `16` `–£5.00`
**Blanc 2000, Asda**
Superb value: elegance, richness, subtlety, texture and a smart finish.

**Undurraga** `16` `–£5.00`
**Gewürztraminer 2000**
At last! A really accomplished Undurraga wine: spicy, balanced, rich and very elegant. Selected stores.

**Valdivieso Malbec Rosé** `16.5` `–£5.00`
**2000**
One of the most delicious rosés I've tasted. Terrific spicy cherry and very subtle blackberry fruit with fine acids and an excellent texture. Brilliant thirst quencher, barbecue food wine and all-round civilised household friend. Selected stores.

## BOOTHS WHITE

**Casablanca Barrel** `16.5` `£5–7`
**Fermented Chardonnay 1999**
Superb! The finest white wine at Booths? Possibly. Has gorgeous woody richness, ripe fruit and teasing acids. A very fine Chardonnay indeed.

**Isla Negra Chardonnay** 15.5 £5–7
1999
Oily, rich, deep and charmingly
disorganised and slightly raffish.
Good quaffing companion.

**Sierra Sauvignon Blanc** 13.5 −£5.00
2000
Bit numb.

**Subsol Chardonnay** 14 −£5.00
Sauvignon 2000
Interesting oriental food wine.

**Subsol Chardonnay** 13 −£5.00
Sauvignon Vistamar
1999

**Tocornal White NV** 13.5 −£5.00
Dry and good value for PTA
parties.

## BUDGENS WHITE

**Paso del Sol Sauvignon** 13 −£5.00
Blanc 2000
Oddly ill at ease for a Chilean
wine.

**Terra Andina** 13.5 −£5.00
Chardonnay 2000
Has some richness and texture
but seems unbalanced as it
finishes.

## CO-OP WHITE

**Four Rivers** 13.5 −£5.00
Chardonnay 2000
Rich and soft and perfect with
tandoori cod or hake.

**Long Slim Chardonnay** 13 −£5.00
Semillon 2000
Long, yes, slim too.

**Santa Carolina** 16.5 −£5.00
Chardonnay 1999
Concentrated elegance here, but
not a hair is out of place; nothing
overdone. Understated? Maybe,
but very classy.

## KWIK SAVE WHITE

**Chilean Chardonnay** 15.5 −£5.00
2000, Somerfield
Dry melon nuttiness and calmly
textured ripeness. Pear and
pineapple on the finish.

**Chilean White 2000,** 14 −£3.50
Somerfield
Crisp and fresh.

## M & S WHITE

**Barrera Chardonnay** 13.5 −£5.00
2000
Bit short on the finish. Fatness
where it should have fitness.

**Casa Leona** 14 −£5.00
Chardonnay 2000
Not as insistently fruity and
exciting as previous vintages.

**Los Claveles** 13.5 −£5.00
Gewürztraminer 2000
The most oddly packed Gewürz
I've tasted – ever. Lacks varietal
spice and chutzpah. (That's what
you get from mucking it about by
adding 20% Chardonnay.)

**Pirque Estate** `13` `£7–10`
**Chardonnay 2000**
Curious cosmetic feel to it. The
lemon juice finish disturbs the
palate rather than smoothes it.

**Pirque Estate** `13` `£7–10`
**Sauvignon Blanc 2000**
£7.50? £2.99!

## MORRISONS WHITE

**35 South Chardonnay** `14.5` `–£5.00`
**2000**
A rich oriental food wine.

**Antu Mapu Reserva** `13` `–£5.00`
**Rosé 1999**

**Condor Chilean** `13` `–£5.00`
**Chardonnay 2001**
Very fat and fleshy. Bit too over-
exuberant for me.

**'M' Chilean Sauvignon** `13` `–£5.00`
**Blanc 2000**
Another fat and fleshy Morrisons
white wine under four quid. Can
we change the recipe, Stuart?

**Montes Alpha** `17.5` `£7–10`
**Chardonnay 1998**
Chile's Montrachet – if that isn't
to insult it. It has a creamy
vegetality, beautiful smooth
texture, subtle complex charms
on the tongue, and a lingering
smokiness as it descends – and
hits the soul.

**Villa Montes Sauvignon** `14` `–£5.00`
**Blanc 1999**

## SAFEWAY WHITE

**Aresti Gewürztraminer** `13` `–£5.00`
**2000**
Dry touch awkward on the finish.
Selected stores.

**Casa Lapostolle Cuvee** `17` `£7–10`
**Alexandre Chardonnay**
**1999**
The best white wine at Safeway:
subtle, dry (yet insistent and
coolly rich), layered, oily and
textured, stretching and
languorous on the taste buds and
very very accomplished. Has
complexity and real class.
Selected stores.

**Chilean Dry White** `16` `–£3.50`
**2000, Safeway**
Quite superb subtly grassy yet
rich-to-finish fruit. Much better
than a hundred Sancerres.

**Chilean Sauvignon** `16` `–£5.00`
**Blanc 2000, Safeway**
Superb value for money. Crisper
and more compelling than
Sancerre.

**Santa Rita Chardonnay** `16` `£5–7`
**1999**
Gorgeous melon, raspberry and
lemon fruit, hint of nut,
suggestion of minerality. Gentle
yet engrossing. Most stores.

## SAINSBURY'S WHITE

**Chilean Chardonnay** `16` `–£5.00`
**NV, Sainsbury's**
Length of flavour (Ogen melon
with very subtle spicing) and

concentration here provide a delicious mouthful.

**Chilean Sauvignon** `16.5` `–£5.00`
**Blanc NV, Sainsbury's**
Combines the hint of minerality classic Sauvignon must convey with delicate melon/lemon fruit with a hint of lime and pear.

**Errázuriz Wild** `17` `£7–10`
**Ferment Chardonnay,**
**Casablanca 1999**
It's most like a wild Meursault with its hint of vegetality and very lingering, creamy woodiness. Has a long-delayed richness, complex and fine, which demands the drinker employs a brain, to mull over the wine's effects, as well as the usual organs. Limited distribution.

**MontGras Chardonnay** `15.5` `£5–7`
**Reserva 1999**
Rich, ripe fruit with a hint of roasted nuts and toffees. Finishes with a resounding thwack of fruit. Most stores.

**MontGras Chardonnay** `15` `£5–7`
**Reserva 2000**
Very sticky toffee with the two thousand vintage, and more dry lemon. Most stores.

**Stowells Chilean** `15.5` `–£3.50`
**Sauvignon Blanc NV (3**
**litre box)**
Price band indicates the 75cl equivalent.

## SOMERFIELD WHITE

**Chilean Chardonnay** `15.5` `–£5.00`
**2000, Somerfield**
Dry melon nuttiness and calmly textured ripeness. Pear and pineapple on the finish.

**Chilean Sauvignon** `16` `–£5.00`
**Blanc 2001, Somerfield**
Tangy tenacity and lovely rolling acids.

**Chilean Semillon** `16` `–£5.00`
**Chardonnay 2000,**
**Somerfield**
Fantastically elegant and well-tailored for the money. Like M&S shirts twelve years ago.

**Chilean White 2000,** `14` `–£3.50`
**Somerfield**
Crisp and fresh.

**Cono Sur Viognier 2000** `15` `£5–7`
Very acute apricot richness with an added layer of stewed berries on the finish. Limited distribution.

**Errázuriz Chardonnay** `16` `£5–7`
**2000**
If it's not an overworked word in my limited vocabulary: delicious and scrumptious, elegant, buttery, delicate, wonderful. Selected stores.

**Isla Negra Chardonnay** `15` `£5–7`
**2000**
Dry and purposeful: lemon undertone to melon richness.

**Terrarum Sauvignon** `15` `–£5.00`
**Blanc 2000**
A high class dry contender for crab and prawn dishes.

## SPAR WHITE

**Canepa Chilean**   15.5   £5–7
**Chardonnay 1999, Spar**
Some good ripe fruit here, melon,
pear and pineapple, nicely
textured form to finish.

**Canepa Chilean**   14   –£5.00
**Sauvignon Blanc 1999,**
**Spar**
Chewy, ripe, baked gooseberry
edge.

**Tocornal Chilean**   13   –£5.00
**White 2000, Spar**
Dry richness which doesn't quite
reach an exciting finish.

## TESCO WHITE

**Chilean Chardonnay**   16   –£5.00
**Reserve 2000, Tesco**
Superb casual elegance to the
fruit here as though the wine was
born not made. Has unalloyed
deliciousness and charming
unpretentious richness. Part of
Tesco's 'Finest' range. Most
stores.

**Chilean Chardonnay,**   14   –£5.00
**Tesco**

**Chilean Sauvignon**   14.5   –£5.00
**Blanc NV, Tesco**

**Chilean White NV,**   14.5   –£3.50
**Tesco**

**Errázuriz Chardonnay**   16   £5–7
**1999**
Very distinguished in feel as it
slithers over the taste buds,

proving, if any further proof were
necessary, that Chile makes
abundantly toothsome
Chardonnays at a remarkable
price.

**Errázuriz Chardonnay**   17   £7–10
**Reserva 1997**
Superb! Like an exotic Meursault!
Not at all stores.

**Isla Negra Chardonnay**   15   –£5.00
**2000**
Dry and purposeful: lemon
undertone to melon richness.

**Luis Felipe Edwards**   16.5   –£5.00
**Chardonnay 1999**
Beautiful subtlety and creamy
richness which reveal gentle
layers of melon, wood, lemon,
pineapple and cream on the
finish. Most stores.

**Santa Ines Sauvignon**   16   –£5.00
**Blanc 2000**
Not typically Sauvignon in
character except as the dry, crisp
fruit dries out in the back of the
throat and the tang of gooseberry
is detectable. Most stores.

**Stowells Chilean**   12   –£5.00
**Sauvignon Blanc NV**

**Terra Mater**   14.5   –£5.00
**Chardonnay 2000**
Dry melon and raspberry fruit
with a touch of pineapple.

**Two Tribes White NV**   14   –£5.00
Ripe pear undertone, touch of
coriander, fresh lemon. Hits the
spot when the weather's sultry.

Valdivieso Malbec Rosé 16.5 −£5.00
2000
One of the most delicious rosés
I've tasted. Terrific spicy cherry
and very subtle blackberry fruit
with fine acids and an excellent
texture. Brilliant thirst quencher,
barbecue food wine and all-round
civilised household friend.
Selected stores while stocks last.

## WAITROSE WHITE

35 South Sauvignon 14.5 −£5.00
Blanc 2000
Very good with baked cod with
saffron mash.

Caliterra Chardonnay 15.5 −£5.00
2000
Has a wonderful crisp edge with a
soft fruit centre – delicious.

Canepa Semillon 2000 14.5 −£5.00
Excellent crisp dry peach/pear
fruit.

Gracia Temporal 15 £7–10
Reserva Superior
Chardonnay 1997
A food Chardonnay, most likely a
perfect marriage with scallops.
The wine has a richness which
tempers any elegance it might
had laid claim to.

# CYPRUS

The possibilities exist for greatness – some day.

## CO-OP RED

**Island Vines Cyprus Red 2000, Co-op**  `13`  –£3.50
Has a baked plum overtone.

**Mountain Vines Reserve Cabernet/ Maratheftiko 1999, Co-op**  `16`  –£5.00
The Maratheftiko adds a curious nutty, cooked, almost herby/ spicy element to the dry, peppery Cabernet and the result is some extremely engaging fruit of lingering lushness. Superstores only.

## CO-OP WHITE

**Island Vines Cyprus White 2000, Co-op**  `14.5`  –£3.50
Good tangy gooseberries, limes and a hint of raspberry.

**Mountain Vines Semillon 1998, Co-op**  `14`  –£5.00
Interesting edge of ripe plum and gooseberry with fresh acids, with a slight vegetal hint, surging alongside. Not at Convenience Stores.

# ENGLAND

Ah, those brave bulldog vine-growers of the Merrie Island – mostly mediocre.

## BUDGENS WHITE

**Three Choirs Phoenix** 11 –£5.00
**1999**
Odd greasy finish.

## SAINSBURY'S WHITE

**Chapel Down Premium** 12.5 –£5.00
**Medium Dry 1999**
Rich, off-dry, and good for spicy fish stews. Expensive, though. Limited distribution.

**Chapel Down** 11 £5–7
**Schonburger 1999**

Seems to make a reasonable start then turns austere and falls short. Limited distribution.

## WAITROSE WHITE

**Chapel Down** 15 –£5.00
**Downland Oak NV**
Heaven help us! A drinkable English white under a fiver. Delicious gooseberry and lime fruit.

**Chapel Down Flint Dry** 13.5 –£5.00
**1998**

# FRANCE

Look to the Languedoc and Roussillon for the great wines of the future.

## ASDA RED

**Beaune 1er Cru Antoine de Peyrache 1998** `10` `£10–13`
Why bother? There are Asda reds at half the price three times more interesting.

**Buzet Cuvee 44 1997** `15` `–£5.00`

**California Old Vine Estates Carignan NV** `13.5` `–£5.00`
Juicy, ripe, and manifestly curry friendly.

**Château Biston Brillette Moulis 1997** `16.5` `£7–10`
Classic cheroot aroma, superb tannins and real sumptuous texture. Brilliant fruit. High class stuff. Limited distribution.

**Château Clauzet St-Estèphe 1997** `13` `£10–13`
Compared to the average Chilean Cab/Merlot it's overpriced by at least three times.

**Château 'D' de Dassault St-Emilion 1998** `16` `£10–13`
What elegance and balanced charms, delicious tannins, lovely blackcurrant fruit. Limited distribution.

**Château d'Arsac Margaux 1999** `15` `£10–13`
Lovely tannins. Not ferocious exactly . . . but superb with red meat and rare game. Limited distribution.

**Château du Gaby Cannon-Fronsac 1998** `13.5` `£7–10`
Bit loose and sweet on the finish. Limited distribution.

**Château Gigault Premières Côtes de Blaye 1998** `16.5` `£7–10`
Superb structure! Lovely blackcurrant spiciness and earthy richness with delightful tannins. Very elegant, fruity and deep. Hugely attractive wine for rich food.

**Château Haut Canteloupe Médoc 1998** `16.5` `£7–10`
Lovely sweet/tannin finish on it gives it great lingering classiness. It is a complex claret, possessing remarkable quaffability.

**Château La Chene de** 15.5 £5–7
**Margot Premières**
**Côtes de Blaye 1998**
Very dry and tannic but superb
with rare game and meat
dishes.

**Château Lamarzelle St-** 14.5 £13–20
**Emilion Grand Cru**
**1997**
The true name of this château is
Grand-Barrail-Lamarzelle-Figeac
and thirty-five years ago I was
advised that this collation of
syllables made the wine
impossible to sell. Hence it was
cheap. Now it's shorter in name
and longer in price. No longer a
bargain but marvellous fluency
between fruit and tannins.

**Château Lynch-** 15 £13–20
**Moussas Pauillac 1997**
Delightfully spicy (coriander?)
fruit with dashing and concise
tannins. Lot of money but has
some class.

**Château Maucaillou** 15 £13–20
**Moulis 1997**
Energy here and very cultured
tannins. Limited distribution.

**Château Sociando** 12 £20+
**Mallet Haut-Médoc**
**1997**
Very ripe with a sour edge to the
blackcurrant. Lovely tannins but
. . . £25? Limited distribution.

**Château Vieux Gabiran** 14 –£5.00
**1999 (organic)**

**Châteauneuf-du-Pape** 13.5 £10–13
**Domaine Giraud 1998**

Very juicy and ripe for eleven
quid. Selected stores.

**Cornas 1998** 14 £7–10
Juicy, ripe, hint of coal-tar on the
finish. Very good casserole wine.
Limited distribution.

**Côte de Beaune-** 11 £5–7
**Villages Michel Pont**
**1998**
Another crude Burgundy barely
deserving of the taste buds.

**Côtes du Rhône Cuvée** 15.5 –£3.50
**Spéciale 2000, Asda**
I laughed when I saw cuvée
spéciale on the label but was
forced to swallow my disdain. It
is special. Very special – for under
three quid. It has lively tannins
and rich berried fruit. Classy
finish, too.

**Côtes du Rhône Jean** 15.5 –£5.00
**Berteau 1999**
Simply classic Rhône quaffing
under-a-fiver. Has herbs, earth,
touches of warm hedgerows,
good tannins, and a very upright
structure.

**Crozes-Hermitage Les** 16 £5–7
**Haut de Pavières 1999**
A classic Crozes where the
immediate plummy richness (and
blackcurrants) goes marvellously
dry, smoky and chewy and goes
on developing layers of tarry fruit
as it soothes the throat.

**Domaine de** 16 –£5.00
**Montplaisir Cabernet**
**Franc VdP d'Oc 2000**
Lovely textured chewiness, gentle

chocolate-edged richness, raunchy tannins, and a really lingering finish. An exceptionally characterful wine for the money.

**French Connection Reserve Merlot 2000**

Excellent balance of fruit, tannins, and acids with the tannin pulling away on the finish. Has touches of soft leather and berries (black and blue). A bruising experience, then.

**Gigondas Domaine St Damien 1999**

Sweet liquorice. Wonderful tannins. Good grip. Marvellous with refined Indian cuisine. Selected stores.

**Hermitage 1998**

Lots of ripe juice plus a hint of tobacco. Limited distribution.

**J. Frelin Organic Côtes du Rhône NV** 14 −£5.00

Nice touch of fruity earthiness. Spiced plums mostly.

**La Montagne Fitou Réserve 1999** 15 −£5.00

Seems big and soupy at first quaff then goes berries and bustling with tannins.

**La Vieille Ferme, Côtes du Ventoux 1999** 16 −£5.00

Classic oomph from the fruit which offers herbs, tannins, berries and bounce. Also it has dry, textured tenacity and drive. Selected stores.

**Les Crouzels Fitou 1999**

When you try to lift the bottle you know this is a wine which takes itself seriously. And it does. It has a very classy texture, polished berries, and firmish tannins.

**Les Fiefs de La Grange St-Julien 1998** 14 £13–20

Lot of money. Very svelte tannins. Limited distribution.

**Nuits-St-Georges 1988** 10 £13–20

Lot of money but not a lot of excitement. Would have been better five or six years ago. Getting raw and stale on the edge. Limited distribution.

**Organic Claret Château Vieux Georget, Bordeaux 1998** 15.5 £5–7

**Pommard Jean-Marc Bouley 1998** 14.5 £13–20

Bitter cherries and very fine-grained, deep tannins. Limited distribution.

**Rasteau Côtes du Rhône-Villages Domaine de Vallambreuse 2000**

One of my favourite villages in the Rhône known for its rich dry reds – but not at this remarkable price. Here we are presented with berries and coffee, lovely warm tannins, a suspicion of spice, and a lovely cuddly finish.

**Syrah VdP d'Oc 2000**

Curious sticky fruit from which

berries slowly emerge and then pretty strident tannins which contribute hugely to its effect and its rating.

**Tramontane Red VdP** `16` `−£3.50`
**de l'Aude 1999, Asda**
Brilliant earthy richness and ripeness. Real bargain here.

**Vacqueyras Domaine** `16.5` `£5–7`
**de l'Oiselet 1999**
Superbly herby and ripe, rivulets of leather/plump blackcurrant fruit and marvellous alert tannins. Gorgeous fruit of great style here.

**Volnay Antoine de** `10` `£7–10`
**Peyrache 1998**
It was only a pleasure to spit it out.

## BOOTHS RED

**Bergerac Rouge NV,** `13` `−£3.50`
**Booths**

**Bourgogne Rouge** `13` `£5–7`
**Joillot 1999**

**Cahors 1999** `15` `−£5.00`
Intensely dry and deep. Wonderful meaty stuff. Tannins like shark's teeth.

**Château Cluzan** `15.5` `−£5.00`
**Bordeaux 1999**
Brilliant value claret. Has presence and poise.

**Château Ducla,** `15` `£5–7`
**Bordeaux 1997**

**Château l'Euzière Pic** `16.5` `£7–10`
**St Loup 1998**

Wonderful biscuity tannins, herbs, earthiness to the tannins, tension to the rich finish. Wonderful wine.

**Château Mayne-Vieil,** `16` `£5–7`
**Fronsac 1998**
Coal-edged chewiness to beautiful tannins and firmly textured fruit. A lovely claret for the money.

**Château Pierrail** `15.5` `£5–7`
**Bordeaux Supérieur**
**1998**
Intense dry fruit of great concentration and class.

**Chaume Arnaud** `17` `£7–10`
**Domaine Côtes du**
**Rhône-Villages 1998**
**(organic)**
It develops on the palate with insidious deliciousness providing herbs, savoury tannins, a hint of rustic orchards, and a deal of characterful texture. Marvellous stuff.

**Côtes du Rhône-** `13.5` `£5–7`
**Villages Georges**
**Darriaud 1998**

**Domaine de la Bastide** `8` `−£3.50`
**VdP Hautrive 1999**
So sweet and ripe it stuns the palate.

**Domaine de Petit** `15.5` `−£5.00`
**Roubie Syrah VdP d'Oc**
**NV (organic)**
Superb tannins, rich and ready, to deep plums and cherries.

**Domaine les Yeuses la** `14` `−£5.00`
**Soure VdP d'Oc 1999**

Dark, rich, thick.

**Faugères Gilbert Alquier 1998**  `15.5`  `£7–10`
Dry plums (intense, interesting, incisive) and firm, deep tannins. An outstandingly herby Rhône red.

**Fitou Madame Parmentier 1998**  `13.5`  `–£5.00`

**Gigondas Domaine Paillere et Pied 1998**  `16`  `£7–10`
Superb lesson in integrated rich, soft tannicity and herb-drenched plums, blackberries and baked earth. Hugely civilised tippling.

**Honoré de Berticot Merlot Côtes de Duras NV**  `15.5`  `–£5.00`
Delicious depth of fruit here: herby, ripe and soft to finish.

**La Passion Rouge VdP de Vaucluse 2000**  `14`  `–£3.50`
Brilliant little party wine. Has an easygoing earthiness.

**La Réserve du Reverend Corbières 1999**  `13.5`  `–£5.00`

**Marcillac 1997**  `15`  `–£5.00`

**Morgon Côte du Py 1998**  `13`  `£5–7`

**Oak Aged Claret Bordeaux Supérieur NV, Booths**  `14`  `–£5.00`

**Old Git Grenache Syrah 1999**  `15.5`  `–£5.00`

**Pernands Vergelesses Domaine Rossignol Cornu 1998**  `14`  `£7–10`
One of the driest Burgundies I've tasted for some time. The tannins are crunchy and deep.

**Vin Rouge NV, Booths**  `11`  `–£3.50`

## BUDGENS RED

**Chapelle St Laurent Côtes du Marmandais 1999**  `12`  `–£5.00`
Raw tannins to fruity juice.

**Château St Louis Corbières 2000**  `13`  `–£5.00`
Bit rough on the finish.

**Côtes du Rhône-Villages 2000**  `11`  `–£5.00`
Juicy and overripe.

**Fleurs de France Merlot Syrah Devereux NV**  `12`  `–£3.50`
Very soupy and ripe.

**Fortant de France Grenache VdP d'Oc 2000**  `16`  `–£5.00`
Absolutely delicious glugging here. The wine has depth, personality, structure and weight – and calm complexity on at least two levels. Yes, it's immediate and gently lush but its charm is huge.

**Fortant de France Syrah 1999**  `15`  `–£5.00`
Juicy berries but has terrific tannins to give it backbone. Has personality and flavour.

**French Connection
Syrah Grenache 2000**  `14.5`  `−£5.00`
Good blackcurrants and fine
tannins. Stylish finish.

**La Baume Syrah 1998**  `15`  `−£5.00`
Ripe but with some chewy
texture to the tannins. Overall, a
firm Syrah uniting a Rhône
dryness with an Aussie spiciness:
somewhere in the middle.

**La Nature French Red
VdP de l'Hérault 2000**  `11`  `−£5.00`
Very very . . . uninteresting.

**Oaked Côtes du Rhône
Prestige Les
Faisandines 2000**  `15.5`  `−£5.00`
Delicious collusion of herby
berries and warm tannins. Has
character and style, this wine.

**Premium Oaked
Cabernet Sauvignon/
Syrah VdP d'Oc,
Devereux NV**  `14`  `−£5.00`
Has some amusing tannins on the
berried finish.

**Rhône Valley Red
Côtes du Ventoux 2000**  `13.5`  `−£3.50`
Very ripe, hint of tannins, big rich
finish.

## CO-OP RED

**Beaujolais NV, Co-op**  `12`  `−£5.00`
Jammy.

**Beaujolais-Villages
Nouveau 2000**  `9`  `−£3.50`
Horrible experience. Bananas and

coconut with the texture of
bubble gum.

**Calvet Réserve Red
1998**  `10`  `£5–7`
Typical Bordeaux at its basic and
most boringly dry and costive.
Superstores only.

**Château de l'Hospital
Graves 1997**  `13`  `£7–10`
Not a tenner's worth of grapes
here. Superstores only.

**Château Fourtanet
Côtes de Castillon 1997**  `15`  `£5–7`
Raw, naked, dry claret for lovers
of dark tannins, savourily deep,
and a finish with hints of stale
cheroot.

**Château Laurencon
Bordeaux Supérieur
1998**  `14`  `−£5.00`

**Château Pierrousselle
Bordeaux 1999**  `14`  `−£5.00`

**Château Thezannes
Corbières 1998**  `15`  `−£5.00`
Good character to the wine – has
depth, daring and balanced
richness of elements. Superstores
only.

**Château Villeranque
Haut-Médoc 1997**  `15`  `£7–10`
A pert little claret of substance
and class. Very drinkable, dry and
meaty. Superstores only.

**Chevalière Réserve
Grenache Vieilles
Vignes 1999**  `13`  `−£5.00`
Very juicy.

**Claret NV, Co-op**  `15`  `−£3.50`

**Corbières Rouge NV,** `15` −£3.50
**Co-op**

**Corso Merlot 1999** `12` −£5.00
Merlot? Could have fooled me.
Superstores only.

**Domaine les Combelles** `13.5` −£5.00
**Minervois 1998**

**Fleurie 2000** `12` £5–7
Expensive. Superstores only.

**French Organic Merlot** `13.5` −£5.00
**Syrah 2000, Co-op**
Curious disparateness between
the leathery Merlot and the juicy
Syrah. Not at Convenience
Stores.

**French Organic Red** `14` −£5.00
**2000, Co-op**
Juicy but has very good tannin
structure to hold it all together.
Not at Convenience Stores.

**Merlot VdP des Portes** `12` −£3.50
**de Mediterrenee 1999**
Pretty basic, rustic, dry, good
with cigarette smoke, card games,
and crepuscular company.
Superstores only.

**Nuits-St-Georges 1996** `9` £7–10
Disgraceful. Should be locked up
and the key thrown away.
Superstores only.

**Oak Aged Claret NV,** `13` −£5.00
**Co-op**

**Rhône Valley Red 1999** `14.5` −£3.50

**Vin de Pays d'Oc** `15` −£3.50
**Cabernet Sauvignon**
**NV, Co-op**
Deliciously dry blackcurranty

richness, earthiness and gentle
herbiness. A marvellous little glug
for the dosh.

**Vin de Pays d'Oc Fruity** `14.5` −£3.50
**Red NV, Co-op**
Cheap, very cheerful, great with
mildly spicy food. Has depth of
fruit and daintiness of tannins.
Great little glug for the money.
Not at Convenience Stores.

**Vin de Pays d'Oc** `14` −£3.50
**Merlot NV, Co-op**
Jammy and ripe, deep and full.
Great pasta plonk.

**Vin de Pays d'Oc Syrah** `12.5` −£5.00
**Mourvèdre NV, Co-op**
Superstores only.

**Vin de Pays d'Oc Syrah** `14.5` −£3.50
**NV, Co-op**
Juicy yet dry. Good with sausages
and mash. Not at Convenience
Stores.

**Vin de Pays d'Oc** `15.5` −£5.00
**Syrah/Malbec, Co-op**
**(vegetarian)**
Delicious fruit here of bounce and
richness. Good tannins, herbs and
characterful ripeness without
puerility. The veggie reference
ignore (unless you are one).

## KWIK SAVE RED

**Brouilly Les Celliers de** `14` £5–7
**Bellevue 2000**
Drinkable, textured, expensive.

**Cabernet Sauvignon** `14` −£3.50
**d'Oc 2000, Somerfield**

Some good earthy fruit here of character and charm.

**Claret 2000, Somerfield** | 15 | −£3.50
Among the world's best value claret and no disgrace to a once-noble tradition. Has tannins and character.

**Corbières Rouge 2000, Somerfield** | 13 | −£3.50

**Côtes du Rhône 2000, Somerfield** | 13 | −£3.50
Sweet basic fruit.

**Les Oliviers French Red NV** | 13.5 | −£2.50
What do you expect for £1.99? The remarkable thing is you get more than you bargained for.

**Skylark Hill Red 2000** | 12 | −£3.50

## M & S RED

**Beaune Cent-Vignes 1er Cru 1999** | 12 | £13–20
Has some texture, I can grudgingly concede.

**Benjamin de Pontet Pauillac 1997** | 16 | £10–13
Impressive weight on the price tag leads the critical drinker to expect some weight, fruit and this is delivered: richly, softly, lingeringly and even a touch lushly (though the tannins are firm and flavoursome).

**Bin 121 Merlot/Ruby Cabernet 2000** | 14 | −£5.00
Has some active tannins but it's the sweet cherries which

predominate. Good with spicy food.

**Bourgogne Hautes-Côtes de Nuits Genevrières 1999** | 11 | £7–10
Ten quid? It's a joke. In bad taste.

**Bourgogne Rouge Sordet 1998** | 11 | £7–10
Dull.

**Château d'Artix Minervois 1999** | 16.5 | £5–7
Lovely chocolate richness, superb tannins, great blackcurrants and plums, a touch of spice, and a delicious thwack of individuality as it surges home and down. A very engaging wine.

**Château de Surville Costières de Nîmes 1999** | 17 | £5–7
Gripping performance from fine-grained tannins, rich plums, cherries and berries, touches of thyme and rosemary and a warm-hearted, textured finish.

**Château Gallais Bellevue Cru Bourgeois, Médoc 1998** | 13.5 | £5–7
Interesting sweet edge to it. Most untypical.

**Château Gressina, Bordeaux Supérieur 2000** | 14 | −£5.00
Dry, vegetal, good with rare meats.

**Château Haut Duriez Haut-Médoc 2000** | 15 | £5–7
Smells of stale stogie, tastes of dry

charcoal-edged plums, and finishes with a touch of floorboard. Classic claret, some would say.

**Château La Roseraie Dumont Puisseguin Saint-Emilion 2000**  16.5  £5–7
One of the best under £7 clarets I've tasted. Lovely warm tannins, cassis-edged plums, and a fine texture holding it all convincingly together.

**Château Lataste Premières Côtes de Bordeaux 1996**  16  −£5.00
A ripe, ready claret at a sensible price. Has deliciously smooth tannins and a delightful cigar-box tang to the blackcurranty, leathery fruit. Balanced, positive fruit at a fantastic price.

**Coeur de Vallée VdP d'Oc 2000**  14.5  −£5.00
Some good savoury tannins here.

**Côtes du Parc, Coteaux du Languedoc 2000 (organic)**  16  −£5.00
Very spicy, creamy fruit with most uncommon touches of bay leaf and banana – all this is subtle because the tannins give bite and backbone.

**Domaine Galetis Cabernet/Merlot VdP d'Oc 2000**  15  −£5.00
Good rich fruit, rustic yet civilised, with good tannins and weight on the finish. Tastes like a minor claret but has more oomph and smoothness on the finish.

**Domaine St Pierre VdP de l'Hérault 2000**  13  −£3.50
Rough, rustic roustabout.

**Gold Label Cabernet Sauvignon VdP d'Oc 2000**  15  −£5.00
Ripe and juicy but with marvellous saucy tannins.

**Gold Label Reserve Barrel Aged Syrah VdP d'Oc 1998**  16.5  £5–7
Superb meaty fruit, touch of old cheroot to the spicy plums and blackberries, and a great rousing finish of oregano and coriander. Brilliant dinner party companion.

**Gold Label Syrah VdP d'Oc 2000**  14.5  −£5.00
Mild, cool fruit of plummy richness with some real energy from the tannins.

**House Red Wine, VdP du Comte Tolosan 2000**  13.5  −£3.50
Bungalow more like. One storey fruit. But perfectly acceptable as a communion wine.

**La Colonie VdP des Collines de la Moure 1998**  16.5  £5–7
Lovely, quite brilliant, savoury, almost meaty richness and polished tannins. The texture is superbly pleasurable and finely wrought.

**Les Romaines VdP d'Oc 1998**  17  £7–10

A magical level of warm tannins, insistent yet impish, and huge dollops of catering chocolate bitterness harnessed to blackberries, cherries and soft fruit. The finish is like a long bite of chocolate heaven. A sinful, hedonistic experience, this fruit.

**Margaux 1997**　13.5　£10–13

**Mercurey 1er Cru**　11　£7–10
**Domaine Levert 1998**
Yet more M&S Burgundy of no charm to this drinker.

**Rock Ridge Cabernet**　15.5　−£5.00
**Sauvignon 2000**
Ripe blackberries and very savoury hint-of-chocolate plums. Very good tannins here, too. Highly quaffable, food-friendly and classy.

**St-Joseph, Cuvée Côte-**　16　£7–10
**Diane, 1998**
Intense, mysterious perfume, slightly exotic, leads to coal-black fruit of burnt-edge cherries and blackberries and full rich tannins.

**Silver Tree Shiraz 1999**　14　£7–10
Very juicy and ripe and ready for spicy food.

**Terre du Lion St-Julien**　15.5　£7–10
**1997**
Very mature considering its youth and the tannins are superb. A fruity claret of class and impressive impactfulness. Compact, soft fruit of some style here.

**Volnay 1er Cru 1999**　13.5　£13–20

Lovely tannins here and a good level of ripe fruit of some class but at £18 I really find it difficult to rave about this when £18 is a ravingly high price. I'd buy this wine at £4.99 but it doesn't begin to compare with an M&S Minervois.

## MORRISONS RED

**Bouches du Rhône**　15　−£3.50
**Merlot NV**
Cheekily priced, properly fruity, very well organised. Has good tannins, hint of leather and deep plums.

**Château Cadillac**　15　£5–7
**Legourgues Bordeaux**
**1997**

**Château de Candale**　15　£7–10
**Haut-Medoc 1996**

**Château Saint Galier**　14　−£5.00
**Graves 1999**
Very dry claret for Conservative Club members.

**Claret Bordeaux NV,**　13.5　−£3.50
**Morrisons**

**Falcon Ridge Cabernet**　16　−£3.50
**Sauvignon, VdP d'Oc**
**1999**
Brilliant dryness and hugely arresting blackcurrant richness. Fantastic value.

**Falcon Ridge Merlot**　14　−£3.50
**VdP d'Oc 2000**
Very soft and gluggable with elegant tannins.

Falcon Ridge Syrah
VdP d'Oc 2000
`14.5` `−£3.50`
Plump, smokey and deep.

Heritage des Caves des
Papes Côtes du Rhône
1999
`16` `−£5.00`
Rich herbs, soft tannins, some
well organised, deep flavoured
touches here.

La Chasse du Pape
Réserve Côtes du
Rhône 2000
`16` `−£5.00`
Stern-visages richness and tannic
dryness – has hints of raspberry
and cassis.

Les Planels Minervois
1999
`14` `−£5.00`
Herby, rustic richness and dry-to-
finish fruit.

'M' Côtes du Rhône
NV
`13` `−£3.50`

'M' Côtes du
Roussillon Red NV
`13` `−£3.50`

Minervois Cellier la
Chouf NV
`13` `−£3.50`

Morgon Domaine de
Chatelet 1999
`13` `£5–7`

Old Git Grenache
Syrah 2000
`14` `−£3.50`
Nothing old gittish about it. It's
young and soft, gently plump and
charming.

Pic St-Loup d'Une Nuit
1999
`14` `−£5.00`
Simple, smooth fruit of cherries,
soft tannins and plums.

St-Emilion NV,
Morrisons
`14` `£5–7`

Sichel Médoc NV `13` `£5–7`

Winter Hill Red VdP
d'Oc 1999
`14` `−£3.50`

## SAFEWAY RED

Anciennes Vignes
Carignan, VdP de
l'Aude 2000
`14` `−£5.00`
Juicy and very dry to finish. Most
stores.

Baron de Lestac,
Bordeaux 1998
`14.5` `−£5.00`
Soft, rich, plummy fruit with
good tannins. A claret of some
decency and decorum. Dry but
engagingly fruity.

Beaune 1998, Safeway `10` `£7–10`
Utterly bereft of wit. Selected
stores.

Beaune Premier Cru,
Les Epenottes 1998
`13.5` `£13–20`
Bitter cherry finish gives it some
back-up to the tannins but it lacks
that hint of the daredevil which
great Pinot must exhibit.

Bourgueil Les
Chevaliers 2000
`16` `−£5.00`
I love this style of severe, dry
raspberries/plums/cherries and
dusty, slate-tile tannins. Lovely
stuff. Most stores.

Cabernet Sauvignon
VdP d'Oc 2000,
Safeway
`15.5` `−£5.00`
Good ripe blackcurrants, tight

tannins and a surging finish. Very good value for money.

**Château Boisset Cuvée** `16.5` `£5–7`
**Eugenie La Clape,**
**Coteaux du Languedoc**
**2000**
Remarkably textured, highly herby, piles of soft fruit flavours and gorgeous tannins. Selected stores.

**Château Chaubinet** `16` `–£5.00`
**Bordeaux 1999**
Amazing quality of tobacco-edged fruit for under four quid. Fine savoury tannins and plump blackberries.

**Château Clos de la** `14.4` `£7–10`
**Chesnaie, Lalande-de-**
**Pomerol 1998**
Very classy, and stylish rich finish.

**Château d'Agassac,** `13.5` `£10–13`
**Haut-Médoc Cru**
**Bourgeois 1998**
Dry, good fruit – cellar it for two hundred years and it'll reach fourteen points. Selected stores.

**Château de Coulaine,** `16` `£5–7`
**Chinon 1999 (organic)**
An organic red of mellow-textured, raspberry and cherry fruit with a delicious dry, slatey edge. 75 stores.

**Château de Lausières,** `16.5` `–£5.00`
**Coteaux du Languedoc**
**1999**
Smacks of savoury fruit and lithe tannins. A telling recipe of layered

lushness and deep dry fruit. Excellent food wine. Selected stores.

**Château de** `16.5` `£7–10`
**Villenouvette, Cuvée**
**Marcel Barsalou**
**Corbières 1998**
Intense, warm, gently spicy, savoury, characterful, softly yet determinedly tannic and huge value for money. A lovely wine. 70 stores.

**Château du Tasta,** `13` `–£5.00`
**Premières Côtes de**
**Bordeaux 1998**
Dry, very dry. Selected stores.

**Château Jouanin Cuvée** `15` `£5–7`
**Prestige, Côtes du**
**Castillon 1998**

**Château La Rose** `16` `£10–13`
**Brisson St-Emilion**
**Grand Cru 1998**
Deliciously woody and dry but this sensation is dispersed by the cassis-edged finish. An impressively cultured and perfectly mature claret.

**Château Liversan, Cru** `12` `£7–10`
**Bourgeois, Haut-Médoc**
**1997**

**Château Maison Neuve** `15.5` `£7–10`
**Montagne-St-Emilion**
**1998**

**Château Montbrun de** `16` `–£5.00`
**Gautherius Corbières**
**2000**
The texture is superb – close-knit tannins hand-in-leather-glove

with the rich fruit. Selected stores.

**Château Philippe de** `15.5` `−£5.00`
**Vessière, Costieres de**
**Nîmes 1997**

**Château Pouchard-** `15` `£5–7`
**Larquey Bordeaux 1998**
Very typical '98 minor claret.
Drink it now. The tannins will
outlast the fruit.

**Château Pouchard-** `15.5` `£5–7`
**Larquey, Bordeaux**
**1998 (organic)**

**Château Rozier, St-** `13.5` `£10–13`
**Emilion Grand Cru**
**1998**
Too expensive for my pocket.
Too dry for my tongue (and that
is an instrument which relishes
dry things). Selected stores.

**Château Salitis** `15` `£5–7`
**Cabardès 1998**
Extremely rich and deep with a
very meaty finish. Selected stores.

**Château Teyssier** `15` `£7–10`
**Montagne-St-Emilion**
**1998**
Severe claret but the Merlot saves
the Cabernet from extinction. Big
tannins. Best cellared for three or
four years yet. Selected stores.

**Château Tour du Mont,** `14` `£5–7`
**Haut-Médoc 1999**
Severe claret. Selected stores.

**Château Troupian** `14` `£7–10`
**Haut-Médoc 1998**
Austere, bitter tannins to young

brisk fruit. Possibly better cellared
for another three to four years.

**Château Villespassans** `17` `−£5.00`
**St-Chinian 2000**
High class texture, thick yet not
too dense, and the fruit
delightfully illuminates the
tannins. A quite terrific red for
under a fiver. Most stores.

**Château Vircoulon** `16.5` `−£5.00`
**Bordeaux 1999**
Fantastically well-textured and
chewy, this seems more like a
premier cru than the humble
bumpkin it is. Gorgeous fullness
and depth. Quite scrumptious
finish.

**Châteauneuf-du-Pape** `12` `£7–10`
**1999, Safeway**
Very ripe and almost volatile.

**Chevalier de Malle,** `14` `£7–10`
**Graves 1998**

**Claret NV, Safeway** `16` `−£5.00`
Amazing deep chocolate fruit.
Behind that pleonastic label lies a
superbly well-textured claret of
great style. Lovely rich tannins.

**Corbières 2000,** `13.5` `−£3.50`
**Safeway**
Very dry and earthy.

**Crozes-Hermitage** `15` `£5–7`
**Etienne Barret 2000**
Has hints of typical coal-cellar-
edged richness of Crozes but has
more jammy berries than most.

**Domaine Chris** `15.5` `£5–7`
**Limouzi, Corbières**
**1998**

Ineffably quaffably fruity and soft-minded. Hints of herbs and sunshine. Selected stores.

**Domaine de l'Auris** 16 £5–7
Syrah, Côtes du
Roussillon 1998
Marvellous turn of speed to the tannins, which whips the fruit into such delicious shape. Selected stores.

**Domaine de Tudery St-** 16.5 £5–7
Chinian 1998
Chewy cocoa and coffee fruit (mainly black and logan berries) finish off a beautifully textured, tannically svelte red of great style. 70 selected stores.

**Domaine des Lauriers,** 17 £5–7
Faugères 1998
No nods to the New World here and what a triumph of plummy richness, spice, herbs and lovely polished, textured tightness it is. A delightfully daring wine. Selected stores.

**Domaine La Tour du** 15 –£5.00
Maréchal Merlot, VdP
de l'Hérault 2000
(organic)
Exceedingly plump and rounded in the mouth and then the tannins mug the palate with clods of earth. Selected stores.

**Domaine Montmija,** 14 –£5.00
Corbières 1999
(organic)
Good herby ripeness and tannins.

**Enclos des Cigales** 16 –£5.00
Merlot, VdP d'Oc 2000

Severely tannic but the fruit still combats this forcefully to make its plummy, herby point. Resoundingly good quaffing here. Selected stores.

**Enclos des Cigales** 15.5 –£5.00
Syrah, VdP d'Oc 1999

**Fitou 1999, Safeway** 13.5 –£5.00
Very straightforward, simple quaffing with rather less impactful richness on the finish.

**Fleurie Domaine des** 14 £5–7
Raclets 2000
Nice cherry fruit with excellent tannins. A serious red of surprising texture.

**Gevrey-Chambertin** 12 £13–20
Domaine Rossignol-
Trapet 1998
Higgledy-piggledy tannins and fruit – for £16 a poor buy.

**Jean Louis Denois** 15 –£5.00
Grenache/Syrah/
Mourvèdre, VdP d'Oc
2000
Modern fruit, old-fashioned tannins. A dry, deep, rich wine of great interest to food. Selected stores.

**Jean Louis Denois** 13.5 £5–7
Mourvèdre/Grenache,
VdP d'Oc 1999
Very ripe and palate pounding. Selected stores.

**L'Enclos Domeque** 15.5 –£5.00
Syrah/Malbec, VdP
d'Oc 2000
Deliciously smooth and rich and

with lovely warm, soft tannins. A terrific mouthful of textured fruit for the money.

**L'If Merlot/Carignan,** `16.5` `−£5.00`
**VdP du Torgan 2000**
Combines the best of both worlds, characterful tannins and rich, gently spicy fruit. Loads of flavour, buckets of personality, yet not OTT.

**La Cuvée Mythique** `16` `£5–7`
**VdP d'Oc 1998**
One of the Oc's most elegant and well-structured reds. Runs the gamut from Syrah to Cabernet Sauvignon brilliantly.

**La Nature Rhône** `14` `−£5.00`
**Valley Red 2000**
Country bumpkin style of tannins and grouchy fruit.

**La Source Merlot/** `16` `−£5.00`
**Syrah VdP d'Oc 2000**
Very polished and full of fruit but has an undertone of characterful tannins and acids. Most impressive.

**Merlot Reserve Mont** `17.5` `£7–10`
**Tauch, VdP du Torgan**
**1999**
Lovely rich colour and entertaining bouquet of chocolate and cigars. Terrific classy texture, hint of spice, complex layers of tannin and berried fruit and a very stylish finish. Selected stores.

**Merlot Vin de Pays** `16` `−£3.50`
**d'Oc 2000, Safeway**
Super leathery texture (more Gucci than saddle bag) and lovely

blackcurranty fruit. Excellent welcoming attitude and decisive finish. Fantastic value for money.

**Minervois 2000,** `15.5` `−£3.50`
**Safeway**
Fantastic value here: earthy, herby, juicy yet dry. Great tippling and good with food.

**Minervois Domaine de** `14` `£5–7`
**Bayac 'Les Pierres**
**Blanches' 1999**
Touch of ripe plums to the tannins. Selected stores.

**Mont Tauch Merlot,** `17` `£7–10`
**Barrel Matured, VdP du**
**Torgan 1998**
Superb tobacco undertones to the leather and plummy spiciness. The Pétrus of the Midi? Extraordinarily complex and beautifully textured richness. Selected stores.

**Moulin de Ciffre** `13` `£5–7`
**Faugères 1999**
Too juicy. Selected stores.

**Pinot Noir d'Autrefois** `14` `−£5.00`
**VdP d'Oc 2000**
Rustic and ready. Interesting tannins and characterful fruit.

**Pommard Premier Cru** `12` `£13–20`
**Les Arvelets 1996**

**Red Burgundy 1999** `13` `£5–7`
Rather austere on the finish.

**Syrah VdP d'Oc 2000,** `15.5` `−£3.50`
**Safeway**
Soft, spicy fruit of very yielding tannins. Has touches of

blackberry and leather, raspberry and plum.

**Vacqueyras Domaine la** `14` `£5–7`
**Bouscatière 1999**
Intensely soft and ripe. Not usual for this appellation. Selected stores.

**Val Bruyère Côtes du** `14` `–£5.00`
**Rhône-Villages 2000**
Nice plummy polish to it. Most stores.

**'Yellow Jersey' Rhône** `14` `–£5.00`
**Valley Côtes de**
**Ventoux 2000**
This Syrah/Grenache blend celebrates the Tour de France with simple plum and blackberry richness.

**Young Vatted** `15` `–£3.50`
**Grenache VdP de**
**l'Ardèche 1999**

## SAINSBURY'S RED

**Beaujolais NV,** `13.5` `–£5.00`
**Sainsbury's**

**Beaujolais-Villages Les** `12` `£5–7`
**Roches Grillées 1999**

**Bourgogne Pinot Noir,** `13` `£5–7`
**Louis Max 1999**
It's all right. Not bad. Passable – well, almost. Selected stores.

**Cabernet Sauvignon** `16` `–£3.50`
**d'Oc NV, Sainsbury's**
Astonishing quality of fruit for a non-discounted £2.99 wine. JS must be congratulated for finding such rich, textured blackcurrants

with their hint of cocoa, excellent tannins, and overall class.

**Cabernet Sauvignon** `14.5` `–£3.50`
**d'Oc NV, Sainsbury's (3**
**litre box)**
Price band indicates the 75cl equivalent.

**Celliers des Dauphins** `14.5` `–£5.00`
**Côtes du Rhône 2000**
The Rhône's worst label but not the ugliest wine. Oh no, for there are real tannins here, touch chauvinistic in their overbearance, but a wine of character emerges. Most stores.

**Château Barreyres Cru** `14` `£7–10`
**Bourgeois, Haut-Médoc**
**1998**
A sweet little claret, i.e. it has charm to its fruit, but eight quid? Hmm . . . Selected stores.

**Château Cazal-Viel St-** `13.5` `£13–20`
**Chinian Larmes des**
**Fées 1998**
The fairies weep for the price (£19 which is mad) and sigh over the lovely tannins . . . but it's the price which sticks in the throat. 10 selected stores.

**Château Coufran Cru** `13` `£10–13`
**Bourgeois, Haut-Médoc**
**1996**

**Château Fonreaud Cru** `13.5` `£10–13`
**Bourgeois, Listrac 1998**
Lot of money for an average claret. 138 selected stores.

**Château Gaubert,** `15.5` `–£5.00`
**Corbières 2000**

Strong hints of tobacco to rich blackcurrants and damsons, touch of peach and raspberry. Has fine tannins to buttress this display of fruit. Selected stores.

**Château La Tour**   16   £13–20
**Carnet, Haut-Médoc**
**1998**
No denying the toothsome presence of finely wrought tannins and very classy fruit. Other claret producers please copy. (Even at £20 the bottle.) 138 selected stores.

**Château La Vieille**   16.5   £10–13
**Cure Fronsac 1997**
Great value claret offering stylish cedar wood and tobacco fruit with fine-grained tannins. A wine to muse over – as you read Tristram Shandy. Selected stores.

**Château Moulin**   16.5   £7–10
**Canon-Fronsac 1996**
Wonderful aroma of charred wood and baked fruit with great tannins spiking the rich, deep warm fruit. Has great style and wit this wine. An outstanding claret. Selected stores.

**Château Semeillan**   14   £13–20
**Mazeau Cru Bourgeois,**
**Listrac 1996**

**Château Tassin**   15   −£5.00
**Premières Côtes de**
**Bordeaux 1999**

**Claret Cuvée Prestige,**   16   −£5.00
**Sainsbury's**
Perfect ascension as the Sainsbury's own label clarets rise in price, so does the quality and rich fruit. Here there are superbly classy tannins and rich berries in first class, textured collusion. Most stores.

**Claret, Sainsbury's**   15   −£3.50
Amazing! A three quid claret which gives you a penny change and makes a change from the usual run of such things with lovely rich charcoal-edged fruit and mild tannins.

**Claret, Sainsbury's (3**   15.5   −£5.00
**litre box)**
Burnt fruit in fine fettle here and this slightly spicy, charred approach to claret makes for a really filling, savoury mouthful. Price band indicates the 75cl equivalent.

**Classic Selection**   13   £5–7
**Brouilly 1999,**
**Sainsbury's**
Has some meatiness about the fruit but is not entirely meet to my mind at seven quid. Most stores.

**Classic Selection**   15   £7–10
**Châteauneuf-du-Pape**
**1998, Sainsbury's**

**Classic Selection St-**   15.5   £7–10
**Emilion 1998,**
**Sainsbury's**
Lovely texture, plump and gently edged with fine tannins. Has concentration and class.

**Côtes du Rhône NV,**   13.5   −£3.50
**Sainsbury's**

**Côtes du Rhône NV,** `15.5` `−£3.50`
**Sainsbury's (3 litre box)**
Rich, dry, gently earthy and deep,
this is a very soft wine of gentle
tannins and determined longevity
in the mouth. Combines gutsiness
with delicacy. Price band
indicates the 75cl equivalent.

**Crozes-Hermitage** `16.5` `£5–7`
**Cave de Tain 1999**
Amazing chocolate chewiness
here and coal-edged tannins.
Terrific texture, thick and darkly
balsamic. Brilliant hearty quaffing
– deliciously old-fashioned – and
great with food. It has great
exuberance and style, this wine.

**Crozes-Hermitage** `15.5` `£7–10`
**Petite Ruche 1997**

**Devereux Portan/** `14.5` `−£3.50`
**Carignan, VdP de**
**l'Aude 2000**
A simple, fruity party and pasta
plonk. Most stores.

**Domaine de Mas Blanc** `10` `£13–20`
**Coullioure 'Les**
**Cosprons Levant' 1997**
Sweet, old-fashioned, ludicrously
expensive, porty and raisiny.
Presumably it would have been
turned into dessert wine, the red
Maury, but who drinks this
nowadays? 10 selected stores.

**Domaine des Bouziers** `16.5` `−£5.00`
**Cabernet Franc VdP**
**d'Oc 2000**
Quite superb class to the texture,
hints (heavy) of black cherries,
plums and blackberries, good

tannins (well-integrated) and an
overall concentrated richness of
calm, controlled deliciousness.
Selected stores.

**Domaine Ellul-** `17` `£5–7`
**Ferrieres Vignes VdP**
**d'Oc 1998**
It fills the nose and mouth with
the pure, racy smells and flavours
of Provence: sun on warm stones,
Gitanes in yellow teeth, mimosa
on dry hillsides, and earth as
fecund as it's possible to be. 30
selected stores.

**Eliane's Single** `16` `−£5.00`
**Vineyard Corbières**
**'Gruissan' 2000**
Curious elderflower and
blackberry aroma leads to ripe
fruit and assertive, clinging
tannins. Classy, stylish, delicious.
120 selected stores.

**Eliane's Single** `16` `−£5.00`
**Vineyard Minervois**
**2000**
Begins with sweet cherries, ends
with chocolate and currants – a
really delightful charmer for the
palate. 120 selected stores.

**Fitou 'Les Douzes'** `15.5` `£5–7`
**Mont Tauch 1998**
Dainty opening soon opens up to
reveal hedgerow fruit, light
tannins, and a very soft finish. 140
selected stores.

**Fleurie La Madone 2000** `14` `£7–10`
Not bad, has tannins and
personality and is even, vaguely,
Fleurie-like.

**French Revolution Le Rouge 1999**  16 −£5.00

Hugely different from its white cousin, in that there is real character and effortless fruit here. Great depth, marvellous tannins, firm, rich texture.

**Gevrey-Chambertin Rodet 1998**  11 £13–20

The meaning of life? It can stink. As does fine Burgundy. This is not amongst such. 140 selected stores.

**Hautes-Côtes de Nuits Dames Huguettes 1998**  13.5 £7–10

**Heritage du Rhône 1999**  15 −£5.00

Beefy country-bumpkin style glugging. Has dry, earthy touches to the plums and blackberries. Limited distribution.

**Jacques Frelin Crozes Hermitage 1999** 13 £7–10

(organic)

Very very juicy which the tannins can do nothing to check. 80 stores.

**La Chasse du Pape Côtes du Rhône 1999** 14 −£5.00

Younger and softer in feel than previous vintages and lacking in bite. Selected stores.

**Le Catalan Old Vine Carignan 2000**  16 £5–7

What does the Carignan lack, by half a point, that the Grenache flaunts so spectacularly? Just a touch less adult dryness. 150 selected stores.

**Le Catalan Old Vine Grenache 2000**  16.5 £5–7

Huge personality, chocolate-edged richness to a depth of plummy ripeness which stays judiciously the right side of overripeness. Great food wine. 100 selected stores.

**Le Midi Cabernet Sauvignon 2000**  17 −£5.00

Utterly astonishing texture for the money (Médocs: eat your heart out) which brings together gorgeous tannins, concentrated blackcurrants and plums and a lingering finish. Selected stores.

**Le Midi Merlot 2000** 16.5 −£5.00

Terrific rascally fruit which combines a louche, aromatic richness (herbs, earth, old stoves) with polished leathery lushness. Great stuff. Selected stores.

**Le Véritable Laurent Miquel Syrah Mourvèdre VdP d'Oc 2000** 15 −£5.00

A sweet cherry finish, touches of spice and cheroot, make this a spicy food red of aplomb and style. Selected stores.

**Les Cassagnes Merlot VdP d'Oc 2000** 15.5 −£5.00

Delicious roasted fruit, nutty, herby, dry and rich and lovely savoury tannins. The finish is soft and classy. Most stores.

**Louis Bernard Côtes du** 16.5 −£5.00
**Rhône-Villages 1999**
Superb rustic charmer with
sophisticated manners and tannic
style. Lovely herbs, earth and
deep plum fruit which is
gloriously unpretentious.

**Marsannay Domaine** 15 £7–10
**Bertagna 1998**

**Mercurey Clos La** 13 £13–20
**Marche 1997**

**Merlot VdP de La Cite** 15.5 −£5.00
**de Carcassonne,**
**Caroline de Beaulieu**
**2000**
A mildly-dispositioned but
delicious Merlot which oozes
charm and good breeding.

**Minervois 2000,** 14.5 −£3,50
**Sainsbury's**
A charming party wine of
character and bite – not simply all
gooey fruit. Most stores.

**Old Git Grenache** 15.5 −£5.00
**Syrah 1999**

**Red Burgundy NV,** 12 £5–7
**Sainsbury's**
When I taste a Burgundy like this
I question the meaning of life.
The answer? Now, that would be
telling.

**Régnié Duboeuf 1999** 11 £5–7
Not as joyous as its label would
pretend. Rather manufactured in
feel. Selected stores.

**Réserve du General,** 15 £13–20
**Margaux 1997**
The general has taste and his

Margaux is suitably reserved – a
real warrior's tipple: brave, soft at
heart, not remotely, outwardly,
brusque. 80 selected stores.

**Special Reserve Claret,** 16 −£5.00
**Sainsbury's**
A bit special, but not reserved at
all: rich, dry blackcurrants, hint of
raspberry, touch of nut, and rich,
fluent tannins. A fine little claret
of class and clout.

**Stowells of Chelsea** 15 −£3.50
**Merlot VdP d'Oc (3**
**litre box)**
Price band indicates the 75cl
equivalent.

**Syrah VdP d'Oc 2000,** 13 −£5.00
**Sainsbury's (organic)**
Sweet and ever so mildly yawn-
inducing. Selected stores.

**Valréas Domaine de La** 14.5 £5–7
**Grande Bellane 1999**
**(organic)**
Ripe, but has good tannins,
touches of earth, and some herby
richness.

**Van Rouge, VdP de** 15 −£3.50
**Vaucluse NV**
Simply charming, conceptually
and fruitily. Has tannins and a
hint of the sunny Provençal
garrigues to back up its soft, easy-
going fruit.

**Vin de Pays des** 14.5 −£3.50
**Bouches-du-Rhône NV,**
**Sainsbury's**

Vin Rouge de France `13` —£3.50
NV, Sainsbury's (3 litre
box)
Price band indicates the 75cl
equivalent.

Brouilly Les Celliers de `14` £5–7
Bellevue 2000
Drinkable, textured, expensive.

Cabernet Sauvignon `14` —£3.50
d'Oc 2000, Somerfield
Some good earthy fruit here of
character and charm.

Château Blanca, `15.5` —£5.00
Bordeaux 2000
Tangy blackberries, chewy
tannins and a delightful charcoal
undertone.

Château Cazal Viel, `16` £5–7
Cuvée des Fées St-
Chinian 1999
Delightful cherries and plums and
low-lying tannins which strike
surprisingly softly and stealthily.
Selected stores.

Château Plaisance, `14.5` £7–10
Montagne-St-Emilion
1997
Expensive but has elegance and
class to its brisk fruit softened by
its tannins (rather than the other
way round). Selected stores.

Château St-Benoit `15.5` —£5.00
Minervois 1999
It's the brilliant texture which
wins it its points.

Château Valoussière `16` —£5.00
Coteaux de Languedoc
1997
Text book French red under-a-
fiver: has bistro savouriness, bite
and rich characterfulness.

Châteauneuf-du-Pape `14` £7–10
Domaine La Solitude
1999
Rampancy and richness here –
with matching price tag.

Claret 2000, Somerfield `15` —£3.50
One of the world's best value
claret and no disgrace to a once-
noble tradition. Has tannins and
character.

Corbières Rouge 2000, `13` —£3.50
Somerfield

Côte Sauvage Syrah `16` —£5.00
Mourvèdre 2000
So superbly quaffable.
Delightfully vibrant wine of rich,
soft classiness and depth.

Côtes du Rhône 2000, `13` —£3.50
Somerfield
Sweet basic fruit.

Côtes du Rhône- `14` —£5.00
Villages 1999,
Somerfield
Very ripe sweet fruit with tannins
to take the curse off its simplicity.

Côtes du Roussillon `15` —£3.50
2000, Somerfield
Delicious fresh, uncluttered fruit.
Total pure fruit charm.

Domaine de Courtilles `16` £5–7
Côte 125 Corbières
1999

Soft and ripe but with hints of herb, touches of earth, and lovely subtle tannins. Selected stores.

**Domaine La Tuque Bel** 15.5 £5–7
**Air, Côtes de Castillon**
**1998**
One of my favourite Somerfield clarets – to be wholly decanted three to four hours before drinking. Or cellared for two or three years more (at most).

**Fitou Rocher d'Ambrée** 14 –£5.00
**2000, Somerfield**
Very chewy chocolate-edged fruit.

**Gouts et Couleurs** 15.5 –£5.00
**Syrah Mourvèdre VdP**
**d'Oc 2000**
Terrific warmth of soft blackberries and plums with soft, silken tannins.

**Hautes-Côtes de** 11 £7–10
**Beaune 1999**

**Médoc 2000, Somerfield** 14.5 –£5.00
Lovely savoury tannins to the berries.

**Merlot VdP l'Ardèche** 14 –£3.50
**2000, Somerfield**
Party wine.

**Oak Aged Claret 2000,** 14 –£5.00
**Somerfield**
Soft and ripe and not overly tannic and claret-like.

**Old Git Grenache** 14 –£5.00
**Syrah 2000**
Nothing old gittish about it. It's

young and soft, gently plump and charming.

**Organic Merlot Vin de** 15.5 –£5.00
**Pays NV**
Superb tannins here connected to tobacco-subtle blackberry/plum fruit of excellent texture.

**Red Burgundy 1998,** 10 £5–7
**Somerfield**
Sweet yet dry and unforgiving on the finish.

**St-Emilion 2000,** 14 £5–7
**Somerfield**
Lip-puckering tannins and gripping fruit.

**Stowells of Chelsea** 12 –£5.00
**Merlot VdP d'Oc NV**
Boring.

**Syrah VdP de l'Ardèche** 13 –£3.50
**2000, Somerfield**

**Vacqueyras, Vignerons** 16.5 £5–7
**Beaumes-de-Venise**
**2000**
Gorgeous plums and blackberries with a hint of raspberry. Then there's the herbs (thyme), a touch of black olive, and the tannins. Quite a mouthful.

**VdP de l'Ardèche** 13.5 –£3.50
**Rouge 2000, Somerfield**

**Vin de Pays Hérault** 11.5 –£3.50
**2000, Somerfield**

**Winter Hill Rouge,** 15 –£5.00
**VdP de l'Aude 2000**
Strikingly rich and ready to please.

## SPAR RED

**Beaujolais NV, Spar**  10  –£5.00
The astonishing thing is that one
assumes it comes from grapes.

**Claret NV, Spar**  15  –£5.00

**Coteaux du Languedoc**  13  –£5.00
**2000, Spar**
Rich and deep and very casserole
compatible.

**Côtes du Rhône 1999,**  13.5  –£5.00
**Spar**
Dry plums here, bit stretched on
the finish.

**Côtes du Ventoux, Spar**  14.5  –£5.00
**1999**
Good simple unpretentious
plums, cherries, earth and
tannins.

**Crozes-Hermitage**  13  £5–7
**1999, Spar**
Dry and fails to clinch more
points because of the aridity of
the finish.

**Fitou NV, Spar**  16  –£5.00
Touch of tar, tobacco, coffee,
then blackcurrants, herbs and
earth. A wonderful rustic
mouthful.

**French Country Red**  12  –£3.50
**NV, Spar (1 litre)**
Roughly rustic yet little character.
Very dry. Price band shows the
75cl equivalent.

**Gevrey-Chambertin**  12  £13–20
**Les Caves des Hautes-**
**Côtes 1994**

**Hautes-Côtes de**  10  £5–7
**Beaune 1995, Spar**

**La Côte Syrah Merlot**  13.5  –£5.00
**VdP d'Oc 1999, Spar**
Dry yet has touches of blackberry
richness and tannins.

**Le Monstre Grenache**  15  –£5.00
**Noir 2000**
Drinkable casserole red. Has
some tannins of interest and fruit
of depth. Selected stores.

**Oaked Merlot 1999,**  14  –£5.00
**Spar**
Ripe plums, soft tannins. Decent
quaffing style.

**Salaison Shiraz/**  16  –£5.00
**Cabernet VdP d'Oc**
**1998, Spar**
Brilliant vivacious berries and
classy tannins, tightly packed, and
a terrific finish.

**Shiraz VdP d'Oc 1999,**  13.5  –£5.00
**Spar**
Rounded and very ripe.

**Vin de Pays de lAude**  10  –£3.50
**NV, Spar**
To call it basic flatters it. It has
little to interest the wine drinker.

**Wild River Grenache**  13  –£5.00
**1999**
The sweet fruit and the dry
tannins don't quite gel.

**Wild River Merlot 1999**  15.5  –£5.00
Better than the Barolo (qv) for
the money for it has similar
tannins and equally gripping fruit.

**FRENCH RED**

## TESCO RED

**Beaujolais NV, Tesco**  `11` −£3.50

**Beaujolais Villages**  `12` −£5.00
**2000, Tesco**
One of Tesco's so-called 'Finest'
range.

**Bordeaux Réserve**  `14.5` £5–7
**Calvet 1998**
Very good warm claret with hints
of smoked blackcurrant and
charred plum. Has a very firm
texture. Most impressive for the
money. Selected stores.

**Cabernet Sauvignon**  `15.5` −£5.00
**Prestige VdP d'Oc NV,**
**Tesco**
Terrific hint of tobacco to the
tannins and blackcurrants. Superb
texture and non-OTT ripeness
here. Great quality glugging.

**Cabernet Sauvignon**  `15.5` −£5.00
**Réserve 1998, Tesco**

**Cabernet Sauvignon**  `14` −£3.50
**VdP d'Oc NV, Tesco**

**Château Clement**  `13` £13–20
**Pichon, Cru Bourgeois**
**Haut-Médoc 1996**

**Château de Côte de**  `16` £5–7
**Montpezat, Côtes de**
**Castillon 1998**
I love the savoury richness,
almost charcoal-edged, to the rich
fruit and its tannins are equally
impressive. A brilliant wine for
game dishes and rare roast dishes.
Selected stores.

**Château La Fleur**  `14` −£5.00
**Bellevue Premières**
**Côtes de Blaye 1998**

**Château La Tour de**  `13.5` £13–20
**Mons Bordeaux 1996**

**Château Lafarque**  `12` £10–13
**Pessac-Léognan 1996**

**Château Liliane-**  `12` £13–20
**Ladouys Cru Bourgeois**
**Supérieur St-Estèphe**
**1996**

**Chinon Baronnie**  `16.5` £5–7
**Madeleine, Couly**
**Dutheil 1999**
Superb cherries, blackcurrants,
raspberries, lead pencils (the
tannins) and a lingering finish of
spicy cherry and walnut. A lovely
elegant red of class and textured
richness.

**Claret, Tesco**  `12.5` −£3.50

**Clarity Bordeaux**  `14` −£5.00
**Rouge 1998**

**Corbières NV, Tesco**  `13.5` −£3.50

**Corbières Réserve La**  `13.5` −£5.00
**Sansoure 2000, Tesco**
One of Tesco's so-called 'Finest'
range. Most stores.

**Côtes du Rhône NV,**  `13.5` −£3.50
**Tesco**

**Côtes du Rhône-**  `16` −£5.00
**Villages 2000, Tesco**
Superb fruit here, touch sweet
but the tannins save the day. A
real approachable Rhône red of

texture and depth. Great glugging.

**Côtes du Rhône-Villages Réserve Domaine de La Grande Retour 2000, Tesco** 15 −£5.00
Rich, meaty, soft. Excellent casserole companion. One of Tesco's so-called 'Finest' range. Most stores.

**Crozes-Hermitage Cave de Tain 1999** 16.5 £5−7
Amazing chocolate chewiness here and coal-edged tannins. Terrific texture, thick and darkly balsamic. Brilliant hearty quaffing – deliciously old-fashioned – and great with food. It has great exuberance and style, this wine. Most stores.

**Domaine du Soleil Syrah/Malbec VdP d'Oc NV** 14.5 −£5.00

**Domaine Richeaume Organic Syrah Côtes de Provence 1999** 16.5 £13−20
Impressively dry and deep, herby and splendidly rustic, but, and it's a delicious but, it has masses of class and concentrated charm. At Wine Advisor Stores.

**Dorgan VdP de l'Aude NV** 14 −£3.50
Simple party plonk. Good with not-too-robust casseroles (for it has some tannins to it).

**Fitou NV, Tesco** 14.5 −£3.50

**Fitou Réserve Baron de La Tour 1999, Tesco** 16 −£5.00
Excellent balance and bounteous tannins, herbs and warm, rich fruit of layered lushness yet dryness. One of Tesco's so-called 'Finest' range. Most stores.

**Fleurie Louis Josse 1999** 11 £5−7
Rather bland, if it does have some tannins (so we know, or rather we think we know, that perhaps grapes were used in its manufacture). Most stores.

**French Cabernet Sauvignon Réserve, VdP d'Oc 1998** 16 −£5.00
One of Tesco's so-called 'Finest' range. Deliciously superior to the general run of claret, this warmly textured, sensually-fruited wine has immense character, layered richness, and charm.

**French Merlot VdP d'Oc NV, Tesco** 14.5 −£3.50

**Gamay NV, Tesco** 10 −£3.50
I confess to finding it the least charming wine at Tesco. It's spineless. Most stores.

**Gevrey-Chambertin Jean-Philippe Marchand 1998** 12 £13−20
Unconscionably overpriced. Shocking example of Burgundy at fifteen quid. If it was £4.99 it might be different. Has some tannins to talk about. Limited distribution.

**Grenache Prestige VdP d'Oc NV, Tesco** 13 −£5.00

Very dry and difficult to catch as it finishes.

**Grenache VdP d'Oc** `14.5` `–£3.50`
**NV, Tesco**
Very fruity but not OTT. Has good tannins and ripe cherry/strawberry fruit. Good chilled with barbecues. Most stores.

**Hautes-Côtes de** `13` `£5–7`
**Beaune Les Caves des**
**Hautes-Côtes 1998**
Juicy, authentic, dry, almost good – but at seven quid who needs it? Most stores.

**Hautes-Côtes de Nuits** `12` `£5–7`
**Louis Josse 1998**
Sweet yet dry, and basically dull. Most stores.

**Juliénas Georges** `13` `£5–7`
**Duboeuf 1999**
Has some tannins. Selected stores.

**Les Etoiles French** `13` `–£5.00`
**Organic Red Wine NV**

**Louis Jadot Beaujolais-** `14` `£5–7`
**Villages 2000**
Not bad at all for a Beaujolais. Has some cru-level tannins and it firms up nicely on the finish.

**Margaux 1998, Tesco** `14` `£10–13`
Ripe and ready but curiously muted tannin-wise. One of Tesco's 'Finest' range.

**Médoc 1998, Tesco** `16` `£5–7`
Remarkably couth tannins, blackcurrants and strawberries, deep, roasted tannins, and a very very very smooth texture. High

class claret and very far from a high class price. Under the tutelage of Tesco Bordeaux can deliver. One of Tesco's 'Finest' range.

**Merlot Prestige VdP** `15` `–£5.00`
**d'Oc NV, Tesco**
Nice warm richness and subtle savouriness here. Good casserole red.

**Minervois NV, Tesco** `14` `–£3.50`

**Oak Aged Red** `13.5` `£5–7`
**Burgundy 1998, Tesco**

**Oaked Côtes du Rhône** `13.5` `–£5.00`
**NV**

**Perrin Vacqueyras 1998** `14` `£7–10`
Juicy and ripe with attendant, rather over-obedient, tannins. Selected stores.

**St-Emilion 1999, Tesco** `16` `£7–10`
Has an unusually soft and baked fruit richness which gives texture, tenacity and real class. An impressive wine of dryness, leatheriness and classiness. Most stores.

**Valréas Domaine de La** `14.5` `£5–7`
**Grande Bellane 1999**
**(organic)**

**Vintage Claret 1998** `14` `–£5.00`
One of Tesco's so-called 'Finest' range, this has soft fruit of very typically claret dryness and blackcurrantiness.

**Yvecourt Claret** `13.5` `–£5.00`
**Bordeaux 1999**
A tautological specimen of very

tannic richness. Somewhat one-sided, I ached to blend it with a soft Aussie.

## WAITROSE RED

**Abbotts Ammonite** `14` `−£5.00`
Côte du Roussillon
1999
Very fruity and ripe. Good with robust vegetable dishes with tomato sauces.

**Beauchatel Claret,** `12` `−£5.00`
Bordeaux 1999

**Bistro Rouge VdP d'Oc** `14.5` `−£5.00`
2000
A good bistro food companion it is.

**Boulder Creek Red** `13` `−£3.50`
VdP du Vaucluse 2000

**Cahors 1999** `15` `−£5.00`
A true Cahors. 100% Cot (or Malbec as it's called in Bordeaux). Dry, herby, uncompromising.

**Château Beauchene** `13` `£7–10`
Châteauneuf-du-Pape
1999
Good aromatic opening, seems to go too sweet and hedgerow.

**Château Calon Ségur** `14` `£13–20`
Bordeaux 1997
Typical St-Estèphe, best left for another five years for the tannins to really soften. Could be a classic.

**Château Cazal Viel,** `16` `£5–7`
Cuvée des Fées St-Chinian 1999

Delightful cherries and plums and low-lying tannins which strike surprisingly softly and stealthily.

**Château d'Aiguilhe** `15` `£7–10`
Côtes de Castillon 1997
Lovely smoked fruit and tannins. Mail Order only.

**Château de Caraguilhes** `13.5` `£5–7`
Corbières 1998
(**organic**)
Sweeter than other vintages as I recall and less tannically tenacious.

**Château de Castres** `15` `£7–10`
Graves 1998
Very elegant and ripe. Good gripping tannins.

**Château de Targ,** `15.5` `£5–7`
Saumur 1999
A very delicious affront to those who say Loire reds are too austere. Here the prolonged cherry fruit finishes with mildly tannic precision.

**Château des Jacques,** `13` `£7–10`
Moulin-à-Vent 1999

**Château du Glana Cry** `14` `£10–13`
Bourgeois St-Julien
1997
Very aromatic and dry. Lot of money, though, for a performance like that.

**Château Haut d'Allard** `15` `£5–7`
Côtes de Bourg 1998
Exciting time to be had here with the tannins.

Château Haut-Nouchet 15.5 £10–13
Pessac-Léognan 1998
(organic)
A very gripping claret of some
weight and undoubted class.

Château l'Evangile, 16 £20+
Pomerol 1997
A beautifully structured claret of
presence and power. Superb
texture to it. Mail Order only.

Château Léoville- 15.5 £20+
Barton 2eme Cru
Classé, St-Julien 1997
Beautiful high class texture and
tannins. A very ready St-Julien.
Mail Order only.

Château Léoville-Las- 16 £20+
Cases 2eme Cru Classé,
St-Julien 1994
Superb tannins and ripe, soft
structured texture. Only from
Waitrose Direct.

Château Pavie-Macquin 12 £20+
St-Emilion Grand Cru
Classé 1996
Not at the price I'm afraid. It's an
eight quid wine at most. Mail
Order only.

Château Pech-Latt, 15 £5–7
Corbières 1999
One of the more elegant of
southern French organic reds.

Château Rauzan-Segla 13.5 £20+
2eme Cru Class,
Margaux 1997
Mail Order only.

Château Tayac Cru 13 £13–20
Bourgeois, Margaux
1995

Châteauneuf-du-Pape 16 £7–10
Clos St-Michel 1999
A juicy C-d-P with lovely dry
savoury hints from the tannins.

Chinon Les Petites 13.5 £5–7
Roches 2000
Light cherries with slight flavour.
Might be best cellared for fifteen
months more.

Chorey-les-Beaune 14.5 £7–10
Domaine Maillard 1998
Roasted aroma, good texture and
some weight to the finish. Fully
decant two hours, maybe more,
beforehand. Has some
pretensions to class and, if
cellared three to four years more,
a higher points rating.

Côtes du Rhône 2000, 13 –£5.00
Waitrose

Côtes du Ventoux 2000 13.5 –£5.00

Crozes-Hermitage 13 £10–13
Domaine de Thalabert
1998

Domaine de Courtille 15 £7–10
Corbières 1999
Has sweet cherries mingling with
herbs and hedgerows. Light
tannins.

Ermitage du Pic Saint- 16.5 £5–7
Loup Coteaux du
Languedoc 1999
The tannins dally with the rich,
herby fruit so daintily and

delicately yet so deliciously and decisively, you relax and simply bathe in this lovely civilised red wine.

**Fleurie Montreynaud 2000**   `12`   `£7–10`

**Fortant Grenache VdP d'Oc 2000**   `16`   `–£5.00`
Absolutely delicious glugging here. The wine has depth, personality, structure and weight – and calm complexity on at least two levels. Yes, it's immediate and gently lush but its charm is huge.

**Gevrey-Chambertin Domaine Heresztyn 1999**   `13`   `£13–20`
Sweet touches.

**Good Ordinary Claret Bordeaux NV, Waitrose**   `13`   `–£5.00`

**Hermitage Le Pied de La Cote, Paul Jaboulet Aine 1998**   `12`   `£13–20`

**La Colombe Côtes du Rhône 1999 (organic)**   `14`   `–£5.00`

**La Cuvée Mythique VdP d'Oc 1998**   `16`   `£5–7`
One of the Oc's most elegant and well-structured reds. Runs the gamut from Syrah to Cabernet Sauvignon brilliantly.

**La Nature Oaked Merlot VdP d'Oc 2000**   `14.5`   `–£5.00`
Juicy plums with dry cherries as an aftertaste, with gently grilled nuts and tannic richness on the finish.

**Les Quarterons St-Nicolas de Bourgueil 2000**   `15.5`   `£5–7`
Delicious cherries and plums with a tang, an undertone, of minerality.

**Maury, Les Vignerons du Val d'Orbieu NV**   `16`   `–£5.00`
A sweet red wine for chocolate-based puddings. Did I say sweet? It hardly does this complex wine justice.

**Maury Vin Doux Naturel NV (half bottle)**   `16`   `–£5.00`
The absolute acme of chocolate-to-go red wines and so it suits chocolate desserts brilliantly. Has confitured tannins, most preposterous and delicious.

**Mercurery Rouge 1er Cru 'Les Puillets', Château Le Hardi 1998**   `13`   `£10–13`

**Merlot/Cabernet Sauvignon VdP d'Aigues 2000**   `16`   `–£3.50`
Has tobacco hints and coffee but mostly it's the tannins which take the palate by storm.

**Oaked Merlot VdP d'Oc 1999**   `14`   `–£5.00`

**Parallele 45 Côtes du Rhône, Paul Jaboulet 1998**   `16`   `£5–7`
Has a sense of rugged certitude to the herby softness and richness. Superb class.

Pommard Premier Cru `12.5` `£13–20`
Les Boucherottes 1999
Good tannins here.

Prieurs de Foncaire, `15.5` `–£5.00`
Buzet Grande Réserve
1998

Saint Roche VdP du `13.5` `–£5.00`
Gard 1999 (organic)

Savigny-les-Beaune `13` `£7–10`
Caves des Hautes-
Côtes 1999

Seigneurs d'Aiguilhe `13` `£7–10`
Côtes de Castillon 1998

Spécial Réserve Claret `13` `–£5.00`
Bordeaux 1999,
Waitrose
Has some tannins at least.

Spécial Réserve Claret, `16` `–£5.00`
Côtes de Castillon
Limited Edition
Millennium Magnum
1996 (magnum)
Bargain claret in a big sexy bottle
– the fruit is subtly sensual too
and wears a thick, winter coat of
nicely knitted tannins. Price
bracket shows the 75cl
equivalent.

St-Emilion Yvon Mau `13` `£5–7`
NV

Volnay 1er Cru Les `10` `£20+`
Caillerets, Clos des 60
Ouvrées, Domaine de
La Passe d'Or 1996
Mail Order only.

Volnay 1er Cru Les `13.5` `£20+`
Chevrets 1999

I grudgingly admit it has some
class but thirty quid? No way.

Winter Hill Shiraz, `14` `–£5.00`
VdP d'Oc 2000
Really unpretentious quaffing:
berries and smooth tannins in fine
collusion.

## ASDA WHITE

Chablis Premier Cru `15` `£10–13`
Fourchame 1999
Nice tangy mineral laziness. Hint
of chewiness on the edge lends
charm. Selected stores.

Chardonnay, Jardin de `14` `–£3.50`
la France 1999

Château Perruchot `12` `£13–20`
Meursault 1998
Bit sharp – like the price tag.
Limited distribution.

Chenin Blanc Loire `14` `–£3.50`
1999, Asda

French Connection `14.5` `–£5.00`
Viognier VdP d'Oc
2000
Has a dry apricot opening which
seems to turn faintly nutty then
goes dry and peachy – not a huge
variation in fruit then (or
complexity).

L'Enclos Domeque Dry `14` `–£5.00`
Muscat VdP d'Oc 2000
It is dry and the grapey spiciness a
suggestion only. An aperitif style
of shy fruitiness.

Louis Maynard Anjou `13.5` `–£3.50`
Blanc NV

A trifle sweet but not sweet like a trifle – thus it has some chillable acidic qualities which make it acceptable as a torrid weather whistle-wetter.

**Louis Maynard** `14.5` `–£3.50`
**Sauvignon Blanc**
**Ackerman NV**
Has a good raspberry fruitiness, a firm texture and a very faint herbaceous undertone.

**Mâcon-Villages La** `14` `–£5.00`
**Colombier 2000, Asda**
Nutty, faintly vegetal, dry white wine of agreeable restraint. Has a good nuttiness on the finish.

**Pouilly-Fuissé Antoine** `13` `£7–10`
**de Peyrache 1999**
Has some flinty charm but the price sucks.

**Pouilly-Fumé Les** `14` `£7–10`
**Cornets 1999**
Nice chewy fruit. Most engaging – till you see the price tag. Selected stores.

**Sancerre Les Noble** `13` `£5–7`
**Villages Caves de**
**Sancerre 2000**
Has some tangy edges to conventional fruit with a slightly tart undertone.

**Sancerre Vieilles** `14.5` `£7–10`
**Vignes Patient Collat**
**1999**
More concentration and crispness from this Sancerre and the gooseberry fruit has a disarmingly restrained richness. Has an elegant, classy finish.

**Tramontane Sauvignon** `14.5` `–£5.00`
**Blanc 2000, Asda**
Nice touch of ripe gooseberry to the minerals. Great fish wine. Selected stores.

**Vouvray Denis** `10` `–£5.00`
**Marchais 1999**

**Xanadu Secession** `13.5` `£5–7`
**Sémillon Chardonnay**
**2000**
Ripe blend of melon and lemon – fairly straightforward approach – some texture on the finish.

## BOOTHS WHITE

**Bergerac Blanc NV,** `14` `–£3.50`
**Booths**

**Bourgogne Chardonnay** `12` `£5–7`
**Domaine Joseph**
**Matrot 1999**

**Chablis Domaine de** `12` `£7–10`
**l'Eglantière 1999**

**Château Crabitan** `16.5` `£5–7`
**Bellevue St Croix du**
**Mont 1996**
Delicious waxy, honeyed fruit with hints of strawberry and crème brulée. Too delicate for complex puds, treat it as an aperitif.

**Château Lamothe** `14` `–£5.00`
**Vincent, Bordeaux 2000**
Dry but has pleasing lilt of gooseberry on the finish. Good fish wine.

**Château Petit Roubie,** `15.5` `–£5.00`
**Picpoul du Pinet 2000**
**(organic)**
Great change from Chardonnay.
Has dry fruit of bite and wit.

**Château Turcaud** `13` `–£5.00`
**Entre-Deux-Mers 2000**
Very austere. Touch of raw grass
to the finish.

**Clos de Monestier** `12` `–£5.00`
**Bergerac Blanc 2000**
Dry and unresponsive to
affection.

**Clos de Monestier** `14` `–£5.00`
**Bergerac Rosé 2000**
Dry, cherryish fruit.

**Côtes du Rhône** `15` `£7–10`
**Domaine Chaume**
**Arnaud 1999**
Sweet liquorice and blackberries.
Very attractive on the rich finish.

**Domaine de Pellehaut** `14` `–£5.00`
**Côtes de Gascogne**
**2000**
Great value fruity slurping.

**Gewürztraminer** `16` `£5–7`
**d'Alsace Turckheim**
**2000**
Very rich roseate fruit of spice
and vibrancy. Perfect with
oriental food.

**James Herrick** `16` `–£5.00`
**Chardonnay VdP d'Oc**
**1999**
Always one of southern France's
most elegant examples of this
absurdly fashionable grape
variety.

**La Passion Blanc VdP** `14` `–£3.50`
**de Vaucluse 2000**
Has a touch of cloying pear to the
melon and the result is most
effective.

**Louis Chatel sur Lie** `14.5` `–£3.50`
**VdP d'Oc 2000**
Very dry and fish friendly.

**Muscadet sur Lie La** `13` `–£5.00`
**Roche Renard 2000**
Very dry and austere.

**Pouilly-Fumé Les** `13.5` `£7–10`
**Cornets, Cailbourdin**
**2000**
Bit expensive for the style of the
fruit.

**Riesling d'Alsace Aime** `14.5` `£5–7`
**Stentz 1999**
Very elegant aperitif or for robust
support for smoked fish.

**St-Véran Domaine des** `16` `£5–7`
**Deux Roches 1999**
Lovely texture to this vintage
gives the vegetality reach, depth
and elegance.

**Vermentino Les Yeuses** `15` `–£3.50`
**VdP d'Oc 2000**
Delicious dry charm here. Has
balance and bite.

**Vin Blanc NV, Booths** `12` `–£3.50`

## BUDGENS WHITE

**Bordeaux Sauvignon** `13.5` `–£5.00`
**NV, Budgens**

**Chardonnay VdP d'Oc** `13.5` `–£3.50`
**NV, Budgens**

Fat-edged melony fruit with a hint of ripe melon.

**Devereux Premium** `15.5` `−£5.00`
**Cuvée Viognier NV**
Delicious textured ripeness and classy apricot finesse – has good assistance from the acids. Overall, a very charming, well-balanced wine. Excellent value for money.

**Domaine Fouassier** `13` `£7–10`
**Sancerre Les**
**Chasseignes 2000**
Bit flat on the finish and for eight quid who needs a flat cap?

**French Connection** `14` `−£5.00`
**Grenache Sauvignon**
**Blanc 2000**
Rich, hint of spice, good with Thai food.

**Kiwi Cuvée** `14` `−£5.00`
**Chardonnay VdP du**
**Jardin de la France 2000**
Ripe, rather lemony richness. A very good fish wine.

**Kiwi Cuvée Sauvignon** `14` `−£5.00`
**Blanc, VdP du Jardin de**
**la France 2000**
Herbaceous and very crisp. Has a touch of celery to the undertone.

**'L' Grande Cuvée VdP** `15.5` `£5–7`
**d'Oc 1999**

**La Baume Sauvignon** `15.5` `−£5.00`
**Blanc 2000**
Classy style of nuttiness, melonosity and fine, interwoven lemon acids.

**Premium Oaked** `14` `−£5.00`
**Chardonnay VdP d'Oc,**
**Devereux NV**

## CO-OP WHITE

**Alsace Gewürztraminer** `16.5` `£5–7`
**2000**
Superb texture, chewy and rich, lovely rosy fruit with hints of mango and lychee, and altogether gently spicy enough for Thai food. Superstores only.

**Calvet Reserve White** `11` `−£5.00`
**1999**
Strives to be ordinary – and succeeds triumphantly.

**Chardonnay-Chenin** `12.5` `−£5.00`
**Vegetarian NV, Co-op**

**Château Pierrousselle** `14.5` `−£5.00`
**Entre-Deux-Mers 2000**
Great shellfish candidate.

**Chevalière Réserve** `12` `−£5.00`
**Chardonnay 1999**

**French Organic** `14` `−£5.00`
**Chardonnay Sauvignon**
**Blanc 2000, Co-op**
Rich and good with grilled tuna.

**French Organic White** `14` `−£5.00`
**2000, Co-op**
Chewy simplicity. Great with fish 'n' chips.

**James Herrick** `16` `−£5.00`
**Chardonnay 1999**
Always one of southern France's most elegant examples of this absurdly fashionable grape variety.

**Monbazillac Domaine** `16.5` `−£5.00`
**du Haut-Rauly 1998**
**(half bottle)**
Superb waxy richness here.
Gorgeous honeyed fruit with
touches of Brazil nut, lemon,
mango, lychee and . . . ugli fruit.
Well I never. Superstores only.

**Montagny Premiere** `13` `£7–10`
**Cru 1998**

**Orchid Vale** `13.5` `−£5.00`
**Chardonnay Grenache**
**Blanc 1999**

**Rhône Valley White** `14` `−£3.50`
**1999**

**Sancerre Domaine** `13` `£5–7`
**Raimbault 1998**

**Vin de Pays d'Oc** `13.5` `−£5.00`
**Chardonnay Viognier**
**NV, Co-op**
Works with shellfish. Superstores
only.

**Vin de Pays d'Oc** `12` `−£5.00`
**Chenin Chardonnay**
**NV, Co-op (vegetarian)**

**Vin de Pays d'Oc Syrah** `11` `−£3.50`
**Rosé NV, Co-op**

**Vin de Pays des Côtes** `14.5` `−£3.50`
**de Gascogne, Co-op**

**Vin de Pays du Jardin** `12` `−£3.50`
**de la France Sauvignon**
**Blanc NV, Co-op**
Pretty dull. Superstores only.

## KWIK SAVE WHITE

**Les Oliviers French** `14.5` `−£2.50`
**White NV**
Astonishing value for money. It
has graceful lemon fruit of
surprising charm.

**Muscadet 2000,** `13` `−£3.50`
**Somerfield**

**Skylark Hill VdP du** `15` `−£3.50`
**Comte Tolosan 2000**
Quite delicious tangy lemon fruit.

**Winter Hill White 2000** `14` `−£5.00`
Has a good texture and warmth
to it with a fresh edge as it
finishes.

## M & S WHITE

**Bordeaux Sauvignon** `16` `−£5.00`
**2000**
A very elegant labelling fully
echoing the very elegant fruit
within. Has soft-fruit tension with
good acids. A very accomplished
white wine.

**Chablis Grand Cru** `14` `£20+`
**Grenouille 1995**
A very fine Chablis offering
under-ripe melon, subtle lemon,
sesame seeds and a controlled
texture of elegance and
elongation. However, £23 is a lot
of money.

**Chablis Premier Cru** `13.5` `£10–13`
**Fourchaume 1997**
Nutty and elegant but poor value
compared with M&S white
Aussies.

**Chassagne-Montrachet** `10` `£20+`
**Premier Cru Morgeot**
**'Les Senteurs' 1998**
When you spend £27 on a white
you generally expect excitement
and a haute-couture cut. This
wine, au contraire, seems ragged
to me. I'd much rather drink the
M&S St-Véran at a fraction of the
price.

**Château La Gordonne** `13.5` `–£5.00`
**Côtes de Provence**
**Rosé 2000**
Very dry and absent-fruited.

**Coeur de Vallée VdP** `16.5` `–£5.00`
**d'Oc 2000**
The label's stuck on crooked but
the fruit's straight, bounteous
(yet delicate on the finish) and
very charming. It treats the taste
buds to a courteous medley of
ripe pear, pineapple and very very
subtle passion fruit. All this
fandango, however, is gentle.

**Domaine de Castellas** `15` `–£5.00`
**Côtes de Roussillon**
**2000**
Even has a few tannins to play
with and it is a deliciously playful,
cherry-dry rosé of some class.

**Domaine de Chevaunet** `15.5` `–£5.00`
**Touraine Sauvignon**
**Blanc 2000**
Elegant, clean, fresh, very crisp,
delicious.

**Domaine de La** `15` `–£5.00`
**Pouvraie Vouvray 2000**
Lovely dry-honey, lime and good
undertoning minerals. Finishes

very clean and steely. However,
cellar it for five to eight years and
a really brilliant wine will emerge.

**Domaine Galatis** `15.5` `–£5.00`
**Chardonnay/Viognier**
**VdP d'Oc 2000**
Delicious blend of rich melon and
delicate apricot: bold, refreshing,
very modern.

**Domaine Mandeville** `15` `–£5.00`
**Viognier 2000**
Quiet apricots, subdued lemons,
judicious acids – a muted
performance? Not at all: just
subtle.

**Gold Label Barrel** `15.5` `£5–7`
**Fermented Chardonnay**
**Reserve 2000**
What elegance! What quiet
resolve! What simple fruity
deliciousness! The harmony of
wood and fruit is perfect.

**Gold Label** `16` `–£5.00`
**Chardonnay VdP d'Oc**
**2000**
More oak than I remember on
this established M&S brand and it
adds complexity and depth and
more weight to the wine's main
argument – which is, take me
seriously.

**Gold Label Sauvignon** `15.5` `–£5.00`
**Blanc VdP d'Oc 2000**
Touches of richness to the firm
crisp fruit give it food versatility
and solid quaffability.

**Les Ruettes Sancerre** `14.5` `£7–10`
**2000**
Hints of celery, coriander to the

regulation gooseberry which is very crisp and fresh. A very individual interpretation of success.

**Mâcon-Villages 2000**   15   £5–7
A very sound, solidly-packed white Burgundy of some class.

**Mercurey Premier Cru**   15   £10–13
**Domaine de La Grangerie 1999**
Nicely textured creaminess to the mild fruit but I'd be inclined to cellar this for two to three years to let its vegetal Burgundianess to develop and, possibly, bloom to greater deliciosity.

**Pouilly-Fumé Les**   15.5   £7–10
**Vignes de Saint-Laurent-l'Abbaye 2000**
Classic style with an undertone of fine melon, lemon, minerals and steely acids. Very elegant, prim, correct.

**Rosé d'Anjou 2000**   12   –£5.00
Slightly sweet and very simple on the finish.

**Rosé de Syrah VdP**   15.5   –£5.00
**d'Oc 2000**
One of the most gripping rosés I've tasted. Has delicious dry cherries and tart plums in perfect collusion.

**St-Véran Les Monts**   16   £5–7
**1999**
A marvellous white Burgundy of unpretentious yet telling richness (creamy yet not OTT), gentle vegetality and very insistent fruitiness on the finish. Yet, for all

this, it has serious class and texture.

**St-Aubin Premier Cru**   13.5   £10–13
**Domaine du Pimont 1998**
Bit austere and awkward on the finish to rate higher. And I think cellaring will make it finer.

**Sancerre Domaine**   13   £7–10
**Hubert Brochard 2000**
Rather pricey and has a subtle bitter edge. Overpriced.

**Silver Tree Chardonnay**   14.5   £5–7
**2000**
Some weight and richness here, much of it from the wood ageing, but it seems a bit raw on the finish.

**VdP des Côtes de**   14   –£3.50
**Gascogne 2000**
A pleasing little tipple with hints of pineapple and pear. A good aperitif style.

**Vin de Pays du Gers**   15   –£3.50
**2000**
Delightful fresh fruit, tangy and light, recalling pear and pineapple.

## MORRISONS WHITE

**Château Lafont Menaut**   16   £7–10
**Pessac-Leognan, Graves 1999**
Brilliant chewy texture and well textured fruit. Lovely ripe feel, good acids, pert finish.

**Falcon Ridge** `14.5` `−£3.50`
**Chardonnay 2000**
A remarkable price for such good
clean underripe melon fruit.

**Falcon Ridge** `15` `−£3.50`
**Sauvignon Blanc 2000**
Excellent lemony fruit and
touches of gooseberry.

**Gewürztraminer Preiss** `15.5` `£5−7`
**Zimmer 2000**
Hints of lychee and rich rose
petals and a touch of cumin.
Delicious oriental food wine.

**Haut-Poitou Sauvignon** `14` `−£3.50`
**Blanc NV**

**Pinot Blanc Preiss** `14` `−£5.00`
**Zimmer 2000**
Delicious lemony fruit.

**St-Véran 2000** `14.5` `£5−7`
Gentle plump melon and very
subtle lemon acids. Has elegance
and class.

**Sancerre La Renardière** `12` `£7−10`
**1999**

**Sichel Premières Côtes** `12.5` `−£5.00`
**de Bordeaux Blanc NV**

**Vouvray Les Grands** `16` `−£5.00`
**Mortiers, Pierre Guery**
**2000**
Terrific! One of the most
adventurous white wines in the
store. Dry honey and pineapple,
lovely acids and . . . and the
capacity to develop, if cellared,
for six or seven years.

## SAFEWAY WHITE

**Alsace Gewürztraminer** `15` `£5−7`
**2000, Safeway**
Rich and typical (roses, touch of
lychee and gooseberry) but better
kept for eighteen months
(Christmas 2002) to develop more
and high rating charms.

**Chablis Premier Cru** `13` `£10−13`
**Beauroy 1999**
Rather a lot of pretence, not a lot
of substance – except on the price
tag.

**Chablis Laroche 1999** `12` `£7−10`

**Château de La** `16` `−£5.00`
**Gravelle, Muscadet de**
**Sèvres-et-Maine Sur Lie**
**2000**
Has more concentration than the
de l'Ecu and more lilting minerals
on the finish. A very stylish
Muscadet.

**Château Magneau,** `15` `£5−7`
**Graves 1999**

**Chenin VdP du Jardin** `13.5` `−£3.50`
**de la France 2000,**
**Safeway**
Very respectable balance but a
touch woolly on the finish.

**Corbières Rosé 2000** `13.5` `−£5.00`
Dry plums, touch of black cherry.

**Domaine de Bosquet** `15.5` `£5−7`
**Chardonnay VdP d'Oc**
**2000**
Dry but has a fleshy edge of
under-ripe melon. A Safeway
theme with its 2000 whites – this
dryness. Selected stores.

## FRENCH WHITE

**Domaine de Ciffre** `13.5` `£5–7`
Viognier VdP d'Oc
2000
Very dry and unyielding. Selected
stores.

**Domaine de l'Ecu** `15.5` `–£5.00`
Muscadet de Sèvres-et-
Maine sur Lie 2000
Deliciously tangy – almost
Sauvignon-like in its
gooseberryishness. Classy hint of
mineral depths.

**Domaine La Tour du** `15.5` `–£5.00`
Maréchal Chardonnay,
VdP de l'Hérault 2000
(organic)
An intensely dry specimen of
Chardonnay but very crisp. Great
food wine. Selected stores.

**Domaine Lafage** `14` `–£5.00`
Muscat Sec, VdP d'Oc
1999

**French Revolution Le** `14` `–£5.00`
Blanc 1999
Crisp but with a bitter finish.

**James Herrick** `16` `–£5.00`
Chardonnay VdP d'Oc
1999
Always one of southern France's
most elegant examples of this
absurdly fashionable grape
variety.

**La Source** `15.5` `–£5.00`
Chardonnay/
Roussanne VdP d'Oc
2000
Terrific plump fruit, oily and
deep, and it has excellent
balancing tannins.

**'Les Caudanettes'** `13` `–£3.50`
Anjou Blanc 2000
Slightly sweet finish.

**Montagny Premier Cru** `14` `£7–10`
1998, Safeway

**Pinot Blanc Alsace** `15.5` `–£5.00`
2000, Safeway
Lovely rich apricot touches with
an undertone of subtle toastiness.

**Pouilly-Fuissé 1998,** `12` `£7–10`
Safeway
Absurd price for such dried out
views on life. Selected stores.

**Sancerre 'Les Bonnes** `11` `£7–10`
Bouches' 2000
Bad value lacklustre fruit.
Selected stores.

**Sauvignon Blanc Cuvée** `13.5` `–£5.00`
Réserve VdP d'Oc 2000
Almost there. Selected stores.

**St-Véran 1997** `13` `£5–7`

**Touraine Sauvignon** `15.5` `–£5.00`
2000
Lovely crisp, dry wine of great
interest to food – and fun-lovers.
It is quintessentially French and
stylish. Finishes with aplomb.
Selected stores.

**VdP de l'Ardèche Rosé** `13` `–£3.50`
2000, Safeway
Light cherry fruit.

**Via Domitia** `13` `£5–7`
Chardonnay/Viognier
Réserve Spéciale, VdP
d'Oc 2000
Bit fat and muddy on the finish.
Selected stores.

**Viognier Cuvée**   `14`  `–£5.00`
**Réserve, VdP d'Oc**
**2000**
Mild apricots in dry array.
Selected stores.

## SAINSBURY'S WHITE

**Ackerman Anjou Blanc**  `14.5`  `–£5.00`
**2000 (organic)**
Touch of sweet melon to the
gentle lemon richness. Touch
forward? Maybe. But as a hot-
weather refresher it has much to
commend it. Selected stores.

**Antonin Rodet**   `12`   `£13–20`
**Meursault 1998**
Difficult to justify the juice when
it comes with so lush a price.

**Big Frank's Deep Pink**  `13`  `–£5.00`
**2000**
Playful, adolescent, cherry-ripe
fruit. Selected stores.

**Bordeaux Blanc,**   `15.5`  `–£3.50`
**Sainsbury's**
Remarkable price for such clean,
crisp fruit (mainly under-ripe
gooseberry and vague melon).
The label sucks, but the fruit
sings.

**Bourgogne**   `15.5`  `£5–7`
**Chardonnay, Louis**
**Max 1999**
Delightful stuff, showing how
elegant and subtly vegetal le vrai
bourgogne blanc can be. Dry, a
touch delicate, it's decisively
delicious. Most stores.

**Chablis Calvet 1999**   `14`   `£5–7`

Has some texture, a hint of
melony plumpness, and some
degree of class.

**Chablis Premier Cru**   `16`  `£10–13`
**Côtes de Jouan,**
**Brocard 1999**
Expensive but fine. Has
concentration, crisply tailored
classiness, and a delicate yet
decisive finish.

**Chardonnay VdP d'Oc**  `15.5`  `–£5.00`
**NV, Sainsbury's**
**(organic)**
Even has some tannins to it! This
gives it a slightly chewy texture to
its fruity, fresh, concentrated
finish. Remarkable value. Most
stores.

**Chardonnay VdP d'Oc,**  `15.5`  `–£3.50`
**Sainsbury's (3 litre box)**
Price band indicates the 75cl
equivalent.

**Château de Rully**   `13`  `£10–13`
**Blanc, Rodet 1998**
Rather boredom-inducing for so
extravagant a bar code. Selected
stores.

**Château Tassin**   `14.5`  `–£5.00`
**Bordeaux Clairet 2000**
Serious dry rosé. Great with food,
entertaining with mood. Selected
stores.

**Classic Selection**   `16`  `£7–10`
**Chablis Domaine**
**Sainte Cecil 1999,**
**Sainsbury's**
Well, well! Indeed it's classic: dry
and minerally, and with that

sedate crispness which good
Chablis has. Most stores.

**Classic Selection** 16 £7–10
**Pouilly-Fumé 2000,**
**Sainsbury's**
I confess to liking it. To finding it
crisp and steely, minerally and
fresh, elegant and subtle. To
confess is good for the soul.

**Classic Selection** 15.5 £7–10
**Sancerre 2000,**
**Sainsbury's**
Am I getting old? or is Sancerre
getting more amusing? I suspect
the latter. I fear the former.
Selected stores.

**Condrieu Guigal 1998** 15.5 £13–20

**Cuvée Victoria Rosé de** 14.5 £5–7
**Provence 2000**
Nice bitter nut and sour peach
aftertaste as the cherry fruit goes
down. Selected stores.

**Domaine de Pellehaut** 14 −£5.00
**Côtes de Gascogne**
**2000**
Great value fruity slurping. Most
stores.

**Domaine de Sours** 14 £5–7
**Bordeaux Rosé 2000**
Serious, sober, plum/cherry rosé.
Expensive, yes. But if you must
have rosé . . . then . . . Selected
stores.

**Domaine Leonce** 15.5 £5–7
**Cuisset, Saussignac**
**1998 (50cl)**
Sainsbury characterise this as a
dessert wine but its sweet

delicacy is more pre- than post-
prandial. It is honeyed, yes, but it
has a finesse which brutal puds
will smother. Limited
distribution.

**Duo Rosé d'Anjou and** 14.5 −£3.50
**Anjou Blanc NV (3 litre**
**box)**
This is a novel twin-tap wine box
with the rosé on the bottom and
the blanc on top. This is not quite
how it works out point-wise: the
blanc rates 14 points, the rosé
14.5. A commendable initiative
from Sainsbury's buying team
which will undoubtedly be
copied. Most stores.

**French Revolution Le** 14 −£5.00
**Blanc 1999**
Crisp but with a bitter finish.

**Le MD de Bourgeois** 15 £10–13
**Sancerre 1999**
An interesting Sancerre with few
rich minerals but a beautiful
textured plumpness not
Rubenesque so much as
Giacomettiesque. Expensive but
classy. Limited distribution.

**Le Midi Rosé,** 13.5 −£5.00
**Languedoc 2000**
A good barbecue fish wine.
Selected stores.

**Le Midi Viognier 2000** 16 −£5.00
Delicious! Dry apricots, hint of
nut, touch of lemon/melon on
the finish. Classy stuff, very
crisply and smartly turned out.
Selected stores.

**Mercurey Blanc** `14` `£13–20`
**Domaine La Marche**
**Les Rochelles 1998**
Expensive but has a lingering
richness reminiscent of the real
thing, i.e. posh farmyards
complete with cow dung. Limited
distribution.

**Meursault Clos de** `11` `£20+`
**Mazeray, Domaine**
**Jacques Prieur 1998**
A lot of money, not a lot of
excitement. Limited distribution.

**Mouton Cadet Blanc** `12` `£5–7`
**1999**
Rather dull and overpriced.

**Numero Un Bordeaux** `13.5` `–£5.00`
**Blanc 2000**
Dry. Selected stores.

**Petit Chablis Jean** `15.5` `–£5.00`
**Brocard NV (3 litre**
**box)**
Amazing! Real Chablis in a box.
Here is style and steeliness in
vibrant Chablis form in three
litres of generous cardboard
luxury. Has classic mineral
richness. Price band indicates the
75cl equivalent.

**Picpoul de Pinet 'Les** `16` `£10–13`
**Flacons' Coteaux du**
**Languedoc 1999**
A very engagingly textured, finely
wrought white wine. It's classier
and more impactfully individual
than many a white Burgundy
which would look askance at this
wine on the same shelf.

**Puilly-Fuissé Georges** `13.5` `£10–13`
**Duboeuf 1998**
Lot of money, not entirely a lot
of wine for eleven quid. A four
quid wine masquerading as
something else. Limited
ditribution.

**Réserve St Marc** `16.5` `–£5.00`
**Sauvignon Blanc, VdP**
**d'Oc 2000**
Superb tang of gooseberries,
limes, minerals and tightly packed
acids. Very classy and finely
styled. Most stores.

**Touraine Sauvignon Le** `15.5` `–£5.00`
**Chalutier 2000**
Quite delicious citrussy fruit.
Selected stores.

**Van Blanc, VdP de** `14.5` `–£3.50`
**Vaucluse NV**
A perfectly charming, dry, crisp
white of style and texture. Has a
fine tang to its finish. Selected
stores.

**Vin Blanc de France,** `12` `–£3.50`
**Sainsbury's (3 litre box)**
Price band indicates the 75cl
equivalent.

**Vin de Pays des Côtes** `15` `–£3.50`
**de Gascogne,**
**Sainsbury's (3 litre box)**
Price band indicates the 75cl
equivalent.

**Vouvray La Couronne** `15.5` `–£5.00`
**des Plantagenets 2000**
Brilliant new vintage of this off-
dry wine which is more sec than
it might appear. It has lovely
minerals to the dry fruit and it

ages superbly. I'm drinking the '94 at home now.

White Burgundy NV, `14` `£5–7`
Sainsbury's

## SOMERFIELD WHITE

Anjou Blanc 2000, `12` `–£3.50`
Somerfield

Bordeneuve Blanc VdP `13` `–£5.00`
des Côtes de Gascogne
1999

Chablis 1998, `12.5` `£7–10`
Somerfield
Has some mildly amusing texture
to it.

Chablis Premier Cru `11.5` `£10–13`
Cottin Freres 1999

Chardonnay VdP d'Oc `14` `–£5.00`
2000, Somerfield
Has some vague melon fruit.

Côte Sauvage `15` `–£5.00`
Chardonnay Viognier
2000
Delicious apricot/melon/
hazelnut and lemon fruit. Dry,
expressive, individual. Selected
stores.

Côte Sauvage Cinsault `15` `–£5.00`
Rosé d'Oc 2000
Lovely dry cherries and
strawberries. Remarkable couth
fruit.

Domaine du Bois `15` `£5–7`
Viognier, Maurel
Vedeau 1999
Dry peachy fruit of some charm.

Domaine Sainte Agathe `15` `£5–7`
Oak Aged Chardonnay
1999, Somerfield
More texture and interesting
vegetal fruit than many a white
Burgundy.

Gewürztraminer `16` `£5–7`
d'Alsace, Turckheim
2000
Superb nuttiness here with a
lingering lychee and rose petal
finish. Predictable but not dull.
Very good value. Selected
stores.

Hautes-Côtes de `13` `£7–10`
Beaune Blanc, Georges
Desire 1998
Bit expensive . . . more than a
bit . . .

James Herrick `15` `–£5.00`
Chardonnay VdP d'Oc
2000
So far Penfolds haven't screwed it
up. But why the cork, Penfolds?
Screwcap it, you cowards!

Kiwi Cuvée Sauvignon `14` `–£5.00`
Blanc, VdP du Jardin de
la France 2000
Herbaceous and very crisp. Has a
touch of celery to the undertone.

La Baume Viognier `14.5` `–£5.00`
VdP d'Oc 2000
Lemon and dried peach and fig
fruit.

Laroche Chardonnay `14.5` `£5–7`
2000
Rich yet not OTT. Selected
stores.

**Muscadet 2000,** `13` `—£3.50`
Somerfield

**Old Tart Terret** `13.5` `—£5.00`
Sauvignon 2000

**Rosé d'Anjou 2000,** `12.5` `—£3.50`
Somerfield
Too sweet – a touch.

**Sancerre Domaine des** `13` `£7–10`
Grand Groux 2000,
Somerfield
Oddly fat and chewy.

**VdP de l'Ardèche Blanc** `15` `—£3.50`
2000, Somerfield
Simple lemon fruit of striking
charm for the money.

**VdP du Comte Tolosan** `15` `—£3.50`
2000, Somerfield
Quite delicious tangy lemon fruit.

**Vouvray 2000,** `14` `—£5.00`
Somerfield
Off-dry – and has good honey and
minerals. It will cellar well for
three of four years and become
very interesting.

**White Burgundy 2000,** `13.5` `£5–7`
Somerfield
Decently assembled, gently
vegetal fruit with a crisp finish.

**Winter Hill White 2000** `14` `—£5.00`
Has a good texture and warmth
to it with a fresh edge as it
finishes.

**Chablis 1998, Spar** `15` `£5–7`
Good, genuinely classy fruit, hints

of soft vegetality and a classic
finish. Good mature fruit.

**French Country VdP de** `13` `—£5.00`
l'Hérault White NV

**La Côte Chasan** `14` `—£5.00`
Chardonnay 1999
A good balance of fleshy fruit and
pert acidity.

**Salaison Chardonnay** `13.5` `—£5.00`
Sauvignon 1999, Spar
Rather austere on the finish.

**Unoaked Chardonnay** `13` `—£5.00`
1999, Spar
Mild, inoffensive fruit of gentle
citricity.

**Vin de Pays de l'Aude** `14` `—£3.50`
NV, Spar
Simple, fruity, tangy, lemony.

**White Burgundy** `13` `£5–7`
Chardonnay 1996, Spar

**Wild River Terret** `14` `—£5.00`
Sauvignon 1999
Has some melon character and
some underpinning lemon.

**Alsace Gewürztraminer** `17` `£5–7`
1999, Tesco
What a wonderfully complex,
rich yet subtle, energetic, spicy
wine of huge charm. At its price
it's a marvel: lemon, lime, apple,
pear, gooseberry and ripe melon
yet . . . not OTT. Brilliant with
Chinese food, beautiful with
literary mood. One of Tesco's so-

called 'Finest' range. At most stores.

**Alsace Riesling 1999, Tesco** `14.5` `£5–7`

Very dry and gently mineral-tinged. Terrific fish wine – brilliant with fruits de mer. Part of Tesco's so-called 'Finest' range. At most stores.

**Anjou Blanc NV, Tesco** `13` `–£3.50`

**Bergerac Blanc NV, Tesco** `14.5` `–£3.50`

Utterly unpretentious. Supremely slurpable and refreshing: crisp, clean, uncluttered. Most stores.

**Cabernet de Saumur Rosé NV, Tesco** `14.5` `–£5.00`

**Celsius Cabernet Sauvignon Rosé, VdP d'Oc 2000** `14` `–£5.00`

Rich, energetic, touch toffee-edged, and dry. Good food rosé.

**Celsius Medium Chardonnay, VdP d'Oc 2000** `13.5` `–£5.00`

Sweet edged but good with Chinese spicy food. Most stores.

**Chablis 2000, Tesco** `15` `£5–7`

**Chablis Premier Cru 1998, Tesco** `16` `£10–13`

An exceptionally rich and complex Chablis of considerable concentration and class. One of Tesco's so-called 'Finest' range.

**Chardonnay Barrel-aged Reserve, VdP d'Oc 1999** `15` `–£5.00`

One of Tesco's so-called 'Finest' range, so it might be good and it is. It displays well-integrated melon/lemon/nutty fruit with a softness and richness balanced by the gentle woodiness.

**Chardonnay Réserve 1999, Tesco** `14` `–£5.00`

**Château Baratet Blanc 1999 (organic)** `14` `–£5.00`

**Château Talmont 2000** `16` `–£5.00`

Interestingly tangy white Bordeaux of crisp fruit attack and huge shellfish friendliness without tartness. Superb value for money. Selected stores.

**Côtes du Rhône Blanc NV, Tesco** `15` `–£3.50`

**Côtes du Rhône Rosé, AC Côtes du Rhônes 2000** `14` `–£5.00`

Mild, dry cherry fruit.

**Domaine Cazal Viel Viognier 1999** `16` `£5–7`

The moment the beautiful golden liquid flows into the glass and you raise it to the eye, then the nose, you know you're in for a treat. And so it transpires as you raise the wine to the lips and the taste buds revel in subtle apricot fruit, lemon and a hint of nuttiness. A lovely, elegant wine of some class and smoothly textured delivery.

**Domaine du Soleil Chardonnay VdP d'Oc NV** `14` `–£5.00`

**Domaine du Soleil** `14` `−£5.00`
Sauvignon/
Chardonnay VdP d'Oc
NV

**Entre-Deux-Mers NV,** `13.5` `−£5.00`
Tesco

**French Chardonnay** `13.5` `−£3.50`
NV, Tesco

**French Chenin Blanc** `14.5` `−£3.50`
NV, Tesco

**French Viognier VdP** `16` `−£5.00`
d'Oc 2000, Tesco
Interesting edge to the wine
makes it less full, more quirky
than the New World versions of
this grape. It's a grassiness.
Brilliant for food. Most stores.

**Kiwi Cuvée Sauvignon** `14` `−£5.00`
Blanc, VdP du Jardin de
la France 2000
Herbaceous and very crisp. Has a
touch of celery to the undertone.

**Les Estoiles Organic** `13.5` `−£5.00`
Chardonnay/Chenin
VdP d'Oc NV

**Les Quatre Clochers** `15.5` `£5–7`
Chardonnay 1998

**Mâcon-Villages Blanc** `15` `−£5.00`
2000, Tesco
Unusually fruity for this
appellation. In the New World
mould, almost. Most stores.

**Muscadet NV, Tesco** `14.5` `−£3.50`
Amazingly well-meaning, crisp,
clean-finishing Muscadet of
charm and character. Superb

shellfish partner. Remarkable
value for money.

**Muscadet sur Lie 2000,** `14` `−£5.00`
Tesco
Fresh and crisp. Hint of mineral
undertone but it's just a hint. One
of Tesco's so-called 'Finest' range.

**Oak Aged Bordeaux** `13` `−£5.00`
NV, Tesco
Finishes well but in the mid-
palate it seems lost and ill-
defined. Most stores.

**Oak Aged White** `13` `£5–7`
Burgundy 1999, Tesco
Bit ordinary compared to the
glorious New World
Chardonnays Tesco sells. Part of
Tesco's 'Finest' range. Most
stores.

**Petit Chablis 1999,** `15` `£5–7`
Tesco

**Pouilly-Fuissé Louis** `11` `£13–20`
Jadot 1998

**Pouilly-Fumé Cuvée** `13` `£7–10`
Jules 1999
Bit ho-hum on the finish for
seven quid.

**Sancerre 2000, Tesco** `16` `£5–7`
Goodness, what a crisp clean
specimen of subtle
gooseberriness. Excellent price for
a real classic Sancerre. One of
Tesco's so-called 'Finest' range.
Most stores.

**Vouvray, Tesco** `12` `−£5.00`

## WAITROSE WHITE

**Alsace Gewürztraminer** `16` `£5–7`
**1999, Waitrose**
Superb spicy succulence without over-ripeness.

**Alsace Pinot Blanc,** `14` `–£5.00`
**Paul Blanck 1999**

**Anjou Blanc Ackerman** `13` `–£3.50`
**1999**

**Bordeaux Blanc** `12` `–£3.50`
**Medium Dry, Yvon**
**Mau NV**

**Bordeaux Sémillon** `15.5` `–£5.00`
**2000**
Very elegant, well-textured fruit of great charm.

**Boulder Creek White** `13` `–£3.50`
**2000**

**Chablis Gaec des** `14.5` `£7–10`
**Reugnis 1998**

**Chablis Grand Cru** `11` `£13–20`
**Vaudésir 1998**

**Chablis, William Fèvre** `13` `£7–10`
**1999**
Oily, slightly austere finish.

**Chardonnay VdP du** `13.5` `–£5.00`
**Jardin de la France**
**2000, Waitrose**
Touch tart on the finish.

**Chassagne-Montrachet** `13` `£20+`
**Bouchard Père 1999**

**Château Carsin Cuvée** `15` `£7–10`
**Prestige 1998**
Very elegant and accomplished feel to it.

**Château Climens** `13` `£13–20`
**Barsac 1996 (half bottle)**
Very sweet and monodimensionally so. Mail Order only.

**Château de Caraghuiles** `14` `£5–7`
**Organic Rosé 2000**
Elegant and serious-minded.

**Château La Garenne** `13.5` `£13–20`
**Sauternes 1997**
Needs ageing, five to ten years of it.

**Château Liot Sauternes** `14` `£7–10`
**1997 (half bottle)**
Still rather sweet and little else, so cellar it for five years.

**Château Petit Roubie,** `15.5` `–£5.00`
**Picpoul du Pinet 2000**
**(organic)**
Great change from Chardonnay. Has dry fruit of bite and wit.

**Château Rieussec,** `15` `£13–20`
**Sauternes 1996 (half**
**bottle)**
Lovely oily and waxy honeyed stuff. Still five to seven years off its best, though. Mail Order only.

**Château Saint-Jean-des-** `10` `£5–7`
**Graves, Graves 2000**

**Château Thieuley,** `15` `£5–7`
**Bordeaux 2000**
Lovely style to the texture and subtle, vegetal fruit.

**Château Vignal Labrie,** `16` `£7–10`
**Monbazillac 1997**
Lovely honeyed, waxy fruit with

nuts and raspberries. Will age
well for five to eight years more.

**Coteaux du Giennois** `14.5` `£5–7`
**Blanc 1999**
Classy stuff.

**Fortant 'F' Limited** `13` `£7–10`
**Release Chardonnay,**
**VdP d'Oc 1998**
Far too expensive. Touch of
creamy oak is unsettling rather
than sympathetic.

**Huet Clos de Bourg** `17.5` `£7–10`
**Demi-sec, Vouvray**
**1999**
Don't be put off by the demi-sec
bit – it has superb acids which
give it great balance (and fifteen
years of cellaring capacity). It has
hay, minerals, honey and
butterscotch, and a lingering
finish of pear soufflé.

**La Baume Viognier** `14.5` `–£5.00`
**VdP d'Oc 2000**
Has some good dry apricots.

**La Cité Chardonnay,** `13` `–£5.00`
**VdP d'Oc 2000**

**Mâcon-Villages** `14` `–£5.00`
**Chardonnay, Cave de**
**Lugny 2000**
A mildly entertaining white
Burgundy.

**Mercurey Blanc** `12` `£10–13`
**Château le Hardi 1999**

**Montagny Premier Cru** `10` `£7–10`
**Bouchard Père 1998**
Over ripe and too extracted in
feel. Tries too hard.

**Muscadet sur Lie 'Fief** `14` `–£5.00`
**Guerin' 1999**

**Muscat Sec Domaine** `16` `–£5.00`
**de Provenquiere, VdP**
**d'Oc 2000**
Wonderful dry grapeyness with
hints of nuts, pear and peach, and
a deep finish.

**Muscate de Beaumes-** `15.5` `–£5.00`
**de-Venise NV (half**
**bottle)**
Lovely thick texture and very
vague hint of sweet marmalade
on the finish. For ice creams and
fresh fruit puddings.

**Pinot Gris Grand Cru** `18.5` `£20+`
**Rangen de Thann Clos**
**St Urbain, Domaine**
**Zind Humbrecht 1996**
Magnificent beast! Has sesame
seeds, figs, raspberries and
melons, plus minerals and fine
acids. Still young, it'll age eight to
ten years more but it's great now.
Only from Waitrose Direct.

**Pouilly-Fuissé Château** `11` `£10–13`
**Vitallis 2000**

**Pouilly-Fumé Masson** `14.5` `£7–10`
**Blondelet 1999**
Extremely dry, impishly lemony
and dry. Very steely and stylish.

**Puligny-Montrachet** `13` `£20+`
**Premier Cru Champs**
**Gains 1997**

**Quincy La Boissière** `13` `£5–7`
**1999**

**Rosé d'Anjou 2000,** `11` `–£5.00`
**Waitrose**

50% Grolleau grape variety is too much, I feel.

Saumur Blanc 'Les Andides' Saint Cyr-en-Bourg 1999    `14`   `–£5.00`

Tokay Pinot Gris Heimbourg, Domaine Zind Humbrecht 1998    `17`   `£20+`
17 now, possibly 20 in three to five years. Quite wonderful sweet apricots and wild raspberries with delicious mineral acids. A great French white wine of world class structure.

Top 40 Chardonnay VdP d'Oc 1999    `17`   `£5–7`
Better than many a Meursault this creamy, woody wine. It has delicacy yet lingering power and real deep class.

Touraine Sauvignon Blanc 2000, Waitrose    `12`   `–£5.00`

Vin Blanc Sec VdT Francais NV, Waitrose    `12`   `–£3.50`

Winter Hill Syrah Rosé, VdP d'Oc 2000    `13`   `–£5.00`
Very ripe and sweet.

Winter Hill VdP d'Oc 1999    `15`   `–£3.50`

# GERMANY

Crushed by UK consumer indifference. However, the great estates can still produce the greatest white wines on the planet.

## TESCO RED

**Fire Mountain Pinot Noir 1999**  10  −£5.00
The label, at least, is stuck on straight. Selected stores.

## WAITROSE RED

**Dornfelder Pfalz Lergenmüller 1999**  16  £5–7
Love it! It's like dry Beaujolais with a touch of dry Rhône. Joyous and full-throated fruit.

## ASDA WHITE

**Grans Fassian Trittenheimer Riesling Kabinett Altarchen 1999**  13.5  £5–7
Cellar it for eight years. It'll put on four or even five points of weight, complexity and concentration.

## BOOTHS WHITE

**Dr 'L' Riesling, Loosen Mosel 1999**  14  £5–7
Needs to be cellared for three or four years yet.

**Fire Mountain Riesling 1999**  14  −£5.00
Simple aperitif style with a hint of fat melon to an edge of lime.

**Gau-Bickelheimer Kurfurstenstuck Auslese 1998**  13  −£5.00

**Liebfraumilch NV, Booths**  13  −£3.50
Very off-dry style, not fully sweet, with a nuttiness – an excellent spritzer component.

**Piesporter Michelsberg NV, Booths**  12  −£5.00
Very sweet and simple.

**Riesling Louis Guntrum 1999**  14  −£5.00

**Villa Wolf Pinot Gris, Loosen Pfalz 1999**  16  £5–7
Exceedingly civilised peach, apricot, pineapple and lemon fruit. A most striking German dry white of great charm.

## BUDGENS WHITE

**Devil's Rock Riesling 2000** `14` –£5.00

Nothing wrong with this. Pity it doesn't have a screw cap.

## CO-OP WHITE

**Bockenheimer Grafenstuck Beerenauslese 1998 (half bottle)** `16` –£5.00

Lovely limey acids and mineral hints to ripe honey fruit with an undertone of raspberry and mango. Best cellared for another five to eight years to achieve almost perfection. Superstores only.

**Devil's Rock Riesling 2000** `14` –£5.00

Nothing wrong with this. Pity it doesn't have a screw cap.

**Graacher Himmelreich Riesling Spätlese 1999** `13` –£5.00

Excellent spritzer. Superstores only.

**Kendermans Dry Riesling 1999** `11` –£5.00

I've lost my patience with this dullard. Not at Convenience Stores.

**Twin Rivers Riesling 2000** `13` –£5.00

Screw-capped and mildly fruity. Not at Convenience Stores.

## KWIK SAVE WHITE

**Hock NV, Somerfield** `14.5` –£2.50

## MORRISONS WHITE

**Franz Reh Auslese 1999** `16` –£5.00

Delicious undertone of crème brulée to the honeyed raspberries and pears. Brilliant wine to have after a meal just by itself.

**Kendermans Dry Riesling 1999** `11` –£5.00

I've lost my patience with this dullard.

**Noble House Riesling 2000** `14` –£5.00

A fine off-dry aperitif.

**Urziger Wurzgarten Spätlese 1999** `14.5` £5–7

Bit young and will improve if cellared for up to five years. Has sweet pineapple and good acids.

## SAFEWAY WHITE

**Langenbach St Johanner Spätlese, Rheinhessen 2000** `10` –£5.00

Bit bare of excitement. Has some sugar if you like that sort of thing.

**Mertes Riesling Classic Medium, Pfalz 1999** `11` –£3.50

Pretty. Nothing much.

**Peter Mertes Dry Riesling 1999** `12.5` –£3.50

Sweet edged simpleton.

SA Prum Wehlener    16    £5–7
Sonnenuhr Riesling
Kabinett 1997
Lovely lime, pear, raspberry and
melon richness which never goes
sweet because of the superb
liveliness of the acids.

## SAINSBURY'S WHITE

Devil's Rock    13    –£5.00
Masterpiece, St Ursula
1999
Crisp but finishes with a nod to
sweetness. A masterpiece it is not.
Most stores.

Dr Pauly Riesling 1999    13    £5–7
Lay it down for five years.
Selected stores.

Hock, Sainsbury's (3    14.5    –£3.50
litre box)
Price band indicates the 75cl
equivalent.

Liebfraumilch,    14    –£3.50
Sainsbury's (3 litre box)
Price band indicates the 75cl
equivalent.

Ockfener Bockstein    15.5    –£5.00
Riesling Spätlese 1999
Terrific lemony, almost sweet
custardy fruit. Has a gentle
chewiness which gives it class. A
lovely aperitif or to go with
smoked fish.

Querbach Hallgartener    16    £5–7
Schonhell Rheingau
Riesling 1997
Has good structure and texture
with subtle touches of melon,

raspberry and lemon, with
attendant minerals in good array.
Will improve in bottle for ten
years more. 70 selected stores.

Schloss Wallhausen    16    £7–10
Riesling Kabinett 1999
Delicious apricot/strawberry/
lime fruit with the typical
regional fix (Nahe) on Riesling
which provides a rich undertone
to the excellent minerally acids.
75 selected stores.

## SOMERFIELD WHITE

Blue Nun Riesling 1999    13.5    –£5.00
Not bad – but expensive for the
label.

Hock NV, Somerfield    14.5    –£2.50

Kendermann Mosel    14.5    –£5.00
Riesling 1999
Sweet and sour with hints of
tanginess. Great Thai food wine.

Kendermann Pinot    15    –£5.00
Grigio 1999
Extraordinary! As good as the real
thing from Italy. Nuts, peaches
and a dry crisp finish. Selected
stores.

Morio Muskat 2000    15.5    –£3.50
Lovely Muscat richness tempered
by limes and pineapple. Great
refreshing stuff. Selected stores.

Niersteiner Gutes    12    –£3.50
Domtal 1999,
Somerfield
Good spritzer ingredient, though.

And if you add mint and cucumber, even better.

**Niersteiner Gutes Domtal, Johannes Egberts 1999**  `14`  −£5.00
Lay it down for five years and achieve some bargain 16.5 fruit of honey, lime, raspberry and cherries.

**Niersteiner Spiegelberg 1999, Somerfield**  `14`  −£3.50
Try it with Peking duck.

**Oppenheimer Krotenbrunner Rheinhessen Spätlese, Johannes Egberts 1999**  `12`  −£5.00

**Rheingau Riesling 2000, Somerfield**  `15`  −£5.00
Lovely dry honey and lemon. Superb torrid weather aperitif.

**Rheinhessen Spätlese 1999, Somerfield**  `13`  −£5.00
A sweetish ingredient for a spritzer.

**Rudesheimer Rosengarten 2000, Somerfield**  `11`  −£3.50

**St Ursula Dry Riesling 2000**  `14.5`  −£5.00
It works! Try it! Try it with fish 'n' chips – they need each other.

## SPAR WHITE

**Grans Fassian Riesling 1996**  `16`  £5–7
Lovely sherbet lemon and mineralised rich fruit of great class. Only just beginning to open up, this wine; it could be cellared for up to ten or fifteen years more.

## TESCO WHITE

**Bernkasteler Graben Riesling Kabinett 1999**  `15`  £5–7
Interesting ripe melon edge with the mineral citrus of the Riesling typicity showing up as it slides down the throat. Best left to age for five to seven years more when it will rate even higher. Selected stores.

**Carl Erhard Rheingau Riesling 1999**  `14`  −£5.00

**Fire Mountain Riesling 1999**  `14`  −£5.00
Simple aperitif style with a hint of fat melon to an edge of lime.

**Grans Fassian Riesling 1999**  `14.5`  £5–7
Needs time to develop: five or six years yet but has some evidence of its quality already in its rich fruit and acids.

**Steinweiler Kloster Liebfrauenberg Kabinett, Tesco**  `14`  −£5.00

**Steinweiler Kloster Liebfrauenberg Spätlese, Tesco**  `13`  −£5.00

## WAITROSE WHITE

**Bernkasteler Badstube Spätlese Dr Thanisch 1997**  `14`  £7–10

A warm weather aperitif.

**Devil's Rock** `13` `–£5.00`
**Masterpiece, St Ursula
1999**
Crisp but finishes with a nod to
sweetness. A masterpiece it is not.

**Dr Loosen Wehlener** `15` `£10–13`
**Sonnenuhr Riesling
Spätlese 1995**
Extruded minerals and honey
richness which achieves impact
yet subtlety. A gorgeous, civilised
aperitif.

**Dr Wagner Ockfener** `15` `£5–7`
**Bockstein Riesling 2000**
Delicious change from
Chardonnay: rich melons and
great acids with a touch of honey.

**Erdener Treppchen** `15.5` `£7–10`
**Riesling Auslese 1990**
Mature Mosel for nine quid! Snap
it up! It's a brilliant aperitif.

**Erdener Treppchen** `16.5` `£5–7`
**Riesling Spätlese 1997**
Superb minerals, packed inside
melons, pears, limes and
raspberries, and they emerge on
the finish as going gently
petroleum-like and fine. Will age
for the next eight to ten years and
actually improve. A great wine
for nigh-peanuts.

**Hedgerow Rheinhessen** `13` `–£5.00`
**2000**

**Kendermann Vineyard** `13.5` `–£5.00`
**Selection Dry Riesling
1998**

**Riesling Bassermann** `13` `£5–7`
**Jordan, Pfalz 2000**
16 in five to seven years. So cellar
it!

**Scharzhofberger** `10` `£20+`
**Riesling Auslese, Egon
Müller 1999**
10 points now. 20 points in 2015.
Sixty pounds is a lot of money. 20
points is a lot of points. But can
you wait a decade and a half?
Mail Order only.

**Scharzhofberger** `13` `£13–20`
**Riesling Kabinett, Egon
Müller 1999**
Must not be drunk now. Cellar it
until the end of New Labour's
third term . . . Mail Order only.

**Villa Wolf Pinot Gris** `14` `£5–7`
**1999**
Charming if a touch delicate in a
way which walks a thin line
between Alsatian Pinot Gris and
Friuli Pinot Grigio.

**Wehlener Sonnenuhr** `17` `£13–20`
**Riesling Auslese 1990**
One of the finest aperitifs in the
world. Trouble is, what follows?
Only from Waitrose Direct.

**Wehlener Sonnenuhr** `15` `£13–20`
**Riesling Spätlese, JJ
Prum 1994**
Getting richer and more
minerally as it ages. But still a
decade off its 18.5 point best. Mail
Order only.

# GREECE

The world's biggest curate's egg.

## BOOTHS RED

**Vin de Crete Kourtaki** 12 —£5.00
**1999**

## TESCO RED

**Grande Reserve** 14 £5–7
**Naoussa 1996**
Tannins nudge the vague plum
and blackcurrant fruits into
richness – needs robust Greek
roast lamb to be at its best.

## WAITROSE RED

**Pathos Xinomavrou,** 15 —£5.00
**Tsantali 1999**
Very beefy and rich and a
wonderful companion with like
minded plates.

## BOOTHS WHITE

**Kretikos Vin de Crete** 13 —£5.00
**Blanc Boutari 1999**
Odd sweet edge of under-ripe
melon. Needs spicy food.

## TESCO WHITE

**Santorini 1999** 16 —£5.00
Lovely richness and acidic
freshness combined in a very
stylish way. An exceptionally
striking Chardonnay under a
fiver. Most stores.

# HUNGARY

Not living up to the promise of its best estates.

## BUDGENS RED

Riverview Kékfrancos/ `13.5` −£5.00
Merlot 2000
Very juicy.

## CO-OP RED

Hungarian Country `13` −£3.50
Wine NV, Co-op

Kékfrancos Oaked `13` −£5.00
Merlot 1999, Co-op
Very jammy and half-baked. Not
at Convenience Stores.

## SAFEWAY RED

Riverview Kékfrancos/ `13.5` −£5.00
Merlot 2000
Very juicy. Most stores.

## SPAR RED

Misty Mountain Merlot `13` −£5.00
NV, Spar

## TESCO RED

Reka Valley Hungarian `13` −£3.50
Merlot, Tesco

Riverview Kékfrancos/ `13.5` −£5.00
Merlot 2000
Very juicy. Most stores.

## ASDA WHITE

Badger Hill Hungarian `14` −£3.50
Sauvignon 1999

Hungarian Medium `12` −£3.50
Chardonnay 1999, Asda

## BOOTHS WHITE

Chapel Hill Oaked `13.5` −£3.50
Chardonnay, Balaton
Boglar NV
Lemony and dry.

Tokaji Harslevelu `13.5` −£5.00
Castle Island 2000
Edgy fruit.

## BUDGENS WHITE

Riverview `15` −£5.00
Chardonnay/Pinot
Grigio 2000
Bargain fruity tippling. Not a
brash edge in sight.

## CO-OP WHITE

Chapel Hill Irsai Olivér 2000    13    −£3.50
Slightly spicy.

Gyöngyös Estate    14    −£5.00
Chardonnay 1999
Fresh with a sense of frolicsome fruit.

Hungarian White NV,    13.5    −£3.50
Co-op

Riverview    15    −£5.00
Chardonnay/Pinot
Grigio 2000
Bargain fruity tippling. Not a brash edge in sight.

## MORRISONS WHITE

Ideal with Friends    12.5    −£3.50
Chardonnay NV

'M' Ideal with Friends    13    −£3.50
Sauvignon Blanc NV

Oliver Irsai Olivér 2000    12    −£5.00
Spicy. Good with gung-ho chillied chicken from Nepal.

## SAFEWAY WHITE

Hilltop Virgin Vintage    16    £5–7
Sauvignon Blanc 1999
In the Kiwi '96 vintage class: grassy and greengage fruited. Most stores.

Irsai Olivér 2000,    14    −£3.50
Safeway
Delicious, fruitily spicy aperitif. Most stores.

Karolyi Estate Private    13.5    −£5.00
Reserve 2000
Bit austere and taut. Most stores.

Mátra Mountain    14    −£5.00
Sauvignon Blanc 2000,
Safeway
Dry, simple, for fish. Most stores.

Riverview    15    −£5.00
Chardonnay/Pinot
Grigio 2000
Bargain fruity tippling. Not a brash edge in sight. Most stores.

Riverview    14    −£5.00
Gewürztraminer 2000
Very mild and a touch uncertain. Will age well for the Christmas stocking. Selected stores.

Riverview Sauvignon    15    −£5.00
Blanc 2000
Nice grassy touch to the gooseberry finish. Selected stores.

## SAINSBURY'S WHITE

Hungarian Cabernet    11    −£3.50
Sauvignon Rosé NV,
Sainsbury's

## SPAR WHITE

Misty Mountain    13    −£5.00
Chardonnay NV, Spar

## TESCO WHITE

Emerald Hungarian    15.5    −£5.00
Sauvignon Blanc 2000
Has an interesting herbaceous undertone which fits nicely with

the melon fruit and lemon acidity. Terrific value for money. Not at all stores.

**Nagyrede Estate Barrel** `16` `−£5.00`
**Aged Pinot Grigio/**
**Zenit 1998**
Superb little throat charmer! Highly stylised, rich/dry fruit, with a solidly engaging finish. Terrific price for the class. 100 selected stores.

**Reka Valley** `12` `−£3.50`
**Chardonnay NV, Tesco**

**Riverview** `15` `−£5.00`
**Chardonnay/Pinot**
**Grigio 2000**
Bargain fruity tippling. Not a brash edge in sight.

## WAITROSE WHITE

**Deer Leap** `16.5` `−£5.00`
**Gewürztraminer,**
**Zemplen 2000**

Superbly elegant gewurz, with subdued spice, beautiful texture and a lychee finish.

**Deer Leap Sauvignon** `16` `−£5.00`
**Blanc 2000**
Fantastic value for such classy, gooseberry fruit. Better than many Sancerres.

**Matra Springs 2000** `14` `−£3.50`
A very acceptable warm weather aperitif. Very elegant screwcap to it.

**Nagyrede Cabernet** `14` `−£3.50`
**Sauvignon Rosé 2000**
A light cherryish rosé of light charms.

**Riverview** `15` `−£5.00`
**Chardonnay/Pinot**
**Grigio 2000**
Bargain fruity tippling. Not a brash edge in sight.

# ITALY

Fantastic potential from top to bottom.

## ASDA RED

**Barolo Veglio Angelo** `14` `£7–10`
**1996**

**Big Mamma's Italian** `14` `–£5.00`
**Red NV**
Tastes like a tomato and olive
pasta sauce already.

**Cantele Zinfandel** `14` `–£5.00`
**Salento 2000**
Made by Aussie in Italy's heel
using California nomenclature
(Primitivo's the local name for
the Zin grape) and so the result is
exuberant fruitiness brilliantly
capable of dining out, or indeed
in, with Indian food.

**Chianti 1999, Asda** `12` `–£3.50`

**Chianti Classico** `14` `£5–7`
**Riserva 1997, Asda**

**Puccini Chianti Reserva** `14` `–£5.00`
**1997**

**Ruvello Cabernet** `17` `£7–10`
**Sauvignon Passito 1998**
An individual Cabernet of
urgency yet complex, lingering,
slow-moving finishing strength.
Dry yet rich and delicate, earthy
yet not inelegant, gentle tannins

with tension and great class. A
delicious mouthful.

**Solara Organic Rosso,** `15` `–£3.50`
**Nero d'Avola 2000**
Very fruity and full of flavour but
doesn't overplay its hand here
courtesy of good balancing acids.

**Villa Cerna Chianti** `15` `£5–7`
**Classico 1998**
Lovely savoury herby fruit and
rich tannins. Selected stores.

## BOOTHS RED

**A Mano Primitivo** `15.5` `£5–7`
**Puglia 2000**
Delicious ripe plums, touches of
chocolate and tobacco and dark
cherries and this is all stitched
together by warm tannins.

**Amarone Classico** `16.5` `£13–20`
**Brigaldara 1996**
Sweet liquorice and fig fruit, fine
tannins, textured and ripe, and
black cherries to finish.

**Archidamo Pervini** `15.5` `£5–7`
**Primitivo di Manduria**
**1997**

Barocco Rosso del Salento 1999   11  −£3.50
Sweet plums with earthy tannins. Good curry red.

Chianti Leonardo 2000   14  £5−7
Dry and earthy yet finishes with an interesting cherry herbiness.

Col di Sasso Toscana 1998   14  −£5.00

I Promessa Sangiovese Puglia 1999   13.5  −£5.00

La Piazza Rosso 1999 (Sicily)   13.5  −£3.50
Sweet tobacco fruit.

Valpolicella Classico Superiore, Viviani 1997   15  £7−10
Rich and rampant, sweet and dry – the usual paradox where Valpol is concerned.

Valpolicella Classico, Viviani 1999   13  £5−7
Not in the class of its more expensive cousin.

Veneto Salice Salento Vallone 1998   15  −£5.00
Raisiny ripe damsons and cherries. Great pasta plonk.

Vigna Flaminio, Brindisi Rosso 1997   14  £5−7
Sweet, thick and curry friendly.

## BUDGENS RED

Il Padrino Sangiovese 2000 (Sicilia)   15.5  −£5.00
Elegant, ripe, textured and concentrated. Food will love it.

Trulli Primitivo Salento 1999   14.5  −£5.00
Sweet dry-to-finish fruit excellent with curried chicken dishes.

Valpolicella NV, Budgens   12  −£3.50
Juicy.

## CO-OP RED

Barrelaia NV, Co-op   13  −£5.00

Bona Terra Organic Merlot 1999   13  −£5.00
Ho hum. Superstores only.

Il Padrino Rosso Sicilia 1999   15  −£5.00

Inycon Merlot 1999 (Sicily)   15.5  −£5.00
Juicy but not injudiciously so and the savoury tannins are excellent. Terrific food wine.

Otto Santi Chianti Classico 1999   13  £5−7
Oddly inconclusive finish. Superstores only.

Puglia Primitivo Sangiovese 2000, Co-op   15  −£5.00
Delicious raspberries and plums with hearty tannins and touches of basil. Vibrant personality here.

Trulli Primitivo del Salento 1998   14.5  −£5.00

Valpolicella NV, Co-op   12  −£3.50

Zagara Nero d'Avola Cabernet 2000   12  −£5.00
Juicy and paranoid. Not at Convenience Stores.

## KWIK SAVE RED

**Montepulciano d'Abruzzo 2000, Somerfield**  `14`  `−£5.00`
Very dry yet very juicy. A conundrum solved by spicy food.

## M & S RED

**Amarone Classico della Valpolicella Villalta 1997**  `16.5`  `£10–13`
Combines figs, raspberries, savoury tannins, plums and cassis, cocoa and chocolate – this is a full rich spread from a great wine.

**Barolo 1996**  `13.5`  `£13–20`

**Canfera 1997**  `14.5`  `£7–10`

**Chianti Classico Basilica Cafaggio Single Estate 1999**  `16`  `£7–10`
Delicious tobacco-rich fruit, fine tannins, elegance to the texture, grip to the finish. Very classy stuff.

**Italian Table Red Wine NV (1 litre)**  `14`  `−£3.50`
A screwcapped litre of simple plums. Has a soft, rich, very quaffable texture. Price band indicates the 75cl equivalent.

**Montepulciano d'Abruzzo 2000**  `15.5`  `£7–10`
Great energy from the ripe plums and dashing tannins.

**Reggiano Rosso Single Estate 2000**  `13`  `−£5.00`

Sweet and curry friendly.

**Rosso di Puglia 2000**  `15`  `−£3.50`
Very bright and breezy fruit with good tannic grip nevertheless.

**Sangiovese di Puglia 2000**  `15.5`  `−£5.00`
Tastier than many a Chianti. Has the same grape . . . But . . . has added warmth and sensual tannins.

**Valpolicella Classico Single Estate 1999**  `15`  `−£5.00`
Lovely texture offering integrated cherries and plums with tannins. Very soft and yielding.

## MORRISONS RED

**Casa di Monzi Merlot 1999**  `13`  `−£5.00`

**Inycon Merlot 2000**  `16.5`  `−£5.00`
One of Italy's greatest Merlots: brilliant texture and richness here.

**Montepulciano d'Abruzzo Uggiano 1999**  `14`  `−£5.00`
Brisk tannins to ripe cherries and dry plums.

**Vino Rosso di Puglia NV**  `13.5`  `−£3.50`
Cheerful enough with bangers and mash.

## SAFEWAY RED

**Alto Varo Rosso di Puglia 2000**  `13`  `−£5.00`
Selected stores.

**Araldica Albera Barbera** `14` `–£5.00`
**d'Asti Superior,**
**Piemonte 1999**
Sweet cherries and a touch of
herb. Most stores.

**Canaletto Nero** `13` `–£5.00`
**d'Avola/Merlot 2000**
Most stores.

**D'Istinto Sangiovese** `13.5` `–£5.00`
**Merlot 1999 (Sicily)**
Very dry and brooding.

**Italia Negroamaro 2000** `13` `–£5.00`
A simple juicy curry red.

**Italia NV** `13` `–£5.00`

**La Nature Organic** `14` `–£5.00`
**Nero d'Avola 2000**
**(Sicily)**
Nice plumpness and texture to
the rich fruit. Selected stores.

**Melini Chianti 1998** `12` `–£5.00`
Rather dull and obvious.

**Sentiero NV** `13` `–£3.50`

**Sentiero Rosso NV (3** `11` `–£3.50`
**litre box)**
Ordinary, very ordinary. Most
stores.

**A Mano Primitivo** `15.5` `£5–7`
**Puglia 2000**
Delicious ripe plums, touches of
chocolate and tobacco and dark
cherries and this is all stitched
together by warm tannins. Most
stores.

**Alario Barolo Riva 1995** `10` `£20+`

Dry, dusty, some grudging
tannins, but little Barolo
classicism. Currently at two
stores, but will extend to thirty
early in 2001.

**Alessandra Colonna** `13.5` `£13–20`
**Barbera del Monferrato**
**1998**
A lovely rich fulsome expression
of richness and softness – but at
£5.99 not £15.99. 50 selected
stores.

**Allora Negroamaro** `14` `£5–7`
**2000**
A sweet curry wine of ripeness
and richness.

**Araldica Albera Barbera** `14` `–£5.00`
**d'Asti Superior,**
**Piemonte 1999**
Sweet cherries and a touch of
herb. Most stores.

**Barbera d'Alba** `16.5` `£7–10`
**Fontanelle, Ascheri**
**1999**
Superb liquorice, figs, black
cherries and fine tannins.
Compelling price for such riches.
Selected stores.

**Barco Reale di** `16` `£7–10`
**Carmignano Capezzana**
**1999**
Very impressive class of tannin
you encounter here and this
dominates the sweet fruit which,
thus tamed, can simply get on
with entertaining the palate
sweetly and suavely. Selected
stores.

**Barking Mad 15%** `15` `−£5.00`
**Primitivo 2000**
Not remotely insane. The balance
of alcohol and tannin is perfect,
sane, very tasty. Most stores.

**Barolo Cantine Rocca** `15` `£10–13`
**Ripalta 1995**

**Chianti la Capannuccia** `14.5` `−£3.50`
**1999**
Amazing value. Dry, rich fruit,
slightly smoky and spicy, with
deep and decisive tannins. A great
pasta plonk.

**Classic Selection Barolo** `13.5` `£10–13`
**1996, Sainsbury's**
A lot of money for a wine of
moderate impressiveness. 200
selected stores.

**Classic Selection** `15.5` `£5–7`
**Chianti Classico 1997,**
**Sainsbury's**

**Emporio Nero d'Avola** `15` `−£5.00`
**Merlot 2000**
Sweet berries, rich dark tannins,
and a soupy texture of ripeness
and readiness. Leaps out of the
glass, so eager is it. Good spicy
food companion. Not at all stores.

**Inycon Syrah 2000** `16` `−£5.00`
**(Sicily)**
Beautiful fruit, quite beautiful.
The tannins' subsidiary role is
entirely proper here for the fruit
richly and ripely strides forward
with great confidence.

**Morellino di Scansano** `16` `£7–10`
**Riserva 1997**
A wonderful food wine of great
energy and elongated, fruity
richness. Warmly textured and
extremely deep – like an old
knitted cardigan worn by Isaiah
Berlin. 100 stores.

**Natio Organic Chianti,** `13.5` `£5–7`
**Cecchi 1998**

**Poliziano Rosso di** `15.5` `£7–10`
**Montepulciano 1999**
Touches of baked Tuscan
earthiness to ripe plums and a
hint of cherry custard. Fine
tannins, too. 100 selected stores.

**Promessa Rosso** `15.5` `−£5.00`
**Salento 2000**
Lovely ripe, soft fruit, slightly
richly baked, but has fine tannins.
Most stores.

**Rosso di Provincia di** `12` `−£3.50`
**Verona NV, Sainsbury's**
Screwcapped, as all wines ought
to be, this has mild sweet fruit of
medium impact.

**Sangiovese di Sicilia** `13.5` `−£5.00`
**2000, Sainsbury's**
A fine wine. To take to the
Tandoori Caf.

**Sicilia Red, Sainsbury's** `15` `−£3.50`

**Teuzzo Chianti** `15` `£5–7`
**Classico 1998**
Has some interesting tannins and
dry plummy fruit, but a touch
overpriced for the style.

**Valpolicella,** `12` `−£3.50`
**Sainsbury's (3 litre box)**
Price band indicates the 75cl
equivalent.

## SOMERFIELD RED

**Bardolino 2000,** `12` `–£5.00`
**Somerfield**
Cherries, thin on top.

**Bright Brothers** `14` `–£5.00`
**Negroamaro Cabernet**
**Sauvignon 1999**
Raspberry, blackcurrant, figs –
very rich, dry fruit.

**Cabernet Sauvignon** `13` `–£5.00`
**delle Venezie 2000,**
**Somerfield**

**Chianti Serristori 2000,** `13` `–£5.00`
**Somerfield**

**D'Istinto Sangiovese** `13.5` `–£5.00`
**Merlot 1999 (Sicily)**
Very dry and brooding.

**Il Padrino Syrah di** `16` `–£5.00`
**Sicilia 2000**
Soft and ripe, polished yet deep,
rich and very ready. A lovely
wine.

**Inycon Merlot 2000** `16.5` `–£5.00`
One of Italy's greatest Merlots:
brilliant texture and richness here.

**Merlot delle Venezie** `14` `–£5.00`
**2000, Somerfield**
Cheering cherry-ripe stuff.

**Montepulciano** `14` `–£5.00`
**d'Abruzzo 2000,**
**Somerfield**
Very dry yet very juicy. A
conundrum solved by spicy
food.

**Sicilian Red 2000,** `14` `–£3.50`
**Somerfield**

Warm and richly textured. Great
with mildly spicy food.

**Terrale Sangiovese di** `16.5` `–£5.00`
**Puglia 2000, Somerfield**
Brilliant tarry texture with lovely
liquorice, blackberries, plums,
strawberries and figs.

**Tre Uve Ultima 1999** `16.5` `£5–7`
So vivacious yet elegant. So rich
yet understated. So potent yet
precise and unfussy. So tightly
textured and teasing. Selected
stores.

**Tre Uve VdT 2000** `16` `–£5.00`
Vibrant cherries and dark damson
fruit with remarkable tannins.

**Tuscan Red 2000,** `12` `–£5.00`
**Somerfield**
Intensely dry and austere.

**Valpolicella 2000,** `12` `–£3.50`
**Somerfield**

## SPAR RED

**Barolo 'Costa di Bussia'** `15` `£13–20`
**1996**
The second best red at Spar? Over
thirteen quid it ought to be for it
has classy tannins, big deep
berries and a lingering, stylish
finish. Very compacted wine.

**Chianti 1999, Spar** `11` `–£5.00`
Doesn't add up to £4.50's worth
of fruit in my book.

**Chianti Classico Le** `10` `£7–10`
**Fioraie 1995**
Outpriced by a considerable

factor. Underfruited in proportion.

**Montepulciano d'Abruzzo 1999, Spar**  `12`  −£5.00
Sweet and juicy.

**Pasta Red NV, Spar (1 litre)**  `11`  −£3.50
Price band indicates the 75cl equivalent.

**Riva Vino da Tavola NV, Spar**  `10`  −£3.50
I was glad to spit it out.

**Sangiovese del Rubicone Arienta NV, Spar**  `11`  −£5.00
Very thin and meagre as it finishes.

**Valpolicella NV, Spar**  `10`  −£5.00
Cosmetic aroma, dry dull fruit, haywire finish.

## TESCO RED

**Badia a Coltibuono Chianti Classico 1998**  `14`  £7–10
One of the more engaging expensive Chiantis. Very fine tannins. Selected stores.

**Barbera d'Asti Calissano 1999**  `14`  −£5.00
Barbera with curried lamb's brains? Why not? OK, try it with mushroom risotto instead.

**Chianti 1999, Tesco**  `12`  −£3.50
Very thin to finish.

**Chianti Classico Riserva 1998, Tesco**  `16.5`  £5–7

Ah! A Chianti to get excited about. Has elegance yet bite, personality yet many subtle nuances, delicious tannins, and real depth and class as it finishes. Why isn't Classico always this accomplished? One of Tesco's 'Finest' range.

**Chianti Rufina 1999, Tesco**  `15.5`  −£5.00
Rufina is one of Chianti's great secrets. This example is smoother, more polished (yet not lacking in character or tannins) than regular Chiantis and it has a lovely plummy dryness as it quits the throat.

**Inycon Merlot 1999 (Sicily)**  `15.5`  −£5.00
Juicy but not injudiciously so and the savoury tannins are excellent. Terrific food wine. Most stores.

**Inycon Syrah 2000 (Sicily)**  `16`  −£5.00
Beautiful fruit, quite beautiful. The tannins' subsidiary role is entirely proper here for the fruit richly and ripely strides forward with great confidence.

**La Gioiosa Merlot 2000**  `15.5`  −£5.00
Delicious leathery herbaceous fruit of class and richness with delightful dry, savoury, slightly herby depth. Very versatile with food. Can be chilled and drunk with fish.

**Merlot del Piave NV, Tesco**  `11`  −£5.00

**Monte d'Abro** `15` `−£5.00`
**Montepulciano**
**Abruzzo NV**
Brambly fruit offset by dry
tannins. Terrific tension to the
fruit as these elements fight it out
with deft stroke play.

**Pendulum Zinfandel** `15.5` `−£5.00`
**1999**

**Pinot Noir del Veneto** `11` `−£5.00`
**NV, Tesco**

**Sicilian Red NV, Tesco** `14` `−£3.50`

**Terra Viva Organic** `14` `−£5.00`
**Red 2000**
Very dry with plum and
raspberry richness. Decent
savoury tannins.

**Terre Dego 2000** `15.5` `−£5.00`
Delightful meaty richness, good
tannins and a real textured finish
accommodating blackberries and
herb and a touch of the forest
floor.

**Tre Uve Ultima 1998** `16` `£5−7`
Superb depth of tannic richness
geared to smoothly run alongside
smooth plum/blackberry fruit.
Selected stores.

**Trulli Primitivo Salento** `14.5` `−£5.00`
**1999**
Sweet dry-to-finish fruit excellent
with curried chicken dishes.

**Valpolicella Classico** `13` `−£5.00`
**1999, Tesco**

**Villa Pigna Rosso** `14` `−£5.00`
**Piceno 1998**

## WAITROSE RED

**Amarone della** `15` `£20+`
**Valpolicella Classico**
**Riserva, Zenato 1993**
On the edge of late middle-age,
but still full of figs and raisins and
black cherries, and superb
tannins. Mail Order only.

**Amativo Negroamaro** `15.5` `£5−7`
**Primitivo 1999**
Delicious vibrant cherries and
plums with a hint of spice.

**Araldica Albera Barbera** `14` `−£5.00`
**d'Asti Superior,**
**Piemonte 1999**
Sweet cherries and a touch of
herb.

**Arcano Chianti Colli** `15.5` `£5−7`
**Senesi, Cecchi 1999**
**(organic)**
A rare organic Chianti with
vigorous baked plums and berries
and active tannins. Good firm
savoury finish.

**Barolo Terre da Vino** `13.5` `£10−13`
**1997**
Too pricey.

**Bonarda Sentito,** `15.5` `−£5.00`
**Oltrepo Pavese 1999**

**Buonasera, Argiolas NV** `15` `−£5.00`
**(Sardegna)**
Toffeed richness and texture,
excellent for robust foods.

**Capitel dei Nicola** `15.5` `£5−7`
**Valpolicella Classico**
**Superiore 1997**
Figs, cherries, hint of liquorice,

rich plums and very dry tannins. Terrific stuff.

**Castello di Fonterutoli Chianti Classico Riserva 1997**  `14`  `£20+`
Far too much money for the tannins which, exciting though they are, can be experienced elsewhere for one third of the price.

**Chianti 1999, Waitrose**  `13.5`  `−£5.00`

**Chianti Classico Fattoria di Capraia, Rocca di Castagnoli 1998**  `13.5`  `£7–10`
Very sweet.

**Emporio Barrel Aged Syrah 1998 (Sicilia)**  `15`  `£5–7`

**Il Padrino Sangiovese 2000 (Sicilia)**  `15.5`  `−£5.00`
Elegant, ripe, textured and concentrated. Food will love it.

**La Rena Salice Salento Leone de Castris 1998**  `16`  `£5–7`
Gorgeous tannins coating juicy cherries and blackcurrants with a hint of liquorice.

**Mezzomondo Negroamaro 1999**  `16`  `−£5.00`
Brilliant value food wine with rich, herby fruit and delicious spicy tannins. Has a first-class texture and concentration of flavours.

**Natural State Montepulciano d'Abruzzo 1999 (organic)**  `16.5`  `−£5.00`

Utterly superb wine at a glorious price: cherries, plums, nuts all beautifully knitted together and texturally fine. Wonderful stuff.

**Nero d'Avola Syrah, Firriato 2000 (Sicilia)**  `14.5`  `−£5.00`
Sweet, cherry-ripe, rich and will adhere firmly to Indian spices.

**Pendulum Zinfandel 1999**  `15.5`  `−£5.00`

**Planeta Cabernet Sauvignon 1998**  `17`  `£13–20`
So much more impressive than more expensive Bordeaux. Lovely structure and balance of elements. Mail Order only.

**Sangiovese Marche, Waitrose**  `13`  `−£3.50`

**Tenute Marchese Antinori Chianti Classico Riserva 1997**  `16`  `£10–13`
Expensive elegance it is impossible not to like or to rate lower. Tremendously smooth cassis and tannins.

**Terra Viva Merlot del Veneto 2000 (organic)**  `14`  `−£5.00`
Juicy and ripe but firmly textured and food friendly.

**Tignanello 1997**  `13`  `£20+`
Hugely overrated and overpriced. Not worth more than twelve or fifteen pounds. The luxury is there and the tannins but why pay so much more for this label? Mail Order only.

**Valpolicella 2000, Waitrose**  `13`  `−£3.50`

Thin, slightly earthy plums and cherries.

**Vigna Alta Merlot/** 16.5 −£5.00
**Cabernet Venosa,**
**Basilicata 2000**
Superb tanginess here (the volcanic soil), leathery and blackcurranty and with lithe tannins of great alertness. A lovely texture to the wine gives it great class.

## ASDA WHITE

**Cantele Chardonnay** 14 −£5.00
**Salento 2000**
Not your big New World in-yer-face Chard but one of subtle richness and acidic limpidity.

**Lambrusco Bianco NV,** 13.5 −£3.50
**Asda**

**Lambrusco Rosato NV,** 13 −£2.50
**Asda**

**Solara Organic White** 15 −£3.50
**Inzolia 2000**
Inzolia is the grape which makes Sicily's contribution to ichthyophilogastry: the love of eating fish. It is delightfully crisp and fresh and nutty.

## BOOTHS WHITE

**La Piazza Bianco 2000** 14 −£3.50
**(Sicily)**
Spicy food wine. Take it to the BYOB Thai restaurant.

**Le Rime Pinot Grigio/** 13 −£5.00
**Chardonnay 2000**
Very rich and ripe.

**Sentito Cortese DOC** 14 −£5.00
**Oltrepo Pavese 1999**
Dry and rather prim.

**Soave Classico Pra 2000** 13.5 £5−7
Rather expensive.

**Viña Ruspo Rosado** 14 £5−7
**Capezzana 2000**
Intense damson dryness. Good fish wine.

## BUDGENS WHITE

**Il Padrino Grecanico/** 14.5 −£5.00
**Chardonnay, Sicily**
**2000**
Rich yet refreshing. Good texture.

**Marc Xero Chardonnay** 15 −£5.00
**NV**

**Sartori Pinot Grigio** 14 −£5.00
**delle Venezie 2000**
Charm to the dry, peachy fruit.

**Soave Dry NV,** 12 −£3.50
**Budgens**
Dry it certainly is.

**Trulli Chardonnay del** 16 −£5.00
**Salento 2000**
Deliciously elegant and easy-going.

## CO-OP WHITE

**Chardonnay** 12 −£5.00
**dell'Umbria 1999,**
**Co-op**
Not at Convenience Stores.

## ITALIAN WHITE

**Chardonnay** 15 −£5.00
**Vallagerina 2000, Co-op**
Delicious warm nutty fruit.

**Puglia Chardonnay** 12 −£5.00
**Bombino 1999, Co-op**

**Villa Lanata Gavi 2000** 16.5 −£5.00
Superb individuality of effort
offering dry peaches, walnuts,
raspberries and fine acids.
Superstores only.

**Zagara Catarratto** 16.5 −£5.00
**Chardonnay Firriato**
**2000 (Sicily)**
Delicious rich, nutty fruit, finely
textured and gently oily, with an
elegant finish of great class.

## KWIK SAVE WHITE

**Sicilian White 2000,** 14 −£3.50
**Somerfield**
Good nutty edge to it.

**Soave 2000, Somerfield** 13.5 −£5.00

## M & S WHITE

**Frascati Superiore** 15.5 −£5.00
**Single Estate 2000**
Beautifully nutty, crisp and
whistle-clean. Lovely pureness to
it.

**Orvieto Single Estate** 16 −£5.00
**2000**
Remarkably delicious fruit –
classically walnutty and dry –
which has great elegance and
style as it lingers in the throat.

**Pinot Grigio/** 14.5 −£5.00
**Garganega 2000**
Dry and crisp. The orgy
suggested by the label is indeed in
its early throes.

**Soave Superiore Single** 16 −£5.00
**Estate 2000**
Lovely wine of consummate
class, brilliant value, and double-
layered elegance. Finishes with a
bright fruity lilt.

**Villa Masera Organic** 15 −£5.00
**Wine 2000**
Slight yoghurt edge to the finish.
Crisp, clean attack opens up the
performance.

## MORRISONS WHITE

**Casa de Monzi** 13 −£5.00
**Chardonnay delle**
**Venezie 1999**

**Chardonnay di Puglia** 13 −£3.50
**NV**

**Chianti Colli Fiorenti** 13 −£5.00
**Uggiano 1998**
Dry. Very dry.

**Inycon Chardonnay** 16 −£5.00
**2000 (Sicily)**
Gorgeous! Brilliant layered fruit.

**Uggiano Orvieto** 12 −£5.00
**Classico 2000**
Flat on the finish.

## SAFEWAY WHITE

**Arcadia Veronese** 14.5 −£5.00
**Rosata 2000**

The usual pert cherries but with the added drama of a plummy lilt on the finish. Selected stores.

**Inycon Chardonnay 2000 (Sicily)**  `16`  `–£5.00`
Gorgeous! Brilliant layered fruit. Selected stores.

**Sentiero Bianco NV**  `15`  `–£3.50`
A bargain. Goes with smoked salmon and intelligent conversation.

**Sentiero Bianco NV (3 litre box)**  `13.5`  `–£3.50`
Party wine box for parties where you leave early. Most stores.

**Trulli Chardonnay 1999**  `16`  `–£5.00`
Marvellously fluent fruit. Dry, crisp, complex, elegant. Selected stores.

**Verdicchio dei Castelli di Jesi Classico 2000**  `16`  `–£5.00`
Very impressive layered fruit, fine acidity, and a pineapple/pear/lemon finish.

## SAINSBURY'S WHITE

**Bianco di Provincia di Verona NV, Sainsbury's**  `14`  `–£3.50`
Curious perfumed fruit of a fish-friendly disposition.

**Ca'Donini Bianco di Custoza 2000**  `15.5`  `–£5.00`
Deliciously crisp and fresh. Really delivers elegance and bite. Most stores.

**Classic Selection Pinot Grigio 2000, Sainsbury's**  `15`  `£5–7`
Lovely dry, minerally apricots. Superbly well-textured and crisp-as-a-lettuce finish. Most stores.

**Figli di Augusto Pinot Bianco 2000**  `15.5`  `£5–7`
Delightful minerals lurk amongst the crisp, clean fruit. 140 selected stores.

**Grecanico di Sicilia 2000, Sainsbury's**  `15.5`  `–£5.00`
Characterful, very dry, deliciously insistent fruit of class and charm.

**Inycon Chardonnay 2000 (Sicily)**  `16`  `–£5.00`
Gorgeous! Brilliant layered fruit.

**Orvieto Classico Amabile le Cimmelle 2000**  `15`  `–£5.00`
Medium-dry spicy pears and melon with a hint of herb. Good aperitif.

**Pinot Grigio Veneto Borgo Paveri 2000 (organic)**  `14.5`  `–£5.00`
Has a fruity classiness and texture to it. Very quaffable stuff. 105 selected stores.

**Sartori Organic Soave 2000**  `13.5`  `–£5.00`
Words fail me. Except: it smells and tastes of melons.

**Sicilian White, Sainsbury's**  `13.5`  `–£3.50`

**Soave, Sainsbury's (3 litre box)**  `15`  `–£3.50`

Price band indicates the 75cl equivalent.

**Villa Bianchi** `16` `—£5.00`
**Verdicchio Classico dei**
**Castelli di Jesi 2000**
Concentrated richness and nuttiness of great class. Not at all stores.

## SOMERFIELD WHITE

**Alfresco Vino da** `14` `—£3.50`
**Tavola Bianco NV,**
**Somerfield**
Party wine solely.

**Alfresco Vino da** `13` `—£3.50`
**Tavola Rosso NV,**
**Somerfield**

**Bright Brothers** `14` `—£5.00`
**Greganico Inzolia 2000**
Has the usual Italian dry nuttiness.

**Chardonnay delle** `14.5` `—£5.00`
**Venezie 2000,**
**Somerfield**
Underripe melon. Good with fish cakes.

**Chiaro di Luna Bianco** `15.5` `—£5.00`
**di Custoza 2000**
Very delicious dry, underripe fruit with apples and lemon, very restrained and elegant.

**D'Istinto Catarratto** `13` `—£5.00`
**Chardonnay 1999**

**Inycon Chardonnay** `16` `—£5.00`
**2000 (Sicily)**
High class stuff. Terrific style on the restrained finish.

**La Luna Bianco di** `15.5` `—£5.00`
**Custoza 2000**
Lovely gooseberry, lemon, cobnut fruit. Finishes crisply and firmly.

**Marc Xero Chardonnay** `14` `—£5.00`
**2000**
Lemony with a hint of fat melon.

**Pinot Grigio delle** `14.5` `—£5.00`
**Venezie 2000,**
**Somerfield**
Classic Italian dry nuttiness. Good fish wine.

**Sicilian White 2000,** `14` `—£3.50`
**Somerfield**
Good nutty edge to it.

**Soave 2000, Somerfield** `13.5` `—£5.00`

**Trulli Chardonnay del** `16` `—£5.00`
**Salento 2000**
Deliciously elegant and easy-going. Selected stores.

## SPAR WHITE

**Colli Albani NV, Spar** `14` `—£5.00`
Citrussy opening with a finish, chewy, of indefinable fruit.

**Pasta White NV, Spar** `13` `—£3.50`
**(1 litre)**
Price band indicates the 75cl equivalent.

**Riva Vino da Tavola** `15` `—£3.50`
**NV, Spar**
Delicious hints of apricot, lemon and pineapple. Fantastic value for money.

**Verdicchio dei Castelli** `14` `−£5.00`
**di Jesi 1999, Spar**
Nervous acids and dry melon
undertone. Good fish wine.

## TESCO WHITE

**Antinori Orvieto** `13` `−£5.00`
**Classico Secco 1999**

**Asti NV, Tesco** `13` `−£5.00`

**Cataratto Chardonnay** `15.5` `−£5.00`
**Sicilia NV, Tesco**
Terrific blend of grapes which
gives it individuality and poise.
Lovely fruit of class and style.

**'I Portali' Basilicata** `16` `−£5.00`
**Greco 1999**
A splendidly vigorous wine of
dry, mineral freshness and rich
crispness. Selected stores.

**Inycon Chardonnay** `16` `−£5.00`
**2000 (Sicily)**
Gorgeous! Brilliant layered fruit.

**Italia Pinot Grigio 2000** `12.5` `−£5.00`
Goes fat and flabby after some
initial tanginess.

**La Gioiosa Pinot Grigio** `15` `−£5.00`
**2000**
Has that delicious peachy edge
with a cobnut undertone.

**Lamberti Pinot Grigio** `16` `−£5.00`
**2000**
Simply one of the most elegant
and delicious Pinot Grigios I've
tasted. Delicious balanced style,
subtle apricot ringed with lemon
edging. Most stores.

**Terra Viva Organic** `14` `−£5.00`
**Soave Superiore 2000**
Tangy and crisp.

**Terra Viva Organic** `15.5` `−£5.00`
**White 2000**
Nutty, gently rich, relaxed fruit
which has poise, control and a
lovely gooseberry finish. Has
tanginess and purity of style.

**Trulli Dry Muscat 2000** `15` `−£5.00`
Very dry grapeyness here, of
some elegance, and it makes a
pert aperitif as well as a good fish
wine.

**Verdicchio Classico dei** `14.5` `−£5.00`
**Castelli di Jesi 2000,**
**Tesco**
Nutty, crisp, clean – very Italian
underripeness and food
friendliness.

**Viña Clara Frascati** `14.5` `−£5.00`
**Classico Superiore 2000**
Classic lemon, nut and underripe
melon fruit. One of Tesco's so-
called 'Finest' range.

## WAITROSE WHITE

**Buongiorno Argiolas** `16` `−£5.00`
**Sardegna NV**
Brilliant texture and layered
richness. Lovely class to it.

**Inycon Chardonnay** `16` `−£5.00`
**2000 (Sicily)**
Gorgeous! Brilliant layered fruit.

**Lugana Villa Flora 2000** `16` `£5–7`
Marvellous texture and
compressed dry fruit.

**Mezzo Mondo** `15` `−£5.00`
**Chardonnay 2000**
Sunny and engaging. Suits
barbecued fish splendidly.

**Orvieto Classico** `15.5` `−£5.00`
**Cardeto 2000**
Evolves slowly and deliciously on
the taste buds to telling effect.

**Pinot Grigio Alto Adige** `15.5` `£5−7`
**San Michele-Appiano**
**2000**
Apricots, slightly ripe, conceal, at
the finish, the classiness of the
opening and the middle palate
polish.

**Planeta Chardonnay** `18` `£13−20`
**1999**
One of Italy's greatest
Chardonnays: oily, rich, complex,
lingering and very very stylish as
it finishes. A truly wonderful
Chardonnay of excitement and
brilliance. Mail Order only.

**Sauvignon Friuli, San** `15.5` `−£5.00`
**Simone 2000**
Terrific tanginess and texture.

**Soave Classico Vigneto** `16.5` `−£5.00`
**Colombara 2000**
Defines how classy Soave can
become. It mingles gooseberries
and raspberries with bright acids
and a textured richness of style
and wit. Superb stuff.

**Verdicchio dei Castelli** `14` `−£5.00`
**Jesi, Moncaro 2000**
Nice dry peach and gooseberry.

**Zagara Catarratto** `16.5` `−£5.00`
**Chardonnay Firriato**
**2000 (Sicily)**
Delicious rich, nutty fruit, finely
textured and gently oily, with an
elegant finish of great class.

# LEBANON

Oddities of interest only.

## BOOTHS RED

**Hochar Red 1998** `13.5` `£5-7`
Ripe yet dry, rich and sweet to
finish.

# MEXICO

Has pockets of fascination.

## SOMERFIELD RED

L A Cetto Petite Sirah 15 −£5.00
1999
Juicy, spicy, berried – plus well-ordered tannins.

## TESCO RED

Mexican Cabernet 13 −£5.00
Sauvignon 1999, Tesco

## WAITROSE RED

L A Cetto Petite Sirah 16 −£5.00
1998
Terrific texture and controlled ripeness. The tannins are so classy and calm. The whole effect is highly drinkable yet serious.

## TESCO WHITE

Mexican Chardonnay 15 −£5.00
1999, Tesco

# MOROCCO

Great potential.

**Baraka Private Reserve** `14` `−£5.00`
**Cabernet Merlot 1999**
Sweet, overbaked, very ripe – it
must have a Balti! It cries out:
help me! Pair me with a Balti!
Selected stores.

**Moroccan Cabernet** `13.5` `−£5.00`
**Sauvignon 2000,**
**Sainsbury's**

Fine for Moroccan food and
Moroccan mood: ripe, dry to
finish, rampant, very eager.
Selected stores.

**Moroccan Syrah 2000,** `14.5` `−£5.00`
**Sainsbury's**
A brilliant, if very saucy, red for
spicy food especially curries of
full-blooded hotheadedness.
Selected stores.

# NEW ZEALAND

The world's most elegant Sauvignons, with improving reds.

## BUDGENS RED

**Helderberg Pinotage 2000** | 13 | −£5.00
Touch of tannin on the finish does save the fruit from soppiness but the initial juiciness of the fruit is the theme of the wine.

**Montana Cabernet Sauvignon/Merlot 2000** | 15 | £5–7
Ripe and very forward. Even the tannins are ripe and slightly half-baked.

## CO-OP RED

**Terrace View Cabernet Merlot 1999** | 13 | −£5.00
Jam with a grassy undertone.

## M & S RED

**Kaituna Hills Cabernet Merlot 1999** | 16 | £5–7
Superbly well-kitted out with warm, basil-edged fruit, olives and fine tannins. A very safely textured, fine wine.

**Kaituna Hills Reserve Cabernet Merlot 1999** | 15.5 | £7–10
Has more woody richness than its two-quid cheaper sister but I don't see it's worth two quid more.

**Kaituna Hills Reserve Pinot Noir 1999** | 10 | £7–10
Pretty juicy and sweet for me.

## MORRISONS RED

**Montana Cabernet Sauvignon/Merlot 2000** | 14 | £5–7
Ripe and very forward. Even the tannins are ripe and slightly half-baked.

## SAFEWAY RED

**Delegat's Reserve Cabernet Sauvignon 1999** | 16.5 | £7–10
Superb class here: rich, complex, beautiful tannin structure, fine acidity and a superb balance of these elements. Very classy texture. 75 stores.

**Montana Reserve Pinot Noir 1999** | 13.5 | £7–10
Sweet and jammy. Touch of

tannins, true. But it's a faint touch with faint Pinot Noir punch. Selected stores.

**Villa Maria Cellar** 15 £7–10
**Selection Cabernet/**
**Merlot 1998**
Dry, purposeful, balanced, well-tailored tannins. 75 stores.

**Villa Maria Reserve** 13.5 £13–20
**Cabernet Sauvignon/**
**Merlot 1998**
Far too expensive. A collector's folly. It is drinkable and well formed but Languedoc has it beaten hollow at a third of the price. Selected stores.

## SAINSBURY'S RED

**Montana East Coast** 15 £5–7
**Cabernet Sauvignon**
**Merlot 1999**
Unusually soft and ripe blend from Montana. Subtle tannins give it some backbone and character. A wholly quaffable wine. Selected stores.

## TESCO RED

**Babich Cabernet** 13.5 £5–7
**Franc/Pinotage 1999**
Juicy and odd. Most stores.

**Babich Winemaker's** 15 £7–10
**Reserve Syrah 1998**

**Montana Cabernet** 14 £5–7
**Sauvignon/Merlot 2000**
Ripe and very forward. Even the

tannins are ripe and slightly half-baked.

**Montana Pinotage 2000** 14 £5–7
Nice tannins and tension. Most stores.

**Montana Reserve** 15 £7–10
**Merlot 1999**
A very well-wrought wine of some medium-weight class and richness. I'm not crazy about its price.

## WAITROSE RED

**Church Road Cabernet** 15.5 £7–10
**Sauvignon/Merlot 1998**
Always one of NZ's more enterprising and elegant Cab/Merl blends.

**Montana Cabernet** 15 £5–7
**Merlot 1999**

**Montana Reserve Pinot** 13.5 £7–10
**Noir 1999**
Sweet and jammy. Touch of tannins, true. But it's a faint touch with faint Pinot Noir punch.

**Unison Selection,** 12 £13–20
**Hawkes Bay 1998**
Absurd price for such a construct.

**Wither Hills Pinot Noir** 13 £10–13
**1999**

## ASDA WHITE

**Babich Semillon** 15 £5–7
**Chardonnay 2000**
Terrific fish cake wine in its fluidity with spicy, fishy fare.

**Corbans Sauvignon** `15.5` `£5–7`
**Blanc 1999**
Lovely hints of grass to the firm
rich fruit. Excellent price for such
lean Kiwi charms.

**Nobilo Sauvignon** `14` `£5–7`
**Blanc 1999**
Tangy gooseberries.

**Villa Maria Private Bin** `17` `£5–7`
**Sauvignon Blanc 1999**
Utterly utter – that is to say,
haiku-like in its concentrated
richness of theme, pointedness of
acidity and marvellous
uncomplicated structure.

## BOOTHS WHITE

**Dashwood Sauvignon** `17` `£7–10`
**Blanc 2000**
Quite beautiful the Dashwood.
More dash than wood, of course:
balanced, subtly rich, finely acidic
– and a great finish. Very classy.

**Jackson Estate** `16.5` `£7–10`
**Sauvignon Blanc 2000**
Richer style of Sauvignon with a
sense of opulence to the well-
textured fruit but what is so
satisfying about it is its
indescribable dryness yet
fruitiness.

## BUDGENS WHITE

**Corban's White Label** `12` `–£5.00`
**Muller Thurgau/**
**Sauvignon Blanc 2000**
Rather ho-hum on the finish.

**Corbans Sauvignon** `13.5` `£5–7`
**Blanc 2000**
Grassy, rich, fish friendly.

**Montana Unoaked** `16` `£5–7`
**Chardonnay 2000**
Lemon, melon and gooseberry –
standard top-notch Kiwi recipe?
Perhaps but this is a superior
example and no wood gives it
more purity than most.

## CO-OP WHITE

**Explorer's Vineyard** `14` `£5–7`
**Sauvignon Blanc 2000,**
**Co-op**
A very dry, fresh wine for
shellfish.

**Matua Valley** `16.5` `£5–7`
**Sauvignon Blanc 2001**
Superb lemon and gooseberries
with hints of orange peel and
raspberry. Lovely fresh fruit wine.
Superstores only.

**Oyster Bay** `15.5` `£5–7`
**Marlborough**
**Chardonnay 2000**
Ripe, ready fruit of depth and
substance.

**Oyster Bay Sauvignon** `16` `£5–7`
**Blanc 2000**
Classic mineral-edged Sauvignon
with subtle gooseberry and lemon
undertones. Utterly marvellous.

**Stoneleigh Chardonnay** `15.5` `–£5.00`
**1999**
Rich and very ready with fine
texture and well-knitted acids and

gooseberry/melon fruit.
Superstores only.

## M & S WHITE

**Kaituna Blue** `13` `–£5.00`
**Sauvignon Semillon**
**2000**
Very odd stalky fruit. Repulsive
blue bottle, too.

**Kaituna Hills** `15.5` `£5–7`
**Chardonnay 2000**
A mild salade de fruits with
pineapple acids. Controlled
exuberance from the New World.

**Kaituna Hills Reserve** `13.5` `£7–10`
**Chardonnay 2000**
Has some interesting nuances as
it opens but does flag a bit on the
finish. An eight quid wine? Only
in part.

**Kaituna Hills Reserve** `14` `£7–10`
**Sauvignon Blanc 1999**

**Kaituna Hills** `14` `£5–7`
**Sauvignon Blanc 2000**
Old-fashioned grassy gutsiness.

**Shepherds Ridge** `13.5` `£7–10`
**Chardonnay 1999**
Expensive, bit flash.

**Shepherds Ridge** `13` `£7–10`
**Sauvignon Blanc 2000**
Doesn't quite finish the theme it
opens up with.

## MORRISONS WHITE

**Moa Ridge Chardonnay** `13.5` `£5–7`
**1999**

Very ripe and smokey and
unsubtle.

**Moa Ridge Sauvignon** `14` `£5–7`
**Blanc 2000**
Rich and very firmly textured.

## SAFEWAY WHITE

**Delegat's Reserve** `16.5` `£7–10`
**Chardonnay, Barrel**
**Fermented 1999**
Superb texture, so gripping and
subtly oleaginous. Has loads of
fruit yet there's a toasty
undertone, oil, and cream on the
finish. Selected stores.

**Lawsons Dry Hills** `16.5` `£7–10`
**Chardonnay,**
**Marlborough 1999**
Open it four to five hours
beforehand and fully decant it.
Delicious richness, subtle yet
striking, and dry, classy acids.
Selected stores.

**Montana Unoaked** `16` `£5–7`
**Chardonnay 2000**
Lemon, melon and gooseberry –
standard top-notch Kiwi recipe?
Perhaps but this is a superior
example and no wood gives it
more purity than most.

**Oyster Bay** `15.5` `£5–7`
**Marlborough**
**Chardonnay 2000**
Ripe, ready fruit of depth and
substance.

**Oyster Bay Sauvignon** `16` `£5–7`
**Blanc 2000**
Classic mineral-edged Sauvignon

with subtle gooseberry and lemon undertones. Utterly marvellous.

**Villa Maria Reserve** `16.5` `£7–10`
**Wairau Valley**
**Sauvignon Blanc 2000**
Delicious texture to it which adheres to the taste buds with a gently oily richness of gooseberry, raspberry, lime and pineapple (all very subtle). Very classy stuff. Selected stores.

## SAINSBURY'S WHITE

**Nobilo Sauvignon** `14` `£5–7`
**Blanc 2000**
Grassy richness with touches of gooseberry and lemon. Dry finish of some length. Curiously old-fashioned NZ style. Most stores.

**Shingle Peak Pinot** `15.5` `£5–7`
**Gris, Marlborough 2000**
A vivid example of this grape: apricots and strawberries, a hint of Ogen melon, a tangy undertone of acid minerality. This is a richly entertaining wine of some depth.

**The Sanctuary** `17` `£5–7`
**Sauvignon Blanc 2000**
Superb layers of minerals, melon, lemon, raspberry, cobnuts and apples. Beautifully thought-provoking, keenly priced and deliciously keenly-fruited. Has a high stepping crisp finish. Not at all stores.

## SOMERFIELD WHITE

**Montana Sauvignon** `15.5` `£5–7`
**Blanc 1999**

**Nobilo White Cloud** `13` `–£5.00`
**2000**
Bit ho-hum on the finish.

**Villa Maria** `16.5` `£5–7`
**Chardonnay 1999**
Superbly well-textured and classy where the full virtues of emphatic rich fruit and understated acidity triumphantly emerge into a deliciously drinkable whole. Selected stores.

## SPAR WHITE

**Saint Clair** `13.5` `£5–7`
**Marlborough**
**Sauvignon 1996**
Grassy lemons, rather expensive.

## TESCO WHITE

**Azure Bay** `13.5` `–£5.00`
**Chardonnay/Semillon**
**2000**
Slightly bruised fruit undertone.

**Jackson Estate** `16.5` `£7–10`
**Sauvignon Blanc 2000**
Richer style of Sauvignon with a sense of opulence to the well-textured fruit but what is so satisfying about it is its indescribable dryness yet fruitiness.

**Lawsons Dry Hills** `17` `£7–10`
**Sauvignon Blanc 2000**

Extremely classic Sauvignon of
high class, subtle richness and
delicacy. A wine of finesse yet
fulsomeness, depth yet delicacy,
richness yet restraint. Great value,
too, for it is superior to more
expensive Kiwis.

**Marlborough** `16` `£5–7`
**Sauvignon Blanc 2000,**
**Tesco**
Fat on the one edge, grassy on
the other, this presents problems
for the classicist but for those
who regard wine as wine and not
cultural icons, this is irrelevant.
Here is a patently individual,
thought-provoking wine. Part of
Tesco's so-called 'Finest' range.
Most stores.

**Montana Reserve** `17` `£7–10`
**Chardonnay 1999**
Intensely classy and enormously
creamy and rich without being
too ripe and obvious. A
provocative blend of smokey
melon and fine acids. Has
elegance, elongation and ease of
effort.

**Montana Reserve** `16.5` `£7–10`
**Sauvignon Blanc,**
**Marlborough 2000**
Quite gorgeous richness yet
subtlety here: herbaceousness
with fine, cutting acidity and a
great texture. A lovely wine of
some class.

**Montana Unoaked** `16` `£5–7`
**Chardonnay 2000**
Lemon, melon and gooseberry –
standard top-notch Kiwi recipe?

Perhaps but this is a superior
example and no wood gives it
more purity than most. Most
stores.

**New Zealand Dry** `13.5` `–£5.00`
**White, Tesco**

**Nobilo White Cloud** `15` `–£5.00`
**1999**
An excellent wine to have handy
when eating takeaway Chinese
duck with plum sauce. Most
stores.

**Villa Maria Private Bin** `15` `£5–7`
**Sauvignon Blanc 2000**
Needs six months to pile on more
points but it has classic
gooseberry fruit with a touch of
celery.

## WAITROSE WHITE

**Azure Bay** `13.5` `–£5.00`
**Chardonnay/Semillon**
**2000**
Slightly bruised fruit undertone.

**Craggy Range Old** `14.5` `£7–10`
**Renwick Vineyard**
**Sauvignon Blanc 2000**
Has some mild tannins to it,
uncommon in a white wine.

**Craggy Range Winery** `16` `£10–13`
**Chardonnay, Hawkes**
**Bay 1999**
Splendid treat of a wine, nutty,
caramely, rich and lingering.
Individual and very stylish.

**Jackson Estate** `16.5` `£7–10`
**Sauvignon Blanc 2000**

Richer style of Sauvignon with a sense of opulence to the well-textured fruit but what is so satisfying about it is its indescribable dryness yet fruitiness.

**Montana Reserve** `16.5` `£7–10`
**Barrique Fermented**
**Chardonnay 1999**
Very accomplished wine of aplomb and weight. Lovely wood integration. Fine fruit and gentle vegetality.

**Montana Riesling 2000** `14` `–£5.00`
Cellar it for five years and get 16.5 points.

**Oyster Bay** `15.5` `£5–7`
**Marlborough**
**Chardonnay 2000**
Ripe, ready fruit of depth and substance.

**Oyster Bay Sauvignon** `16` `£5–7`
**Blanc 2000**
Classic mineral-edged Sauvignon with subtle gooseberry and lemon undertones. Utterly marvellous.

**Stoneleigh Vineyard** `15` `£5–7`
**Sauvignon Blanc 2000**
Rich and ready for moules marinières.

**Tiki Ridge Dry White** `13` `–£5.00`
**2000**

**Villa Maria Private Bin** `16` `£5–7`
**Riesling 2000**
Delicious certainty of fruit: minerally, rich, balanced, eminently cellar-worthy.

**Wither Hills Sauvignon** `15` `£7–10`
**Blanc 2000**
Tangy ripeness and richness. Will develop well over the next two years if not longer.

# PORTUGAL

Failed to deliver after a promising new beginning.

## BOOTHS RED

**Alianca Foral Douro Reserva 1997** `15.5` `−£5.00`

**Alta Mesa Red 1999** `12` `−£3.50`
Very sweet and thin.

**Bela Fonte Baga, Beiras 1999** `14` `−£5.00`
Rich and curry-friendly.

**Dão Dom Ferraz 1999** `15` `−£5.00`
Delightful tannins sprinkled over ripe, chocolate-sweet fruit. The mouth puckers in pleasure.

**Portada Red Estremadura 1999** `13.5` `−£5.00`
A juicy curry red.

**Quinta da Villa Freire Douro 1996** `15` `£5–7`

**Quinta de la Rosa 1998** `15.5` `£5–7`
Very elegant richness and cherry-ripe fruit. Great tannins.

## BUDGENS RED

**Dão Dom Ferraz 1999** `15` `−£5.00`
Delightful tannins sprinkled over

ripe, chocolate-sweet fruit. The mouth puckers in pleasure.

**Segada Portuguese Red 2000** `13` `−£5.00`
Very sweet.

## CO-OP RED

**Big Baga 1999, Co-op** `13.5` `−£5.00`

**Portada Tinto 2000** `13` `−£5.00`
Very jammy ripeness – lush (the wine, not me). Superstores only.

**Star Mountain Oak Aged 1997** `13.5` `−£5.00`
Juice with raw tannins. Not at Convenience Stores.

**Star Mountain Touriga Nacional 1997** `14` `−£5.00`

**Terra Boa Portuguese Red 2000** `13` `−£5.00`
Bit thin – even with the tannins. Not at Convenience Stores.

## MORRISONS RED

**Dão Dom Ferraz 1999** `15` `−£5.00`
Delightful tannins sprinkled over

ripe, chocolate-sweet fruit. The mouth puckers in pleasure.

Tamara Red Vinho Regional Ribatejo 1999 `13` −£3.50

## SAFEWAY RED

Bela Fonte Jaen 1999 `13` −£5.00
Hint of sweet chocolate struggling under the tannins. Selected stores.

Bright Brothers Trincadeira Preta 1997 `14` −£5.00

Falcoaria, Almeira 1997 `14.5` £5−7

Miradouro, Terras do Sado 1999 `12` −£3.50

Palmela 1998 `14.5` −£5.00

Tamara Ribetajo 1999 `13` −£5.00

## SAINSBURY'S RED

Quinta de Bons-Ventos 1999 `14` −£5.00

Quinta do Crasto 1999 `15.5` £5−7
Rich, berried, deep, good meaty edge to the tannins, classy structure, some heft to the texture, and a finish of mild aplomb. Most stores.

Segada Trincadeira Preta-Castelao 2000 `12` −£5.00
So ripe! It's like fruit salad with gravy.

## SOMERFIELD RED

Bright Brothers Atlantic Vines Baga 1999 `14.5` −£5.00
Bright as its name. Offers dry cherries and blackberries.

Pedras do Monte 1999 `16` −£5.00
Gorgeous savoury tannins allied to sweet cherries and dry plums and blackcurrants. Selected stores.

Portada Red Estremadura 1999 `13.5` −£5.00
A juicy curry red.

Portuguese Red 2000, Somerfield `13.5` −£3.50
Dry and ripe.

## TESCO RED

Dão, Tesco 1999 `14.5` −£5.00
Big, rich fruit, developed tannins, and a precise finish.

Portuguese Red NV, Tesco `14.5` −£3.50

## WAITROSE RED

Altano 1999 `14` £5−7
Touch sweet but has some tannic decency.

Terra de Lobos, Quinta do Casal Branco 2000 `14` −£5.00
Very rich and baked and ripe. Suits very spicy food.

Trincadeira Joao Portugal Ramos 1999 `14` £7−10
Nice civilised tippling. Not to civil

is the price tag.

**Vila Santa Alentejano** `15` `£7–10`
**1999**
Superior aroma and texture,
touch of spice, good firm texture.

**Vinho do Monte,** `15` `–£5.00`
**Alentejo 1999**
Good level of plummy fruit allied
to soft tannins. Respectable
performance.

## ASDA WHITE

**Vale de Rosas Fernão** `15` `–£5.00`
**Pires 1999**
A fish wine pre-eminently –
sardines spring to mind. It has
some poise and meaty richness.

**Vinho Verde 1999,** `10` `–£3.50`
**Asda**

## CO-OP WHITE

**Fiuza Chardonnay 1999** `16` `–£5.00`
Rather dainty at first and then it
really surges into fruity action.
Captivating final richness here.

**Portuguese** `14.5` `£5–7`
**Chardonnay 1999,**
**Co-op**

Ripe and gently toffeed texture.
Great wine for smoked fish and
complex shellfish plates.
Superstores only.

## SAFEWAY WHITE

**Globus Ribetajo 1999** `11` `–£5.00`

**Tamara Ribetajo White** `14.5` `–£3.50`
**1999**

## SOMERFIELD WHITE

**Bright Brothers Fernão** `15.5` `–£5.00`
**Pires Chardonnay 1998**
Interesting blend of strikingly
individual components. Has
refreshing elements and food
friendly ones.

## TESCO WHITE

**Dry Vinho Verde,** `13.5` `–£5.00`
**Tesco**

## WAITROSE WHITE

**Terras do Rio Quinta** `15` `–£3.50`
**de Abrigada 1998**

# ROMANIA

Not quite as exciting as it seemed a decade ago.

## CO-OP RED

**Prahova Valley Pinot Noir 1999** `12.5` −£3.50
Struggling . . . Not at Convenience Stores.

**Prahova Valley Special Reserve Merlot 1999** `15` −£5.00
Tangy tannins and tight, well-composed plums and berries. Superstores only.

**Romanian Prairie Merlot 1999, Co-op** `14.5` −£3.50

## MORRISONS RED

**Prahova Valley Reserve Merlot 1999** `13.5` −£5.00
Dry, has tannins, will go with food. Thus, no florid metaphors come to mind.

**Proles Pontica Merlot 1995** `13` −£5.00
Very dry and mature, hints of meat and gravy. Bit too old for me, Stuart.

**Romanian Classic Pinot Noir 1998** `11` −£3.50

**Special Reserve Pinot Noir 1998** `10` −£5.00

**Special Reserve Sangiovese 1998** `10` −£5.00

## SAFEWAY RED

**Idle Rock Merlot 1998** `12` −£5.00

## SAINSBURY'S RED

**Prahova Valley Reserve Pinot Noir 1999** `13` −£5.00
Fairly innocuous, unfairly priced. Selected stores.

**Romanian Pinot Noir NV, Sainsbury's** `13.5` −£3.50
A juicy curry wine. Some cherried Pinot character but thinner than previous vintages.

## SOMERFIELD RED

**Eagle Valley Romanian Merlot 1999** `15` −£5.00
Lovely dry blackberries and plums. Good soft tannins give it backbone.

## TESCO RED

Reka Valley Romanian `15.5` −£3.50
Pinot Noir, Tesco

## WAITROSE RED

Willow Ridge Pinot `15.5` −£5.00
Noir/Merlot 1999
Interesting ripe/leathery chewy
edge the Merlot gives the Pinot.
Highly civilised quaffing here.

## SAFEWAY WHITE

Château Cotnari, Blanc `10` −£5.00
de Cotnari 1998

## SAINSBURY'S WHITE

Romanian Merlot Rosé `14` −£3.50
NV, Sainsbury's

## TESCO WHITE

Shaw & Smith `16` £7–10
Unoaked Chardonnay
1999
Delicious class and richness here
with an elongated elegance of
fruit which is subtle and fine.
Limited distribution.

## WAITROSE WHITE

Willow Ridge `15` −£3.50
Sauvignon Blanc/
Feteasca 2000
Interesting chewiness to the wine.
Brilliant for Thai food.

# RUSSIA

I'm sorry? Are you serious?

## SAFEWAY RED

**Caucasus Valley,** `15` −£5.00
**Matrassa, Georgia 1998**

**Odessos Steppe** `13` −£5.00
**Cabernet Sauvignon,**
**Ukraine 1998**

**Tamada Saperavi,** `15.5` −£5.00
**Georgia 1998**
Lush as a Beaujolais but has
much more character and bite
from the tannins – which are
great.

# SOUTH AFRICA

The Cape sizzles with vibrant reds and vivacious whites.

## ASDA RED

**Beyerskloof Pinotage, Stellenbosch 2000** `15.5` `-£5.00`
Rubbery, spicy fruit, deep tannins, coffee-edged rich fruit and a roaring finish.

**Carnby Liggle 2000** `12` `-£5.00`
Needs a good kick up the backside via a good Balti.

**Dumisani Ruby Cabernet/Merlot 1999** `15.5` `-£5.00`

**Graham Beck Coastal Shiraz 1999** `16.5` `£5-7`
Deeply integrated elements provide superbly well textured berries, touch of tobacco to dry cassis fruit and a plump, textured richness and great class. A really exceptional Shiraz. Selected stores.

**Kumala Cabernet Sauvignon Shiraz 2000** `16` `-£5.00`
Huge juice and tannins. Lovely meaty edge.

**Landskroon Merlot Reserve 1999** `16` `£5-7`
Gigantic hedgerow fruitiness. The wine simply swims with flavours.

Utterly seductive from nose to throat.

**Linton Park Cabernet Sauvignon 1998** `13.5` `£10-13`
A huge gravy of a wine with such savoury richness it clogs the throat. A most unusual and cloying Cabernet, absurdly overpriced, but of interest to plutocrats eating game dishes. Only at the Bristol Supercentre.

**Middelvlei Cabernet Sauvignon 1998** `15.5` `£5-7`
Very striking tannins here and very couth blackcurrants. Limited distribution.

**Neil Ellis Cabernet Sauvignon 1998** `16.5` `£7-10`
Delightful aroma of spicy blackcurrants, elegant layered fruit, delicious integrated acids and a lovely lilting finish. Terrific Cabernet. Limited distribution.

**Pinotage Reserve 1999, Asda** `14` `-£5.00`

**Porcupine Ridge Syrah 1999** `16` `£5-7`
There used to be two styles of Syrah: the Rhône's (dry) and the

Aussie's (very rich). Now comes the Cape's Crusader. And it makes a very strong, rich case for itself.

**Railroad Cabernet** `15` `−£5.00`
**Sauvignon Shiraz 1999**
Positive ripe glugging. Good tannins, firmly and confidently structured. Selected stores.

**Savanha Merlot 1999** `14` `£5–7`
Odd cosmetic richness and spiciness.

**South African Cabernet** `14` `−£5.00`
**Sauvignon 1999, Asda**

**South African Pinotage** `13.5` `−£5.00`
**1999, Asda**

**Spier Unexpected** `16` `−£5.00`
**Pleasures Cabernet**
**Sauvignon 1999**
At first I was flummoxed. Was it too dry? Too . . . well, too many things. Perhaps, infuriatingly, it is accurately labelled. The pleasures of it are unexpected . . . the lingering tannins, the bite of the blackcurrants. Great with food.

**Van Loveren Cabernet** `13` `−£5.00`
**Shiraz 1999**

## BOOTHS RED

**Goats Do Roam** `14` `−£5.00`
**Fairview, Paarl 2000**
Sweet Rhône fruit with elegant tannins. Greatly quaffable and unpretentious (the name apart).

**Helderberg Shiraz 1999** `15` `−£5.00`

**Spice Route Andrew's** `16.5` `£5–7`
**Hope Cabernet**
**Sauvignon/Merlot 1999**
Vibrates with rich cherries, plums, blackberries and fine tannins.

**Welmoed Merlot 1999** `16` `£5–7`
Hints of heather, spice and fresh blackberries – terrific pace to the fruit helped by great tannins.

## BUDGENS RED

**Kumala Cinsault** `13.5` `−£5.00`
**Pinotage 2000**
Curry red.

**Long Mountain Merlot** `13.5` `£5–7`
**Shiraz 2000**
Touch expensive for the sweetness of the style.

## CO-OP RED

**Cape American Oak** `14` `−£5.00`
**Pinotage 1999, Co-op**

**Cape Indaba Pinotage** `13` `−£5.00`
**1998**

**Cape Red NV, Co-op** `11` `−£3.50`
Well, it's ripe and ready, but not for my glass it's not . . .

**Cape Ruby Cabernet,** `13` `−£5.00`
**Oak Aged 2000, Co-op**
Curry-friendly jamminess.

**Elephant Trail** `15` `−£5.00`
**Cinsault/Merlot 2000,**
**Co-op**

**Fire Engine Red 1999** `15.5` `−£5.00`
Indeed, it tastes burnt as it quits

the throat – though the fire is, as promised by the label, out. The fruit is well-built and handsome. Superstores only.

**Goiya Giaan 2000**  `13`  `−£5.00`
Rubbery and dry. Remarkable feat to achieve. Not at Convenience Stores.

**Kumala Ruby Cabernet**  `15`  `−£5.00`
**Merlot 2000**
Baked, almost grilled, rich fruit of depth and clarity.

**Natural State Cape**  `15`  `£5–7`
**Soleil Organic Shiraz**
**1999**

**Oak Village Cabernet**  `13`  `−£5.00`
**Sauvignon 1999**
Cabernet as fruit juice. Not at Convenience Stores.

**Pinnacle Merlot 1998**  `16`  `£5–7`
Very thrusting style, taking no prisoners, and it has something to say for itself. 'I am utterly hedonistic and delicious.' Amen to that. Superstores only.

**Railroad Cabernet**  `15`  `−£5.00`
**Sauvignon Shiraz 1999**
Positive ripe glugging. Good tannins, firmly and confidently structured. Selected stores.

**Spice Route Cabernet**  `16.5`  `£7–10`
**Sauvignon/Merlot 1998**
Roasted nuts, ripe raspberries, blackcurrants, plums, spices, herbs, integrated soft tannins and an overall demeanour of determinacy and deliciousness. Superstores only.

**Three Worlds Pinotage**  `15.5`  `£5–7`
**Shiraz Zinfandel 1999,**
**Co-op**

**Winds of Change**  `14`  `−£5.00`
**Pinotage/Cabernet**
**Sauvignon 1999**
Juicy curry wine.

## M & S RED

**Cape Country**  `13`  `−£5.00`
**Cinsault/Ruby**
**Cabernet 2000**
Great with a takeaway chicken tandoori.

**Monate Cabernet**  `13`  `£7–10`
**Sauvignon 1999**
Sweet and sour fruit. Not a £10 wine.

**Monate Shiraz 2000**  `15.5`  `£7–10`
Brilliant spicy richness, tobacco-edged blackberries and baked plums and a surprising turn of speed to the tannins. Terrific texture to it, too.

**Rock Ridge Pinotage**  `14`  `−£5.00`
**2000**
Very fit and sweetly dispositioned for spicy food. Burnt rubber undertone to some raunchy fruit.

**Warwick Estate**  `12`  `£7–10`
**Trilogy 1997**
Not the wine it was. I remember it had real panache and luminosity. Now it seems even a touch soppy. What's going on here?

## MORRISONS RED

**Cathedral Cellars** `13` `£7–10`
**Merlot 1996**

**Fairview Malbec 2000** `16.5` `£5–7`
Elegance, power with finesse,
complexity plus luxury extras like
aroma, chutzpah and great
tannins.

**Namaqua Classic Red** `11.5` `–£3.50`
**NV (3 litre box)**
Price band indicates the 75cl
equivalent.

**Old Cellar Cabernet** `13` `–£5.00`
**Sauvignon 1995**
Ripe finish with an echo of
linoleum.

**Spice Route Andrew's** `16.5` `£5–7`
**Hope 1998**
Thundering riches abound here:
blackcurrants, tar, violets,
rosewater, leather and a subtle
spicy tang. Great stuff.

## SAFEWAY RED

**Apostle's Falls** `16.5` `£5–7`
**Cabernet Sauvignon**
**1998**
What wouldn't they give in
Bordeaux for such ripeness, such
texture, such savoury richness
with austerity. A beautiful
performer, this specimen, on
every front.

**Arniston Bay Ruby** `13` `–£5.00`
**Cabernet/Merlot 1999**

**Bellingham Cabernet** `13` `£10–13`
**Franc 1998**
Selected stores.

**Cape Soleil Organic** `9` `–£5.00`
**Pinotage 1998**
Thin and insubstantial. Why sell
organic wine as puny as this just
to see the word organic on shelf?

**Goiya Glaan 1999** `16` `–£5.00`
Very ripe and rich, firmly
textured, delicious plums,
blackcurrants and spice. Really
gushes with flavour whilst
retaining a serious depth. Selected
stores.

**Kanonkop 'Kadette'** `15.5` `£5–7`
**Estate Wine 1998**

**Kleinbosch Reserve** `14` `£5–7`
**Cabernet Sauvignon**
**1999**

**Landskroon Shiraz,** `15` `£5–7`
**Paarl 1998**
Juicy, ripe, raunchy and ready.
Hint of cigar to the hedgerow
fruit.

**Simsberg Pinot Noir,** `13.5` `£5–7`
**Paarl 1998**

**South African Pinotage** `16` `–£5.00`
**2000, Safeway**
Quirky, smokey, dry, jammy,
deep, spicy and very dry. Tarry
texture gives it huge food
compatibility.

**Stellenbosch Cabernet** `14` `–£5.00`
**Sauvignon 1999**

**Stellenbosch Merlot** `15.5` `–£5.00`
**1999**

**Young Vatted Pinotage,** `15` `–£5.00`
**Paarl 1999, Safeway**

## SAINSBURY'S RED

**Bellingham Pinotage** `13` `–£5.00`
**1999**
Bit juicy for me.

**Clos Malverne** `13` `£5–7`
**Cabernet Sauvignon**
**Pinotage 1999**
Very sweet and a touch
simpering. Not at all stores.

**Flagship Vergelegen** `14` `£13–20`
**Bordeaux Blend 1998**
Soft, ripe, highly drinkable.
Eighteen quid is overloading it,
though. Limited distribution.

**Goats Do Roam** `14` `–£5.00`
**Fairview, Paarl 2000**
Sweet Rhône fruit with elegant
tannins. Greatly quaffable and
unpretentious (the name apart).

**Graham Beck Merlot** `13` `£5–7`
**1999**
Why are many of this retailer's
SA reds so sweet? They used to
imprison reds in this country
once. Maybe they should consider
bringing it back – for wines like
these. Selected stores.

**Kumala Cabernet** `16` `–£5.00`
**Sauvignon Shiraz 2000**
Huge juice and tannins. Lovely
meaty edge.

**Kumala Cabernet** `15.5` `–£5.00`
**Shiraz NV (3 litre box)**
Boisterous, bouncy, full of
vivaciously layered fruit and fun-
filled riches. A lovely devil-may-
care wine of entertaining depth,
food friendly fullness, and

generous-to-finish heartiness.
(Heartiness often disguises
shallowness but not here.)
Selected stores. Price band
indicates the 75cl equivalent.

**Railroad Cabernet** `13` `–£5.00`
**Sauvignon Shiraz 2000**
Juicy, yet dry to finish. Selected
stores.

**South African Cabernet** `15.5` `–£5.00`
**Sauvignon NV,**
**Sainsbury's**

**South African Pinotage** `12` `–£5.00`
**NV, Sainsbury's**
New label, sour. New blend,
sweet.

**South African Red NV,** `15` `–£3.50`
**Sainsbury's**

**South African Reserve** `16` `£5–7`
**Selection Pinotage**
**2000, Sainsbury's**
Unusually dry and serious-sided
Pinotage with more Pinot
character than age. Yes it's young
and vibrant but the plums and
meaty blackberries are
handsomely rigged. Most stores.

**Spice Route Andrew's** `16.5` `£5–7`
**Hope Cabernet**
**Sauvignon/Merlot 1999**
Vibrates with rich cherries,
plums, blackberries and fine
tannins. Most stores.

**Spice Route Pinotage** `16` `£7–10`
**1999**
One of the Cape's more effective
Pinotages where tobacco, a hint
of coffee and roasted berries

harmonise sweetly yet dryly. Selected stores.

**SSW Ruby Cabernet** `14` −£5.00
**NV (1 litre)**
A brilliant curry wine. Sweet but firm to finish. Most stores. Price band indicates the 75cl equivalent.

**Stowells of Chelsea** `15.5` −£5.00
**Cinsault Pinotage**
**Sainsbury (3 litre box)**
Price band indicates the 75cl equivalent.

**Vergelegen Merlot 1998** `13` £10−13
We can exempt this Merlot from the sweet censure referred to elsewhere but this wine displays other criminal tendencies: beginning with the felonious price tag. Limited distribution.

## SOMERFIELD RED

**Andrews Hope Spice** `15.5` £5−7
**Route Cabernet Merlot**
**2000**
Terrific value for the rich, tangy fruit on offer.

**Bellingham Pinotage** `13` £5−7
**1999**
Bit juicy for me. Selected stores.

**Cape Soleil Organic** `12.5` −£5.00
**Pinotage 2000**
Bitter nuts as an undertone to dry plums.

**Kumala Cinsault** `13.5` −£5.00
**Pinotage 2000**
Curry red.

**Kumala Reserve** `15` £7−10
**Cabernet Sauvignon**
**1998**
Chocolate and cocoa, with sweet plums. Selected stores.

**South Africa Dry Red** `12.5` −£5.00
**2000, Somerfield**
Rather dry and a touch incomplete on the finish.

**South African Cabernet** `16` −£5.00
**Sauvignon 2000,**
**Somerfield**
Brilliant tobacco and dry cassis fruit with superb tannins.

**South African Cinsault** `12` −£5.00
**Ruby Cabernet 2000,**
**Somerfield**
Sweet and simple.

**South African Pinotage** `13` £5−7
**2000, Somerfield**
Try it with bacon and eggs. And please e-mail me at *superplonk.com* and let me kow how you and the wine got on.

**Spice Route Pinotage** `16.5` £7−10
**2000**
Exuberant, spicy, rich, deep, berried, chocolatey, tannic – it has it all. Selected stores.

**Spice Route Shiraz 2000** `16.5` £7−10
Oz!! Look to your fruity laurels! There are tannins here to die for. Selected stores.

## SPAR RED

**Chiwara Cinsaut/Ruby** `14.5` −£5.00
**Cabernet 1999**

A good vibrant richness of attack and fine tannins. Has some character and food compatibility (mild curries etc).

**Chiwara Pinotage 2000,** 12 −£5.00
**Spar**
Sweet and sour fruit with a wry burnt edge to the finish.

## TESCO RED

**African Legend** 13 −£5.00
**Pinotage 1999**
Curry friendly. Not at all stores.

**Apostles Falls Cabernet** 15 £5−7
**Sauvignon 1999**
Blackcurrants, spice, and very energetic tannins give this wine personality and punch.

**Apostles Falls Merlot** 15.5 £5−7
**1999**
Ripe, soft and very immediate (a second or two's breathing is more than enough). This wine has spice, substance and great depth.

**Beyers Truter Pinotage** 16 −£5.00
**NV, Tesco**
Brilliant burnt rubber soup – I mean wine – and its tannins excite the palate also. Great with all sorts of meat and chicken dishes and supremely good with Indian food. Part of Tesco's 'Finest' range. Most stores.

**Cape Cinsault NV,** 13.5 −£5.00
**Tesco**
Ripe and curry-friendly.

**Cape Cinsault/** 15 −£5.00
**Pinotage NV, Tesco**
Very dry and tobacco-edged, and has deep tannins – excellent casserole-friendly fruit.

**Fairview Shiraz 1999** 16.5 £5−7
One of the meatiest and most munch-worthy Shirazes around for the money: vibrant tannins, delicious layered fruit with hints of at least fourteen different spices, and a classy finish.

**Goats Do Roam** 14 −£5.00
**Fairview, Paarl 2000**
Sweet Rhône fruit with elegant tannins. Greatly quaffable and unpretentious (the name apart).

**Goiya Glaan 2000** 15 −£5.00
Interesting ripe tannins and hugely plummy richness. A bold wine of depth and flavour.

**Kumala Cabernet** 15 −£5.00
**Sauvignon Shiraz 2000**
Huge juice and tannins. Lovely meaty edge.

**Kumala Cinsault/** 14 −£5.00
**Cabernet Sauvignon**
**2000**
Sweet edge – needs curry.

**Kumala Reserve** 15 £7−10
**Cabernet Sauvignon**
**1999**
Big and rich and engagingly fruity.

**Landskroon Premier** 14 £5−7
**Reserve Cabernet**
**Sauvignon 1998**

**Oak Village Vintage Reserve 2000** `15` `−£5.00`
Good firm tannins which are well hitched to blackberry richness and dryness. Has a slightly exotic (herbs?) tang on the finish.

**Rylands Grove Cabernet/Merlot 2000** `16.5` `−£5.00`
Real crunchiness to the rich tannins, tobacco, coffee and cassis to the fruit, and an elongated, dry finish of calm, controlled fruitiness. A real lip-smacking bargain. At most stores.

**Rylands Grove Cinsaut/Tinta Barocca 2000** `13` `−£5.00`
Bit too jammy for me. At most stores.

**South African Red NV, Tesco** `11` `−£3.50`
Pretty basic. Very dry.

**South African Reserve Cabernet NV, Tesco** `12` `−£5.00`

**Winds of Change Cabernet Sauvignon/Pinotage 2000** `14.5` `−£5.00`
Spicy, food friendly, dry. Good rich finish.

## WAITROSE RED

**Andrew's Hope Spice Route Pinotage 2000** `15.5` `£5−7`
Juicy yet dry, tannic yet fruity, elegant yet ripe.

**Clos Malverne Basket Pressed Pinotage, Stellenbosch 1999** `16` `£5−7`
Rich, aromatic, deep, full and gently spicy. Has oodles of berries and ripe nutty tannins.

**Culemborg Cape Red 2000** `12` `−£5.00`
Very sweet and simpering.

**Goats Do Roam Fairview, Paarl 2000** `14` `−£5.00`
Sweet Rhône fruit with elegant tannins. Greatly quaffable and unpretentious (the name apart).

**Graham Beck The Ridge Shiraz 1999** `15` `£7−10`
Good tannins here and a rich throughput of ripe fruit. Has an incipient raunchiness.

**Natural State Shiraz 1999 (organic)** `14.5` `£5−7`
Very chewy tannins, slightly creamy, roasted finish.

**Spice Route Cabernet Sauvignon/Merlot 1998** `16.5` `£7−10`
Roasted nuts, ripe raspberries, blackcurrants, plums, spices, herbs, integrated soft tannins and an overall demeanour of determinacy and deliciousness.

**Spice Route Flagship Merlot 1998** `17` `£13−20`
A big, rich special occasion Merlot of massive depth, lingering tannins and huge food compatibility. Not at all stores.

**Villiera Merlot, Paarl 1998** `14.5` `£7−10`

Sweet, a touch, and saved by
some earthy tannins.

## ASDA WHITE

**Big South African** 14.5 −£3.50
**Chardonnay 2000 (1.5
litres)**
Great lip-smacking fun. Tangy
and not OTT. Selected stores.
Price band indicates the 75cl
equivalent.

**Interlude Blanc,** 13 £5–7
**Verdun Estate 1999**
Curious blend of Sauvignon,
Gewürztraminer and Chenin
which comes across ill-knit. Only
at the Bristol Supercentre.

**Kumala Chenin** 15 −£5.00
**Chardonnay 2000**
Biting, clean, nicely fruity.

**Porcupine Ridge** 16 −£5.00
**Sauvignon Blanc 2000**
Disarmingly prickly and
classically styled in everything
except the lingering hint of
creamy pineapple and peach.

**Speir Chenin Blanc** 15 −£5.00
**2000**
Touched by a charming ripeness
of apricot, melon and lemon. Not
crisp so much as creamy.

**Speir Sauvignon Blanc** 15.5 −£5.00
**2000**
Delicious nut and ripe gooseberry
fruit.

**Van Loveren Blanc de** 14 −£5.00
**Noirs 2000**

## BOOTHS WHITE

**Altus Sauvignon Blanc** 13.5 −£5.00
**2000**
Very dry.

**Jordan Chardonnay** 16 £7–10
**1999**
Delicious creamy fruit with hints
of raspberry and ripe melon.
Good finish, if somewhat wild
and whacky.

**Landema Falls** 15 −£3.50
**Colombard
Chardonnay NV**

**Welmoed Sauvignon** 13.5 −£5.00
**Blanc 2000**
Very ripe and rich.

## BUDGENS WHITE

**Cape White NV,** 11 −£3.50
**Budgens**

**Clear Mountain Chenin** 13.5 −£5.00
**Blanc NV**

**Kumala Colombard/** 14 −£5.00
**Chardonnay 2000**
Rich apricots, gooseberries and
lemons. Good for spicy oriental
food.

**Long Mountain** 13 −£5.00
**Sauvignon Blanc 2000**
Grassy undertone to rich melon
overtone.

**Stowells of Chelsea** 13 −£5.00
**Chenin Blanc NV**

## CO-OP WHITE

**Cape Chenin Blanc, Oak Aged 2000, Co-op**   `13.5` `-£5.00`
Sticky lime fruit with hints of lychee.

**Cape Soleil Organic Chardonnay 1999, Co-op**   `13` `-£5.00`
Has a fat, creamy edge which mars the natural freshness of the squeezed grapes.

**Cape White NV, Co-op**   `13` `-£3.50`
Cheap and cheerful.

**Elephant River Colombard/ Chardonnay 2000, Co-op**   `14` `-£3.50`

**First Release Chardonnay 2000**   `13.5` `-£5.00`

**Goiya Kgeisje Chardonnay Sauvignon Blanc 2000**   `15` `-£5.00`

**Not Too Dry Chardonnay 2001**   `12` `-£5.00`
Very ripe and Chinese food friendly. Superstores only.

**Oak Village Sauvignon Blanc 1999**   `13` `-£5.00`

**Pendulum Pink 2001**   `12` `-£5.00`
Pretty horrible bottle. Not at Convenience Stores.

**Robert's Rock Chardonnay Semillon 2000**   `13.5` `-£5.00`
Pacy, zippy and keen. Doesn't quite put the ball in the net, though.

**Spice Route Chenin Blanc 1998**   `16` `£5-7`
Fat but far from out of condition or flabby. Has a lush peachy ripeness relieved by a lovely texture and nutty-edged acidity. Not at all stores.

**Stowells South African Chenin Blanc NV**   `13` `-£5.00`

## M & S WHITE

**Cape Country Chenin Blanc 2001**   `14.5` `-£5.00`
An excellent party wine which will raise eyebrows as it raises your neighbourhood esteem.

**'Life from Stone' Sauvignon Blanc, Springfield Estate 2000**   `13.5` `£5-7`
Dry, touch lacking. Austere on the finish. Seems, somehow, incomplete, dissatisfied with itself.

**Rockridge Chardonnay 2000**   `14` `-£5.00`
Pleasant, if unexciting, fruit which starts underripely but finishes with more upbeat richness.

## MORRISONS WHITE

**Danie de Wet Chardonnay Sur Lie 2000**   `16` `-£5.00`
Amazing price for such delicacy

and precision. The best white wine for the money in the store.

**Fair Cape Chenin Blanc** `14.5` `−£3.50`
**2000**
Cheap and very cheerful. Dry fruit with touches of lemon and pineapple.

**Fairview Chardonnay** `16` `£5–7`
**2000**
This is a different sort of Chardonnay with melon, gooseberry and apricot and it expresses its difference via a subtle richness of some sort of herb and nut and in its lovely texture.

**Namaqua Classic Dry** `15` `−£3.50`
**White NV (3 litre box)**
Price band indicates the 75cl equivalent.

**Spice Route Abbotsdale** `16` `−£5.00`
**Colombard/Chenin Blanc 1998**
Very subtle but vibrant and sensual in its delicious fruity finish.

**Van Loveren Blanc de** `14` `−£5.00`
**Noirs 2000**

**Van Loveren Semillon** `14` `−£5.00`
**1999**

of underripe gooseberry. Selected stores.

**Echo Bay Colombar** `13` `−£5.00`
**1999**
Bit sour on the finish.

**Fairview Semillon 1999** `16` `£5–7`
Exciting biting here: richness, texture, tanginess and lovely subtle fruit. Most stores.

**Kumala Colombard/** `14` `−£5.00`
**Chardonnay 2000**
Rich apricots, gooseberries and lemons. Good for spicy oriental food.

**Lyngrove Chenin** `13` `−£5.00`
**Blanc/Colombard 2000**

**Neil Ellis Groenekloof** `16.5` `£7–10`
**Sauvignon Blanc 2000**
Very elegant dry gooseberry, touches of mineral hardness, hint of herbaceousness. Very classy.

**Sea of Serenity Dry** `14` `−£3.50`
**Muscat 2000**

**Vale of Peace** `14` `−£5.00`
**Colombard 2000**

**Versus 2000 (1 litre)** `16` `−£5.00`
Delicious crisp fruit. A most stylishly demure wine. Price band indicates the 75cl equivalent.

## SAFEWAY WHITE

**Douglas Green** `15.5` `−£5.00`
**Sauvignon 2000**
Rich, ready, dry to finish. A very crisp overtone with an undertone

## SAINSBURY'S WHITE

**Bellingham** `15.5` `£5–7`
**Chardonnay 2000**
Rich creamy melon with some good lemon backup.

**Kumala Chardonnay** `16.5` `−£5.00`
NV (3 litre box)
Throbs with purpose and plump
melonople, a touch of pear and
pineapple, and a subtle undertone
of baked fruit. If this sounds a bit
of a mouthful, I apologise. The
wine, is, withal, rather witty in a
box. Price band indicates the 75cl
equivalent.

**Pendulum Chardonnay** `15` `−£5.00`
(3 litre box)
Like getting your teeth stuck into
an overripe Canteloupe melon
with lemon juice and alcohol
added. For plates brimful of spicy
Thai takeaway this is the wine to
go with.

**Pendulum Rosé (3 litre** `14` `−£5.00`
box)
Subdued walnut and cherry fruit,
very dry. Good barbecue food
wine.

**Reserve Selection** `15.5` `£5−7`
South African
Sauvignon Blanc 2001,
Sainsbury's
Very dry gooseberries with a faint
mineral tang as it finishes. Has
some elegance to its structure.
Most stores.

**Rhona Muscadel 1996** `16` `£5−7`
Wonderful textured syrupy
richness of concentrated
sweetness and ripeness. Pour it
over ice-cream or drink it with
raspberries and cream. 70 stores.

**South African** `15.5` `−£5.00`
Chardonnay 2001,
Sainsbury's
Another clean Sainsbury
Chardonnay − as if it were
becoming a house style. Perish
the thought. But celebrate, if you
prefer, this consistency of
approach with this delicious
wine.

**South African Chenin** `14` `−£3.50`
Blanc NV, Sainsbury's

**South African Chenin** `14.5` `−£3.50`
Blanc NV, Sainsbury's
(3 litre box)
Price band indicates the 75cl
equivalent.

**South African Medium** `13` `−£3.50`
White NV, Sainsbury's

**SSW Chardonnay** `12` `−£5.00`
Chenin Blanc 1999 (1
litre)
Unsubtle, overripe, rather crude
and clumsy on the palate. Most
stores. Price band indicates the
75cl equivalent.

**Vergelegen** `14` `£5−7`
Chardonnay 2000
Very woody and ripe. Needs
food. 140 selected stores.

**Arniston Bay South** `14.5` `−£5.00`
African Chenin
Chardonnay 2001
Crisp, chewy edge of ripe melon
and gooseberry.

**Bellingham** 15.5 £5–7
**Chardonnay 2000**
Rich creamy melon with some
good lemon backup. Selected
stores.

**Bellingham Sauvignon** 16.5 –£5.00
**Blanc 2000**
A high class, high-wire act where
fine acids tiptoe along a fine wire
of gooseberry-rich fruit.
Delicately poised yet potent, this
is a lovely wine.

**Bush Vines Semillon** 13.5 –£5.00
**2001, Somerfield**
Bitter hints of pea soup and lime.
Interesting with fish dishes
(spicy).

**Danie de Wet** 16 –£5.00
**Chardonnay 2001**
Lovely elegant fruit. Bargain for
such accomplished, subtle
richness.

**Kumala Colombard** 14 –£5.00
**Sauvignon 2001**
Tangy hints of satsuma and
lemon.

**Porcupine Ridge** 15 £5–7
**Sauvignon Blanc 2001**
Elegant bite of quality acids
coating spiky fruit. Selected
stores.

**South Africa Dry White** 13 –£3.50
**2001, Somerfield**
Grassy, edgily rich.

**South African** 15.5 –£5.00
**Chardonnay 2001,**
**Somerfield**
Rich, balanced, satisfying, well-
packed without being OTT.

**South African Chenin** 14.5 –£5.00
**Blanc 2001, Somerfield**
Good gooseberries and lime fruit.

**South African** 15 –£5.00
**Colombard 2001,**
**Somerfield**
Good rich pickings here.

**South African** 15.5 –£5.00
**Colombard**
**Chardonnay 2001,**
**Somerfield**
Charm and precision – edges of
lemon and melon. Excellent with
food (fish) and mood (blue).

**Van Loveren South** 15 –£5.00
**African Sauvignon**
**Blanc 2001**
Good tanginess of tangerine and
gooseberry.

## SPAR WHITE

**Chiwara Colombard/** 14 –£5.00
**Sauvignon 1998, Spar**
An interesting companion for
oriental food.

## TESCO WHITE

**African Legend** 14 –£5.00
**Colombard 2000**
Crisp nutty edge to faintly
pineapple and apple fruit.

**Apostles Falls** 13 £5–7
**Chardonnay 2000**
Bit flat (yet fat) on the finish.

**Arniston Bay Rosé 2000** 13 –£5.00

**Cape Chenin Blanc NV,** `15` `−£3.50`
**Tesco**

**Fairview Chardonnay** `16` `£5−7`
**2000**
This is a different sort of
Chardonnay with melon,
gooseberry and apricot and it
expresses its difference via a
subtle richness of some sort of
herb and nut and in its lovely
texture.

**Fairview Goats do** `16` `−£5.00`
**Roam Rosé 2000**
Superb rosé richness, textured
and fine, with a hint of tannin, a
touch of lemon and lime, and
more than a suggestion of plum
and blackberry all dry and dainty.
Terrific food and mood wine.
Selected stores.

**Fire Finch Sauvignon** `15.5` `−£5.00`
**Blanc 2000**
Delicious herbaceous, nutty fruit
with touches of fresh vine-
tomato, gooseberry and basil.
Delicious bundle of nervous
energy to activate a slice of grilled
turbot.

**Goiya Kgeisje 2001** `15` `−£5.00`
Hints of pear, pineapple and lush
lemon. Very refreshing and
simple.

**Oak Village Sauvignon** `14` `−£5.00`
**Blanc 2000**
Very tangy and crisp. Good with
prawns.

**Rylands Grove Barrel** `15.5` `−£5.00`
**Fermented Chenin**
**Blanc 2000**
Great value here: fruit of
nuttiness and refined depth and a
lovely dry peach/raspberry finish
of subtlety and charm.

**Rylands Grove Dry** `15` `−£5.00`
**Muscat 2000**
Lovely grapey richness tempered
by dryness and a firm texture.
Excellent with mildly spiced Thai
food or any fish dish using mint
and/or coriander leaves.

**Rylands Grove** `14.5` `−£5.00`
**Sauvignon Blanc 2000**

**South African** `15` `−£5.00`
**Chardonnay 2000,**
**Tesco**

**South African** `14` `−£5.00`
**Chardonnay/**
**Colombard NV, Tesco**

**South African Medium** `13` `−£3.50`
**Sweet White NV,**
**Tesco**

**Third Millennium** `14` `−£5.00`
**Chenin Chardonnay**
**2001**
One of the blue bottle crowd.
Stands out in this respect. A very
rich, oriental food wine.

**Van Loveren Blanc de** `14` `−£3.50`
**Noir Red Muscadel**
**Rosé 2000**

**Winds of Change** `13` `−£5.00`
**Chardonnay 2000**

## WAITROSE WHITE

**Colombard** 14.5 −£5.00
**Chardonnay 2000,**
**Waitrose**
Witless label but charming wit to
the fruit.

**Culemborg Cape White** 13 −£3.50
**2000**

**Culemborg Unwooded** 12.5 −£5.00
**Chardonnay, Western**
**Cape 2000**

**Diamond Hills Chenin** 12 −£5.00
**Blanc/Chardonnay**
**2000**

**Excelsior Estate** 15 −£5.00
**Sauvignon Blanc 2000**
Some pleasantly rich touches.

**Fairview Viognier,** 16.5 £7−10
**Paarl 2000**
Extremely elegant apricot-scented
and fruited wine of superb
texture. Quite gorgeously stacked
with subtle surprises.

**Jordan Chardonnay** 15.5 £7−10
**2000**
Lively, rich, aromatic, deep and
hugely suitable for all kinds of
spicy fish and poultry dishes.

**Kumala Colombard/** 14 −£5.00
**Chardonnay 2000**
Rich apricots, gooseberries and
lemons. Good for spicy oriental
food.

**Spice Route Abbotsdale** 15 £7−10
**Colombard/Chenin**
**Blanc 1999**

**Springfield Sauvignon** 14.5 £5−7
**Blanc Special Cuvee**
**2000**
One of the Cape's most couth
Sauvignons.

**Steenberg Sauvignon** 13.5 £7−10
**Blanc 2000**
Dry and very constrained.

**Steenberg Semillon** 16 £7−10
**1999**
Unusual grassiness to the rich
melon and lemon − great finish of
impactful deliciousness.

**Warwick Estate** 16 £5−7
**Chardonnay,**
**Stellenbosch 2000**
Superb class of fruit here, subtle
yet ripe, excellent texture and a
high class, confident finish.

# SPAIN

The ability to produce great variety, high quality and tasty bargains.

## ASDA RED

**Conde de Navasques** 15.5 −£5.00
1997

**Don Darias Tinto NV** 15.5 −£3.50

**Mont Marcal Crianza** 14 −£3.50
1997

**Torres Coronas** 16 £5–7
Tempranillo 1999
Excellent layers of firm, plump cherries and blackberries, lovely tannins and all round elegance. Why can't Rioja producers turn out Tempranillo like this?

## BOOTHS RED

**Amezola de la Mora** 12.5 £7–10
Rioja Crianza 1997
Very ripe and squashy (like wine made from windfall fruit).

**Artadi Vinas de Gain** 15.5 £7–10
Crianza, Rioja 1997
Dry, cherry-rich, food friendly.

**Casa de la Viña** 15 −£5.00
Valdepeñas 2000
Delicious.

**Casa Morena,** 14 −£3.50
Valdepeñas NV

**Castillo de Almansa** 15.5 −£5.00
Reserva Bodegas
Piqueras 1995
Rich soft plum fruit of substance and depth.

**Guelbenzu Blue Label** 16 £5–7
Navarra NV
Vibrant tannins of delicious immodesty and personality help the berried fruit to a fine finish.

**La Poema Garnacha** 13 −£5.00
Viñas Viejas 1999

**Mas Donis Capcanes** 16.5 −£5.00
Taragona 2000
Superb texture, polished yet characterful, to blackberries and plums. Has very elegant tannins.

**Ochoa Tempranillo** 15 −£5.00
Garnacha 1999

**Viña Alarba, Calatayud** 13 −£3.50
2000
Sweet young thing.

**Viña Albali Gran** 15 £5–7
Reserva 1993

Viña Borgia Campo de `13` `−£5.00`
Borja 1999

puckers the cheeks without
compensating depth of fruit.

## BUDGENS RED

Berberana Dragon `14` `−£5.00`
Tempranillo 1999
Ripe and very curry friendly.

Berberana Rioja `14` `£5–7`
Tempranillo 1999
Svelte and soft and highly
quaffable.

Masia Monistrol `14.5` `−£5.00`
Tempranillo Garnacha
Penedés 2000
A firm meaty red with
characterful tannins (tenacious on
the finish) and solid berried fruit.
Rather what one might call, old-
fashionedly, a bistro red.

Palacio de la Vega `15.5` `£5–7`
Cabernet Sauvignon/
Tempranillo 1998
Coffee, cassis, tannins, touch of
leather, hint of cream of
cauliflower soup – enough of a
meal for anyone here.

Piedemonte Merlot `13` `−£5.00`
Cabernet Sauvignon,
Navarra 1999
Very juicy. Suits . . . you know
what it suits.

Viña Albali Bataneros `13` `−£5.00`
Barrel Aged
Tempranillo,
Valdepeñas 1999
Very dry on the finish. Really

Viña Albali Gran `15` `£5–7`
Reserva 1993

Viña Sardana `14.5` `−£5.00`
Tempranillo, Calatayud
1999
Good brisk tannins and a hint of
chocolate on the finish.

## CO-OP RED

Berberana Rioja `14` `−£5.00`
Tempranillo 1999
Svelte and soft and highly
quaffable.

Berberana Rioja Viura `13` `−£5.00`
1999
Bit too woody. Overwhelms the
fruit. Not at Convenience Stores.

Campo Rojo Cariñena `12` `−£3.50`
NV
Sheer juice.

Chestnut Gully `15.5` `−£5.00`
Monastrell-Merlot
1999, Co-op
Delicious chocolate and, indeed,
roasted chestnut fruit.
Remarkable texture to it, chewy
and deep. Not at Convenience
Stores.

Rioja Tinto, Viña Gala `13.5` `−£5.00`
NV, Co-op

Tempranillo Oak Aged `13` `−£3.50`
NV, Co-op

Tierra Sana Organic `17` `−£5.00`
Wine 1999, Co-op

A thrilling organic, unfiltered wine of huge substance and thrillingly deep and all-enveloping fruit which is absurdly inexpensive. Lovely savoury bouquet, big blackcurrant and cherry fruit and a lushly tannic finish. A real beaut of a bargain.

**XV Monastrell 2000** `16` `−£5.00`
Sports the cheekiest label I've seen for years with the alcohol content, 15%, scrawled large. And what a big, deep wine it is, full of interest and nuances. Superstores only.

## KWIK SAVE RED

**Don Darias Red NV** `14.5` `−£3.50`
Old war horse in fighting fettle.

**Flamenco Red NV** `11` `−£3.50`

**Viña Cana Rioja** `14` `−£5.00`
**Crianza 1998,**
**Somerfield**
Good tangy stuff.

## M & S RED

**Almuran Monastrell** `15` `−£5.00`
**2000**
Soft, ripe, handsomely textured and warm.

**Las Falleras 2000** `13.5` `−£3.50`
A brisk, characterful barbecue wine. Full of toasty flavours.

**Marisa Tempranillo** `13` `−£5.00`
**2000**

Very very very soft. Good to pour over sausages and mash.

**Rioja Roseral Crianza** `13` `£5–7`
**1998**
Dry finish, bit bony, after a plummy opening of no great impact.

## MORRISONS RED

**Baldoma Tinto Seleccio** `14` `−£5.00`
**1999**
Ripe yet dry to finish.

**Gran Feudo Navarra** `13` `−£5.00`
**Crianza 1997**

**Poema Old Vine** `14` `−£5.00`
**Garnacha 2000**
Plummy fruit with hints of nut and herb. Suit spicy food. And being chilled.

**Rio Rojo Tinto NV** `14` `−£3.50`

**Torres Sangre de Toro** `14` `£5–7`
**1999**
The bullnecked brand with simple plummy fruit and gentle tannins.

**Vega del Rio Reserva** `13` `£7–10`
**Rioja 1994**

**Vega del Rio Rioja 1998** `13` `£5–7`
Very coconutty and dry.

## SAFEWAY RED

**Baltasar Gracian** `13` `−£5.00`
**Tempranillo 1999**

**Campo Viejo Crianza** `12` `£5–7`
**1998**

Finishes on its face instead of its feet.

**Castillo Ygay Rioja** `13.5` `£13–20`
**Gran Reserva 1989**
Old-fashioned, subtly oxidised, pruney style – good for rich game dishes – with hints of liquorice and gravy. Almost sweet as it finishes.

**Ceremonia, Utiel** `16.5` `£7–10`
**Requena 1996**
Stunning class here. Loads of woody flavours, hedgerow and orchard fruits and superb tannins. It's a very potent red. 48 stores.

**Cosme Palacio y** `17` `£5–7`
**Hermanos, Rioja 1998**
The essence of how truly elegant and fine Rioja can become.

**Faustino I Gran** `11` `£10–13`
**Reserva 1994**
I like the tannins . . . but on any other wine but this . . .

**Faustino V Rioja** `12.5` `£7–10`
**Reserva 1996**
Has some bulk to its fruit but overall rather too much bulk on the price tag in relation to this fruit is what spoils the experience.

**Marques de Murrieta** `10` `£7–10`
**Reserva Tinto 1997**
So fruitless it's like looking for life on Pluto. Selected stores.

**Marques de Riscal Rioja** `10` `£13–20`
**Gran Reserve 1994**
You breathe in coconut. You spit out tannins. Selected stores.

**Navasques Navarra** `16` `–£5.00`
**1999**
Energy, bite, character and class – has fine, savoury tannins, touches of thyme, and hints of cocoa to the berries.

**Siglo 1881 1999** `10` `–£5.00`
Dire. Selected stores.

**Valdepeñas Reserva** `15` `–£5.00`
**Aged in Oak 1995,**
**Safeway**

**Young Vatted** `15` `–£3.50`
**Tempranillo 1999,**
**Safeway**
Very dry, aromatic and full of interesting edges – including a tannic one. Highly drinkable and food friendly.

## SAINSBURY'S RED

**Alteza 600 Old Vines** `16` `–£5.00`
**Garnacha NV**
Burnt leaves and ripe plums, dry tannins, vivid acidity and fruit balance. Superb for food or mood. Selected stores.

**Alteza 750 Tempranillo** `16` `–£5.00`
**NV**
Why drink expensive Rioja when there is this compelling reason to spend so much less? Gorgeously rich fruit which stays firm and dry even as it strikes with such vivacity. Most stores.

**Alteza Tempranillo** `14` `–£5.00`
**Cabernet Sauvignon La**
**Mancha 1999**
More Temp than Cab, this very

energetic wine has loads of spicy, food-friendly richness and rampant ripeness. Most stores.

**Dama de Toro 1998**   15.5   −£5.00
A very civilised, softly fruity quaffing wine composed of plums, berries and cherries. Most stores.

**Epulum Rioja Crianza,**   13.5   £5–7
**Bodegas Olarra 1998**
Very ripe, baked overtone on the finish.

**Jumilla NV, Sainsbury's**   15.5   −£5.00

**Navarra NV,**   16   −£5.00
**Sainsbury's**
Superb bargain. Lovely tobacco-edged fruit, classy and rich, with loads of freshness and depth behind it. Terrific quaffing wine.

**Ochoa Gran Reserva,**   16   £10–13
**Navarra 1993**
A distinguished grandee of a rich treat: tobacco-edged, rich, very dry and subtly figgy (and a touch raisiny), this is an unusually mature wine to find in a supermarket. It's at its peak of drinkability. Limited distribution.

**Ondarre Reserva Rioja**   15   £7–10
**1996**
Oddly obvious and soft for a Rioja, extremely fruity and full. Great with robust food – and robust company. Limited distribution.

**Stowells of Chelsea**   13   −£3.50
**Tempranillo NV (3 litre box)**

Price band indicates the 75cl equivalent.

**Valencia Oak Aged NV,**   13.5   −£5.00
**Sainsbury's**

**Viña Albali Gran**   15   £5–7
**Reserva 1993**

**Viña Ardanza Rioja**   13.5   £10–13
**Reserva 1994**

## SOMERFIELD RED

**Don Darias Red NV**   14.5   −£3.50
Old war horse in fighting fettle.

**Espiral Tempranillo**   15.5   £5–7
**Barrique Somontano 1999**
Delicious. And perkier than many a Rioja costing more. Selected stores.

**Pergola Tempranillo**   13   −£5.00
**2000, Somerfield**
Very juicy.

**Santa Elisa La Mancha**   10   −£3.50
**Red 1999**
Bananas? Crème of vanilla, too.

**Sierra Alta Cabernet**   16   −£5.00
**Sauvignon 1999**
Superb texture and classic soft blackberries. Terrific tannins here. Selected stores.

**Sierra Alta Tempranillo**   14.5   −£5.00
**1999**
Very dry, very. Has plums in it and old boots.

**Valencia Red NV,**   13.5   −£3.50
**Somerfield**
PTA party wine – good wine for heavy smokers.

Viña Cana Rioja `14` `−£5.00`
Crianza 1998,
Somerfield
Good tangy stuff.

Viña Cana Rioja `15` `£5–7`
Reserva 1995,
Somerfield
Very solemn tannins mitigate the
smiling generosity of the warm
fruit.

## SPAR RED

Rioja Crianza 1997, `13` `£5–7`
Spar
Has some good plummy richness,
expensive, but of interest to Balti
eaters.

Rioja NV, Spar `12` `£5–7`
Bit thin on the finish. Bones
showing through the flesh (what
there is of it).

Valencia Soft Red NV, `12.5` `−£3.50`
Spar
Has a dry finish to some plummy
fruit.

## TESCO RED

Campillo Reserva Rioja `13` `£10–13`
1995

Campo Viejo Crianza `13` `£5–7`
1997

Don Darias NV `15.5` `−£5.00`

Huge Juicy Red NV, `15.5` `−£5.00`
Tesco
Lives up to its name and very
vivaciously so. Brilliant texture,
tannins and tenacious richness.
Brilliant with spicy Balti dishes.
Most stores.

Las Postas Rioja 2000 `14` `−£3.50`
Incredible value but requires
spicy food to show off its best.

Marques de Chive `14.5` `−£5.00`
Reserva 1995, Tesco
Dry, plump, deep, flavoursome –
almost over-ripe. However, with
food (very necessary) it'll perform
small miracles.

Marques de Chive `15` `−£3.50`
Tempranillo NV, Tesco

Marques de Grinon `16` `£5–7`
Rioja 1999
Consistently one of the most
classy Riojas, polished yet
characterful, and in this vintage
softer and riper than previous
ones.

Orobio Tempranillo `16` `−£5.00`
Rioja 1999
Superb example of Rioja which
puts to arid shame many much-
vaunted compatriots pounds
more expensive. Has complex
levels of flavour, fine tannins, a
very classy finish, and overall a
really compelling texture. A
remarkable bargain under-a-fiver.
And only a very vague hint of the
dreaded wood vanilla.

Senorio de los Llanos `14` `−£5.00`
Valdepeñas Gran
Reserva 1994

Senorio de los Llanos | 14 | −£5.00
Valdepeñas Reserva
1996

Simply Garnacha 1999, | 14 | −£3.50
Tesco

Tempranillo 1999, | 15 | −£5.00
Tesco

Torres Coronas | 16 | £5–7
Tempranillo 1999
Excellent layers of firm, plump
cherries and blackberries, lovely
tannins and all round elegance.
Why can't Rioja producers turn
out Tempranillo like this?

Torres Sangre de Toro | 14 | £5–7
1999
The bullnecked brand with
simple plummy fruit and gentle
tannins.

Viña Mara Gran | 13 | £7–10
Reserva Rioja 1994
Another Tesco 'Finest' wine.
Expensive, not as compact as the
cheaper Viña Mara, and finishes
less emphatically.

Viña Mara Rioja | 15.5 | £7–10
Reserva 1996, Tesco
One of Tesco's so-called 'Finest'
range, this is a superior example
of the breed for it has highly
civilised tannins balancing rich,
deep fruit of class and precision.

Viña Mara Rioja, Tesco | 14 | −£5.00

Viña Montana | 16 | −£5.00
Monastrell/Merlot 1998
Superb texture here, classy, ripe
and all-enveloping and the soft

tannins are yielding up meaty
undertones.

Zorro Tempranillo/ | 14 | −£5.00
Monastrell 2000
Ripe, dry and hugely curry
friendly.

## WAITROSE RED

Chivite Coleccion 125 | 16 | £13–20
Reserva 1996
Very elegant and rich, and
superbly well-organised. Lovely
stuff.

Cosme Palacio Rioja | 15 | £5–7
1998
Smooth, rich and deep. Very
elegantly tailored.

Espiral Oaked | 15 | £5–7
Tempranillo 1998

Espiral Tempranillo/ | 16 | −£5.00
Cabernet Sauvignon
1998
Tobacco, tannins, concentration,
class – plus character and bite.
Terrific stuff.

Marques de Grinon | 17 | £10–13
Dominio de Valdepusa
Syrah 1998
A great Spanish wine offering a
wonderful concentrated richness
and lithe plumpness: plums,
liquorice, chocolate and coffee
plus, would you credit, coriander
and cowslips. A heady brew here
of Wordsworthian grandiosity.

Palacio de Otazu | 16 | £7–10
Reserva, Navarra 1996

Super texture and tightness to the ripe fruit. Very elegant and excitingly biting for the palate.

**Torneo Reserva, Valdepeñas 1996**    14    −£5.00
A juicy, spicy food wine.

**Torres Gran Sangre de Toro Reserva 1996**    16    £5–7
Wonderful vintage of the old warhorse – the best for some time. Great tannins, herbs, richness of layered fruit and a striking finish.

**Totally Tinto Tempranillo NV**    14    −£5.00
Ripe curry wine.

**Totally Two Thousand Tempranillo NV (magnum)**    15.5    −£3.50

**Viña Fuerte Garnacha, Calatayud 2000**    15.5    −£5.00
Brilliant value: spiced berries, deep tannins and a long rich finish of weight and wit.

**Viña Herminia Graciano Reserva Rioja 1995**    14    £7–10
Vanilla and roasted coconut aroma you either like or loathe.

**Viña Herminia Rioja Crianza 1996**    14    £5–7
Dusting of tannins keeps some semblance of sanity as the fruit goes sodden.

**Viña Lanciano Reserva 1995**    13    £13–20
Very juicy and expensive.

## ASDA WHITE

**Baron de Ley Rioja Blanco 1999**    13.5    −£5.00
Somewhat muted and limping on the finish.

**Bodegas Cerrosol Sauvignon Rueda 1998**    15    −£5.00

**Moscatel de Valencia NV, Asda**    16    −£3.50
Brilliant sweet wine for crème brulées, ice creams and fruit salad. Has a delicious undertone of marmalade.

**Spanish Oaked White NV, Asda**    15.5    −£3.50

## BOOTHS WHITE

**Castillo de Maluenda Blanco 2000**    15    −£3.50
What a price for such dry, elegant fruit.

**Castillo de Maluenda Rosado 2000**    13.5    −£3.50

**Estrella, Moscatel de Valencia NV**    16    −£5.00
Superb muscat sweetness and hints of marmalade. Marvellous with ice cream.

**Palacio de Bornos Rueda 2000**    15    −£5.00
Excellent texture, gently oleaginous and ripe, but not remotely OTT.

**Santa Lucia Viura, Vino de la Tierra Manchuela 1999**    14    −£3.50
Bargain – bonny bargain.

## SPANISH WHITE

**Viña Albali Rosado** `13.5` −£5.00
2000
Plums and dry lemons.

## BUDGENS WHITE

**Blanco, La Nature** `13.5` −£5.00
**Organic, La Mancha**
**2000**
Expensive, dry, hints of raspberry
and lemon. Disappointing for
organic grapes.

**Castillo de Liria** `15.5` −£5.00
**Moscatel de Valencia**
**NV**

**Masia Monistrol** `13` −£5.00
**Chardonnay Macabeo**
**2000**
Bit confused as it surges.

## CO-OP WHITE

**Gandia Grenache Rosé** `14.5` −£5.00
**1999**
Superb little cherry-ripe rosé of
some class. Superstores only.

**Jaume Serra** `16` −£5.00
**Chardonnay 1999**
From one of the unsung heroes of
Catalan winemaking. A
ridiculously well priced, rich,
handsomely textured, charming
wine of mannered complexity
and style.

**Torres Viña Sol 2000** `15.5` −£5.00
Lovely tangy melons and lemons.
Superstores only.

## KWIK SAVE WHITE

**Moscatel de Valencia,** `16` −£3.50
**Somerfield**
Delicious honey and subtle
orange marmalade fruit.
Marvellous with complex, rich
puddings.

## M & S WHITE

**Moscatel de Valencia** `16` −£5.00
**2000**
Lovely waxy richness with fine
honeyed fruit with touches of
raspberry and very subtle
marmalade.

## MORRISONS WHITE

**Poema Sauvignon** `13.5` −£5.00
**Blanc 2000**
Perfumed and oriental food
friendly.

**Torres San Valentin** `12` −£5.00
**2000**
Sweet, fat, rich fruit of little
subtlety.

**Viña Albali Rosado** `13.5` −£3.50
**2000**
Plums and dry lemons.

## SAFEWAY WHITE

**El Velero Rosé** `12` −£3.50
**Valdepeñas 2000**
Terribly insubstantial. Almost the
ghost of a rosé.

**Faustino V Rioja** `5` £5−7
**Crianza NV**

Horrific overwoody fruit. Might as well suck a plank of balsa and chew a melon.

**Marques de Murrieta** `12` `£7–10`
**Capellania 1996**
Too much chewy wood.

## SOMERFIELD WHITE

**Castillo Imperial** `13.5` `–£3.50`
**Blanco NV, Somerfield**

**Don Darias White NV** `14` `–£5.00`

**Mimbral Penedés** `14` `–£5.00`
**Chardonnay 2000**
Fatter edged Chardonnay with touches of walnut and lemon.

**Moscatel de Valencia,** `16` `–£3.50`
**Somerfield**
Delicious honey and subtle orange marmalade fruit. Marvellous with complex, rich puddings.

**Pergola Oaked Viura** `15` `–£5.00`
**2000, Somerfield**
Dry, nutty, hint of lemon. Very fresh and crisply styled.

**Viña Cana Rioja Blanco** `14.5` `–£5.00`
**2000, Somerfield**
A more adventurous style of white Rioja and very good it is: crisper, fresher, more Italian in feel.

## SPAR WHITE

**Perfect for Parties** `10` `–£3.50`
**White NV, Spar (1 litre)**

Price band indicates the 75cl equivalent.

**Valencia Dry White** `13.5` `–£3.50`
**NV, Spar**

## TESCO WHITE

**Moscatel de Valencia,** `16` `–£3.50`
**Tesco**
Quite superb! Has an overtone of orange marmalade to the honey and the raspberry and pear sweetness. Wonderful taint-free screwcap!

**Torres Viña Sol 2000** `15.5` `–£5.00`
Lovely tangy melons and lemons.

## WAITROSE WHITE

**Albarino Pazo de** `12` `£7–10`
**Seoane, Rias Baixas**
**2000**

**Cune Monopole Rioja** `14` `£5–7`
**Blanco 1998**
Very ripe. Suits Tandoori prawns.

**Lustau Moscatel de** `16` `–£5.00`
**Chipiona NV**
Superb spicy honey here. Brilliant wine to accompany sweet pastry desserts.

**Palacio de Bornos** `15` `–£5.00`
**Rueda 2000**
Excellent texture, gently oleaginous and ripe, but not remotely OTT.

**Torres Viña Sol 2000** `15.5` `–£5.00`
Lovely tangy melons and lemons.

# TUNISIA

Can grow fine wine grapes . . . but . . .

## SAINSBURY'S RED

**Accademia del Sole**    11    £5–7
**Carignan 2000**
Ripe, sweet, overpriced and very
over-cooked as a specimen of
fruitiness. Selected stores.

# URUGUAY

Has, in Tannat, its own grape that is the key to making some terrific red wines.

## M & S RED

**Polo Sur Pisano Family** 14 £7–10
**Reserve Tannat 2000**
Finishes with eccentric sweetness
for a ten quid wine.

## SAINSBURY'S RED

**Bright Brothers** 14 –£5.00
**Merlot/Tannat 1998**

**Don Pascual Reserve** 16 £5–7
**Tannat 2000**
Energy and richness, depth and
daring – this is a terrific,
tannically rich red of gallant,
fighting-style richness and
warmth. 174 selected stores.

## SOMERFIELD RED

**Bright Brothers Tannat** 16 –£5.00
**Cabernet Franc 2000**
Wow! It explodes with flavour
and personality. Great food wine.

## WAITROSE RED

**Pisano Family Reserve** 13 £7–10
**Tannat 1999**
Very sweet.

## SOMERFIELD WHITE

**Bright Brothers** 15.5 –£5.00
**Uruguayan Sauvignon/**
**Semillon 2000**
Immensely quaffable, crisp/soft
fruit, refreshing to finish. Lovely
aperitif.

# USA

Vast untapped potential in more States than you would believe possible.

## ASDA RED

**Rosemount 'V' NV** `14` `£5–7`
Rather a guilty edge of richness.
A parvenu conscience perhaps?

**Garnet Point Shiraz** `15.5` `–£5.00`
**Cabernet 2000**
Rich savoury fruit, touch of spice,
soft accessible tannins. Perfect
vegetable quaffing and bangers-
and-mash-friendly fruit. Has a
warm, ready charm.

**Talus Merlot 1998** `13` `£5–7`
More sweets packed in a bottle.

**Talus Zinfandel 1998** `13` `£5–7`
Very sweet.

## BOOTHS RED

**Stonybrook Merlot** `15.5` `£5–7`
**1999**
Lovely dry leather and cassis fruit.

**Turning Leaf Cabernet** `12` `£5–7`
**Sauvignon 1998**
Makes a good marinade for a
dead cow but not so thrilling for a
live tongue.

## BUDGENS RED

**Garnet Point Shiraz** `15.5` `–£5.00`
**Cabernet 2000**
Rich savoury fruit, touch of spice,
soft accessible tannins. Perfect
vegetable quaffing and bangers-
and-mash-friendly fruit. Has a
warm, ready charm.

**Glen Ellen Cabernet** `13` `£5–7`
**Sauvignon 1998**

**Marc Xero Merlot 1999** `14` `–£5.00`
Some good tannins to the dry
berries.

**Sutter Home Merlot** `13` `£5–7`
**1998**

## CO-OP RED

**California Premium** `13.5` `–£3.50`
**Red NV, Co-op**
A first rate curry wine. Has
fatness and sweetness and
clingability (to chillies).

**Fetzer Valley Oaks** `14.5` `£5–7`
**Cabernet Sauvignon**
**1998**
Mildly diverting blackberries.

Superstores only.

'Laid Back Ruby'     15    −£5.00
California Ruby
Cabernet 1999, Co-op

Sebastiani Sonoma     15.5    £7–10
Cask Old Vine
Zinfandel 1998
Expensive but luxuriously well
appointed. The scaffolding of the
rich wood does not mar the
brickwork, slightly rococo in
parts, in any way.

## M & S RED

Clear Lake Cabernet     15    −£5.00
Franc 2000
Deliciously textured, soft plums
which has well-balanced tannins
to buttress the fruit.

Freedom Ridge Shiraz     13.5    £5–7
2000
Soft, rich, ripe and very OK with
spicy Middle Eastern meat balls.

Live Oak Road Old     13.5    £7–10
Bush Vine Zinfandel
2000
Very soft, ripe and ready, but ten
quid? Not in my book. If it was a
fiver it would rate 15 for it does
have some gusto on the finish.

Zamora Zinfandel 1999     12    £5–7
Smells like a pear-drop with
raspberry essence on it. The fruit,
struggling to recover from this
chutzpah, is more soft, ripe Cal
squashed fruit.

## MORRISONS RED

Beringer Zinfandel     15    £5–7
1999
Lovely dusky dryness with berries
of some substance at its core.

Blossom Hill California     10    −£5.00
Red NV
Vomit-worthy sweetness.

Blossom Hill Merlot     13    £5–7
1999
Expensive, touch expensive.

Fetzer Bonterra     14    £7–10
Cabernet Sauvignon
1997

Glen Ellen Pinot Noir     9    £5–7
1997
Ugh!

Glen Ellen Zinfandel     13.5    £5–7
1998

Ironstone Vineyards     16    £5–7
Cabernet Franc 1997
Really buzzes with layers of spice,
plums, blackcurrants, raspberries,
chocolate and superbly soft
tannins.

Ironstone Vineyards     14.5    −£5.00
Shiraz 1998

'M' Californian Red NV     14    −£3.50
Very bright and well-packed with
berried fruit. Excellent texture.

Nathanson Creek     14    −£5.00
Cabernet Sauvignon
1999
Deep flavoured, curry-friendly
(yet dry) fruit. Very mouth filling.

Turning Leaf Cabernet Sauvignon 1997 `12` `£5–7`

Turning Leaf Zinfandel 1996 `12.5` `£5–7`

## SAFEWAY RED

Echelon Merlot 1998 `15` `£7–10`

Pacific Coast Ruby Cabernet 2000 `12` `–£5.00`
Selected stores.

Pepperwood Grove Syrah 1999 `13.5` `£5–7`
Very jammy and with ripe tannins. Selected stores.

## SAINSBURY'S RED

Blossom Hill Californian Red NV `10` `–£5.00`
Vomit-worthy sweetness.

Buckeye Vineyard Single Vineyard Series Cabernet Sauvignon, Kendall Jackson 1996 `16.5` `£13–20`
Rather splendid in its isolated, plough-a-lonely-furrow fruitiness and superbly tannic tenacity. Has great individuality and depth, class and richness. Gripping from nose to throat. 3 selected stores.

Four Vines Paso Robles Zinfandel 1997 `11` `£7–10`
Simply too juicy. And the price tag is an outrage. 150 selected stores.

Kendall Jackson Vintners Reserve Pinot Noir 1998 `16` `£7–10`
Superb Pinot aroma of truffles and farmyards and the fruit, though too juicy to be classic, has lovely cherries and wild raspberries. Good tannins. 130 selected stores.

La Crema Pinot Noir 1998 `16` `£10–13`
Lovely dry classic Pinot finish to fine fruit of cherries and plums. Has elegance and rich charm. 35 selected stores.

Marc Xero Merlot 1999 `14` `–£5.00`
Some good tannins to the dry berries.

## SOMERFIELD RED

Californian Dry Red NV, Somerfield `14` `–£5.00`

Hidden Falls Carnelian Merlot 2000 `11` `–£3.50`
Sticky tannins and toffee-rich fruit of great oddity.

Laguna Canyon Zinfandel NV `10` `–£5.00`
Dislike the aroma of fruit salad (baked) and loathe the crudity of the fruit. Not even a Balti would redeem it.

Marc Xero Merlot 1999 `14` `–£5.00`
Some good tannins to the dry berries.

Talus Zinfandel 1998 `13` `£5–7`
Very sweet.

Turning Leaf Cabernet Sauvignon 1997 `12` `£5–7`

Turning Leaf Zinfandel 1996 `12.5` `£5–7`

## SPAR RED

Fetzer Valley Oaks Cabernet Sauvignon 1997 `15.5` `£5–7`

Heritage Red 1999 `14` `−£5.00`
Soupy but has some textured tannins to buttress this. Good pasta plonk.

## TESCO RED

Fetzer Barrel Select Pinot Noir 1997 `15` `£7–10`
Unusual tobacco scented prologue, lovely texture to the cherries and a hint of truffle, and a real classy, if ripe and New Worldy, finish. Overall, a surprisingly accomplished Pinot.

Fetzer Barrel Select Zinfandel 1997 `15.5` `£7–10`
Gushes with ripe, well-meaning fruit, touch sweet on the finish, and the tannins are well integrated and soft. Has a lovely layered richness.

Fetzer Syrah 1997 `12` `£5–7`
Getting old at four years of age and it's lost its vibrancy and the bravura edge to the Pinot.

Gallo Turning Leaf Zinfandel 1998 `12` `£5–7`

Quietly rich and quaffable at four quid but at £6.50 it's very poor value.

West Coast California Cabernet/Shiraz 2000, Tesco `12` `−£5.00`
Don't like the overripeness of the smell on the finish. But with curried goat's liver with pickled okra it might work.

West Coast Merlot Reserve 1999, Tesco `14.5` `£5–7`
Dry, rich, leathery hints to blackcurrant ripeness. One of Tesco's so-called 'Finest' range. Most stores.

West Coast Ruby Cabernet/Merlot 1999, Tesco `15` `−£5.00`

West Coast Zinfandel Reserve 1999, Tesco `13` `£5–7`
Juicy ands simperingly sweet. One of Tesco's so-called 'Finest' range. Most stores.

## WAITROSE RED

Bonterra Vineyards Merlot 1997 (organic) `16.5` `£7–10`
Thrillingly ripe, herby tannins and great levels of fruit (prunes, cherries and blackberries).

Fetzer Valley Oaks Cabernet Sauvignon 1998 `14.5` `£5–7`
Mildly diverting blackberries.

**Hedges Three** `13` `£13–20`
**Vineyards Columbia**
**Valley 1998**
Very tannic and interesting but at
sixteen quid it should have more
elements.

**Ironstone Vineyards** `10` `£5–7`
**Zinfandel 1998**
Not overkeen on its lushness.

**Yorkville Cellars** `14` `£7–10`
**Cabernet Franc 1997**
**(organic)**

**Yorkville Petit Verdot** `16` `£7–10`
**1997**
Much more like it, Yorkville!
Brilliantly bustling tannins to
lovely purple damson fruit. Spicy,
deep, warm.

## ASDA WHITE

**Ca'del Solo Malvasia** `12` `£7–10`
**Bianca, Bonny Doon**
**1998**
Odd cosmetic dryness and near
rawness of expression. Only at
the Bristol Supercentre.

**Garnet Point Semillon** `14.5` `–£5.00`
**Chardonnay 2000**
Refreshing tangy satsumas, lemon
and melon.

## BOOTHS WHITE

**Stonybrook** `14` `–£5.00`
**Chardonnay 2000**
Rich and ripe fruit but the
controlling acids balance it well.

## BUDGENS WHITE

**Garnet Point Semillon** `14.5` `–£5.00`
**Chardonnay 2000**
Refreshing tangy satsumas, lemon
and melon.

## CO-OP WHITE

**Garnet Point** `15.5` `–£5.00`
**Chardonnay-Chenin**
**1997**

**Sebastiani Sonoma** `15.5` `£7–10`
**Chardonnay 1998**
Expensive but luxuriously well
appointed. The scaffolding of the
rich wood does not mar the
brickwork, slightly rococo in
parts, in any way. Superstores
only.

**'The Big Chill'** `13.5` `–£5.00`
**California Colombard**
**Chardonnay 1999,**
**Co-op**

**'The Big Chill'** `13.5` `–£5.00`
**California Colombard**
**Chardonnay 2000,**
**Co-op**
Limey touches to the fruit.

## M & S WHITE

**Clear Lake Chardonnay** `15.5` `–£5.00`
**2000**
Bruised fruit (soft and ripe),
melon, cauliflower and pears. A
lot going on here. Very vivacious.

**Clear Lake Rosé** `12` `–£5.00`
**Merlot/Cabernet 2000**

Adolescent fruit – almost.
Lollipop rich and cheeky.

**Dunnigan Lane Fume** `15.5` `£5–7`
**Blanc 2000**
Very elegant, slightly creamy,
smoky fruit.

**Gardeners Grove** `15.5` `£7–10`
**Chardonnay 2000**
Rich, ready, stylish. Very
controlled undertone of ripeness
which finishes well.

## MORRISONS WHITE

**Glen Ellen Chardonnay** `15.5` `£5–7`
**1998**
Delicious rich fruit combining a
touch of spicy pear to the usual
melon/lemon/pineapple etc.

**Ironstone Chardonnay** `10` `£5–7`
**1998**

**'M' Californian White** `13` `–£3.50`
**NV**
Dry and indelicate. The label is
probably the worst Californian in
existence (5 out of 20 here).

**Nathanson Creek** `11` `–£5.00`
**White Zinfandel 1999**
Very sweet and simpering.

**Wente Johannesburg** `16.5` `–£5.00`
**Riesling 1997**
Terrific spice and lime sherbet
fruit here. Not wholly dry, to be
sure, but it bounces with life and
would be terrific with Thai food.

## SAFEWAY WHITE

**Bonterra Muscat 1999** `14` `£5–7`
**(half bottle) (organic)**

**Pacific Coast** `14` `–£5.00`
**Chardonnay 2000**
Rich, fleshy fruit. Needs Thai
cuisine possibly. Selected stores.

**Pyramid Lake Napa** `8` `–£5.00`
**Gamay Rosé NV**
Revoltingly cosmetic and
'manufactured'. An insult to the
grape.

## SAINSBURY'S WHITE

**Blossom Hill NV** `10` `–£5.00`
So boring you must be careful not
to yawn as you sip. Selected
stores.

**Bonterra Muscat 1999** `14` `£5–7`
**(half bottle) (organic)**

**Fetzer Valley Oaks** `13.5` `£5–7`
**Rosé 2000**
Very rich and ripe. Most stores.

**Kendall Jackson Single** `13` `£10–13`
**Vineyard Series**
**Camelot Chardonnay**
**1998**
Too woody for me. 3 selected
stores.

**Kendall Jackson** `15` `£7–10`
**Vintners Reserve**
**Chardonnay 1998**
Very forward, creamy and rich,
and woody. A brilliant wine to
match with all kinds of poultry
dishes. 130 selected stores.

## AMERICAN WHITE

**Sutter Home** `14` `−£5.00`
**Gewürztraminer 2000**
Sweet rich fruit and peach and
strawberry. Suit Peking duck.
Most stores.

**Sutter Home** `14` `−£5.00`
**Sauvignon Blanc 2000**
Simple lip-smacking gooseberries.
Most stores.

### SOMERFIELD WHITE

**Fetzer Sundial** `14` `£5–7`
**Chardonnay 1999**
Tending to get expensive.

**Sebastiani Sonoma** `15.5` `£7–10`
**Chardonnay 1998**
Expensive but luxuriously well-
appointed. The scaffolding of the
rich wood does not mar the
brickwork, slightly rococo in
parts, in any way.

**Talus Chardonnay 1998** `16.5` `£5–7`
Superb value fruit for you get
authentic California all-surfin'
fruit and sunshine. Deep and
delicious.

### SPAR WHITE

**Heritage Californian** `10` `−£5.00`
**White 1999**
Almost revoltingly cosmetic and
perfumed.

### TESCO WHITE

**Fetzer Barrel Select** `15` `£7–10`
**Chardonnay 1997**

**Fetzer Valley Oaks** `13.5` `£5–7`
**Rosé 2000**
Very rich and ripe. Most stores.

**Gallo Turning Leaf** `13` `£5–7`
**Chardonnay 1999**
Expensive for the level of
excitement on offer. It doesn't
seen complete.

**West Coast California** `14.5` `−£5.00`
**Chardonnay 1999,**
**Tesco**

### WAITROSE WHITE

**Bonterra Muscat 1999** `14` `£5–7`
**(half bottle) (organic)**
Gently honeyed aperitif.

**Fetzer Echo Ridge** `15.5` `£5–7`
**Viognier 2000**
Very well put together fruit and
acids offering tangy peaches and
gentle lemons.

**Mandolin Californian** `11` `£5–7`
**Chardonnay 1999**

# PART 2

# FORTIFIED AND SPARKLING WINES

# FORTIFIED WINES

## ASDA

**Dow's LBV Port 1995** `14.5` `£7–10`
(Portugal)
Has some real texture and the
sweet plums and subtle bitter
cherries are helped, in the end, by
some husky tannins.

**Fine Ruby Port, Asda** `14` `£5–7`

**Graham's LBV Port** `13.5` `£10–13`
1994 (Portugal)
Rich ripe alcoholic plums which
strike warm on the finish.

**Manzanilla, Asda** `17` `£5–7`
A staggeringly well-endowed,
aromatic, yet subtle sherry of
immense charm and richness.
Unusually well-textured and soft
(uniquely so, I suggest) and so
warm and approachable it must
convert those who previously
found the tea leaf and hard
edge of this style of wine too
austere.

**Tawny Port, Asda** `15` `£5–7`

**Warre's Optima 10** `13.5` `£7–10`
Year Old Tawny Port
NV (Portugal) 50cl
Sweet, brown/orange colour,
hint of caramel toffee. Good with
fruit cake.

**Warre's Warrior** `13` `£7–10`
Special Reserve Port
NV (Portugal)
Sweet and rich with a touch of
wet rag on the finish.

## BOOTHS

**Amontillado del** `16` `£7–10`
Puerto, Lustau
Sure, it smells mouldy and too
ripe for comfort but imagine a
glass, well-chilled, with a bowl of
almonds and an absorbing book.
Great combination.

**Banyuls Chapoutier** `14` `£7–10`
1997 (50cl)
Perfect with chocolate at the end
of a meal.

**Churchills Dry White** `13` `£7–10`
Port

**Finest Reserve Port,** `14.5` `£7–10`
Booths

**Fino NV, Booths** `14` `–£5.00`
Has a good chewy texture to its
tangy minerals. Not as bone dry
as some.

**Henriques & Henriques** `13` `£10–13`
**5 Year Old Madeira NV**
Expensive curiosity. Goes with
sweet digestive crackers and the
dentured set.

**Lustau Old East India** `17` `£7–10`
**Sherry**
Magnificent name, recalling the
excesses of the Empire, just as the
intense sweet fruit (molasses and
butterscotch with crème brulée
overtones) is redolent of excess
around Victorian dinner tables. A
taste of history. Quite marvellous
stuff.

**Manzanilla Sherry,** `15` `–£5.00`
**Booths**

**Medium Amontillado** `15.5` `–£5.00`
**NV, Booths**

**Niepoort LBV Port** `14` `£10–13`
**1996**
Sweet, rich, figgy wine – good
with Christmas cake.

**Niepoort Ruby Port** `14` `£7–10`

**Dow's LBV 1995** `14.5` `£7–10`
**(Portugal)**
Has some real texture and the
sweet plums and subtle bitter
cherries are helped, in the end, by
some husky tannins.

**Graham's LBV Port** `13.5` `£10–13`
**1994 (Portugal)**
Rich ripe alcoholic plums which
strike warm on the finish.

**Warre's Warrior** `13` `£7–10`
**Special Reserve Port**
**NV (Portugal)**
Sweet and rich with a touch of
wet rag on the finish.

## MORRISONS

**Dow's LBV Port 1995** `14.5` `£7–10`
**(Portugal)**
Has some real texture and the
sweet plums and subtle bitter
cherries are helped, in the end, by
some husky tannins.

**Fonseca Bin No 27 Fine** `13` `£7–10`
**Reserve Port NV**
**(Portugal)**
Thick, rich, sweet cherries and
custard. A winter warmer for
extremely cold hearts.

**Graham's LBV Port** `13.5` `£10–13`
**1994 (Portugal)**
Rich ripe alcoholic plums which
strike warm on the finish.

**Taylor's Late Bottled** `15` `£7–10`
**Vintage Port 1995**
**(Portugal)**
Good thickness of fruit allied to
rich layers of plums and baked
blackcurrants. Raisins on the
finish, and good lashings of
tannin.

**Warre's Warrior** `13` `£7–10`
**Special Reserve Port**
**NV (Portugal)**
Sweet and rich with a touch of
wet rag on the finish.

## SAFEWAY

**Blandy's Duke of** `16` `£7–10`
**Clarence Rich Madeira**
Wonderful old-fashioned plot:
Dickensian, warm, sweet,
sentimental. Drink it with
Christmas cake. At most stores.

González Byass Tio    14   £7–10
Pepe Fino Muy Sec NV

Marsala Superiore,    16   £5–7
Garibalde Dolce NV
(18% vol)
Staggeringly rich and figgy.
Wonderful for desserts of all
descriptions (even if they all come
served at once on the same grand
plate). Or pour it over ice cream.

Taylor's 10 Year Old    14   £13–20
Tawny Port NV
Sweet but has some rich layers of
fig and roast plum. Needs
sweetmeats to accompany it. Has
a very superior, thick texture.

Taylor's LBV Port 1995    15   £7–10
Good thickness of fruit allied to
rich layers of plums and baked
blackcurrants. Raisins on the
finish, and good lashings of
tannin.

Vintage Character Port,    13   £5–7
Safeway

Warre's Optima 10    13.5   £7–10
Year Old Tawny Port
NV 50cl
Sweet, brown/orange colour,
hint of caramel toffee. Good with
fruit cake.

Warre's Traditional    16.5   £13–20
LBV Port 1990
The best LBV I've tasted which
has lovely tannins and rich sweet
plums and blackcurrants. It'll age
for another fifteen years.

Warre's Warrior Finest    13   £7–10
Reserve Port NV

## SAINSBURY

Cockburn's 10 Year Old    13.5   £7–10
Tawny Port (half
bottle)
Cloying sweet fruit. Most stores.

Cockburn's Light    14.5   £7–10
White Port
Delicious, if absurdly priced.
Selected stores.

Dow's LBV 1995    14.5   £7–10
Has some real texture and the
sweet plums and subtle bitter
cherries are helped, in the end, by
some husky tannins.

Dow's Quinta do    16.5   £13–20
Bonfim Vintage Port
1987
A superbly well-organised, figgily
rich and sweet port with
gorgeous tannins. Beautiful
warmth and texture to it. Limited
distribution.

Fino Sherry,    16   –£5.00
Sainsbury's
Great value for money. Who
needs Tio Pepe?

Fonseca Bin No 27 Fine    13   £7–10
Reserve Port NV
Thick, rich, sweet cherries and
custard. A winter warmer for
extremely cold hearts.

González Byass    16.5   £10–13
Apostoles NV (half
bottle) sherry
Big and bustling yet delicate and
elongated. It's a wine to drink
(one of those dangerous ones)
with Anita Brookner or Michael

Dibdin: a rich, brown, voluptuous, crème-brulée and toffeed wine. Limited distribution.

**González Byass** `17` `£10–13`
**Matusalem NV (half bottle) sherry**
Axel grease to ease the progress of sweetmeats and post-prandial seductions. Limited distribution.

**Graham's 20 Year Old** `14` `£20+`
**Tawny Port**
This is more like what tawny port should be, But those twenty years you have to pay for: £26. The liquid is fine, raisiny and rich. 32 selected stores.

**Graham's LBV Port** `13.5` `£10–13`
**1994**
Rich ripe alcoholic plums which strike warm on the finish.

**Hidalgo Manzanilla la** `16` `£5–7`
**Gitana NV sherry**
Lovely, more textured that JS's own-label Manzanilla. Selected stores.

**Manzanilla, Sainsbury's** `15.5` `–£5.00`
Nuttier, more complex than fino, there's some real intrigue here (especially at this price). Most stores.

**Sainsbury's LBV Port** `15.5` `£7–10`
**1992**

**Solear Manzanilla NV** `16` `£5–7`
Superb baked nuts, tea leaves, hint of Peking duck, and extremely dry minerals. A super aperitif sherry – well-chilled. Limited distribution.

**Tawny Port,** `13` `£5–7`
**Sainsbury's**
Sweet and old-fashioned.

**Taylor's 10 Year Old** `14` `£13–20`
**Tawny Port NV**
Sweet but has some rich layers of fig and roast plum. Needs sweetmeats to accompany it. Has a very superior, thick texture.

**Taylor's 20 Year Old** `12` `£20+`
**Tawny Port NV**
Thirty quid! Seven maybe. Currently at two stores only.

**Taylor's LBV Port 1995** `15` `£7–10`
Good thickness of fruit allied to rich layers of plums and baked blackcurrants. Raisins on the finish, and good lashings of tannin.

**Taylors Vintage Port** `16` `£20+`
**1985**
Again, a corked bottle at first. But, in tip-top condition, this port is extremely voluptuous, hedonistic, richly developed and polished. Currently at two stores only.

**Ten Year Old Tawny** `13` `£10–13`
**Port, Sainsbury's**
Sweet. Pricey.

**Tio Pepe Sherry** `13.5` `£7–10`
A gutsier label can't hide the fact that eight quid is eight quid and Tio Pepe is only marginally more crisp and more aromatic than Sainsbury's £3.99 own-label fino. The choice is yours. Most stores.

**Warre's Optima 10 Year Old Tawny Port (50cl)** `13.5` `£7–10`
Needs a slice of Christmas cake at your elbow. Or a piece of raspberry ripple cheesecake. 130 selected stores.

**Warre's Traditional LBV Port 1990** `16.5` `£13–20`
The best LBV I've tasted which has lovely tannins and rich sweet plums and blackcurrants. It'll age for another fifteen years.

**Warre's Warrior Special Reserve Port NV** `13` `£7–10`
Sweet and rich with a touch of wet rag on the finish.

## SOMERFIELD

**Amontillado Sherry, Somerfield** `15` `–£5.00`
Delicious figgy fruit.

**Cream Sherry, Somerfield** `13` `–£5.00`
Very sweet and grandma friendly.

**Dow's LBV 1995** `14.5` `£7–10`
Has some real texture and the sweet plums and subtle bitter cherries are helped, in the end, by some husky tannins.

**Fino Sherry, Somerfield** `16` `–£5.00`
Remarkable lilt on the finish which stops the wine being characterised as austere. A remarkably toothsome experience.

**Manzanilla Sherry, Somerfield** `16` `–£5.00`
Superb nutty Earl Grey (subtle) tea leaf edge. A wonderful aperitif wine of great distinction.

**Navigators LBV Port 1995, Somerfield** `14.5` `£5–7`
Sweet, yes, but has tannins.

**Navigators Ruby Port, Somerfield** `14` `–£5.00`
Sweet raisins and figs.

**Navigators Vintage Character Port, Somerfield** `14` `£5–7`
Big sweet richness.

**Warre's Optima 10 Year Old Tawny Port NV 50cl** `13.5` `£7–10`
Sweet, brown/orange colour, hint of caramel toffee. Good with fruit cake.

**Warre's Warrior Special Reserve Port NV** `13` `£7–10`
Sweet and rich with a touch of wet rag on the finish.

## SPAR

**Fino Sherry NV, Spar** `14.5` `–£5.00`
Not as saline as many and has a good chewy edge to the finish. Well-chilled this is a classic aperitif.

**Old Cellar LBV Port 1995, Spar** `14` `£7–10`
Sweet and rich and full and wicked with Christmas cake.

**Old Cellar Ruby Port**  `14.5`  `£5–7`
NV, Spar

**10 Year Old Tawny**  `14`  `£10–13`
Port, Tesco
Smells of Christmas cake and
finishes with Christmas fruits and
nuts and raisins. What this wine
goes best with does not require a
PPE degree to figure out.

**Dow's LBV Port 1995**  `14.5`  `£7–10`
Has some real texture and the
sweet plums and subtle bitter
cherries are helped, in the end, by
some husky tannins.

**Dow's Quinta do**  `13`  `£13–20`
Bonfim Vintage Port
1986
Needs another ten to fifteen years
to become truly crusty and
interestingly anecdotal. Worth
laying down at the price.

**Superior Oloroso Seco,**  `16`  `–£3.50`
Tesco
Contemplating that lush amber
hue, like the eyes of a rare snake,
the promise of great things is
evident and so it proves. It is dry
yet it has burnt butter, molasses
(dry), and a wonderful spread of
flavours as it stretches itself over
the palate. A quite superb drink,
well-chilled, by itself, as an
aperitif with nuts etc, and,
supremely, as a bottle to read by.
An Anita Brookner hero would
drink this sherry and smile at life.

**Superior Palo Cortado,**  `16`  `–£5.00`
Tesco
For a pound more you get more

life to the bouquet and a rich,
plumper texture than Tesco's
Superior Oloroso... but the sherry
has many similar features. The
Palo, perhaps, is more elegant
and individual.

**Warre's Otima 10 Year**  `13.5`  `£7–10`
Old Tawny Port NV
50cl
Sweet, brown/orange colour,
hint of caramel toffee. Good with
fruit cake.

## WAITROSE

**10 Year Old Tawny**  `14`  `£10–13`
Port, Waitrose

**Apostoles Palo Cortado**  `18.5`  `£10–13`
Muy Viejo (half bottle)
The ultimate bookworm's lone,
hedonist treat: a sherry of huge
treacly texture (but not
sweetness), baked apple and
cobnut crumble-edged fruit with
touches of liquorice, and a
stunningly gripping finish.

**Dow's LBV Port 1995**  `14.5`  `£7–10`
Has some real texture and the
sweet plums and subtle bitter
cherries are helped, in the end, by
some husky tannins.

**Fino Sherry, Waitrose**  `15.5`  `–£5.00`

**Graham's LBV Port**  `13.5`  `£10–13`
1994
Rich ripe alcoholic plums which
strike warm on the finish.

**Matusalem Oloroso Dulce Muy Viejo (half bottle)** `16.5` `£10–13`
Brilliant sherry to clog the throats of carol singers. Has a rich toffeed undertone of burnt treacle.

**Quinta da Noval 10 Year Old Tawny Port NV** `15` `£13–20`
Delicious fruitcake style of rich sweetness with an underlying dry yet honeyed complexity.

**Solera Jerezana Dry Amontillado, Waitrose** `16` `£5–7`
Stunning rich, dry, crème brulée edge. Marvellous cockle warmer, this sherry.

**Solera Jerezana Old Oloroso, Waitrose** `16.5` `£5–7`
Roast walnuts, herbs, molasses, malt whisky (very subtle) – what a marvellous sherry.

**Vintage Warre Quinta da Cavadinha 1987** `17.5` `£13–20`

A magnificently complete port. It has a chewy texture (vibrant tannins), lovely complex fruit of immense depths and sunny ripeness, and lovely balance. It is a wine to stiffen the sinews, summon up the blood, stun the soul.

**Warre's Optima 10 Year Old Tawny Port NV 50cl** `13.5` `£7–10`
Sweet, brown/orange colour, hint of caramel toffee. Good with fruit cake.

**Warre's Traditional LBV Port 1990** `16.5` `£13–20`
The best LBV I've tasted which has lovely tannins and rich sweet plums and blackcurrants. It'll age for another fifteen years.

**Warre's Warrior Special Reserve Port NV** `13` `£7–10`
Sweet and rich with a touch of wet rag on the finish.

# SPARKLING WINES

## ASDA

Asti Spumante NV, `11` `–£5.00`
Asda (Italy)

Bleasdale Sparkling `16` `£7–10`
Shiraz 1999
The perfect bubbly for the Xmas
fowl. Spicy, rich, full,
overflowing.

Cava Brut, Asda (Spain) `16.5` `–£5.00`
Utterly superb. It's better than
Krug at £100. More authentic
value for money, unpretentious
freshness and classic dryness.

Cava Medium Dry, `13` `–£5.00`
Asda (Spain)

Champagne Brut NV, `13.5` `£10–13`
Asda (France)

De Bregille Vintage `14` `£13–20`
1995 (France)

Nicolas Feuillatte Blanc `13` `£13–20`
de Blancs NV (France)

Rondel Cava NV `14` `£5–7`
(Spain)

Stamps Sparkling 1999 `15` `£5–7`
(Australia)

Vintage Cava 1996, `15.5` `£5–7`
Asda (Spain)

## BOOTHS

Brossault Rosé `13` `£13–20`
Champagne NV

Bruno Paillard `15` `£13–20`
Champagne NV

Champagne Baron- `15` `£10–13`
Fuenté Brut NV

Champagne Fleurie NV `13` `£13–20`
(organic)
Not as brilliantly fresh and
magical as previous blends.

Champagne Gremillet `13.5` `£13–20`
NV
Straightforward clear fruit.

Chandon Argentina `15` `£7–10`
Brut NV

Chapelle de Cray Brut `16` `£5–7`
Rosé 1995 (France)
Delicious, sanely priced bubbly of
dry fruit with an undertone of
cherry.

Concerto Lambrusco `16` `£5–7`
1998 (Italy)
Sparkling red wine? From Italy?
Called Lambrusco? Ah! But this is
the real thing. Magically yet
impishly fruity, it is marvellous

with charcuterie at the start of a meal.

**Crémant d'Alsace Cuvée Prestige NV** `14` `£7–10`
Dry, crisp, elegant to finish.

**Deutz NV (New Zealand)** `15` `£10–13`

**Hunter's Miru Miru 1998 (New Zealand)** `16` `£10–13`
Lovely classic dryness, almost bone, but has echoes of lemon and some indefinable soft fruit.

**Palau Brut Cava NV** `13` `–£5.00`
Odd soapiness to the fruit.

**Piper Heidsieck Brut Champagne NV** `15` `£13–20`

**Prosecco Zonin NV (Italy)** `16` `–£5.00`
One of the world's great unsung bubbly wine bargains. Deliciously dry with a hint of strawberry.

## BUDGENS

**Budgens Brut Champagne NV (France)** `12` `£10–13`

**Budgens Rosé Champagne NV (France)** `10` `£10–13`

**Chandon Australia Brut NV** `13.5` `£7–10`
Touch soupy as it finishes.

**Hardys Stamp Sparkling Chardonnay Pinot Noir NV (Australia)** `14` `£5–7`

**Lindauer Brut NV (New Zealand)** `15` `£5–7`

**Pol Acker Sparkling Chardonnay NV (France)** `10` `–£5.00`
Sweet (almost), dry (almost) sparkling wine (almost).

**Rosemount V Sparkling Chardonnay NV** `14.5` `£7–10`
Very charming plump fruit which manages to stay fresh on the finish.

## CO-OP

**Asti NV, Co-op** `11` `–£5.00`
Sweet and rice puddingy. Not at Convenience Stores.

**Australian Quality Sparkling Wine, Co-op** `14` `–£5.00`

**Blossom Hill NV (USA)** `13` `£5–7`

**Cava Brut NV, Co-op** `14` `–£5.00`

**English Sparkling Brut NV, Co-op** `12` `£5–7`
Like fruit juice with a dodgy finish. Not at Convenience Stores.

**Inanda Brut NV (South Africa)** `15.5` `–£5.00`
Terrific bubbly here. Has fruit yet crispness. Superstores only.

**Jacob's Creek Sparkling Chardonnay/Pinot Noir NV (Australia)** `15` `£5–7`

**Jean de Bracieux Champagne NV (France)** `12` `£10–13`
Drink cava is my advice.

Moscato Spumante NV, `11` −£5.00
Co-op (Italy)

Rosemount V Sparkling `14.5` £5–7
Chardonnay NV
Very charming plump fruit which
manages to stay fresh on the
finish. Superstores only.

Sparkling Chardonnay `12` −£5.00
NV, Co-op (France)
Bit dull on the finish.

Sparkling Saumur NV, `11` £5–7
Co-op
Rather soapy finish. Superstores
only.

Tempranillo Brut Red `13.5` £5–7
NV, Co-op

Y2K Champagne NV `13` £13–20
(France)

## KWIK SAVE

Asti Spumante NV, `11.5` £5–7
Somerfield

Cava Brut NV, `15` −£5.00
Somerfield
Nutty, elegant, dry. More
accomplished than many
Champagnes.

Freixenet Cordon `14` £5–7
Negro Brut NV
Dry and crisp.

Martini Asti Spumante `11` £5–7
NV
Very sweet indeed.

Moscato Fizz, `13` −£2.50
Somerfield (Italy)
Torrid weather thirst quencher.

## M&S

Bluff Hill Brut NV `15` £5–7
(New Zealand)
Creamy digestive fruit gives the
crisp dry finish some real charm.

Cava Brut NV (Spain) `13.5` £5–7

Cava Medium Dry NV `12` £5–7
(Spain)

Champagne de St Gall `15` £13–20
Blanc de Blancs NV

Champagne de St Gall `13.5` £13–20
Brut NV

Champagne Desroches `13.5` £13–20
NV

Champagne Oudinot `16` £13–20
Grand Cru 1997
A very fine Champagne indeed
with beautiful mineral-charged
fruit of elegance and great style.

Cuvée Orpale Grand `12` £20+
Cru 1990

Gold Label Sparkling `16` £5–7
Chardonnay NV
(France)
Excellent, dry, subtly fruity
bubbly – elegance and classic
tailoring at a third of the price of
a comparable Champagne.

Oudinot Brut `13` £10–13
Champagne

Vintage Cava 1997 `16.5` £7–10
Superb classic dryness with a
subtle, but plump, hint of
strawberry. A fantastically classy
bubbly for the money. Better
than Krug.

## MORRISONS

**Barramundi Sparkling NV (Australia)** `16` `−£5.00`
Superb! A really deliciously fruity bubbly which isn't OTT. Terrific tasty yet dry finish.

**Brut de Channay NV (France)** `11` `−£5.00`

**Chapel Hill Chardonnay-Pinot Noir NV (Hungary)** `12` `−£5.00`

**'M' Vintage Cava 1998** `16` `£5–7`
Very classic dry fruit. As elegant as a fancy Champagne.

**Mumm Cuvée Napa Brut NV (California)** `16` `£7–10`
So much better than the French product, this elegant bubbly.

**Nicole d'Aurigny Champagne NV** `14` `£7–10`
As good as Champagne gets – under a tenner.

**Paul Herard Champagne Brut NV** `12` `£10–13`

**Reminger Sparkling Brut NV (France)** `10` `−£5.00`

**Santa Carolina Chardonnay Brut 1996 (Chile)** `13` `£5–7`

**Seaview Brut NV (Australia)** `14` `£5–7`

**Seaview Brut Rosé (Australia)** `13.5` `£5–7`

**Sparkling Zero (alcohol free)** `0` `−£2.50`
And zero is what it scores. Why? It isn't wine. It's a crime.

## SAFEWAY

**Albert Etienne Champagne Brut Rosé NV, Safeway** `10` `£13–20`
Oh come on!

**Albert Etienne Champagne Vintage 1995, Safeway** `12` `£13–20`
Pretty raw.

**Asti Spumante NV, Safeway** `10` `−£5.00`
Sweet gunge.

**Baron de Moncenay Chardonnay Brut NV** `12` `−£5.00`

**Canard-Duchene Champagne Brut NV** `14.5` `£13–20`
Dry, some elegance.

**Chandon Argentina NV** `15` `£7–10`

**Chandon Australia Brut NV** `13.5` `£7–10`
Touch soupy as it finishes.

**Conde de Caralt Cava Brut NV** `16.5` `£5–7`
As elegant a Cava as they come. Knocks a thousand Champagnes into oblivion. Top 280 stores from mid-June.

**Freixenet Cava Rosada Brut NV** `13.5` `£5–7`

**Graham Beck Brut NV (South Africa)** `14` `£5–7`

**Lambrusco Rosé Light, Safeway (4%vol)** `13.5` `−£2.50`

**Le Baron de Moncenay Merlot/Gamay Brut NV** `15` `−£5.00`

Great fun for barbecues and game dishes. Selected stores.

**Le Monferrine Moscato d'Asti 1999 (5%)**   `13`   `−£3.50`

**Lindauer Brut NV (New Zealand)**   `14`   `£7–10`

**Louis Roederer Champagne Brut Premier NV**   `13`   `£20+`

**Piper-Heidsieck Champagne Vintage 1990**   `10`   `£20+`

**Pommery Brut Royal Champagne NV**   `12`   `£20+`

**Seaview Blanc de Blancs 1996**   `13`   `£7–10`
Fails to compete with Cava. Selected stores.

**Sélection XXI, Champagne, Nicolas Feuillatte NV**   `13`   `£13–20`

## SAINSBURY

**Banrock Station Sparkling Shiraz NV (Australia)**   `16.5`   `£7–10`
Staggeringly toothsome and rich. Selected stores.

**Blanc de Noirs Champagne NV, Sainsbury's**   `16`   `£10–13`
Still on form as one of the UK's classiest, richest, most impressive own-label supermarket Champagnes.

**Canard-Duchêne Champagne Brut NV**   `14.5`   `£13–20`
Dry, some elegance.

**Cava Brut NV, Sainsbury's (Spain)**   `16.5`   `−£5.00`
Still a flagship sparkling wine: crisp, clean, fresh, classic. Better than hundreds of Champagnes.

**Cava NV, Sainsbury's (Spain) (1.5 litres)**   `16`   `−£5.00`
A superbly classy and classically crisp bubbly which is in a wonderfully festive big bottle (magnum) with, unfortunately, a very naff label which would make Santa puke. Selected stores. Price band indicates the 75cl equivalent.

**Cava Rosado Brut, Sainsbury's (Spain)**   `15`   `−£5.00`

**Champagne Blanc de Blancs 1997, Sainsbury's**   `13`   `£13–20`
It says it's 'rich and elegant' on the label. I get the rich. I don't get the elegance.

**Champagne Boizel Chardonnay NV (France)**   `16`   `£13–20`
Two stores. Wonderfully elegant, classic richness, subtle yet substantial, with a finish of baked apple.

**Champagne Charles Heidsieck Mis en Cave 1995**   `13`   `£20+`

**Champagne Demi Sec NV, Sainsbury's**   `14`   `£10–13`

**Champagne Duval-Leroy 1995** `13` £13–20
Not twenty quid! Selected stores!

**Champagne E. Barnaut Blanc de Noirs NV (France)** `15.5` £13–20
Two stores again. Very fruity with hints of strawberry. Very elegant for all that.

**Champagne Franck Bonville Blanc de Blancs NV (France)** `17.5` £13–20
Two stores only (the usual poncy pair). This example of great Champagne is toasty, rich yet dry with a huge lingering flavour of croissant and very, very subtle blackcurrant jam. (For all that, it's dry.)

**Champagne Lanson Black Label Brut NV** `13.5` £13–20

**Champagne Laurent-Perrier NV** `13.5` £20+

**Champagne Louis Roederer NV** `13` £20+

**Champagne Nicolas Feuillatte Premier Cru NV** `14` £13–20

**Champagne Palmer 1982 (France)** `16` £13–20
Two stores. Very sprightly and fresh for an eighteen year old and it well justifies its £20 price tag offering as it does the maturity which age brings: a roasted nuttiness of huge elegance and style.

**Champagne Perrier-Jouet Belle Epoque 1995 (France)** `13` £20+
Absurd amount of money for a reasonably drinkable Champagne. Limited distribution.

**Champagne Perrier-Jouet NV** `14` £20+

**Champagne Pommery Brut Royal NV** `13` £20+

**Champagne Premier Cru Extra Dry NV, Sainsbury's** `14` £13–20
Has some cool class to it.

**Chardonnay Brut, Méthode Traditionelle, Sainsbury's (France)** `15` £5–7

**Freixenet Cava Rosada NV** `13.5` £5–7

**Grand Cru Millennium Champagne 1995, Sainsbury's** `13` £13–20

**Green Gold Brut Organic Vin Mousseux NV (France)** `13.5` £5–7
Slightly fat finish mars the crispness of the wine, compared with Cava. Expensive. Selected stores.

**Hardys Nottage Hill Chardonnay Brut 1998** `15` £5–7

**Hardys Stamp of Australia Chardonnay/Pinot Noir Brut NV** `14` £5–7

**Inanda Brut NV (South Africa)** `15.5` –£5.00

Terrific bubbly here. Has fruit yet crispness. Selected stores.

**Krug Grande Cuvée NV**  `10`  `£20+`
Obscenely overpriced and unexciting.

**Millennium Vintage Cava 1997, Sainsbury's (Spain)**  `13`  `£5–7`

**Mumm Champagne Brut NV**  `13`  `£13–20`

**Piper-Heidsieck Brut NV**  `15`  `£13–20`

**Trudon Champagne Festigny Cuvée Sélection NV (France)**  `18`  `£13–20`
Available at two stores. Which two? Cromwell Road in London and Richmond in Surrey. How tragic! This is a magnificent, slightly quirky Champagne, 100% Pinot Meunier (no Chardonnay or Pinot Noir) and it has a lovely crisp nuttiness with a fantastic undertone of subtle wild raspberry. A massive bargain.

**Vin Mousseux Brut, Sainsbury's (France)**  `13`  `–£5.00`

## SOMERFIELD

**Asti Spumante NV, Somerfield**  `11.5`  `£5–7`

**Australian Quality Sparkling NV, Somerfield**  `14`  `£5–7`

**Australian Sparkling Chardonnay 1995, Somerfield**  `14`  `£7–10`

**Bollinger Spécial Cuvée NV**  `13`  `£20+`
Nothing special – except £26 required to buy it.

**Cava Brut NV, Somerfield**  `15`  `–£5.00`
Nutty, elegant, dry. More accomplished than many Champagnes.

**Cava Rosado NV, Somerfield**  `16`  `–£5.00`
Delicious crisp fruit with a hint of strawberry. A superb bubbly for the money.

**Crémant de Bourgogne 1998, Somerfield**  `14`  `£7–10`
As cool and crisp as they come.

**De Vauzelle Champagne NV**  `14`  `£10–13`
OK.

**Freixenet Cordon Negro Brut NV**  `14`  `£5–7`
Dry and crisp.

**Lindauer Brut NV (New Zealand)**  `14`  `£7–10`

**Martini Asti Spumante NV**  `11`  `£5–7`
Very sweet indeed.

**Moscato Fizz, Somerfield**  `13`  `–£2.50`
Torrid weather thirst quencher.

**Mumm Cuvée Napa Brut NV (California)**  `16`  `£7–10`

So much better than the French product, this elegant bubbly.

**Nicolas Feuillatte** `14` `£13–20`
**Champagne Brut NV**
Good basic crispness and nuttiness. Selected stores.

**Prince William Blanc** `13` `£13–20`
**de Blancs Champagne**
**NV, Somerfield**

**Prince William Blanc** `13.5` `£10–13`
**de Noirs Champagne**
**NV, Somerfield**

**Prince William** `14` `£13–20`
**Champagne Premier**
**Cru NV, Somerfield**
Has some elegance to justify that Premier Cru tag.

**Prince William** `12` `£13–20`
**Champagne Rosé NV,**
**Somerfield**

**South African Sparkling** `16` `–£5.00`
**Sauvignon, Somerfield**
Gorgeous, just gorgeous! Loads of personality and flavour – yet it's stylish withal.

**Vintage Cava 1997,** `16` `£5–7`
**Somerfield**
Classic bubbly of great finesse and class. Prefer it to Krug.

## SPAR

**Asti Spumante NV,** `13` `–£5.00`
**Spar**
Sweet old-fashioned thing for sweet old-fashioned things.

**Cava Brut NV, Spar** `13` `–£5.00`

Rather an inconclusive finish.

**Marques de Prevel** `12` `£13–20`
**Champagne NV, Spar**
Sharp and tangy and expensive.

## TESCO

**Australian Sparkling** `13` `–£5.00`
**Wine NV, Tesco**

**Banrock Station** `16.5` `£7–10`
**Sparkling Shiraz NV**
**(Australia)**
Staggeringly toothsome and rich. Selected stores.

**Blanc de Blancs** `15` `£13–20`
**Champagne NV, Tesco**
Delicious lemon style. Most stores.

**Blanc de Noirs** `17` `£10–13`
**Champagne NV, Tesco**
Interesting, classic. Most stores.

**Cava NV, Tesco** `15` `–£5.00`

**Champagne Perrier-** `13` `£20+`
**Jouët Belle Epoque**
**1995 (France)**
Absurd amount of money for a reasonably drinkable Champagne. Limited distribution.

**Cockatoo Ridge Black** `16.5` `£7–10`
**Sparkling Red NV**
Superb chocolatey fruit with raisins and ripe fruits, great tannins and a spicy finish. A wonderful wine for game dishes. Selected stores.

**Demi Sec Cava NV,** `13` `–£5.00`
**Tesco**

Very sweet and ripe but anyone who has received the telegram from Betty at Buck House will love it.

**Demi-Sec Champagne NV, Tesco** | 13.5 | £10–13
Too sweet for me. Selected stores.

**Hardys Stamp of Australia Chardonnay/Pinot Noir Sparkling NV** | 14 | £5–7

**Heidsieck Dry Monopole Blue Top Champagne NV** | 13 | £13–20
I prefer Tesco's Cava to this sourly fruity, dry bubbly.

**Hungarian Sparkling Chardonnay NV, Tesco** | 13.5 | –£5.00

**Jacob's Creek Sparkling Chardonnay/Pinot Noir NV (Australia)** | 15 | £5–7

**Laurent-Perrier Cuvée Rosé Brut NV** | 11 | £20+

**Laurent-Perrier Vintage 1990** | 13 | £20+

**Les Etoiles Organic Sparkling Wine NV** | 12 | £5–7

**Lindauer Brut NV (New Zealand)** | 14 | £7–10

**Lindauer Brut Rosé NV (New Zealand)** | 14 | £7–10
Hint of raspberry to some very dry fruit.

**Lindauer Special Reserve NV (New Zealand)** | 16 | £7–10

Very elegant and classically cut. Very smart on the taste buds.

**Organic Champagne Jose Ardinat NV** | 13.5 | £13–20

**Premier Cru Champagne NV, Tesco** | 15 | £10–13
Yes, yes. Most stores.

**Rosé Cava NV, Tesco** | 15.5 | –£5.00

**Rosé Champagne Brut NV, Tesco** | 14 | £13–20

**South African Sparkling Sauvignon 2000, Tesco** | 12 | –£5.00
Very ripe and fleshy.

**Taittinger Champagne Brut NV** | 12 | £20+

**Vintage Cava 1997, Tesco** | 15 | £5–7
Crisp, clean, classic dryness. An elegant bubbly. One of Tesco's 'Finest' range.

**Vintage Champagne 1995, Tesco** | 14.5 | £13–20
Rather good, rather good – has some lean elegance to it. One of Tesco's so-called 'Finest' range. Selected stores.

## WAITROSE

**Alexandre Bonnet Brut Rosé NV (France)** | 14 | £13–20

**Banrock Station Sparkling Shiraz NV (Australia)** | 16.5 | £7–10
Staggeringly toothsome and rich.

**Brut Vintage 1996, Waitrose** | 14 | £13–20

Stylish edge to the finish.

**Cava Brut NV,** 15 −£5.00
**Waitrose (Spain)**
Exquisite dry fruit.

**Champagne Blanc de** 14 £13–20
**Blancs NV, Waitrose**
**(France)**
Very elegant stuff.

**Champagne Blanc de** 15 £10–13
**Noirs NV, Waitrose**
**(France)**

**Champagne Blanc de** 16 £10–13
**Noirs NV, Waitrose**
**(France)**
Delicious hints of wild strawberry
to the dry dry fruit.

**Champagne Bredon** 12 £7–10
**Brut NV**

**Champagne Brut NV,** 14 £13–20
**Waitrose**

**Champagne Fleury** 13 £20+
**Brut 1993 (France)**

**Champagne Fleury** 13 £13–20
**Brut NV**
Not remotely in the class of
previous blends.

**Champagne Lanson** 12 £20+
**Noble Cuvée 1988**
Absurd fruit. Absurd price.

**Champagne Moët et** 13.5 £20+
**Chandon Brut Imperial**
**Vintage 1992**
Toasty and fine. £29? Not by a
long chalk.

**Chandon Argentina** 13.5 £7–10
**Brut Fresco NV**

**Chandon Australia Brut** 13.5 £7–10
**NV**
Touch soupy as it finishes.

**Chapel Hill Pinot Noir/** 15 −£5.00
**Chardonnay NV**

**Chapel Hill Sparkling** 12 −£5.00
**Chardonnay/Pinot**
**Noir NV (Hungary)**

**Charles Heidsieck** 20 £20+
**Champagne Blanc de**
**Blancs 1982**
Perfect champagne. As good as it
is possible for Chardonnay to get
with bubbles. It is perfectly
mature, rich and complex but
finally dry and delicate. It is so
elegant it defines what
Champagne is. Only from
Waitrose Direct.

**Charles Heidsieck** 16 £20+
**Réserve Mise en Cave**
**1996 (France)**
Compelling dryness and delicacy.
A bubbly to make the heart sing.
To be served to old soldiers on
their deathbeds – for a reward for
all those wounds.

**Clairette de Die** 11 £5–7
**Jadissane NV (organic)**
Sweet thing for immature
drinkers.

**Crémant de Bourgogne** 14 £7–10
**Rosé NV (France)**

**Cuvée Royale** 13.5 £5–7
**Blanquette de Limoux**
**NV**
Dry with a stale lemon edge.

**Deutz Marlborough Cuvée NV** `13` `£10–13`

**Duc de Marre Spécial Cuvée Champagne Brut Non Vintage** `13.5` `£13–20`

**Jacob's Creek Sparkling Chardonnay/Pinot Noir NV (Australia)** `15` `£5–7`

**Lanson Vintage Gold Label 1994** `13` `£20+`
Over-priced.

**Le Mesnil Blanc de Blancs Grand Cru Champagne Brut Non Vintage** `13` `£13–20`

**Lindauer Brut NV (New Zealand)** `14` `£7–10`

**Moët et Chandon L-D 1992 (France)** `14` `£20+`

Difficult to swallow, £28, but easy to similarly deal with the wine. It is delicious.

**Saumur Brut NV, Waitrose** `16` `£5–7`
More strikingly clean and classically dry than many a much-vaunted Champagne.

**Seaview Brut NV (Australia)** `14` `£5–7`

**Seaview Brut Rosé NV (Australia)** `13.5` `£5–7`

**Sparkling Burgundy NV (France)** `12` `£7–10`

**Taittinger Comtes de Champagne Blanc de Blancs 1990** `13` `£20+`

# PART 3

# A TO Z OF RETAILERS

# ASDA

Every retailer in this book was asked the same question for this 2002 edition. 'What is,' I asked, 'in your opinion the strength of your range of wines or the particular style of your way of retailing wine?'

Asda replied:

> *'Providing good quality wines, at great Asda value, from easy drinking afford-able Australian Chardonnay to premium classic French Bordeaux. Particularly focusing on Australia, South America and France – primary customer-favourite wine selections.'*

Asda is not only the first retailer in this book because of the arrangement of the English alphabet, it is also the number one retailer in this book because of the speed of its response to this question.

Asda's view of its range is as easy to swallow as many of its wines. This response hardly does justice to the unusual attention Asda pays to its customers' needs and how well they service them. Its newly revamped, staffed, and energised wine department is hugely committed to value for money. Many stuffy and out-of-touch wine critics find Asda's principles of good value drinkability intolerable, but for me this approach is music to my ears.

Who needs stuffy wine critics when you have a branch of Asda in the locality? Who needs stuffy wine critics when you have an innovative supermarket chain like this one? And not just in wine. In the recent past it has had the chutzpah to offer jewellery in its stores for the first time. It launched a scheme allowing grandparents time off to spend with their new grandchildren, and leave to help with childminding. It erected a motorway sign, similar to those for heritage sites, near Junction 3 of the M66, on the basis that the Bury store should qualify as a tourist attraction since it gets more than 250,000 visitors a year. It introduced a scheme backed by the Campaign for Racial Equality, called Talent Race, to increase recruitment from ethnic minorities. It announced plans to open garden centres in 90 of its branches' car parks. It launched a 'Get involved with Kids' programme, allowing staff a total of 60,000 days out, to work on community projects between now and 2003.

Disasters? Only one. The retailer's Brighton Marina store was forced to close after it was partially demolished by a 4,000 tonne landslide. However, this blip has been offset by ascent in popularity. The *Grocer* trade magazine reported that sales at the three Asda Wal-Mart superstores were in the top five for Wal-Mart worldwide. Small wonder that there were reports of Asda creating 10,000 new jobs. In June 2001, it was widely reported that Asda had 'restarted the price war'. The company announced price cuts, worth £100 million, over a four-month period.

However, and most bizarrely, who would have reckoned that this emphasis on value for money at Asda and its slick trading practices would have inspired the legendary alfresco salesmen of North Africa? As one report had it: 'Street traders in Tunisia, in towns like Monastir, can be heard shouting at potential customers: "I give you good price – I give you Asda price".'

Not much I can add after that sort of encomium.

Asda Stores Limited
Asda House
Great Wilson Street
Leeds
LS11 5AD

Tel 0500 100055 Customer Service Line
Fax 0113 241 8666
www.asda.co.uk

## ARGENTINIAN RED

| Wine | Score | Price |
|---|---|---|
| Argentinian Bonarda 1999, Asda | 14.5 | –£5.00 |
| Argentinian Syrah 1999, Asda | 16 | –£5.00 |
| Casa Latina Shiraz Tempranillo 1999 | 16 | –£5.00 |
| Far Flung El Montero Shiraz Reserva 2000 | 14 | £5–7 |
| Far Flung Malbec 2000 | 15 | –£5.00 |
| La Nature Organic Barbera 2000 | 14 | –£5.00 |
| Nieto Senetiner Bonarda Reserva 2000 | 15 | £5–7 |
| Nieto Senetiner Merlot Reserve 2000 | 14 | £5–7 |
| Santa Julia Tempranillo Reserva 1999 | 16.5 | £5–7 |

## ARGENTINIAN WHITE

Argentinian White NV, Asda | 14 | −£3.50

Argento Chardonnay 2000 | 17 | −£5.00

Candela Viognier 2000 | 15 | £5–7

Far Flung Viognier 2000 | 16.5 | −£5.00

## AUSTRALIAN RED

Andrew Peace Cabernet Merlot 1999 | 15 | £5–7

Fox River Pinot Noir 1998 | 13 | £5–7

Houghtons Shiraz 1998 | 15 | £5–7

La Nature Organic Shiraz Cabernet 1999 | 13.5 | −£5.00

Maglieri Shiraz 1998 | 15.5 | £7–10

Normans Estates Lone Gum Cabernet Merlot 2000 | 12 | −£5.00

Normans Estates Pinot Noir 1999 | 10 | £5–7

Normans Estates Yarra Valley Cabernet 1998 | 14 | £7–10

Secession Xanadu Shiraz/Cabernet 1999 | 15 | £5–7

Temple Bruer Shiraz/Malbec 1998 | 16.5 | £5–7

The Potts Family Bleasdale Malbec 2000 | 13 | £5–7

Vine Vale Grenache 1998 (Peter Lehmann) | 15 | £5–7

Wolf Blass Yellow Label Cabernet Sauvignon 1999 | 14 | £7–10

Wyndham Estate Bin 444 Cabernet Sauvignon 1998 | 15 | £5–7

## AUSTRALIAN WHITE

Cranswick Nine Pines Vineyard Marsanne 1998 | 16.5 | −£5.00

Karalta White 1999, Asda | 14 | −£3.50

La Nature Organic Chardonnay Sauvignon 2000 | 14.5 | −£5.00

Peter Lehmann Eden Valley Riesling 1999 | 16.5 | £5–7

Rosemount GTR 2001 | 13.5 | £5–7

Rosemount 'Hill of Gold' Chardonnay, Mudgee 1999 | 14 | £7–10

Rymill Sauvignon Blanc 1999 | 15.5 | £5–7

Wyndham Estate Bin 222 Chardonnay 1999 | 16 | £5–7

Xanadu Secession Sémillon Chardonnay 2000 | 13.5 | £5–7

## CHILEAN RED

35 South Cabernet Sauvignon 1999 | 17 | −£5.00

Big Chilean Cabernet 2000 (1.5 litres) | 15 | −£3.50

Casas del Bosque Merlot 1999 | 14 | £5–7

Castillo de Molina Cabernet Sauvignon 1998 | 15.5 | £5–7

Cono Sur Cabernet Sauvignon Reserve, Rapel Valley 1999 | 16.5 | −£5.00

Cono Sur Pinot Noir 1999 | 16.5 | −£5.00

Terra Mater Cabernet Sauvignon 1999 | 13 | −£5.00

Terra Mater Carmenère Cabernet Sauvignon 1998 | 14 | −£5.00

Terra Mater Zinfandel Shiraz 2000 | 14 | −£5.00

Valdivieso Single Vineyard Merlot 1998 | 16.5 | £7–10

## CHILEAN WHITE

Casas del Bosque Sauvignon Blanc 1999 | 15 | £5–7

Chardonnay Reserve Cono Sur 1999 | 15.5 | £5–7

Chilean Sauvignon Blanc 2000, Asda | 16 | −£5.00

Undurraga Gewürztraminer 2000 | 16 | −£5.00

Valdivieso Malbec Rosé 2000 | 16.5 | −£5.00

## FRENCH RED

Beaune Premier Cru Antoine de Peyrache 1998 | 10 | £10–13

Buzet Cuvée 44 1997 | 15 | −£5.00

California Old Vine Estates Carignan NV | 13.5 | −£5.00

Château Biston Brillette Moulis 1997 | 16.5 | £7–10

Château Clauzet St-Estèphe 1997 | 13 | £10–13

Château 'D' de Dassault St-Emilion 1998 | 16 | £10–13

Château d'Arsac Margaux 1999 | 15 | £10–13

Château du Gaby Canon-Fronsac 1998 | 13.5 | £7–10

Château Gigault Premières Côtes de Blaye 1998 | 16.5 | £7–10

Château Haut Canteloupe Médoc 1998 | 16.5 | £7–10

Château La Chene de Margot Premières Côtes de Blaye 1998 | 15.5 | £5–7

Château Lamarzelle St-Emilion Grand Cru 1997 | 14.5 | £13–20

Château Lynch-Moussas Pauillac 1997 | 15 | £13–20

Château Maucaillou Moulis 1997 | 15 | £13–20

Château Sociando Mallet Haut-Médoc 1997 `12` `£20+`

Château Vieux Gabiran 1999 (organic) `14` `−£5.00`

Châteauneuf-du-Pape Domaine Giraud 1998 `13.5` `£10–13`

Cornas 1998 `14` `£7–10`

Côte de Beaune-Villages Michel Pont 1998 `11` `£5–7`

Côtes du Rhône Cuvée Spéciale 2000, Asda `15.5` `−£3.50`

Côtes du Rhône Jean Berteau 1999 `15.5` `−£5.00`

Crozes-Hermitage Les Haut de Pavières 1999 `16` `£5–7`

Domaine de Montplaisir Cabernet Franc VdP d'Oc 2000 `16` `−£5.00`

French Connection Reserve Merlot 2000 `15` `−£5.00`

Gigondas Domaine St Damien 1999 `14.5` `£7–10`

Hermitage 1998 `14` `£10–13`

J. Frelin Organic Côtes du Rhône NV `14` `−£5.00`

La Montagne Fitou Réserve 1999 `15` `−£5.00`

La Vieille Ferme, Côtes du Ventoux 1999 `16` `−£5.00`

Les Crouzels Fitou 1999 `16` `£7–10`

Les Fiefs de La Grange St-Julien 1998 `14` `£13–20`

Nuits-St-Georges 1988 `10` `£13–20`

Organic Claret Château Vieux Georget, Bordeaux 1998 `15.5` `£5–7`

Pommard Jean-Marc Bouley 1998 `14.5` `£13–20`

Rasteau Côtes du Rhône-Villages Domaine de Vallambreuse 2000 `16` `−£5.00`

Syrah VdP d'Oc 2000 `14.5` `−£3.50`

Tramontane Red VdP de l'Aude 1999, Asda `16` `−£3.50`

Vacqueyras Domaine de l'Oiselet 1999 `16.5` `£5–7`

Volnay Antoine de Peyrache 1998 `10` `£7–10`

## FRENCH WHITE

Chablis Premier Cru Fourchame 1999 `15` `£10–13`

Chardonnay, Jardin de la France 1999 `14` `−£3.50`

Château Perruchot Meursault 1998 `12` `£13–20`

Chenin Blanc Loire 1999, Asda `14` `−£3.50`

French Connection Viognier VdP d'Oc 2000 `14.5` `−£5.00`

L'Enclos Domeque Dry Muscat VdP d'Oc 2000 `14` `−£5.00`

Louis Maynard Anjou Blanc NV   13.5   −£3.50

Louis Maynard Sauvignon Blanc Ackerman NV   14.5   −£3.50

Mâcon-Villages La Colombier 2000, Asda   14   −£5.00

Pouilly-Fuissé Antoine de Peyrache 1999   13   £7–10

Pouilly-Fumé Les Cornets 1999   14   £7–10

Sancerre Les Noble Villages Caves de Sancerre 2000   13   £5–7

Sancerre Vieilles Vignes Patient Collat 1999   14.5   £7–10

Tramontane Sauvignon Blanc 2000, Asda   14.5   −£5.00

Vouvray Denis Marchais 1999   10   −£5.00

## GERMAN WHITE

Grans Fassian Trittenheimer Riesling Kabinett Altarchen 1999   13.5   £5–7

## HUNGARIAN WHITE

Badger Hill Hungarian Sauvignon 1999   14   −£3.50

Hungarian Medium Chardonnay 1999, Asda   12   −£3.50

## ITALIAN RED

Barolo Veglio Angelo 1996   14   £7–10

Big Mamma's Italian Red NV   14   −£5.00

Cantele Zinfandel Salento 2000   14   −£5.00

Chianti 1999, Asda   12   −£3.50

Chianti Classico Riserva 1997, Asda   14   £5–7

Puccini Chianti Reserva 1997   14   −£5.00

Ruvello Cabernet Sauvignon Passito 1998   17   £7–10

Solara Organic Rosso, Nero d'Avola 2000   15   −£3.50

Villa Cerna Chianti Classico 1998   15   £5–7

## ITALIAN WHITE

Cantele Chardonnay Salento 2000   14   −£5.00

Lambrusco Bianco NV, Asda   13.5   −£3.50

Lambrusco Rosato NV, Asda   13   −£2.50

Solara Organic White Inzolia 2000   15   −£3.50

## NEW ZEALAND WHITE

Babich Semillon Chardonnay 2000   15   £5–7

| | | |
|---|---|---|
| Corbans Sauvignon Blanc 1999 | 15.5 | £5–7 |
| Nobilo Sauvignon Blanc 1999 | 14 | £5–7 |
| Villa Maria Private Bin Sauvignon Blanc 1999 | 17 | £5–7 |

## PORTUGUESE WHITE

| | | |
|---|---|---|
| Vale de Rosas Fernao Pires 1999 | 15 | –£5.00 |
| Vinho Verde 1999, Asda | 10 | –£3.50 |

## SOUTH AFRICAN RED

| | | |
|---|---|---|
| Beyerskloof Pinotage, Stellenbosch 2000 | 15.5 | –£5.00 |
| Carnby Liggle 2000 | 12 | –£5.00 |
| Dumisani Ruby Cabernet/Merlot 1999 | 15.5 | –£5.00 |
| Graham Beck Coastal Shiraz 1999 | 16.5 | £5–7 |
| Kumala Cabernet Sauvignon Shiraz 2000 | 16 | –£5.00 |
| Landskroon Merlot Reserve 1999 | 16 | £5–7 |
| Linton Park Cabernet Sauvignon 1998 | 13.5 | £10–13 |
| Middelvlei Cabernet Sauvignon 1998 | 15.5 | £5–7 |
| Neil Ellis Cabernet Sauvignon 1998 | 16.5 | £7–10 |
| Pinotage Reserve 1999, Asda | 14 | –£5.00 |
| Porcupine Ridge Syrah 1999 | 16 | £5–7 |

| | | |
|---|---|---|
| Railroad Cabernet Sauvignon Shiraz 1999 | 15 | –£5.00 |
| Savanha Merlot 1999 | 14 | £5–7 |
| South African Cabernet Sauvignon 1999, Asda | 14 | –£5.00 |
| South African Pinotage 1999, Asda | 13.5 | –£5.00 |
| Spier Unexpected Pleasures Cabernet Sauvignon 1999 | 16 | –£5.00 |
| Van Loveren Cabernet Shiraz 1999 | 13 | –£5.00 |

## SOUTH AFRICAN WHITE

| | | |
|---|---|---|
| Big South African Chardonnay 2000 (1.5 litres) | 14.5 | –£3.50 |
| Interlude Blanc, Verdun Estate 1999 | 13 | £5–7 |
| Kumala Chenin Chardonnay 2000 | 15 | –£5.00 |
| Porcupine Ridge Sauvignon Blanc 2000 | 16 | –£5.00 |
| Speir Chenin Blanc 2000 | 15 | –£5.00 |
| Speir Sauvignon Blanc 2000 | 15.5 | –£5.00 |
| Van Loveren Blanc de Noirs 2000 | 14 | –£5.00 |

## SPANISH RED

| | | |
|---|---|---|
| Conde de Navasques 1997 | 15.5 | –£5.00 |
| Don Darias Tinto NV | 15.5 | –£3.50 |

| | | |
|---|---|---|
| Mont Marcal Crianza 1997 | 14 | −£3.50 |
| Torres Coronas Tempranillo 1999 | 16 | £5–7 |

## SPANISH WHITE

| | | |
|---|---|---|
| Baron de Ley Rioja Blanco 1999 | 13.5 | −£5.00 |
| Bodegas Cerrosol Sauvignon Rueda 1998 | 15 | −£5.00 |
| Moscatel de Valencia NV, Asda | 16 | −£3.50 |
| Spanish Oaked White NV, Asda | 15.5 | −£3.50 |

## USA RED

| | | |
|---|---|---|
| Rosemount 'V' NV | 14 | £5–7 |
| Garnet Point Shiraz Cabernet 2000 | 15.5 | −£5.00 |
| Talus Merlot 1998 | 13 | £5–7 |
| Talus Zinfandel 1998 | 13 | £5–7 |

## USA WHITE

| | | |
|---|---|---|
| Ca'del Solo Malvasia Bianca, Bonny Doon 1998 | 12 | £7–10 |
| Garnet Point Semillon Chardonnay 2000 | 14.5 | −£5.00 |

## FORTIFIED

| | | |
|---|---|---|
| Dow's LBV Port 1995 | 14.5 | £7–10 |
| Fine Ruby Port, Asda | 14 | £5–7 |

| | | |
|---|---|---|
| Graham's LBV Port 1994 | 13.5 | £10–13 |
| Manzanilla, Asda | 17 | £5–7 |
| Tawny Port, Asda | 15 | £5–7 |
| Warre's Optima 10 Year Old Tawny Port NV 50cl | 13.5 | £7–10 |
| Warre's Warrior Special Reserve Port NV | 13 | £7–10 |

## SPARKLING

| | | |
|---|---|---|
| Kirribilly Riesling Brut 1999 | 15 | £7–10 |
| Asti Spumante NV, Asda (Italy) | 11 | −£5.00 |
| Bleasdale Sparkling Shiraz 1999 | 16 | £7–10 |
| Cava Brut, Asda (Spain) | 16.5 | −£5.00 |
| Cava Medium Dry, Asda (Spain) | 13 | −£5.00 |
| Champagne Brut NV, Asda | 13.5 | £10–13 |
| De Bregille Vintage 1995 (France) | 14 | £13–20 |
| Nicolas Feuillatte Blanc de Blancs NV (France) | 13 | £13–20 |
| Rondel Cava NV (Spain) | 14 | £5–7 |
| Stamps Sparkling 1999 (Australia) | 15 | £5–7 |
| Vintage Cava 1996, Asda (Spain) | 15.5 | £5–7 |

# BOOTHS

In answer to the question I asked every retailer for this edition of *Superplonk*, Booths had a simple response. It stayed mum, though I'm quite sure I asked its PR company to pass on my simple needs to this small, northern supermarket chain. 'What is,' I asked, 'in your opinion the strength of your range of wines or the particular style of your way of retailing wine?'

My answer would be 'Booths is Booths'. It isn't Tesco or Asda, or The Great Northern Wine Company or Fortnum & Mason. The wine range is broad and well-selected by buyer Sally Holloway, and its style is an amalgam of all the aforementioned retailers.

Booths has been busy this year, so I do understand that it didn't have time for tomfool questions. Finally, the company's 25th store was opened, in Kirby Lonsdale, and work also began on another new store in Settle in February. Edwin Booth, chairman, said the company 'was keen to expand further in Yorkshire' and 'further north' with Penrith identified as another target area. The company also reported that sales growth was running at 7.5%, which is a more than healthy trading performance, being well above average.

Booths will never be large enough to challenge the big players, but it doesn't try to. Its presence in a local community gives it all the kudos, and the profits, it needs.

In a Britain where we bemoan the loss of the small family business here is one doing well, prospering, and offering a solid range of wines at all price levels. If you live in a town where there's a Booths store, count yourself lucky.

Booths Supermarkets
4–6 Fishergate
Preston
Lancashire
PR1 3LJ

Tel 01772 251701
Fax 01772 204316
www.booths-supermarkets.co.uk

## ARGENTINIAN RED

El Montonero Bonarda Barbera 1999 — 15.5 — −£5.00

Finca el Retiro Malbec, Mendoza 2000 — 16.5 — £5–7

Libertad Malbec Bonarda 2000 — 14.5 — −£5.00

Mission Peak Red NV — 15.5 — −£3.50

Terrazas Alto Cabernet Sauvignon 1999 — 14.5 — £5–7

## ARGENTINIAN WHITE

Libertad Chenin Sauvignon 2000 — 13 — −£5.00

Terrazas Alto Chardonnay 2000 — 14.5 — £5–7

## AUSTRALIAN RED

Australian Red Shiraz Cabernet Sauvignon NV, Booths — 14 — −£5.00

Brown Brothers Tarrango 2000 — 13 — −£5.00

CV Capel Vale Shiraz 1998 — 14.5 — £7–10

d'Arenberg d'Arrys Original Shiraz/ Grenache 1998 — 15 — £7–10

Ironstone Shiraz Grenache 1998 — 15.5 — £5–7

Knappstein Cabernet Franc 1998 — 15 — £7–10

Marktree Premium Red 1999 — 15 — −£5.00

Oxford Landing Merlot 1999 — 14 — £5–7

Penfolds Bin 407 Cabernet Sauvignon 1996 — 15 — £10–13

Rosemount Estate Shiraz/Cabernet Sauvignon 2000 — 14 — £5–7

The Seven Surveys Peter Lehmann 1998 — 16 — £5–7

## AUSTRALIAN WHITE

Capel Vale CV Unwooded Chardonnay 1999 — 14.5 — £7–10

Capel Vale Verdelho 1999 — 16 — £7–10

Château Tahbilk Marsanne 1998 — 17 — £5–7

Cranswick Botrytis Semillon 1996 (half bottle) — 15 — £10–13

d'Arenberg The Olive Grove Chardonnay, McLaren Vale 2000 — 16.5 — £5–7

Deakin Estate Chardonnay 2000 — 15.5 — −£5.00

Ironstone Semillon Chardonnay 1999 — 16 — £5–7

Marktree White SE Australia 2000 — 13.5 — −£5.00

| Ninth Island Chardonnay 2000 | 14 | £7–10 |
| Oxford Landing Chardonnay 2000 | 15.5 | –£5.00 |
| Oxford Landing Viognier 2000 | 16 | £5–7 |
| Penfolds Bin 21 Rawson's Retreat Semillon/Colombard/Chardonnay 2000 | 14 | –£5.00 |
| Shaw & Smith Sauvignon Blanc 1998 | 15 | £7–10 |

## BULGARIAN RED

| Boyar Cabernet Merlot 1998 | 12.5 | –£3.50 |

## CHILEAN RED

| Apaltagua Carmenère 2000 | 13.5 | £5–7 |
| Carmen Grande Vidure Cabernet Sauvignon 1998 | 16.5 | £7–10 |
| Cono Sur Pinot Noir 2000 | 16 | –£5.00 |
| Sierra Cabernet Sauvignon 2000 | 13.5 | –£5.00 |
| Subsol Cabernet Malbec 1999 | 15 | –£5.00 |

## CHILEAN WHITE

| Casablanca Barrel Fermented Chardonnay 1999 | 16.5 | £5–7 |

| Isla Negra Chardonnay 1999 | 15.5 | £5–7 |
| Sierra Sauvignon Blanc 2000 | 13.5 | –£5.00 |
| Subsol Chardonnay Sauvignon 2000 | 14 | –£5.00 |
| Subsol Chardonnay Sauvignon Vistamar 1999 | 13 | –£5.00 |
| Tocornal White NV | 13.5 | –£5.00 |

## FRENCH RED

| Bergerac Rouge NV, Booths | 13 | –£3.50 |
| Bourgogne Rouge Joillot 1999 | 13 | £5–7 |
| Cahors 1999 | 15 | –£5.00 |
| Château Cluzan Bordeaux 1999 | 15.5 | –£5.00 |
| Château Ducla, Bordeaux 1997 | 15 | £5–7 |
| Château l'Euzière Pic St Loup 1998 | 16.5 | £7–10 |
| Château Mayne-Vieil, Fronsac 1998 | 16 | £5–7 |
| Château Pierrail Bordeaux Supérieur 1998 | 15.5 | £5–7 |
| Chaume Arnaud Domaine Côtes du Rhône-Villages 1998 (organic) | 17 | £7–10 |

Côtes du Rhône-Villages Georges Darriaud 1998 — 13.5 — £5–7

Domaine de la Bastide VdP Hautrive 1999 — 8 — −£3.50

Domaine de Petit Roubie Syrah VdP d'Oc NV (organic) — 15.5 — −£5.00

Domaine Les Yeuses La Soure VdP d'Oc 1999 — 14 — −£5.00

Faugères Gilbert Alquier 1998 — 15.5 — £7–10

Fitou Madame Parmentier 1998 — 13.5 — −£5.00

Gigondas Domaine Paillere et Pied 1998 — 16 — £7–10

Honoré de Berticot Merlot Côtes de Duras NV — 15.5 — −£5.00

La Passion Rouge VdP de Vaucluse 2000 — 14 — −£3.50

La Réserve du Reverend Corbières 1999 — 13.5 — −£5.00

Marcillac 1997 — 15 — −£5.00

Morgon Côte du Py 1998 — 13 — £5–7

Oak Aged Claret Bordeaux Supérieur NV, Booths — 14 — −£5.00

Old Git Grenache Syrah 1999 — 15.5 — −£5.00

Pernands-Vergelesses Domaine Rossignol Cornu 1998 — 14 — £7–10

Vin Rouge NV, Booths — 11 — −£3.50

## FRENCH WHITE

Bergerac Blanc NV, Booths — 14 — −£3.50

Bourgogne Chardonnay Domaine Joseph Matrot 1999 — 12 — £5–7

Chablis Domaine de l'Eglantière 1999 — 12 — £7–10

Château Crabitan Bellevue St-Croix-du-Mont 1996 — 16.5 — £5–7

Château Lamothe Vincent, Bordeaux 2000 — 14 — −£5.00

Château Petit Roubie, Picpoul du Pinet 2000 (organic) — 15.5 — −£5.00

Château Turcaud Entre-Deux-Mers 2000 — 13 — −£5.00

Clos de Monéstier Bergerac Blanc 2000 — 12 — −£5.00

Clos de Monéstier Bergerac Rosé 2000 — 14 — −£5.00

Côtes du Rhône Domaine Chaume Arnaud 1999 — 15 — £7–10

Domaine de Pellehaut Côtes de Gascogne 2000 — 14 — −£5.00

Gewürztraminer d'Alsace Turckheim 2000 — 16 — £5–7

James Herrick Chardonnay VdP d'Oc 1999 — 16 — −£5.00

La Passion Blanc VdP de Vaucluse 2000 — 14 — −£3.50

Louis Chatel Sur Lie VdP d'Oc 2000 — 14.5 — −£3.50

Muscadet sur Lie La Roche Renard 2000 — 13 — −£5.00

Pouilly-Fumé Les Cornets, Cailbourdin 2000 — 13.5 — £7–10

Riesling d'Alsace Aime Stentz 1999 — 14.5 — £5–7

St-Véran Domaine des Deux Roches 1999 — 16 — £5–7

Vermentino Les Yeuses VdP d'Oc 2000 — 15 — −£3.50

Vin Blanc NV, Booths — 12 — −£3.50

## GERMAN WHITE

Dr 'L' Riesling, Loosen Mosel 1999 — 14 — £5–7

Fire Mountain Riesling 1999 — 14 — −£5.00

Gau-Bickelheimer Kurfurstenstuck Auslese 1998 — 13 — −£5.00

Liebfraumilch NV, Booths — 13 — −£3.50

Piesporter Michelsberg NV, Booths — 12 — −£5.00

Riesling Louis Guntrum 1999 — 14 — −£5.00

Villa Wolf Pinot Gris, Loosen Pfalz 1999 — 16 — £5–7

## GREEK RED

Vin de Crete Kourtaki 1999 — 12 — −£5.00

## GREEK WHITE

Kretikos Vin de Crete Blanc Boutari 1999 — 13 — −£5.00

## HUNGARIAN WHITE

Chapel Hill Oaked Chardonnay, Balaton Boglar NV — 13.5 — −£3.50

Tokaji Harslevelu Castle Island 2000 — 13.5 — −£5.00

## ITALIAN RED

A Mano Primitivo Puglia 2000 — 15.5 — £5–7

Amarone Classico Brigaldara 1996 — 16.5 — £13–20

Archidamo Pervini Primitivo di Manduria 1997 — 15.5 — £5–7

Barocco Rosso del Salento 1999 — 11 — −£3.50

Chianti Leonardo 2000 — 14 — £5–7

Col di Sasso Toscana 1998 — 14 — −£5.00

219

I Promessa Sangiovese 13.5 −£5.00
Puglia 1999

La Piazza Rosso 1999 13.5 −£3.50
(Sicily)

Valpolicella Classico 15 £7−10
Superiore, Viviani 1997

Valpolicella Classico, 13 £5−7
Viviani 1999

Veneto Salice Salento 15 −£5.00
Vallone 1998

Vigna Flaminio, 14 £5−7
Brindisi Rosso 1997

## ITALIAN WHITE

La Piazza Bianco 2000 14 −£3.50
(Sicily)

Le Rime Pinot Grigio/ 13 −£5.00
Chardonnay 2000

Sentito Cortese DOC 14 −£5.00
Oltrepo Pavese 1999

Soave Classico Pra 2000 13.5 £5−7

Viña Ruspo Rosado 14 £5−7
Capezzana 2000

## LEBANESE RED

Hochar Red 1998 13.5 £5−7

## NEW ZEALAND WHITE

Dashwood Sauvignon 17 £7−10
Blanc 2000

Jackson Estate 16.5 £7−10
Sauvignon Blanc 2000

## PORTUGUESE RED

Alianca Foral Douro 15.5 −£5.00
Reserva 1997

Alta Mesa Red 1999 12 −£3.50

Bela Fonte Baga, Beiras 14 −£5.00
1999

Dão Dom Ferraz 1999 15 −£5.00

Portada Red 13.5 −£5.00
Estremadura 1999

Quinta da Villa Freire 15 £5−7
Douro 1996

Quinta de la Rosa 1998 15.5 £5−7

## SOUTH AFRICAN RED

Goats Do Roam 14 −£5.00
Fairview, Paarl 2000

Helderberg Shiraz 1999 15 −£5.00

Spice Route Andrew's 16.5 £5−7
Hope Cabernet
Sauvignon/Merlot 1999

Welmoed Merlot 1999 16 £5−7

## SOUTH AFRICAN WHITE

Altus Sauvignon Blanc 13.5 −£5.00
2000

Jordan Chardonnay 16 £7−10
1999

Landema Falls 15 −£3.50
Colombard
Chardonnay NV

Welmoed Sauvignon 13.5 −£5.00
Blanc 2000

## SPANISH RED

| | | |
|---|---|---|
| Amezola de la Mora Rioja Crianza 1997 | 12.5 | £7–10 |
| Artadi Viñas de Gain Crianza, Rioja 1997 | 15.5 | £7–10 |
| Casa de la Viña Valdepeñas 2000 | 15 | –£5.00 |
| Casa Morena, Valdepeñas NV | 14 | –£3.50 |
| Castillo de Almansa Reserva Bodegas Piqueras 1995 | 15.5 | –£5.00 |
| Guelbenzu Blue Label Navarra NV | 16 | £5–7 |
| La Poema Garnacha Vinas Viejas 1999 | 13 | –£5.00 |
| Mas Donis Capcanes Taragona 2000 | 16.5 | –£5.00 |
| Ochoa Tempranillo Garnacha 1999 | 15 | –£5.00 |
| Viña Alarba, Calatayud 2000 | 13 | –£3.50 |
| Viña Albali Gran Reserva 1993 | 15 | £5–7 |
| Viña Borgia Campo de Borja 1999 | 13 | –£5.00 |

## SPANISH WHITE

| | | |
|---|---|---|
| Castillo de Maluenda Blanco 2000 | 15 | –£3.50 |
| Castillo de Maluenda Rosado 2000 | 13.5 | –£3.50 |

| | | |
|---|---|---|
| Estrella, Moscatel de Valencia NV | 16 | –£5.00 |
| Palacio de Bornos Rueda 2000 | 15 | –£5.00 |
| Santa Lucia Viura, Vino de la Tierra Manchuela 1999 | 14 | –£3.50 |
| Viña Albali Rosado 2000 | 13.5 | –£5.00 |

## USA RED

| | | |
|---|---|---|
| Stonybrook Merlot 1999 | 15.5 | £5–7 |
| Turning Leaf Cabernet Sauvignon 1998 | 12 | £5–7 |

## USA WHITE

| | | |
|---|---|---|
| Stonybrook Chardonnay 2000 | 14 | –£5.00 |

## FORTIFIED

| | | |
|---|---|---|
| Amontillado del Puerto, Lustau | 16 | £7–10 |
| Banyuls Chapoutier 1997 (50cl) | 14 | £7–10 |
| Churchills Dry White Port | 13 | £7–10 |
| Finest Reserve Port, Booths | 14.5 | £7–10 |
| Fino NV, Booths | 14 | –£5.00 |
| Henriques & Henriques 5 Year Old Madeira NV | 13 | £10–13 |

| | | |
|---|---|---|
| Lustau Old East India Sherry | 17 | £7–10 |
| Manzanilla Sherry, Booths | 15 | −£5.00 |
| Medium Amontillado NV, Booths | 15.5 | −£5.00 |
| Niepoort LBV Port 1996 | 14 | £10–13 |
| Niepoort Ruby Port | 14 | £7–10 |

## SPARKLING

| | | |
|---|---|---|
| Brossault Rosé Champagne NV | 13 | £13–20 |
| Bruno Paillard Champagne NV | 15 | £13–20 |
| Champagne Baron-Fuenté Brut NV | 15 | £10–13 |
| Champagne Fleurie NV (organic) | 13 | £13–20 |
| Champagne Gremillet NV | 13.5 | £13–20 |
| Chandon Argentina Brut NV | 15 | £7–10 |
| Chapelle de Cray Brut Rosé 1995 (France) | 16 | £5–7 |
| Concerto Lambrusco 1998 (Italy) | 16 | £5–7 |
| Crémant d'Alsace Cuvée Prestige NV | 14 | £7–10 |
| Deutz NV (New Zealand) | 15 | £10–13 |
| Hunter's Miru Miru 1998 (New Zealand) | 16 | £10–13 |
| Palau Brut Cava NV | 13 | −£5.00 |
| Piper-Heidsieck Brut Champagne NV | 15 | £13–20 |
| Prosecco Zonin NV (Italy) | 16 | −£5.00 |

# BUDGENS

In answer to the question I asked every retailer for this edition of *Superplonk*, Christine Sandys, the wine buyer here, was most eloquent.

'What is,' I said, 'in your opinion the strength of your range of wines or the particular style of your way of retailing wine?' She replied:

*'Budgens is essentially a convenience retailer, and as such carries a limited (compared to the major multiples) range of wines, around 300 in our largest stores. We therefore aim to offer a compact, but comprehensive and balanced, range of wines from around the world. Given these parameters I feel that our customers' demand for reliable branded wines from the New World, in particular Australia and California, is well catered for. We also offer a carefully selected yet commercial range of semi-exclusive or less widely available 'soft brands' from other areas of the world such as Spain, Portugal, Eastern Europe and France, and these areas of the range provide the essential Budgens individuality for the more discerning consumer.*

*Budgens are currently experiencing unprecedented levels of growth within the wine category as people lock onto the value of the offers and the variety within the range. As the customer begins to develop more and more confidence in the range then this should allow for a little more experimentation, optimising the delicate balance between the commercial and the innovative, which is ultimately what we are striving for.*

*In terms of price, the emphasis has so far been on the £6 and below bracket, and this has become our strength. As a further enhancement to the range, over the next 12 months or so, I intend to introduce a carefully chosen selection in the £6 to £10 price bracket.*

*All of the above, coupled with our ongoing aggressive promotional activity, should further strengthen Budgens' position as a (progressive!) high street drinks retailer for the foreseeable future.'*

My own response to this question would be to comment that it has little style at the moment and its range is only just beginning to mean something. Christine, who arrived from the Co-op, has had her feet under the table of the wine buying department for a comparatively short time but she is beginning to make her mark – as above 'mission statement' makes clear and the following entries demonstrate.

In a trade magazine interview, Ms Sandys said that one of her prime concerns was the number of bottles of wine being spoilt by tainted cork. How about then, Christine, putting in place a wine range composed entirely of plastic-corked wines and screwcapped bottles? This would give Budgens the edge on all other wine retailers and would guarantee that cork taint would never be found in any of its wines. Think of the effect on all those stuffy wine critics. Most of them have never heard of Budgens. (Many believe Budgens is something to be found in a cage pecking on dried cuttlefish.) And Budgens badly needs to find an edge. Many of its initiatives have not been as successful as hoped, though it continues to make money.

The Budgens direct home-shopping service was abandoned after 18 months because it had been 'suffocated by bigger brands' in the sector. There was, also, the closure of 12 forecourt stores that operated in partnership with petrol company Conoco, only a year after the collaboration was first launched, though the partnership still continues with Total and Q8.

Brighter news came from Budgens' entry into the franchising business. After the opening of its first Local Franchise store in Aylesbury, Bucks, other independent retailers were 'queuing up to join the scheme', it said. Under the 'mutually beneficial trading partnership', Budgens supplies fresh and own-label goods to the stores, which in return convert to the Budgens fascia. The company unveiled its Milton Keynes Local store, the second in the franchise scheme, and reported that it was on target to open 50 in the next two years. Latest news was that the scheme had signed up 21 stores belonging to a former Alldays regional development company. These stores will be converted to the new fascia and format and, presumably, trade as Budgens.

All of which inspired the Irish food group, Musgrave, to acquire a large stake in Budgens, buying it from German retail group, Rewe. The £89.4 million deal gives Musgrave a 28% stake in Budgens, but it said it would not bid for total control for at least a year unless 'a third party' moved on the company. Would anyone launch a takeover bid for Budgens unless they already had a large chunk of it? Doubtful. The latest figures I have showed that pre-tax profits were up by 10.3% to around £9 million on a probable annual turnover of some £500 million.

Slim pickings, then, in supermarketing and further proof that the biggest players in the business have to work on super-thin margins.

Budgens Stores Limited
PO Box 9
Stonefield Way
Ruislip
Middlesex
HA4 0JR

Tel 020 8422 9511
Fax 020 8864 2800
www.budgens.co.uk
info@budgens.com

## ARGENTINIAN RED

| | | |
|---|---|---|
| Argento Malbec 2000 | 17.5 | −£5.00 |
| Etchart Rio de Plata Tempranillo/Malbec 1999 | 14 | −£5.00 |
| La Nature Organic Barbera 2000 | 14 | −£5.00 |

## ARGENTINIAN WHITE

| | | |
|---|---|---|
| Argento Chardonnay 2001 | 15.5 | −£5.00 |
| Etchart Rio de Plata Torrontes/ Chardonnay 2000 | 12 | −£5.00 |
| La Nature Organic Torrontes 2000 | 14 | −£5.00 |

## AUSTRALIAN RED

| | | |
|---|---|---|
| Koonunga Hill Shiraz Cabernet Sauvignon 1999 | 15.5 | £5–7 |
| Oxford Landing Yalumba Cabernet Sauvignon Shiraz 2000 | 14.5 | £5–7 |
| Penfolds Bin 35 Rawsons Retreat Shiraz/Cabernet 1999 | 16 | £5–7 |
| Wolf Blass Yellow Label Cabernet 2000 | 13 | £7–10 |
| Wynns Coonawarra Shiraz 1998 | 15 | £5–7 |

## AUSTRALIAN WHITE

| | | |
|---|---|---|
| Hardys Nottage Hill Chardonnay 2000 | 16 | £5–7 |
| Hardys Stamp Grenache Shiraz Rosé 2000 | 11 | −£5.00 |
| Jacobs Creek Dry Riesling 2000 | 15 | £5–7 |
| Oxford Landing Chardonnay 2000 | 15.5 | −£5.00 |

Penfolds Koonunga
Hill Chardonnay 2000 `16` `£5–7`

Rosemount Semillon/
Chardonnay 2000 `15` `£5–7`

White Pointer 2000 `13` `–£5.00`

## CHILEAN RED

Paso del Sol Cabernet
Sauvignon 1999 `13` `–£5.00`

Stowells of Chelsea
Cabernet Merlot NV `14.5` `–£5.00`

Terra Andina Cabernet
Sauvignon 2000 `12` `–£5.00`

Terra Mater Zinfandel
Shiraz 2000 `14` `£7–10`

## CHILEAN WHITE

Paso del Sol Sauvignon
Blanc 2000 `13` `–£5.00`

Terra Andina
Chardonnay 2000 `13.5` `–£5.00`

## ENGLISH WHITE

Three Choirs Phoenix
1999 `11` `–£5.00`

## FRENCH RED

Chapelle St-Laurent
Côtes du Marmandais
1999 `12` `–£5.00`

Château St-Louis
Corbières 2000 `13` `–£5.00`

Côtes du Rhône-
Villages 2000 `11` `–£5.00`

Fleurs de France Merlot
Syrah Devereux NV `12` `–£3.50`

Fortant de France
Grenache VdP d'Oc
2000 `16` `–£5.00`

Fortant de France
Syrah 1999 `15` `–£5.00`

French Connection
Syrah Grenache 2000 `14.5` `–£5.00`

La Baume Syrah 1998 `15` `–£5.00`

La Nature French Red
VdP de l'Herault 2000 `11` `–£5.00`

Oaked Côtes du Rhône
Prestige Les
Faisandines 2000 `15.5` `–£5.00`

Premium Oaked
Cabernet Sauvignon/
Syrah VdP d'Oc,
Devereux NV `14` `–£5.00`

Rhône Valley Red
Côtes du Ventoux 2000 `13.5` `–£3.50`

## FRENCH WHITE

Bordeaux Sauvignon
NV, Budgens `13.5` `–£5.00`

Chardonnay VdP d'Oc
NV, Budgens `13.5` `–£3.50`

Devereux Premium
Cuvée Viognier NV `15.5` `–£5.00`

Domaine Fouassier
Sancerre Les
Chasseignes 2000 `13` `£7–10`

French Connection Grenache Sauvignon Blanc 2000 `14` `−£5.00`

Kiwi Cuvée Chardonnay VdP du Jardin de la France 2000 `14` `−£5.00`

Kiwi Cuvée Sauvignon Blanc, VdP du Jardin de la France 2000 `14` `−£5.00`

'L' Grande Cuvée VdP d'Oc 1999 `15.5` `£5–7`

La Baume Sauvignon Blanc 2000 `15.5` `−£5.00`

Premium Oaked Chardonnay VdP d'Oc, Devereux NV `14` `−£5.00`

## GERMAN WHITE

Devil's Rock Riesling 2000 `14` `−£5.00`

## HUNGARIAN RED

Riverview Kekfrancos/ Merlot 2000 `13.5` `−£5.00`

## HUNGARIAN WHITE

Riverview Chardonnay/Pinot Grigio 2000 `15` `−£5.00`

## ITALIAN RED

Il Padrino Sangiovese 2000 (Sicilia) `15.5` `−£5.00`

Trulli Primitivo Salento 1999 `14.5` `−£5.00`

Valpolicella NV, Budgens `12` `−£3.50`

## ITALIAN WHITE

Il Padrino Grecanico/ Chardonnay, Sicily 2000 `14.5` `−£5.00`

Sartori Pinot Grigio delle Venezie 2000 `14` `−£5.00`

Soave Dry NV, Budgens `12` `−£3.50`

Trulli Chardonnay del Salento 2000 `16` `−£5.00`

## NEW ZEALAND RED

Helderberg Pinotage 2000 `13` `−£5.00`

Montana Cabernet Sauvignon/Merlot 2000 `15` `£5–7`

## NEW ZEALAND WHITE

Corban's White Label Müller Thurgau/ Sauvignon Blanc 2000 `12` `−£5.00`

Corbans Sauvignon Blanc 2000 `13.5` `£5–7`

Montana Unoaked Chardonnay 2000 `16` `£5–7`

## PORTUGUESE RED

Dão Dom Ferraz 1999 — 15 — -£5.00

Segada Portuguese Red 2000 — 13 — -£5.00

## SOUTH AFRICAN RED

Kumala Cinsault Pinotage 2000 — 13.5 — -£5.00

Long Mountain Merlot Shiraz 2000 — 13.5 — £5–7

## SOUTH AFRICAN WHITE

Cape White NV, Budgens — 11 — -£3.50

Clear Mountain Chenin Blanc NV — 13.5 — -£5.00

Kumala Colombard/ Chardonnay 2000 — 14 — -£5.00

Long Mountain Sauvignon Blanc 2000 — 13 — -£5.00

Stowells of Chelsea Chenin Blanc NV — 13 — -£5.00

## SPANISH RED

Berberana Dragon Tempranillo 1999 — 14 — -£5.00

Berberana Rioja Tempranillo 1999 — 14 — £5–7

Masia Monistrol Tempranillo Garnacha Penedés 2000 — 14.5 — -£5.00

Palacio de la Vega Cabernet Sauvignon/ Tempranillo 1998 — 15.5 — £5–7

Piedemonte Merlot Cabernet Sauvignon, Navarra 1999 — 13 — -£5.00

Viña Albali Bataneros Barrel Aged Tempranillo, Valdepenas 1999 — 13 — -£5.00

Viña Albali Gran Reserva 1993 — 15 — £5–7

Viña Sardana Tempranillo, Calatayud 1999 — 14.5 — -£5.00

## SPANISH WHITE

Blanco, La Nature Organic, La Mancha 2000 — 13.5 — -£5.00

Castillo de Liria Moscatel de Valencia NV — 15.5 — -£5.00

Masia Monistrol Chardonnay Macabeo 2000 — 13 — -£5.00

## USA RED

Garnet Point Shiraz Cabernet 2000 — 15.5 — -£5.00

Glen Ellen Cabernet Sauvignon 1998 — 13 — £5–7

Marc Xero Merlot 1999 — 14 — -£5.00

Sutter Home Merlot 1998 — 13 — £5–7

## USA WHITE

Garnet Point Semillon Chardonnay 2000 `14.5` `–£5.00`

Marc Xero Chardonnay NV `15` `–£5.00`

## SPARKLING

Budgens Brut Champagne NV (France) `12` `£10–13`

Budgens Rosé Champagne NV (France) `10` `£10–13`

Chandon Australia Brut NV `13.5` `£7–10`

Hardys Stamp Sparkling Chardonnay Pinot Noir NV (Australia) `14` `£5–7`

Lindauer Brut NV (New Zealand) `15` `£5–7`

Pol Acker Sparkling Chardonnay NV (France) `10` `–£5.00`

Rosemount V Sparkling Chardonnay NV `14.5` `£7–10`

# CO-OP

Mr Paul Bastard had no excuse for his tardiness. In answer to the question I asked every retailer for this edition of *Superplonk* he stayed silent until two days after the deadline (excusing the delay with the highly plausible tale that the Co-op's e-mail service had gone haywire).

The question was: 'What, Paul old sport, in your opinion is the strength of your range of wines or the particular style of your way of retailing wine?' He replied:

> 'The backbone of our offer is as broad a sweep as possible of countries, grape varieties and wine styles up to the psychological price point of £3.99. (Much more of the esoteric is available but the Opus Ones, Thelemas, etc. represent the spiritual essence of the range not its essential driver.) The background for our offer combines responsible retailing (ingredients labelling; sound sourcing; a move towards organic viticulture), pragmatic retailing (value for money; a necessary branded presence; deep-cut promotions) and imaginative retailing (working by wine not by supplier; industry initiatives, e.g. Cyprus, Argentina; an enhanced own-label premium range; dump bins and wine towers in smaller stores). We are not grinding curmudgeons here; we expend much energy in implementing "the Co-op difference".'

Well, there's a lot here to set us thinking. Has any other retailer pondered more deeply about its purpose in life? I would only add that the Co-op's strength is the loyalty of its customers to all things Co-Opian, as outlined above, and in particular to the keen Bastard nose for a tasty bargain. Its style is its content. There is nothing flashy about the range. There is nothing flashy about the retailer.

Yet the Co-op has, quite splendidly, become the most adventurous wine retailer on the high street in one important respect: on its own-label bottles it provides, in defiance of European regulations, a full list of ingredients even though most leave no residue in the finished wine. No other retailer goes to these lengths. Now you may say, 'Surely wine is just made from grapes and yeast?' But the French routinely add beet sugar to wines from their less solar-charged climates like Bordeaux and Burgundy. In Australia,

South Africa and such clement places tartaric acid may be thrown in (sugar addition being unnecessary because of sufficient sun and in certain countries, like Australia, prohibited). Ascorbic acid, vitamin C, is used as an antioxidant. Potassium phosphate is also an antioxidant and preservative. To encourage yeast growth, diammonium phosphate may be employed. Enzymes may be used to clarify the juice, prior to fermentation, but they can be added after and the result is a fruitier wine. Lactic bacteria may be also welcomed in; they encourage the secondary fermentation where sharp malic acids are transformed into soft lactic acids. The fining agents used to clear fully fermented wine such as egg white, milk or gelatine obviously are not present in the finished wine, but nevertheless offend vegetarians and vegans; bentonite clay is widely used for white wines and offends no one (except the proteins and the larger bacteria it may snare and cause to be deprived of their environment). Polyvinylpolypyrrolidone sounds a repulsive mouthful but after it has been used to take out tannins it leaves no trace of itself. Sulphur (which occurs spontaneously in low levels in wine in any case) is added as an essential preservative to almost all wine, in very tiny amounts, and I've never tasted a wine without it which hadn't gone sour or oxidised in some way. Is there any Co-op wine where all these things are listed on the back label? Yes, Co-op's English Sparkling Wine (see appropriate listing for rating).

This has been a consolidating period for this large retailer, after the merger of the CRS (The Co-op Retail Sociey) and CWS (The Co-op Wholesale Society) into one coherent buying group. It got rid of stores surplus to requirements and bought stores in areas where it was not well represented. This resulted in flogging off two of its superstores – one to Tesco and the other to Sainsbury's – and buying eleven Somerfields. It all begins to sound like the summer football transfer market – especially when some of the players fail to find new teams. Indeed, the CWS closed Leigh, Burnley and Leytonstone superstores, in early 2001, after failing to find anyone interested in buying them.

CWS aims, apparently, to concentrate on its market town and small store concepts and offer 400 newly designed outlets by 2002 – at a cost of £200 million. CWS said it was on target to realise the full potential of the merger with CRS by 2002. In October, however, had come the most radical move of all: after 137 years of trading under CWS its members voted to change its name to the Co-operative Group. It quickly appointed two ad agencies to look after its media planning and buying, Starcom Motive and Mediacom North, and gave them a £12 million budget to play with.

In spring, the Co-operative Group became the first retailer in the UK to put Braille descriptions on packs of its own-label medicines and vitamins. It took two years of development, so it was reported, to find the technology to emboss the cardboard cartons and plastic labels with Braille. Perhaps part of this research was spent in the cellars of the Chapoutier wine company in the Rhône, which has had Braille wine labels for years.

The Co-op also extended its range of Fair Trade goods to include wine. In spite of the absence of agreed international criteria about a Fair Trade wine, the retailer teamed up with *Traidcraft*, the UK's largest fair trade organisation. The result was the establishment of a programme of help and support for the Los Robles co-operative in Chile's Curicó Valley. The Co-op's Fair Trade Carmenère 2000 was available in 1,800 stores at a special price of £3.99 (normal price £4.99). I rate initiatives like this very highly, though it would have helped matters if the retailer had sent samples of the wine, unasked, to leading wine critics. In this regard, the Co-op is still behind its dynamic competitors who never fail to make sure that people like myself are kept up-to-date with new developments and wine samples.

Finally, the Co-operative Group announced its first financial results since the merger of the CWS and CRS. The incorporation of the loss-making CRS did not affect overall profitability, but it did not boost it. The Co-operative Group's trading profit for the year was £130 million, almost the same as the CWS figure for the previous year.

Well, you know how it is with marriage. The first few years are always the stickiest. The other thing is that one of the partners always has some growing up to do, but in this case, whether it should be the CRS or CWS is impossible to say.

The Co-operative Group (CWS) Limited
PO Box 53
New Century House
Manchester
M60 4ES

Tel 0800 068 6727 Customer Careline
Fax 0161 827 6604
www.drinks2u.com

## ARGENTINIAN RED

Adiseno Cabernet Sauvignon Shiraz 1999 `16` `–£5.00`

Adiseno Shiraz Reserve 1999 `16` `£5–7`

Adiseno Tempranillo 2000 `15.5` `–£5.00`

Argentine Malbec 2000, Co-op `16` `–£5.00`

Argentine Malbec Bonarda 2000, Co-op `15.5` `–£5.00`

Argentine Old Vines Sangiovese 2000, Co-op `16` `–£5.00`

Argento Malbec 1999 `16` `–£5.00`

Bianchi Cabernet Sauvignon 1996 `17` `£7–10`

Bin 99 Argentine Cabernet Franc Reserve 1999, Co-op `16` `£5–7`

Corte X Syrah Torrontes 2000, Co-op `13` `–£5.00`

Elsa Barbera 1999 `15.5` `–£5.00`

Graffigna Shiraz Cabernet Sauvignon 1999 `16` `–£5.00`

Graffigna Shiraz Reserve 1999 `15.5` `–£5.00`

La Nature Organic Barbera 2000 `14` `–£5.00`

Lost Pampas Cabernet Malbec 1999, Co-op `14` `–£5.00`

Mission Peak Argentine Red NV `15.5` `–£3.50`

Valentin Bianchi Cabernet Sauvignon 1997 `16` `£7–10`

Weinert Malbec 1994 `16` `£7–10`

## ARGENTINIAN WHITE

Balbi Shiraz Rosé 2000 `13` `–£5.00`

Bright Brothers Viognier Reserve 1999 `15` `£5–7`

Elsa Sémillon Chardonnay 2000 `14.5` `–£5.00`

Etchart Rio de Plata Torrontes 2000 `15.5` `–£5.00`

First Ever Chardonnay 2000 `13.5` `–£5.00`

La Nature Organic Torrontes 2000 `14` `–£5.00`

Lost Pampas Oaked Chardonnay 1999, Co-op `16` `–£5.00`

Mission Peak Argentine White NV `15.5` `–£3.50`

Y2K Chardonnay, San Juan 1999 `16` `–£5.00`

## AUSTRALIAN RED

Andrew Peace Masterpeace Shiraz 2000 `13` `£5–7`

Australian Cabernet Sauvignon 1999, Co-op `13` `–£5.00`

Australian Grenache 2000, Co-op `13.5` `–£5.00`

Australian Merlot 2000, Co-op | 14 | −£5.00

Australian Merlot 2001, Co-op | 15.5 | −£5.00

Brown Brothers Tarrango 1999 | 13.5 | £5–7

Deakin Select Merlot 1999 | 14 | £5–7

E & E Black Pepper Shiraz 1996 | 16 | £20+

Hardys Coonawarra Cabernet Sauvignon 1997 | 16 | £7–10

Jacaranda Hill Shiraz 2000, Co-op | 13 | −£5.00

Leasingham Cabernet Sauvignon/Malbec 1996 | 16.5 | £7–10

Lindemans Cawarra Shiraz/Cabernet 1999 | 13 | −£5.00

Little Boomey Cabernet Merlot 2000 | 15 | £5–7

Rosemount Estate Grenache/Shiraz 2000 | 13 | £5–7

Wolf Blass Yellow Label Cabernet 2000 | 13 | £7–10

## AUSTRALIAN WHITE

Australian Chardonnay 2000, Co-op | 15.5 | −£5.00

Barramundi Semillon/ Chardonnay NV | 16 | −£5.00

Bethany Chardonnay 1998 | 16 | £5–7

Bethany Riesling 2001 | 16 | £5–7

Brown Brothers Late Harvested Orange Muscat & Flora 2000 (half bottle) | 16 | £5–7

Hardys Chardonnay Sauvignon Blanc 1998 | 15 | £5–7

Jacaranda Hill Semillon 2000, Co-op | 13 | −£5.00

Oxford Landing Sauvignon Blanc 2000 | 16 | −£5.00

Rosemount Estate GTR 2000 | 15 | £5–7

Yellow Tail Chardonnay 2000 | 14.5 | −£5.00

## BULGARIAN RED

Bulgarian Cabernet Sauvignon 2000, Co-op | 15 | −£3.50

Mount Sofia Merlot Pinot Noir NV | 14.5 | −£3.50

Oravinifera Cabernet Sauvignon Reserve 1996 | 16 | −£5.00

Sliven Merlot/Pinot Noir NV | 13.5 | −£3.50

## BULGARIAN WHITE

Shumen Chardonnay Sauvignon Blanc 2000 | 14.5 | −£3.50

Shumen Muskat & Ugni Blanc 1999 | 14 | −£3.50

Sliven Valley of the Roses Rosé 2000 | 13.5 | −£3.50

## CHILEAN RED

Antares Merlot 2000          16    −£5.00

Casa Lapostolle Merlot      18    £10–13
Cuvée Alexandre 1997

Chilean Cabernet            15    −£5.00
Sauvignon NV, Co-op

Chilean Fair Trade          15.5  −£5.00
Carmenère 2000, Co-op

Four Rivers Malbec          14    −£5.00
1999

Las Lomas Côt Reserva       15.5  £5–7
1999

Las Lomas Organic           15    −£5.00
Chilean Red 1999

Long Slim Cabernet          16    −£5.00
Merlot 2000

Terra Mater Malbec          15.5  −£5.00
1999

Terra Mater Zinfandel       14    £7–10
Shiraz 2000

Valdivieso Cabernet         17    £7–10
Franc Reserve 1997

Viña Gracia Cabernet        15.5  £5–7
Sauvignon Reserve
1999

Vinã Gracia Carmenère       16    −£5.00
Reserve Especial 1999

## CHILEAN WHITE

Four Rivers                 13.5  −£5.00
Chardonnay 2000

Long Slim Chardonnay        13    −£5.00
Sémillon 2000

Santa Carolina              16.5  −£5.00
Chardonnay 1999

## CYPRIOT RED

Island Vines Cyprus         13    −£3.50
Red 2000, Co-op

Mountain Vines              16    −£5.00
Reserve Cabernet/
Maratheftiko 1999,
Co-op

## CYPRIOT WHITE

Island Vines Cyprus         14.5  −£3.50
White 2000, Co-op

Mountain Vines              14    −£5.00
Sémillon 1998, Co-op

## FRENCH RED

Beaujolais NV, Co-op        12    −£5.00

Beaujolais-Villages         9     −£3.50
Nouveau 2000

Calvet Reserve Red          10    £5–7
1998

Château de l'Hospital       13    £7–10
Graves 1997

Château Fourtanet           15    £5–7
Côtes de Castillon 1997

Château Laurencon           14    −£5.00
Bordeaux Supérieur
1998

Château Pierrousselle       14    −£5.00
Bordeaux 1999

Château Thezannes Corbières 1998 — 15 — −£5.00

Château Villeranque Haut-Médoc 1997 — 15 — £7–10

Chevalière Réserve Grenache Vieilles Vignes 1999 — 13 — −£5.00

Claret NV, Co-op — 15 — −£3.50

Corbierès Rouge NV, Co-op — 15 — −£3.50

Corso Merlot 1999 — 12 — −£5.00

Domaine Les Combelles Minervois 1998 — 13.5 — −£5.00

Fleurie 2000 — 12 — £5–7

French Organic Merlot Syrah 2000, Co-op — 13.5 — −£5.00

French Organic Red 2000, Co-op — 14 — −£5.00

Merlot VdP des Portes de Mediterrenée 1999 — 12 — −£3.50

Nuits-St-Georges 1996 — 9 — £7–10

Oak Aged Claret NV, Co-op — 13 — −£5.00

Rhône Valley Red 1999 — 14.5 — −£3.50

Vin de Pays d'Oc Cabernet Sauvignon NV, Co-op — 15 — −£3.50

Vin de Pays d'Oc Fruity Red NV, Co-op — 14.5 — −£3.50

Vin de Pays d'Oc Merlot NV, Co-op — 14 — −£3.50

Vin de Pays d'Oc Syrah Mourvèdre NV, Co-op — 12.5 — −£5.00

Vin de Pays d'Oc Syrah NV, Co-op — 14.5 — −£3.50

Vin de Pays d'Oc Syrah/Malbec, Co-op (vegetarian) — 15.5 — −£5.00

## FRENCH WHITE

Alsace Gewürztraminer 2000 — 16.5 — £5–7

Calvet Reserve White 1999 — 11 — −£5.00

Chardonnay-Chenin Vegetarian NV, Co-op — 12.5 — −£5.00

Château Pierrousselle Entre-Deux-Mers 2000 — 14.5 — −£5.00

Chevalière Réserve Chardonnay 1999 — 12 — −£5.00

French Organic Chardonnay Sauvignon Blanc 2000, Co-op — 14 — −£5.00

French Organic White 2000, Co-op — 14 — −£5.00

James Herrick Chardonnay 1999 — 16 — −£5.00

Monbazillac Domaine du Haut-Rauly 1998 (half bottle) — 16.5 — −£5.00

Montagny Premier Cru 1998 — 13 — £7–10

Orchid Vale Chardonnay Grenache Blanc 1999 — 13.5 — −£5.00

Rhône Valley White 1999   14   −£3.50

Sancerre Domaine Raimbault 1998   13   £5–7

Vin de Pays d'Oc Chardonnay Viognier NV, Co-op   13.5   −£5.00

Vin de Pays d'Oc Chenin Chardonnay NV, Co-op (vegetarian)   12   −£5.00

Vin de Pays d'Oc Syrah Rosé NV, Co-op   11   −£3.50

Vin de Pays des Côtes de Gascogne, Co-op   14.5   −£3.50

Vin de Pays du Jardin de la France Sauvignon Blanc NV, Co-op   12   −£3.50

## GERMAN WHITE

Bockenheimer Grafenstuck Beerenauslese 1998 (half bottle)   16   −£5.00

Devil's Rock Riesling 2000   14   −£5.00

Graacher Himmelreich Riesling Spätlese 1999   13   −£5.00

Kendermans Dry Riesling 1999   11   −£5.00

Twin Rivers Riesling 2000   13   −£5.00

## HUNGARIAN RED

Hungarian Country Wine NV, Co-op   13   −£3.50

Kekfrancos Oaked Merlot 1999, Co-op   13   −£5.00

## HUNGARIAN WHITE

Chapel Hill Irsai Oliver 2000   13   −£3.50

Gyöngyös Estate Chardonnay 1999   14   −£5.00

Hungarian White NV, Co-op   13.5   −£3.50

Riverview Chardonnay/Pinot Grigio 2000   15   −£5.00

## ITALIAN RED

Barrelaia NV, Co-op   13   −£5.00

Bona Terra Organic Merlot 1999   13   −£5.00

Il Padrino Rosso Sicilia 1999   15   −£5.00

Inycon Merlot 1999 (Sicily)   15.5   −£5.00

Otto Santi Chianti Classico 1999   13   £5–7

Puglia Primitivo Sangiovese 2000, Co-op   15   −£5.00

Trulli Primitivo del Salento 1998   14.5   −£5.00

Valpolicella NV, Co-op   12   −£3.50

Zagara Nero d'Avola Cabernet 2000 — 12 — −£5.00

## ITALIAN WHITE

Chardonnay dell'Umbria 1999, Co-op — 12 — −£5.00

Chardonnay Vallagerina 2000, Co-op — 15 — −£5.00

Puglia Chardonnay Bombino 1999, Co-op — 12 — −£5.00

Villa Lanata Gavi 2000 — 16.5 — −£5.00

Zagara Catarratto Chardonnay Firriato 2000 (Sicily) — 16.5 — −£5.00

## NEW ZEALAND RED

Terrace View Cabernet Merlot 1999 — 13 — −£5.00

## NEW ZEALAND WHITE

Explorer's Vineyard Sauvignon Blanc 2000, Co-op — 14 — £5–7

Matua Valley Sauvignon Blanc 2001 — 16.5 — £5–7

Oyster Bay Marlborough Chardonnay 2000 — 15.5 — £5–7

Oyster Bay Sauvignon Blanc 2000 — 16 — £5–7

Stoneleigh Chardonnay 1999 — 15.5 — −£5.00

## PORTUGUESE RED

Big Baga 1999, Co-op — 13.5 — −£5.00

Portada Tinto 2000 — 13 — −£5.00

Star Mountain Oak Aged 1997 — 13.5 — −£5.00

Star Mountain Touriga Nacional 1997 — 14 — −£5.00

Terra Boa Portuguese Red 2000 — 13 — −£5.00

## PORTUGUESE WHITE

Fiuza Chardonnay 1999 — 16 — −£5.00

Portuguese Chardonnay 1999, Co-op — 14.5 — £5–7

## ROMANIAN RED

Prahova Valley Pinot Noir 1999 — 12.5 — −£3.50

Prahova Valley Special Reserve Merlot 1999 — 15 — −£5.00

Romanian Prairie Merlot 1999, Co-op — 14.5 — −£3.50

## SOUTH AFRICAN RED

Cape American Oak Pinotage 1999, Co-op — 14 — −£5.00

Cape Indaba Pinotage 1998 — 13 — −£5.00

Cape Red NV, Co-op — 11 — −£3.50

Cape Ruby Cabernet, Oak Aged 2000, Co-op — 13 — −£5.00

Elephant Trail `15` `−£5.00`
Cinsault/Merlot 2000,
Co-op

Fire Engine Red 1999 `15.5` `−£5.00`

Goiya Giaan 2000 `13` `−£5.00`

Kumala Ruby Cabernet `15` `−£5.00`
Merlot 2000

Natural State Cape `15` `£5–7`
Soleil Organic Shiraz
1999

Oak Village Cabernet `13` `−£5.00`
Sauvignon 1999

Pinnacle Merlot 1998 `16` `£5–7`

Railroad Cabernet `15` `−£5.00`
Sauvignon Shiraz 1999

Spice Route Cabernet `16.5` `£7–10`
Sauvignon/Merlot 1998

Three Worlds Pinotage `15.5` `£5–7`
Shiraz Zinfandel 1999,
Co-op

Winds of Change `14` `−£5.00`
Pinotage/Cabernet
Sauvignon 1999

## SOUTH AFRICAN WHITE

Cape Chenin Blanc, `13.5` `−£5.00`
Oak Aged 2000, Co-op

Cape Soleil Organic `13` `−£5.00`
Chardonnay 1999,
Co-op

Cape White NV, Co-op `13` `−£3.50`

Elephant River `14` `−£3.50`
Colombard/
Chardonnay 2000,
Co-op

First Release `13.5` `−£5.00`
Chardonnay 2000

Goiya Kgeisje `15` `−£5.00`
Chardonnay Sauvignon
Blanc 2000

Not Too Dry `12` `−£5.00`
Chardonnay 2001

Oak Village Sauvignon `13` `−£5.00`
Blanc 1999

Pendulum Pink 2001 `12` `−£5.00`

Robert's Rock `13.5` `−£5.00`
Chardonnay Semillon
2000

Spice Route Chenin `16` `£5–7`
Blanc 1998

Stowells South African `13` `−£5.00`
Chenin Blanc NV

## SPANISH RED

Berberana Rioja `14` `−£5.00`
Tempranillo 1999

Berberana Rioja Viura `13` `−£5.00`
1999

Campo Rojo Cariñena `12` `−£3.50`
NV

Chestnut Gully `15.5` `−£5.00`
Monastrell-Merlot
1999, Co-op

Rioja Tinto, Viña Gala `13.5` `−£5.00`
NV, Co-op

Tempranillo Oak Aged NV, Co-op | 13 | −£3.50

Tierra Sana Organic Wine 1999, Co-op | 17 | −£5.00

XV Monastrell 2000 | 16 | −£5.00

## SPANISH WHITE

Gandia Grenache Rosé 1999 | 14.5 | −£5.00

Jaume Serra Chardonnay 1999 | 16 | −£5.00

Torres Viña Sol 2000 | 15.5 | −£5.00

## USA RED

California Premium Red NV, Co-op | 13.5 | −£3.50

Fetzer Valley Oaks Cabernet Sauvignon 1998 | 14.5 | £5−7

'Laid Back Ruby' California Ruby Cabernet 1999, Co-op | 15 | −£5.00

Sebastiani Sonoma Cask Old Vine Zinfandel 1998 | 15.5 | £7−10

## USA WHITE

Garnet Point Chardonnay-Chenin 1997 | 15.5 | −£5.00

Sebastiani Sonoma Chardonnay 1998 | 15.5 | £7−10

'The Big Chill' California Colombard Chardonnay 1999, Co-op | 13.5 | −£5.00

'The Big Chill' California Colombard Chardonnay 2000, Co-op | 13.5 | −£5.00

## FORTIFIED

Dow's LBV Port 1995 | 14.5 | £7−10

Graham's LBV Port 1994 | 13.5 | £10−13

Warre's Warrior Special Reserve Port NV | 13 | £7−10

## SPARKLING

Asti NV, Co-op | 11 | −£5.00

Australian Quality Sparkling Wine, Co-op | 14 | −£5.00

Blossom Hill NV (USA) | 13 | £5−7

Cava Brut NV, Co-op | 14 | −£5.00

English Sparkling Brut NV, Co-op | 12 | £5−7

Inanda Brut NV (South Africa) | 15.5 | −£5.00

Jacob's Creek Sparkling Chardonnay/Pinot Noir NV (Australia) | 15 | £5−7

Jean de Bracieux Champagne NV (France) | 12 | £10−13

Moscato Spumante NV, `11` `–£5.00`
Co-op (Italy)

Sparkling Saumur NV, `11` `£5–7`
Co-op

Rosemount V Sparkling `14.5` `£5–7`
Chardonnay NV

Tempranillo Brut Red `13.5` `£5–7`
NV, Co-op

Sparkling Chardonnay `12` `–£5.00`
NV, Co-op (France)

Y2K Champagne NV `13` `£13–20`
(France)

# KWIK SAVE

See Somerfield/Kwik Save, page 293

## AUSTRALIAN RED

Australian Dry Red 2000, Somerfield — 13 — £5.00

Australian Shiraz Cabernet 2000, Somerfield — 14 — £5.00

Banrock Station Shiraz/Mataro 2000 — 15 — £5.00

## AUSTRALIAN WHITE

Banrock Station Colombard Chardonnay 2001 — 14 — £5.00

## BULGARIAN RED

Bulgarian Cabernet Sauvignon 1999. Somerfield — 13.5 — £3.50

Bulgarian Country Red 2000, Somerfield — 13 — £3.50

## CHILEAN RED

Chilean Cabernet Sauvignon Viña La Rosa 2000, Somerfield — 15.5 — £5.00

## CHILEAN WHITE

Chilean Chardonnay 2000, Somerfield — 15.5 — £5.00

Chilean White 2000, Somerfield — 14 — £3.50

## FRENCH RED

Brouilly Les Celliers de Bellevue 2000 — 14 — £5–7

Cabernet Sauvignon d'Oc 2000, Somerfield — 14 — £3.50

Claret 2000, Somerfield — 15 — £3.50

Corbières Rouge 2000, Somerfield — 13 — £3.50

Côtes du Rhône 2000, Somerfield — 13 — £3.50

Les Oliviers French Red NV — 13.5 — £2.50

Skylark Hill Red 2000 — 12 — £3.50

## FRENCH WHITE

Les Oliviers French White NV — 14.5 — £2.50

242

Muscadet 2000, Somerfield    `13`  −£3.50

Skylark Hill VdP du Comte Tolosan 2000    `15`  −£3.50

Winter Hill White 2000  `14`  −£5.00

## GERMAN WHITE

Hock NV, Somerfield  `14.5`  −£2.50

## ITALIAN RED

Montepulciano d'Abruzzo 2000, Somerfield    `14`  −£5.00

## ITALIAN WHITE

Sicilian White 2000, Somerfield    `14`  −£3.50

Soave 2000, Somerfield  `13.5`  −£5.00

## SPANISH RED

Don Darias Red NV    `14.5`  −£3.50

Flamenco Red NV    `11`  −£3.50

Viña Cana Rioja Crianza 1998, Somerfield    `14`  −£5.00

## SPANISH WHITE

Moscatel de Valencia, Somerfield    `16`  −£3.50

## SPARKLING

Asti Spumante NV, Somerfield    `11.5`  £5–7

Cava Brut NV, Somerfield    `15`  −£5.00

Freixenet Cordon Negro Brut NV    `14`  £5–7

Martini Asti Spumante NV    `11`  £5–7

Moscato Fizz, Somerfield (Italy)    `13`  −£2.50

# MARKS & SPENCER

This retailer needs all the support we can give it. Personally, I attend wine tastings kitted out in M&S underpants under M&S chinos and M&S lightweight Italian socks in my M&S casual shoes. My shirt, and often my sweater, has a M&S label (usually so dated it claims descent from St Michael). Only my belt comes from elsewhere.

M&S is more important than the royal family yet it has come in for acres of critical mis-acclaim over its commercial difficulties, its problems over laying off workers in Europe, and its apparent failure to judge the style requirements of its customers. Ironically, in July 2000, it revealed its 'Exclusively for Everyone' advertising slogan for the first time, the centre of a new £27 million advertising campaign, scheduled to begin in September 2000. The slogan may be nonsense but I am the living proof of its truth.

The wines? Some splendid examples, some not so splendid, some patently created to match a perceived need (thus somewhat lacking in character and style). As with all the retailers in this book, I asked M&S the same question: 'What in your opinion is the strength of your range of wines or the particular style of your way of retailing wine?'

It replied:

> 'Marks & Spencer has a highly qualified wine team that works with our wine suppliers and the wine-makers to develop exclusive wines that are unique to M&S. Our first consideration is to always find the highest quality wines. Over the next 18 months we will be expanding the range of our wines, adding 50% to the catalogue, bringing new and exciting wines to our customers, with the reassurance of M&S quality.'

In other words, M&S organises how it sources wines in the same meticulous way it organises how sandwiches are made up and underpants sewn. The strength of the wine range is that it is situated within an M&S store that offers these other things. As for its particular style . . . well, it has none. The M&S stores I walk into have the wines as adjuncts to the food departments and what style there is can be best described as basic or, if you prefer, no-nonsense. There really is not much more to say about the wines, the entries that follow speak for themselves.

However, the company as a whole has had a torrid time, descending from its totemic place in the UK retailing hierarchy to one of widely critical disdain in spite of some interesting initiatives. For example, last summer in an attempt to combat its falling profits M&S reportedly warned suppliers to shave 2% off their prices.

Following hard on the heels of this tough stance and to show it meant business, M&S opened three stores, at Ashford, Cheshire Oaks and Livingston, offering reductions of up to 30%. The M&S chairman, Luc Vandevelde, then issues a call-to-arms to his staff and slammed negative comments made by former chairman, Sir Richard Greenbury. Sir Richard had said on Radio 4 that the 'jury is still out' regarding the future of M&S and he publicly questioned the changes in buying, distribution and head office structure instituted by Mr Vandevelde. 'We'll have to wait and see whether such enormous change was necessary,' he said. In an interview in *The Sunday Times,* in August last year, the former chairman was also critical of the 'revolution' at the store, saying that new designer ranges would alienate traditional customers.

Personally, I thought Sir Richard was right. I'm a trad customer and I thought the new Autograph range, for example, was totally out of place. I visited the section given over to this range many times at a key high street location and only once did I witness a flicker of interest by a cool dude customer. Mr Vandevelde quite rightly was upset by the former chairman's comments and did not mince his words in an e-mail to staff: 'I am shocked that a former chairman has spoken publicly in a way that is clearly damaging to the company and painful to our people.'

Some months later, spring 2001, Mr Vandevelde made an unprecedented personal plea to M&S shoppers to keep faith in the retailer. Posters were put up in the company's 299 stores after the retailer announced its radical restructuring programme. The message read: 'Our plan is to create a more focused organisation so that we are able to get on with what we do best. We are determined to restore an unquestioned reputation for quality, value, service and innovation.'

As long as they don't start employing the sort of sweat shops that got Nike into so much trouble, M&S can count on my support as an underpants and sock wearer. It is, after all, an important British company still doing massive business. The trade magazine *Retail Week* printed a list of the top

500 UK retailers and this showed M&S's turnover had dropped from £6.6 billion in 1999 to £6.48 billion in 2000.

It is widely predicted that turnover will show a further decline in 2001. All I can say is that I'm doing my bit to help. There's still no one else with cheaper socks and pants at the same quality, and though the range of wines cannot make the same claim there are nevertheless some extremely worthy bottles.

Marks & Spencer Plc
Michael House
57 Baker Street
London
W1U 8EP

Tel 020 7268 1234
Fax 020 7268 2380
www.marksandspencer.com

## ARGENTINIAN RED

| | | |
|---|---|---|
| Canale Estate Reserve Merlot 1999 | 16 | £7–10 |
| Rio Santos Bonarda Barbera 2000 | 14.5 | –£5.00 |
| Rio Santos Cabernet Sauvignon Syrah 2000 | 15.5 | –£5.00 |
| Rio Santos Malbec 2000 | 16.5 | –£5.00 |
| San Pablo Estate NV | 16 | £7–10 |
| Villar Cortes Cabernet Sauvignon 1999 | 15.5 | £7–10 |

## ARGENTINIAN WHITE

| | | |
|---|---|---|
| Rio Santos Torrontes 2000 | 14 | –£5.00 |

## AUSTRALIAN RED

| | | |
|---|---|---|
| Cabernet/Shiraz 1999 | 12 | £5–7 |
| Clare Valley Merlot/ Cabernet Sauvignon/ Cabernet Franc/Malbec 1998 | 13.5 | £7–10 |
| Honey Tree Cabernet Merlot 2000 | 15.5 | £5–7 |
| Honey Tree Shiraz Cabernet 2000 | 13 | £5–7 |
| Honey Tree Grenache Shiraz 1999 | 13 | £5–7 |
| Honey Tree Reserve Pinot Noir 1999 | 14 | £7–10 |
| Honey Tree Shiraz Reserve 1998 | 14 | £7–10 |

Lenbridge Forge Pinot Noir 2000 — 12 — £7–10

SE Australian Shiraz 1999 — 15 — £5–7

Shiraz Merlot Ruby Cabernet Bin 312 2000 — 15 — −£5.00

South East Australian Cabernet 2000 — 16.5 — −£5.00

South East Australian Merlot 2000 — 15.5 — −£5.00

South Eastern Australian Shiraz 2000 — 14.5 — −£5.00

Twin Wells Heathcote Shiraz 1999 — 16 — £7–10

## AUSTRALIAN WHITE

Australian Chardonnay/Semillon/Colombard 2000 — 12 — −£3.50

Chardonnay Bin 109 2000 — 15.5 — −£5.00

Honey Tree Gewürztraminer Riesling 2000 — 15 — £5–7

Honey Tree Semillon Chardonnay 2000 — 15 — £5–7

McLean's Farm Riesling, St Hallett 2000 — 13 — £7–10

Semillon Bin 381 2000 — 16 — −£5.00

South Eastern Australian Chardonnay 2000 — 16 — −£5.00

Tumbarumba Chardonnay 1998 — 14.5 — £7–10

## CHILEAN RED

Casa Leona Cabernet Sauvignon 2000 — 16.5 — −£5.00

Casa Leona Merlot 2000 — 16.5 — −£5.00

Cuartel 34 Malbec Reserve 1999 — 16 — £7–10

Leon de Oro Merlot/Cabernet Sauvignon 1999 — 17 — £7–10

Los Claveles Cabernet/Carmenère 2000 — 15 — −£5.00

Pirque Estate Cabernet Sauvignon/Merlot 2000 — 16.5 — £5–7

Sierra Los Andes Merlot Cabernet 1999 — 16 — £5–7

Sierra Los Andes Reserve Cabernet Merlot 1999 — 17.5 — £5–7

Tolten Syrah/Cabernet Sauvignon 1999 — 17 — £7–10

## CHILEAN WHITE

Barrera Chardonnay 2000 — 13.5 — −£5.00

Casa Leona Chardonnay 2000 — 14 — −£5.00

Los Claveles Gewürztraminer 2000 — 13.5 — −£5.00

Pirque Estate Chardonnay 2000 — 13 — £7–10

Pirque Estate Sauvignon Blanc 2000 — 13 — £7–10

## FRENCH RED

Beaune Cent-Vignes Premier Cru 1999 — `12` `£13–20`

Benjamin de Pontet Pauillac 1997 — `16` `£10–13`

Bin 121 Merlot/Ruby Cabernet 2000 — `14` `–£5.00`

Bourgogne Hautes-Côtes de Nuits Genevrières 1999 — `11` `£7–10`

Bourgogne Rouge Sordet 1998 — `11` `£7–10`

Château d'Artix Minervois 1999 — `16.5` `£5–7`

Château de Surville Costières de Nîmes 1999 — `17` `£5–7`

Château Gallais Bellevue Cru Bourgeois, Médoc 1998 — `13.5` `£5–7`

Château Gressina, Bordeaux Supérieur 2000 — `14` `–£5.00`

Château Haut Duriez Haut-Médoc 2000 — `15` `£5–7`

Château La Roseraie Dumont Puisseguin Saint-Emilion 2000 — `16.5` `£5–7`

Château Lataste Premières Côtes de Bordeaux 1996 — `16` `–£5.00`

Coeur de Vallée VdP d'Oc 2000 — `14.5` `–£5.00`

Côtes du Parc, Coteaux du Languedoc 2000 (organic) — `16` `–£5.00`

Domaine Galetis Cabernet/Merlot VdP d'Oc 2000 — `15` `–£5.00`

Domaine St Pierre VdP de l'Hérault 2000 — `13` `–£3.50`

Gold Label Cabernet Sauvignon VdP d'Oc 2000 — `15` `–£5.00`

Gold Label Reserve Barrel Aged Syrah VdP d'Oc 1998 — `16.5` `£5–7`

Gold Label Syrah VdP d'Oc 2000 — `14.5` `–£5.00`

House Red Wine, VdP du Comte Tolosan 2000 — `13.5` `–£3.50`

La Colonie VdP des Collines de la Moure 1998 — `16.5` `£5–7`

Les Romaines VdP d'Oc 1998 — `17` `£7–10`

Margaux 1997 — `13.5` `£10–13`

Mercurey Premier Cru Domaine Levert 1998 — `11` `£7–10`

Rock Ridge Cabernet Sauvignon 2000 — `15.5` `–£5.00`

St-Joseph, Cuvée Côte-Diane, 1998 — `16` `£7–10`

Silver Tree Shiraz 1999 — `14` `£7–10`

Terre du Lion St-Julien 1997 — `15.5` `£7–10`

Volnay Premier Cru 1999 — `13.5` `£13–20`

## FRENCH WHITE

Bordeaux Sauvignon 2000 — 16 — −£5.00

Chablis Grand Cru Grenouille 1995 — 14 — £20+

Chablis Premier Cru Fourchaume 1997 — 13.5 — £10–13

Chassagne-Montrachet Premier Cru Morgeot 'Les Senteurs' 1998 — 10 — £20+

Château La Gordonne Côtes de Provence Rosé 2000 — 13.5 — −£5.00

Coeur de Vallée VdP d'Oc 2000 — 16.5 — −£5.00

Domaine de Castellas Côtes de Roussillon 2000 — 15 — −£5.00

Domaine de Chevaunet Touraine Sauvignon Blanc 2000 — 15.5 — −£5.00

Domaine de la Pouvraie Vouvray 2000 — 15 — −£5.00

Domaine Galatis Chardonnay/Viognier VdP d'Oc 2000 — 15.5 — −£5.00

Domaine Mandeville Viognier 2000 — 15 — −£5.00

Gold Label Barrel Fermented Chardonnay Reserve 2000 — 15.5 — £5–7

Gold Label Chardonnay VdP d'Oc 2000 — 16 — −£5.00

Gold Label Sauvignon Blanc VdP d'Oc 2000 — 15.5 — −£5.00

Les Ruettes Sancerre 2000 — 14.5 — £7–10

Mâcon-Villages 2000 — 15 — £5–7

Mercurey Premier Cru Domaine de la Grangerie 1999 — 15 — £10–13

Pouilly-Fumé Les Vignes de St-Laurent-l'Abbaye 2000 — 15.5 — £7–10

Rosé d'Anjou 2000 — 12 — −£5.00

Rosé de Syrah VdP d'Oc 2000 — 15.5 — −£5.00

St-Véran Les Monts 1999 — 16 — £5–7

St-Aubin Premier Cru Domaine du Pimont 1998 — 13.5 — £10–13

Sancerre Domaine Hubert Brochard 2000 — 13 — £7–10

Silver Tree Chardonnay 2000 — 14.5 — £5–7

VdP des Côtes de Gascogne 2000 — 14 — −£3.50

Vin de Pays du Gers 2000 — 15 — −£3.50

## ITALIAN RED

Amarone Classico della Valpolicella Villalta 1997 — 16.5 — £10–13

Barolo 1996 — 13.5 — £13–20

| | | |
|---|---|---|
| Canfera 1997 | 14.5 | £7–10 |
| Chianti Classico Basilica Cafaggio Single Estate 1999 | 16 | £7–10 |
| Italian Table Red Wine NV (1 litre) | 14 | –£3.50 |
| Montepulciano d'Abruzzo 2000 | 15.5 | £7–10 |
| Reggiano Rosso Single Estate 2000 | 13 | –£5.00 |
| Rosso di Puglia 2000 | 15 | –£3.50 |
| Sangiovese di Puglia 2000 | 15.5 | –£5.00 |
| Valpolicella Classico Single Estate 1999 | 15 | –£5.00 |

## ITALIAN WHITE

| | | |
|---|---|---|
| Frascati Superiore Single Estate 2000 | 15.5 | –£5.00 |
| Orvieto Single Estate 2000 | 16 | –£5.00 |
| Pinot Grigio/ Garganega 2000 | 14.5 | –£5.00 |
| Soave Superiore Single Estate 2000 | 16 | –£5.00 |
| Villa Masera Organic Wine 2000 | 15 | –£5.00 |

## NEW ZEALAND RED

| | | |
|---|---|---|
| Kaituna Hills Cabernet Merlot 1999 | 16 | £5–7 |
| Kaituna Hills Reserve Cabernet Merlot 1999 | 15.5 | £7–10 |
| Kaituna Hills Reserve Pinot Noir 1999 | 10 | £7–10 |

## NEW ZEALAND WHITE

| | | |
|---|---|---|
| Kaituna Blue Sauvignon Semillon 2000 | 13 | –£5.00 |
| Kaituna Hills Chardonnay 2000 | 15.5 | £5–7 |
| Kaituna Hills Reserve Chardonnay 2000 | 13.5 | £7–10 |
| Kaituna Hills Reserve Sauvignon Blanc 1999 | 14 | £7–10 |
| Kaituna Hills Sauvignon Blanc 2000 | 14 | £5–7 |
| Shepherds Ridge Chardonnay 1999 | 13.5 | £7–10 |
| Shepherds Ridge Sauvignon Blanc 2000 | 13 | £7–10 |

## SOUTH AFRICAN RED

| | | |
|---|---|---|
| Cape Country Cinsault/Ruby Cabernet 2000 | 13 | –£5.00 |
| Monate Cabernet Sauvignon 1999 | 13 | £7–10 |
| Monate Shiraz 2000 | 15.5 | £7–10 |
| Rock Ridge Pinotage 2000 | 14 | –£5.00 |
| Warwick Estate Trilogy 1997 | 12 | £7–10 |

## SOUTH AFRICAN WHITE

Cape Country Chenin Blanc 2001 `14.5` `–£5.00`

'Life from Stone' Sauvignon Blanc, Springfield Estate 2000 `13.5` `£5–7`

Rockridge Chardonnay 2000 `14` `–£5.00`

## SPANISH RED

Almuran Monastrell 2000 `15` `–£5.00`

Las Falleras 2000 `13.5` `–£3.50`

Marisa Tempranillo 2000 `13` `–£5.00`

Rioja Roseral Crianza 1998 `13` `£5–7`

## SPANISH WHITE

Moscatel de Valencia 2000 `16` `–£5.00`

## URUGUAYAN RED

Polo Sur Pisano Family Reserve Tannat 2000 `14` `£7–10`

## USA RED

Clear Lake Cabernet Franc 2000 `15` `–£5.00`

Freedom Ridge Shiraz 2000 `13.5` `£5–7`

Live Oak Road Old Bush Vine Zinfandel 2000 `13.5` `£7–10`

Zamora Zinfandel 1999 `12` `£5–7`

## USA WHITE

Clear Lake Chardonnay 2000 `15.5` `–£5.00`

Clear Lake Rosé Merlot/Cabernet 2000 `12` `–£5.00`

Dunnigan Lane Fume Blanc 2000 `15.5` `£5–7`

Gardeners Grove Chardonnay 2000 `15.5` `£7–10`

## SPARKLING

Bluff Hill Brut NV (New Zealand) `15` `£5–7`

Cava Brut NV (Spain) `13.5` `£5–7`

Cava Medium Dry NV (Spain) `12` `£5–7`

Champagne de St Gall Blanc de Blancs NV `15` `£13–20`

Champagne de St Gall Brut NV `13.5` `£13–20`

Champagne Desroches NV `13.5` `£13–20`

Champagne Oudinot Grand Cru 1997 `16` `£13–20`

Cuvée Orpale Grand Cru 1990 `12` `£20+`

**MARKS & SPENCER**

Gold Label Sparkling  `16`  `£5–7`     Vintage Cava 1997  `16.5`  `£7–10`
Chardonnay NV
(France)

Oudinot Brut  `13`  `£10–13`
Champagne

**SEE STOP-PRESS SECTION AT END OF BOOK FOR LAST-MINUTE
ADDITIONS OR UPDATES TO THIS RETAILER'S RANGE.**

# MORRISONS

I must confess that I knew when I asked the senior wine buyer here, Stuart Purdie, the question that I asked every other retailer in this edition of *Superplonk* – 'What in your opinion is the strength of your range of wines or the particular style of your way of retailing wine?' – that he'd be too darned busy to get around to respond quickly so I felt no other course was open to me but to romanticise on his and Morrisons' behalf.

Mr Purdie has been a very busy man and only recently has he acquired another buyer to help him (Suzie Cornwell, who was previously with the Spanish specialists Moreno Wines). Stuart is also a sheep farmer and the recent epidemic of foot and mouth disease has been keeping him occupied. It is said he knows every sheep in his flock by name.

I did not help Stuart's workload when, in the last edition of this book, I invited readers to respond to the vacancy for the second wine buyer's job at Morrisons – now so ably filled by Ms Cornwell – and the store received 23,591 applications, 23,590 of which Stuart personally interviewed (the odd one out was disqualified when she admitted to being teetotal and allergic to pigeons, which Morrisons use as they're safer than e-mail). Competition for the job was so fierce that when the candidates had been whittled down to the final dozen, Sir Ken Morrison flew them to his mountain vineyard in California piloting his own Lear jet from Bradford airport. During the flight Stuart gave each one a grilling, in several languages, as to their knowledge of vine diseases, soil types, and the brands of glue used to adhere labels on bottles. Ms Cornwell obviously knows her cebollas.

Morrisons is not the parochial bumpkin it once was. Last year, it reported a 9.1% increase in pre-tax profits to £86.4 million, in the 27 weeks to 6 August, with turnover up 15% to £1.7 billion in the same period. No wonder the board felt it could fork out a cool £2 million on a TV and press advertising campaign. It also considered giving Stuart his own computer and personal e-mail address (or pigeon), but as yet this is an unconfirmed rumour.

Then, out of the electronic ether, as I was putting the finishing touches to this book, Stuart's answer arrived. It was all of 1,082 words long (eat your heart out, Leo Tolstoy) and I swear I wrote all of the foregoing before it arrived. The coincidences to do with flight are happy ones and only confirm much of what I have written. Below are the edited highlights:

*'Morrisons, that northern bunch of no-nonsense, straight talking, what-you-see-is-what-you-get-retailers, are spreading their wings. When a bird spreads its wings it takes off and Morrisons are no exception. Flying high with 112 stores in tow, its eagle-eyed penetration into the South has put the northern cat among the southern pigeons. With stores in London, the commuter belt and South Wales, linked to its strong base, they are able to bring what's best in retailing to more than just the lucky few up north. Led by that intrepid explorer of our retail world, Sir Ken Morrison, they are as sure-footed as ever. He was knighted last year and the company completed a brilliant triple in being voted "Best Supermarket of the Year" and "Britain's Best Off Licence" soon after.*

*Morrisons is the country's fastest growing national supermarket chain with a range of wines suitable for every pocket and taste, and every occasion. Its 500-strong collection of competitively priced, good value wines is innovative in terms of content, presentation and promotion. The company prides itself on its promotional facilities offering customers a diverse selection of wines, from around the globe. The range is balanced across all price points and regions, is not brand dominant and offers interest at every level.*

*The in-store wine departments are efficiently and effectively merchandised to the highest standards, creating an enjoyable shopping environment. Clearly defined sections arranged country-by-country and by product type, means shoppers can buy their wine of choice easily. Eye-catching point of sale communicates strong promotional offers and low prices, while easy to read shelf-edge descriptors enable customers to make an informed choice about what they are buying. The department's managers are well qualified and are always on hand to give advice to customers. Training days, study trips abroad and regular gatherings ensure managers' knowledge is kept up-to-date.'*

Maintaining our flight theme Stuart can be described as the 'Jumbo Jet' of the team. Those of you who have seen his manly figure striding about your TV screen during the Morrisons company advert will readily see the similarity. Once off the ground, however, Stuart is as eagle-eyed as ever for a bargain or two. Work recently done, on Morrisons' Australian section, as well as Californian and South African, will be revealed by late Summer 2001. So called 'Old World' wines including France, Italy and Eastern Europe will be made to work harder with less space allocated in view of the relentless onslaught of good value, fruit-driven 'New World' styles.

Hardly surprising when you see the reluctance of some French wine-makers to change their ways to produce what many customers want – reliable fruity soft wines that are full of flavours and sunshine.

Suzie Cornwell, not previously mentioned in despatches, has an in-depth knowledge of all things Iberian. Watch out for a new look to Morrisons' Spanish and Portuguese section. Stuart is also getting some free flamenco dance lessons during his lunch breaks.

Not mentioned, as it might be, in this purview is that Mr Purdie's focus on value for money in his range can upset people. Most notably the vast E & J Gallo wine company of California whose wines, in the late summer of 2001, he decided to chuck out. 'We tasted a range of brands, all blind, and Gallo came out badly in comparison with the others,' he told me. 'It strikes me that retailers don't regularly taste all the brands they stock, because such wines look after themselves. But if a brand isn't offering value for money then why should we tolerate it?'

The answer is, because it sells. But Stuart, and Morrisons, I am delighted to report, don't find this sufficient reason for inclusion. This, then, is a retailer that knows its own mind and cares passionately about value for money.

This is a retailer that is really on the move and is no longer, as it was when I first began to write about it ten years ago, a purely northern phenomenon. Last December, it was set to modernise 25 stores and open several new ones. Newcomers included Ipswich and Wellingborough and the chain continued to show interest in extending its presence southwards. It plans to open at least eight new stores over the next two years, bringing the total in the chain to 120. After the announcement that its pre-tax profits for the year were £219 million compared with £189 million the year before, it was established as the UK's fifth biggest grocer by market share on a turnover 18% higher at £3.5 billion.

Morrisons was launched on the FTSE-100 in the spring of 2001 and reported to be under pressure from large investors to appoint independent directors to the board following the retailer's elevation to this unique commercial club of the UK's 100 most fragrant listed companies.

Once you get independent directors on your board, however, directors who think wine is expensive red stuff which comes only from Bordeaux, what will happen to all those marvellous bargains from the unfashionable regions which Stuart regularly digs up? I keep my fingers crossed that Morrisons, and Mr Purdie, will continue to go their own sweet way as always, untrammelled by 'independent directors'.

Wm Morrison Supermarkets
Hilmore House
Thornton Road
Bradford
West Yorkshire
BD8 9AX

Tel 01924 870000
Fax 01924 821300
www.morereasons.co.uk

## ARGENTINIAN RED

| | | |
|---|---|---|
| Balbi Barbaro 1997 | 16 | £7–10 |
| Balbi Malbec 1999 | 15.5 | –£5.00 |
| Balbi Shiraz 1999 | 13 | –£5.00 |
| La Nature Organic Barbera 2000 | 14 | –£5.00 |
| Santa Julia Bonarda Sangiovese 1999 | 16 | –£5.00 |

## ARGENTINIAN WHITE

| | | |
|---|---|---|
| Etchart Rio de Plata Torrontes/ Chardonnay 2000 | 12 | –£5.00 |
| La Nature Organic Torrontes 2000 | 14 | –£5.00 |

## AUSTRALIAN RED

| | | |
|---|---|---|
| Barramundi Shiraz/ Merlot NV | 15.5 | –£5.00 |
| Brown Brothers Barbera 1998 | 13.5 | £5–7 |

| | | |
|---|---|---|
| Cranswick Cabernet Merlot 1999 | 15.5 | –£5.00 |
| Hardys Cabernet Shiraz Merlot 1998 | 15 | £5–7 |
| Lindemans Bin 45 Cabernet Sauvignon 1999 | 15 | £5–7 |
| 'M' Australian Shiraz Cabernet NV | 10 | –£5.00 |
| Nottage Hill Cabernet Sauvignon/Shiraz 1999 | 16.5 | £5–7 |
| Tortoiseshell Bay Mourvedre Shiraz 2000 | 12 | –£5.00 |
| Wakefield Shiraz Cabernet 2000 | 16 | £5–7 |
| Woolpunda Cabernet Sauvignon 1999 | 13.5 | –£5.00 |
| Yellow Tail Shiraz 2000 | 15.5 | –£5.00 |

## AUSTRALIAN WHITE

| | | |
|---|---|---|
| Barramundi Semillon/ Chardonnay NV | 16 | –£5.00 |

Cranswick Estate Botrytis Semillon 1999 (half bottle)　16　−£5.00

Jindalee Chardonnay 1998　16　−£5.00

Lindemans Bin 65 Chardonnay 2000　16　−£5.00

Nottage Hill Chardonnay 1999　16　−£5.00

Oxford Landing Viognier 2000　16　£5–7

Penfolds Koonunga Hill Chardonnay 2000　16　£5–7

Penfolds Rawsons Retreat Semillon/ Chardonnay/ Colombard 1999　14　−£5.00

Rosemount Chardonnay 2000　16　£5–7

Rosemount Estate GTR 2000　15　£5–7

Rothbury Cowra Chardonnay 2000　12.5　−£5.00

Stamp Grenache Shiraz 2000　13　−£5.00

Tortoiseshell Bay Sauvignon Semillon 2000　13.5　−£5.00

Wakefield Unwooded Chardonnay 2001　13　£5–7

Yellow Tail Chardonnay 2000　14.5　−£5.00

Yellow Tail Verdelho 2001　15.5　−£5.00

## BULGARIAN RED

Boyar Iambol Cabernet Sauvignon 1999　14.5　−£3.50

Boyar Premium Oak Merlot 1997　13.5　−£5.00

Danube Red 1999　13.5　−£3.50

## BULGARIAN WHITE

Boyar Pomorie Chardonnay 1998　10　−£3.50

## CHILEAN RED

Antares Merlot 2000　16　−£5.00

Condor Chilean Merlot 2000　14.5　−£5.00

'M' Chilean Cabernet Sauvignon 2000　14.5　−£5.00

Undurraga Carmenère 2000　12　£5–7

Villa Montes Cabernet Sauvignon 1999　15.5　−£5.00

## CHILEAN WHITE

35 South Chardonnay 2000　14.5　−£5.00

Antu Mapu Reserva Rosé 1999　13　−£5.00

Condor Chilean Chardonnay 2001　13　−£5.00

'M' Chilean Sauvignon Blanc 2000　13　−£5.00

Montes Alpha
Chardonnay 1998 `17.5` `£7–10`

Villa Montes Sauvignon
Blanc 1999 `14` `–£5.00`

## FRENCH RED

Bouches du Rhône
Merlot NV `15` `–£3.50`

Château Cadillac
Legourgues Bordeaux
1997 `15` `£5–7`

Château de Candale
Haut-Médoc 1996 `15` `£7–10`

Château Saint Galier
Graves 1999 `14` `–£5.00`

Claret Bordeaux NV,
Morrisons `13.5` `–£3.50`

Falcon Ridge Cabernet
Sauvignon, VdP d'Oc
1999 `16` `–£3.50`

Falcon Ridge Merlot
VdP d'Oc 2000 `14` `–£3.50`

Falcon Ridge Syrah
VdP d'Oc 2000 `14.5` `–£3.50`

Heritage des Caves des
Papes Côtes du Rhône
1999 `16` `–£5.00`

La Chasse du Pape
Réserve Côtes du
Rhône 2000 `16` `–£5.00`

Les Planels Minervois
1999 `14` `–£5.00`

'M' Côtes du Rhône
NV `13` `–£3.50`

'M' Côtes du
Roussillon Red NV `13` `–£3.50`

Minervois Cellier la
Chouf NV `13` `–£3.50`

Morgon Domaine de
Chatelet 1999 `13` `£5–7`

Old Git Grenache
Syrah 2000 `14` `–£3.50`

Pic Saint Loup d'Une
Nuit 1999 `14` `–£5.00`

St-Emilion NV,
Morrisons `14` `£5–7`

Sichel Médoc NV `13` `£5–7`

Winter Hill Red VdP
d'Oc 1999 `14` `–£3.50`

## FRENCH WHITE

Château Lafont Menaut
Pessac-Léognan,
Graves 1999 `16` `£7–10`

Falcon Ridge
Chardonnay 2000 `14.5` `–£3.50`

Falcon Ridge
Sauvignon Blanc 2000 `15` `–£3.50`

Gewürztraminer Preiss
Zimmer 2000 `15.5` `£5–7`

Haut-Poitou Sauvignon
Blanc NV `14` `–£3.50`

Pinot Blanc Preiss
Zimmer 2000 `14` `–£5.00`

St-Véran 2000 `14.5` `£5–7`

Sancerre La Renardière
1999 `12` `£7–10`

| Sichel Premières Côtes de Bordeaux Blanc NV | 12.5 | −£5.00 |
|---|---|---|
| Vouvray Les Grands Mortiers, Pierre Guery 2000 | 16 | −£5.00 |

## GERMAN WHITE

| Franz Reh Auslese 1999 | 16 | −£5.00 |
|---|---|---|
| Kendermans Dry Riesling 1999 | 11 | −£5.00 |
| Noble House Riesling 2000 | 14 | −£5.00 |
| Urziger Wurzgarten Spätlese 1999 | 14.5 | £5–7 |

## HUNGARIAN WHITE

| Ideal with Friends Chardonnay NV | 12.5 | −£3.50 |
|---|---|---|
| 'M' Ideal with Friends Sauvignon Blanc NV | 13 | −£3.50 |
| Oliver Irsai Oliver 2000 | 12 | −£5.00 |

## ITALIAN RED

| Casa di Monzi Merlot 1999 | 13 | −£5.00 |
|---|---|---|
| Inycon Merlot 2000 | 16.5 | −£5.00 |
| Montepulciano d'Abruzzo Uggiano 1999 | 14 | −£5.00 |
| Vino Rosso di Puglia NV | 13.5 | −£3.50 |

## ITALIAN WHITE

| Casa de Monzi Chardonnay delle Venezie 1999 | 13 | −£5.00 |
|---|---|---|
| Chardonnay di Puglia NV | 13 | −£3.50 |
| Chianti Colli Fiorenti Uggiano 1998 | 13 | −£5.00 |
| Inycon Chardonnay 2000 (Sicily) | 16 | −£5.00 |
| Uggiano Orvieto Classico 2000 | 12 | −£5.00 |

## NEW ZEALAND RED

| Montana Cabernet Sauvignon/Merlot 2000 | 14 | £5–7 |
|---|---|---|

## NEW ZEALAND WHITE

| Moa Ridge Chardonnay 1999 | 13.5 | £5–7 |
|---|---|---|
| Moa Ridge Sauvignon Blanc 2000 | 14 | £5–7 |

## PORTUGUESE RED

| Dão Dom Ferraz 1999 | 15 | −£5.00 |
|---|---|---|
| Tamara Red Vinho Regional Ribatejo 1999 | 13 | −£3.50 |

## ROMANIAN RED

| Prahova Valley Reserve Merlot 1999 | 13.5 | −£5.00 |
|---|---|---|

| | | |
|---|---|---|
| Proles Pontica Merlot 1995 | 13 | −£5.00 |
| Romanian Classic Pinot Noir 1998 | 11 | −£3.50 |
| Special Reserve Pinot Noir 1998 | 10 | −£5.00 |
| Special Reserve Sangiovese 1998 | 10 | −£5.00 |

## SOUTH AFRICAN RED

| | | |
|---|---|---|
| Cathedral Cellars Merlot 1996 | 13 | £7–10 |
| Fairview Malbec 2000 | 16.5 | £5–7 |
| Namaqua Classic Red NV (3 litre box) | 11.5 | −£3.50 |
| Old Cellar Cabernet Sauvignon 1995 | 13 | −£5.00 |
| Spice Route Andrew's Hope 1998 | 16.5 | £5–7 |

## SOUTH AFRICAN WHITE

| | | |
|---|---|---|
| Danie de Wet Chardonnay sur Lie 2000 | 16 | −£5.00 |
| Fair Cape Chenin Blanc 2000 | 14.5 | −£3.50 |
| Fairview Chardonnay 2000 | 16 | £5–7 |
| Namaqua Classic Dry White NV (3 litre box) | 15 | −£3.50 |
| Spice Route Abbotsdale Colombard/Chenin Blanc 1998 | 16 | −£5.00 |

| | | |
|---|---|---|
| Van Loveren Blanc de Noirs 2000 | 14 | −£5.00 |
| Van Loveren Semillon 1999 | 14 | −£5.00 |

## SPANISH RED

| | | |
|---|---|---|
| Baldoma Tinto Seleccio 1999 | 14 | −£5.00 |
| Gran Feudo Navarra Crianza 1997 | 13 | −£5.00 |
| Poema Old Vine Garnacha 2000 | 14 | −£5.00 |
| Rio Rojo Tinto NV | 14 | −£3.50 |
| Torres Sangre de Toro 1999 | 14 | £5–7 |
| Vega del Rio Reserva Rioja 1994 | 13 | £7–10 |
| Vega del Rio Rioja 1998 | 13 | £5–7 |

## SPANISH WHITE

| | | |
|---|---|---|
| Poema Sauvignon Blanc 2000 | 13.5 | −£5.00 |
| Torres San Valentin 2000 | 12 | −£5.00 |
| Viña Albali Rosado 2000 | 13.5 | −£3.50 |

## USA RED

| | | |
|---|---|---|
| Beringer Zinfandel 1999 | 15 | £5–7 |
| Blossom Hill California Red NV | 10 | −£5.00 |
| Blossom Hill Merlot 1999 | 13 | £5–7 |

Fetzer Bonterra Cabernet Sauvignon 1997   14   £7–10

Glen Ellen Pinot Noir 1997   9   £5–7

Glen Ellen Zinfandel 1998   13.5   £5–7

Ironstone Vineyards Cabernet Franc 1997   16   £5–7

Ironstone Vineyards Shiraz 1998   14.5   –£5.00

'M' Californian Red NV   14   –£3.50

Nathanson Creek Cabernet Sauvignon 1999   14   –£5.00

Turning Leaf Cabernet Sauvignon 1997   12   £5–7

Turning Leaf Zinfandel 1996   12.5   £5–7

## USA WHITE

Glen Ellen Chardonnay 1998   15.5   £5–7

Ironstone Chardonnay 1998   10   £5–7

'M' Californian White NV   13   –£3.50

Nathanson Creek White Zinfandel 1999   11   –£5.00

Wente Johannesburg Riesling 1997   16.5   –£5.00

## FORTIFIED

Dow's LBV Port 1995   14.5   £7–10

Fonseca Bin No 27 Fine Reserve Port NV   13   £7–10

Graham's LBV Port 1994   13.5   £10–13

Taylor's LBV Port 1995   15   £7–10

Warre's Warrior Special Reserve Port NV   13   £7–10

## SPARKLING

Barramundi Sparkling NV (Australia)   16   –£5.00

Brut de Channay NV (France)   11   –£5.00

Chapel Hill Chardonnay-Pinot Noir NV (Hungary)   12   –£5.00

'M' Vintage Cava 1998   16   £5–7

Mumm Cuvée Napa Brut NV (California)   16   £7–10

Nicole d'Aurigny Champagne NV   14   £7–10

Paul Herard Champagne Brut NV   12   £10–13

Reminger Sparkling Brut NV (France)   10   –£5.00

Santa Carolina Chardonnay Brut 1996 (Chile)   13   £5–7

Seaview Brut NV (Australia)   14   £5–7

Seaview Brut Rosé (Australia)   13.5   £5–7

Sparkling Zero (alcohol free)   0   –£2.50

# SAFEWAY

'What,' I asked Safeway, 'in your opinion is the strength of your range of wines or the particular style of your way of retailing wine?'

Answer came there none. The deadline approached. Then the PR department rang me to confirm the price of a wine in my column, and I gently prodded them. In the days when it had a clearly identified controlling head of its wine department, the iconic (but not laconic) Elizabeth Robertson, I would have received a three-page fax answer to my question within the week. As far as I know, there is now no head of the department, but that does not mean its department lacks direction, or that it does not know where it is going. Though, having said that, a wine journalist like myself does appreciate knowing a retailer has an official department head to whom big questions, and problems, can be referred. Safeway has lacked this since Liz's departure.

However, on the day of the deadline, a fax arrived. How old-fashioned such things seem now we have the Internet. But there it was. Safeway had got there in the end. Here is what it says of itself:

> 'At Safeway we are passionate about wine and focused on the quality of service to our customers. The WOW factor and making every customer feel important is reflected in the quality and depth of our range, the market-leading deals we can source and the exciting, colourful displays in-store. Safeway is the fastest growing supermarket retailer in the UK and we constantly strive to improve and better our offering.'

Make of that what you will. It was not written by a wine buyer, that is for sure, but this offers us a revealing glimpse of the nature of the retailer under review here, which is different from any other in this book. Safeway obviously has bounce, confidence and chutzpah; you can go a long way in this world with these qualities.

Safeway continues to offer an interesting range, some terrific own-labels, and has a real nose for bargain reds from the South of France. Its strength used to be that it had a higher proportion of male wine-buying customers compared with its competitors but this may no longer be true.

It has had an entertaining twelve months since the last guide's introductions were written and.has found itself with publicity it would have wished to avoid. In August last year, for instance, it was the victim of a hoax e-mailer. E-mails were sent to 3,000 Safeway customers who had left their contact details at the Safeway website. They were told that from 13 August all the store's prices would be going up by 25% and if customers did not like it they should 'piss off' and shop at Tesco or Sainsbury's. The retailer sent a statement to these shocked customers apologising and reassuring them that there was no truth in the hoaxer's e-mail and further that this miscreant did not access any customers' personal details.

This irritating happenstance did nothing to dent the company's more buoyant trading performance (sales up 5%) which improved to the extent that, after an absence of 18 months, it volleyed itself back into the FTSE-100 index of top-performing listed companies. It unveiled its newly refurbished St Katharine's Dock store, this three-month revitalisation programme was a major plank in chairman Carlos Criado-Perez's plans to re-energise Safeway. The St Katharine's Dock store will apparently become, according to the trade magazine *The Grocer*, a 'test-bed for many new initiatives'. Let us hope so. I look forward to seeing this book on sale there, in dump bins, in the wine aisles and by the checkouts and if we could have ten-minute announcements of the book's existence broadcast over the store's Tannoy system the publisher would very much appreciate it.

Perhaps, though, the term 'test-bed' referred to Safeway's offer to its customers of a lonely hearts matchmaking service for Valentine's Day. Shoppers filled in a questionnaire and received a free match courtesy of Dateline.

Safeway also claimed a major marketing coup in backing a concert in Hyde Park by Pavarotti to coincide with its 'Viva Italia' Italian food promotion in the summer. Ten new Italian wines were added to the range in case Signor Pavarotti felt thirsty. Mr Carlos Criado-Perez said the promotion and the concert would raise the retailer's profile in the Southeast and boost sales.

It installed photo processing labs in 70 of its stores, to be up and running by the end of the next financial year. It also relaunched its website, *www.safeway.co.uk*, to make it a more effective on-line retailer, and was also reported to be offering travel services 'in collaboration with a third party'. *Madaboutwine.com* has been signed up by Safeway to test a nationwide delivery service for wine with about 80 wines on offer. The joint service was due to go live in spring 2001, but I've had no reports of its success.

It launched a new staff training programme called Safeway School aimed at teaching staff the necessary skills to work in new areas like 'Fresh to Go'. The school offers courses, so I am reliably informed, in pizza throwing, French pastry, Japanese noodles and fresh coffee. I'm unable quite to see how anyone needs to be taught how to throw a pizza (my children's method was to simply lift the offending slice high and hurl), but perhaps if a graduate of the school is reading this (s)he might enlighten me (you can contact me via *superplonk.com*).

Further Safeway food initiatives include the opening of the first of an adventurous style of in-store restaurant at the branch in High Wycombe. Caf Fresco, as it is called, offers that dreadful culinary catch-all 'a Mediterranean-style menu' but more innovatively it stays open in the evening when the store is shut. The concept will, if successful, be repeated in other stores. Useful, I guess, for all those lonely hearts Safeway is so keen to assuage with a suitable partner.

Safeway's first hypermarket in Plymouth loomed large, and was due to have its checkouts up and running by the autumn of 2001. The company is hopeful of opening 70 such hypermarkets over the next three years and I anticipate that these monsters will carry the full range of Safeway's wines. Thus, from being a bit wobbly around the knees a few years back, Safeway is striding forward with a new found confidence. This confidence was boosted when it posted pre-tax profits up by 33% to £314 million amidst ringing claims by the retailer that it has made 'a full recovery'.

I'm delighted to hear it. The only small blip, as far as wine was concerned, was losing the services of one of British supermarketing's most able wine buyers, Mr Neil Sommerfelt, who left Safeway to become an associate director of the fine wine shipper, Laytons of London.

Can we also look forward to a head of department being appointed in Neil's stead? If she wasn't serenely happy and successful at Somerfield I'd suggest they head hunt Angela Mount – if, that is, they can afford to match the yellow\* Ferrari and better the £250,000\*\* a year which Somerfield cough up for her services.

---

\* it has been learned from an impeccable source that Mrs Mount would prefer a black one (if that's not too much trouble).

\*\* this is a *Superplonk* estimate based on the value for money she represents to her present employer. It may be an under-evaluation.

Safeway plc
Safeway House
6 Millington Road
Hayes
UB3 4AY

Tel 01622 712987 Customer Services
Fax 020 8573 1865
www.safeway.co.uk

## ARGENTINIAN RED

Adiseno Reserve
Malbec 1999 — 15 £5–7

Argentinian Bonarda
2000, Safeway — 15 –£5.00

Argentinian Cabernet
Sauvignon 2000,
Safeway — 14 –£5.00

Argentinian Syrah 2000,
Safeway — 15.5 –£5.00

Caballo de Plata
Bonarda/Barbera 2000 — 13 –£3.50

Weinert Malbec 1994 — 16 £7–10

## ARGENTINIAN WHITE

Argentinian
Chardonnay 1999,
Safeway — 16 –£5.00

Caballo de Plata
Shiraz/Malbec Rosada
2000 — 15.5 –£5.00

Caballo de Plata
Torrontes 2000 — 13.5 –£3.50

## AUSTRALIAN RED

Annies Lane Cabernet/
Merlot 1999 — 13.5 £7–10

Australian Oaked
Cabernet Sauvignon
1999, Safeway — 14.5 –£5.00

Australian Oaked
Shiraz 1999, Safeway — 14 –£5.00

Australian Shiraz 1999,
Safeway — 15 –£5.00

Clancy's Shiraz/
Cabernet Sauvignon/
Merlot/Cabernet Franc
1998 — 17 £7–10

CV Capel Vale Shiraz
1998 — 14.5 £7–10

Endeavour Cabernet
Sauvignon 1999 — 12 £7–10

Evans & Tate Shiraz
1999 — 16 £7–10

Hardys Stamp Shiraz/
Cabernet 2000 — 13 –£5.00

Hardys Tintara Shiraz
1998 — 13 £7–10

Haselgrove 'Bentwing' Shiraz, Wrattonbully 1999 — 12 £7–10

Haselgrove 'H' Cabernet Sauvignon/ Merlot 1998 — 15 £13–20

Haselgrove Shiraz, McLaren Vale 1999 — 13 £7–10

Jindalee Merlot 2000 — 12 –£5.00

Jindalee Shiraz 2000 — 13 –£5.00

Masterpiece Shiraz Malbec 2000 — 11 £5–7

Metala Langhorne Creek Shiraz/Cabernet Sauvignon 1998 — 15.5 £7–10

Ninth Island Pinot Noir, Tasmania 1999 — 11 £7–10

Normans Langhorne Creek Cabernet Sauvignon/Cabernet Franc 1996 — 14 £7–10

Penfolds Bin 128 Coonawarra Shiraz 1998 — 13.5 £7–10

Penfolds Organic Merlot Shiraz Cabernet 1998 — 15.5 £7–10

Peter Lehmann The Barossa Shiraz 1998 — 17 £5–7

Rosemount Estate Grenache/Shiraz 2000 — 13 £5–7

Rosemount Estate Merlot 1999 — 15 £7–10

Rosemount 'Hill of Gold' Shiraz, Mudgee 1998 — 17.5 £7–10

Rosemount Shiraz 1999 — 14.5 £7–10

Tatachilla Breakneck Creek Cabernet Sauvignon 2000 — 13.5 £5–7

Tatachilla Foundation Shiraz 1998 — 13.5 £13–20

Tatachilla Padthaway Cabernet Sauvignon 1999 — 16 £7–10

Tatachilla Shiraz 1999 — 15 £7–10

Wakefield Promised Land Shiraz/Cabernet Sauvignon 2000 — 12 £5–7

Wirrega Vineyards Cabernet Sauvignon/ Petit Verdot 1999 — 16 £5–7

Wirrega Vineyards Shiraz 1999 — 13 £5–7

Wolf Blass Yellow Label Cabernet Sauvignon 1999 — 14 £7–10

Woolshed Cabernet/ Shiraz/Merlot, Coonawarra 1998 — 17 £5–7

## AUSTRALIAN WHITE

Alkoomi Riesling, Frankland River 2000 — 14.5 £7–10

Alkoomi Sauvignon Blanc, Frankland River 2000 — 14 £7–10

Annie's Lane Semillon, `15.5` `£5-7`
Clare Valley 1999

Bleasdale Verdelho, `15` `£5-7`
Langhorne Creek 2000

Capel Vale CV `14.5` `£7-10`
Unwooded
Chardonnay 1999

CV Chenin Blanc 2000 `16` `£5-7`

Endeavour Barrel- `14` `£7-10`
fermented Chardonnay,
Limestone Coast 1999

Hardys Tintara `13` `£7-10`
Chardonnay 2000

Haselgrove 'H' `14.5` `£7-10`
Chardonnay 1999

Jindalee Chardonnay `16` `-£5.00`
2000

Leasingham Bin 7 `13.5` `£5-7`
Riesling, Clare Valley
2000

Loxton Low Alcohol `11` `-£3.50`
Chardonnay (1.2% vol)

Mamre Brook `16` `£5-7`
Chardonnay 1999

Nepenthe Vineyards `16` `£7-10`
Sauvignon Blanc 2000

Penfolds Bin 21 `14` `-£5.00`
Rawson's Retreat
Semillon/Colombard/
Chardonnay 2000

Peter Lehmann 'The `16.5` `£5-7`
Barossa' Semillon 1999

Peter Lehmann Vine `16.5` `-£5.00`
Vale Riesling, Barossa
Valley 2000

Robertson Barrel `13` `-£5.00`
Fermented Colombard
1999

Rosemount Estate `16` `£7-10`
Show Reserve
Chardonnay 1999

Rosemount Show `15` `£7-10`
Reserve Chardonnay
1998

Tatachilla Breakneck `16.5` `-£5.00`
Creek Chardonnay
2000

Tatachilla Chardonnay `15.5` `£7-10`
Adelaide Hills 1999

Tatachilla Padthaway `16` `£5-7`
Chardonnay 2000

Wakefield Promised `13` `£5-7`
Land Unwooded
Chardonnay, Clare
Valley 2000

Wakefield St Andrew `14` `£13-20`
Chardonnay, Clare
Valley 1998

## AUSTRIAN WHITE

Cat's Leap Grüner `12` `-£5.00`
Veltliner 1999

## BULGARIAN RED

Azbuka Merlot 1996 `15` `£5-7`

Nazdrave Cabernet `15.5` `-£5.00`
Sauvignon 1999

Sapphire Cove NV `14.5` `-£3.50`

Young Vatted Cabernet | 14 | −£3.50
Sauvignon 2000,
Safeway

Young Vatted Merlot | 12 | −£3.50
2000, Safeway

## BULGARIAN WHITE

Valley of the Roses | 14 | −£3.50
Rosé 2000

## CHILEAN RED

35 South Cabernet | 17 | −£5.00
Sauvignon 1999

Acacias Estate Merlot, | 14 | −£5.00
Maipo Valley 1998,
Safeway

Casa Lapostolle Cuvée | 18 | £7–10
Alexandre Merlot 1999

Chilean Cabernet | 13 | −£5.00
Sauvignon 2000,
Safeway

Concha y Toro | 16.5 | −£5.00
Casillero del Diablo
Cabernet Sauvignon
1999

Cono Sur Cabernet | 17 | −£5.00
Sauvignon, Rapel
Valley 2000

El Cadejo Cabernet | 14 | −£5.00
Sauvignon 2000

Errázuriz Syrah | 15 | £7–10
Reserva 1999

Isla Negra Merlot 2000 | 16.5 | £5–7

Terra Mater Zinfandel | 14 | £7–10
Shiraz 2000

Valdivieso Malbec 2000 | 15 | −£5.00

Valdivieso Single | 16.5 | £7–10
Vineyard Cabernet
Franc 1998

Valdivieso Single | 16.5 | £7–10
Vineyard Merlot 1998

Viña Morande Syrah | 14 | −£5.00
2000

## CHILEAN WHITE

Aresti Gewürztraminer | 13 | −£5.00
2000

Casa Lapostolle Cuvée | 17 | £7–10
Alexandre Chardonnay
1999

Chilean Dry White | 16 | −£3.50
2000, Safeway

Chilean Sauvignon | 16 | −£5.00
Blanc 2000, Safeway

Santa Rita Chardonnay | 16 | £5–7
1999

## FRENCH RED

Anciennes Vignes | 14 | −£5.00
Carignan, VdP de
l'Aude 2000

Baron de Lestac, | 14.5 | −£5.00
Bordeaux 1998

Beaune 1998, Safeway | 10 | £7–10

Beaune Premier Cru, | 13.5 | £13–20
Les Epenottes 1998

Bourgueil Les Chevaliers 2000 — 16 — −£5.00

Cabernet Sauvignon VdP d'Oc 2000, Safeway — 15.5 — −£5.00

Château Boisset Cuvée Eugenie La Clape, Coteaux du Languedoc 2000 — 16.5 — £5–7

Château Chaubinet Bordeaux 1999 — 16 — −£5.00

Château Clos de La Chesnaie, Lalande-de-Pomerol 1998 — 14.4 — £7–10

Château d'Agassac, Haut-Médoc Cru Bourgeois 1998 — 13.5 — £10–13

Château de Coulaine, Chinon 1999 (organic) — 16 — £5–7

Château de Lausières, Coteaux du Languedoc 1999 — 16.5 — −£5.00

Château de Villenouvette, Cuvée Marcel Barsalou Corbières 1998 — 16.5 — £7–10

Château du Tasta, Premières Côtes de Bordeaux 1998 — 13 — −£5.00

Château Jouanin Cuvée Prestige, Côtes du Castillon 1998 — 15 — £5–7

Château La Rose Brisson St-Emilion Grand Cru 1998 — 16 — £10–13

Château Liversan, Cru Bourgeois, Haut-Médoc 1997 — 12 — £7–10

Château Maison Neuve Montagne-St-Emilion 1998 — 15.5 — £7–10

Château Montbrun de Gautherius Corbières 2000 — 16 — −£5.00

Château Philippe de Vessiere, Costières de Nîmes 1997 — 15.5 — −£5.00

Château Pouchard-Larquey Bordeaux 1998 — 15 — £5–7

Château Pouchard-Larquey, Bordeaux 1998 (organic) — 15.5 — £5–7

Château Rozier, St-Emilion Grand Cru 1998 — 13.5 — £10–13

Château Salitis Cabardès 1998 — 15 — £5–7

Château Teyssier Montagne-St-Emilion 1998 — 15 — £7–10

Château Tour du Mont, Haut-Médoc 1999 — 14 — £5–7

Château Troupian Haut-Médoc 1998 — 14 — £7–10

Château Villespassans St-Chinian 2000 — 17 — −£5.00

Château Vircoulon Bordeaux 1999 — 16.5 — −£5.00

Châteauneuf-du-Pape 1999, Safeway — 12 — £7–10

Chevalier de Malle, Graves 1998 — 14 £7–10

Claret NV, Safeway — 16 −£5.00

Corbières 2000, Safeway — 13.5 −£3.50

Crozes-Hermitage Etienne Barret 2000 — 15 £5–7

Domaine Chris Limouzi, Corbières 1998 — 15.5 £5–7

Domaine de l'Auris Syrah, Côtes du Roussillon 1998 — 16 £5–7

Domaine de Tudery St-Chinian 1998 — 16.5 £5–7

Domaine des Lauriers, Faugères 1998 — 17 £5–7

Domaine La Tour du Maréchal Merlot, VdP de l'Hérault 2000 (organic) — 15 −£5.00

Domaine Montmija, Corbières 1999 (organic) — 14 −£5.00

Enclos des Cigales Merlot, VdP d'Oc 2000 — 16 −£5.00

Enclos des Cigales Syrah, VdP d'Oc 1999 — 15.5 −£5.00

Fitou 1999, Safeway — 13.5 −£5.00

Fleurie Domaine des Raclets 2000 — 14 £5–7

Gevrey-Chambertin Domaine Rossignol-Trapet 1998 — 12 £13–20

Jean Louis Denois Grenache/Syrah/Mourvèdre, VdP d'Oc 2000 — 15 −£5.00

Jean Louis Denois Mourvèdre/Grenache, VdP d'Oc 1999 — 13.5 £5–7

L'Enclos Domeque Syrah/Malbec, VdP d'Oc 2000 — 15.5 −£5.00

L'If Merlot/Carignan, VdP du Torgan 2000 — 16.5 −£5.00

La Cuvée Mythique VdP d'Oc 1998 — 16 £5–7

La Nature Rhône Valley Red 2000 — 14 −£5.00

La Source Merlot/Syrah VdP d'Oc 2000 — 16 −£5.00

Merlot Réserve Mont Tauch, VdP du Torgan 1999 — 17.5 £7–10

Merlot Vin de Pays d'Oc 2000, Safeway — 16 −£3.50

Minervois 2000, Safeway — 15.5 −£3.50

Minervois Domaine de Bayac 'Les Pierres Blanches' 1999 — 14 £5–7

Mont Tauch Merlot, Barrel Matured, VdP du Torgan 1998 — 17 £7–10

Moulin de Ciffre Faugères 1999 — 13 £5–7

Pinot Noir d'Autrefois VdP d'Oc 2000 — 14 −£5.00

Pommard Premier Cru Les Arvelets 1996 — 12 — £13–20

Red Burgundy 1999 — 13 — £5–7

Syrah VdP d'Oc 2000, Safeway — 15.5 — –£3.50

Vacqueyras Domaine la Bouscatière 1999 — 14 — £5–7

Val Bruyère Côtes du Rhône Villages 2000 — 14 — –£5.00

'Yellow Jersey' Rhône Valley Côtes de Ventoux 2000 — 14 — –£5.00

Young Vatted Grenache VdP de l'Ardèche 1999 — 15 — –£3.50

## FRENCH WHITE

Alsace Gewürztraminer 2000, Safeway — 15 — £5–7

Chablis Premier Cru Beauroy 1999 — 13 — £10–13

Chablis Laroche 1999 — 12 — £7–10

Château de La Gravelle, Muscadet de Sèvres-et-Maine sur Lie 2000 — 16 — –£5.00

Château Magneau, Graves 1999 — 15 — £5–7

Chenin VdP du Jardin de la France 2000, Safeway — 13.5 — –£3.50

Corbières Rosé 2000 — 13.5 — –£5.00

Domaine de Bosquet Chardonnay VdP d'Oc 2000 — 15.5 — £5–7

Domaine de Ciffre Viognier VdP d'Oc 2000 — 13.5 — £5–7

Domaine de l'Ecu Muscadet de Sèvres-et-Maine sur Lie 2000 — 15.5 — –£5.00

Domaine La Tour du Maréchal Chardonnay, VdP de l'Hérault 2000 (organic) — 15.5 — –£5.00

Domaine Lafage Muscat Sec, VdP d'Oc 1999 — 14 — –£5.00

French Revolution Le Blanc 1999 — 14 — –£5.00

James Herrick Chardonnay VdP d'Oc 1999 — 16 — –£5.00

La Source Chardonnay/ Roussanne VdP d'Oc 2000 — 15.5 — –£5.00

'Les Caudanettes' Anjou Blanc 2000 — 13 — –£3.50

Montagny Premier Cru 1998, Safeway — 14 — £7–10

Pinot Blanc Alsace 2000, Safeway — 15.5 — –£5.00

Pouilly-Fuissé 1998, Safeway — 12 — £7–10

Sancerre 'Les Bonnes Bouches' 2000 — 11 — £7–10

Sauvignon Blanc Cuvée `13.5` `−£5.00`
Réserve VdP d'Oc 2000

St-Véran 1997 `13` `£5–7`

Touraine Sauvignon `15.5` `−£5.00`
2000

VdP de l'Ardèche Rosé `13` `−£3.50`
2000, Safeway

Via Domitia `13` `£5–7`
Chardonnay/Viognier
Réserve Spéciale, VdP
d'Oc 2000

Viognier Cuvée `14` `−£5.00`
Réserve, VdP d'Oc
2000

## GERMAN WHITE

Langenbach `10` `−£5.00`
St Johanner Spätlese,
Rheinhessen 2000

Mertes Riesling Classic `11` `−£3.50`
Medium, Pfalz 1999

Peter Mertes Dry `12.5` `−£3.50`
Riesling 1999

SA Prum Wehlener `16` `£5–7`
Sonnenuhr Riesling
Kabinett 1997

## HUNGARIAN RED

Riverview Kekfrancos/ `13.5` `−£5.00`
Merlot 2000

Hilltop Virgin Vintage `16` `£5–7`
Sauvignon Blanc 1999

Irsai Oliver 2000, `14` `−£3.50`
Safeway

Karolyi Estate Private `13.5` `−£5.00`
Reserve 2000

Matra Mountain `14` `−£5.00`
Sauvignon Blanc 2000,
Safeway

Riverview `15` `−£5.00`
Chardonnay/Pinot
Grigio 2000

Riverview `14` `−£5.00`
Gewürztraminer 2000

Riverview Sauvignon `15` `−£5.00`
Blanc 2000

## ITALIAN RED

Alto Varo Rosso di `13` `−£5.00`
Puglia 2000

Araldica Albera Barbera `14` `−£5.00`
d'Asti Superior,
Piemonte 1999

Canaletto Nero `13` `−£5.00`
d'Avola/Merlot 2000

D'Istinto Sangiovese `13.5` `−£5.00`
Merlot 1999 (Sicily)

Italia Negroamaro 2000 `13` `−£5.00`

Italia NV `13` `−£5.00`

La Nature Organic `14` `−£5.00`
Nero d'Avola 2000
(Sicily)

Melini Chianti 1998 `12` `−£5.00`

Sentiero NV `13` `−£3.50`

Sentiero Rosso NV (3 `11` `−£3.50`
litre box)

## ITALIAN WHITE

| | | |
|---|---|---|
| Arcadia Veronese Rosata 2000 | 14.5 | −£5.00 |
| Inycon Chardonnay 2000 (Sicily) | 16 | −£5.00 |
| Sentiero Bianco NV | 15 | −£3.50 |
| Sentiero Bianco NV (3 litre box) | 13.5 | −£3.50 |
| Trulli Chardonnay 1999 | 16 | −£5.00 |
| Verdicchio dei Castelli di Jesi Classico 2000 | 16 | −£5.00 |

## NEW ZEALAND RED

| | | |
|---|---|---|
| Delegat's Reserve Cabernet Sauvignon 1999 | 16.5 | £7–10 |
| Montana Reserve Pinot Noir 1999 | 13.5 | £7–10 |
| Villa Maria Cellar Selection Cabernet/ Merlot 1998 | 15 | £7–10 |
| Villa Maria Reserve Cabernet Sauvignon/ Merlot 1998 | 13.5 | £13–20 |

## NEW ZEALAND WHITE

| | | |
|---|---|---|
| Delegat's Reserve Chardonnay, Barrel Fermented 1999 | 16.5 | £7–10 |
| Lawsons Dry Hills Chardonnay, Marlborough 1999 | 16.5 | £7–10 |

### ROMANIAN WHITE

| | | |
|---|---|---|
| Montana Unoaked Chardonnay 2000 | 16 | £5–7 |
| Oyster Bay Marlborough Chardonnay 2000 | 15.5 | £5–7 |
| Oyster Bay Sauvignon Blanc 2000 | 16 | £5–7 |
| Villa Maria Reserve Wairau Valley Sauvignon Blanc 2000 | 16.5 | £7–10 |

## PORTUGUESE RED

| | | |
|---|---|---|
| Bela Fonte Jaen 1999 | 13 | −£5.00 |
| Bright Brothers Trincadeira Preta 1997 | 14 | −£5.00 |
| Falcoaria, Almeira 1997 | 14.5 | £5–7 |
| Miradouro, Terras do Sado 1999 | 12 | −£3.50 |
| Palmela 1998 | 14.5 | −£5.00 |
| Tamara Ribetajo 1999 | 13 | −£5.00 |

## PORTUGUESE WHITE

| | | |
|---|---|---|
| Globus Ribetajo 1999 | 11 | −£5.00 |
| Tamara Ribetajo White 1999 | 14.5 | −£3.50 |

## ROMANIAN RED

| | | |
|---|---|---|
| Idle Rock Merlot 1998 | 12 | −£5.00 |

## ROMANIAN WHITE

| | | |
|---|---|---|
| Château Cotnari, Blanc de Cotnari 1998 | 10 | −£5.00 |

## RUSSIAN RED

Caucasus Valley, Matrassa, Georgia 1998 — 15 — −£5.00

Odessos Steppe Cabernet Sauvignon, Ukraine 1998 — 13 — −£5.00

Tamada Saperavi, Georgia 1998 — 15.5 — −£5.00

## SOUTH AFRICAN RED

Apostle's Falls Cabernet Sauvignon 1998 — 16.5 — £5–7

Arniston Bay Ruby Cabernet/Merlot 1999 — 13 — −£5.00

Bellingham Cabernet Franc 1998 — 13 — £10–13

Cape Soleil Organic Pinotage 1998 — 9 — −£5.00

Goiya Glaan 1999 — 16 — −£5.00

Kanonkop 'Kadette' Estate Wine 1998 — 15.5 — £5–7

Kleinbosch Reserve Cabernet Sauvignon 1999 — 14 — £5–7

Landskroon Shiraz, Paarl 1998 — 15 — £5–7

Simsberg Pinot Noir, Paarl 1998 — 13.5 — £5–7

South African Pinotage 2000, Safeway — 16 — −£5.00

Stellenbosch Cabernet Sauvignon 1999 — 14 — −£5.00

Stellenbosch Merlot 1999 — 15.5 — −£5.00

Young Vatted Pinotage, Paarl 1999, Safeway — 15 — −£5.00

## SOUTH AFRICAN WHITE

Douglas Green Sauvignon 2000 — 15.5 — −£5.00

Echo Bay Colombar 1999 — 13 — −£5.00

Fairview Semillon 1999 — 16 — £5–7

Kumala Colombard/ Chardonnay 2000 — 14 — −£5.00

Lyngrove Chenin Blanc/Colombard 2000 — 13 — −£5.00

Neil Ellis Groenekloof Sauvignon Blanc 2000 — 16.5 — £7–10

Sea of Serenity Dry Muscat 2000 — 14 — −£3.50

Vale of Peace Colombard 2000 — 14 — −£5.00

Versus 2000 (1 litre) — 16 — −£5.00

## SPANISH RED

Baltasar Gracian Tempranillo 1999 — 13 — −£5.00

Campo Viejo Crianza 1998 — 12 — £5–7

Castillo Ygay Rioja Gran Reserva 1989 — 13.5 — £13–20

Ceremonia, Utiel Requena 1996 — 16.5 — £7–10

Cosme Palacio y
Hermanos, Rioja 1998 | 17 | £5–7

Faustino I Gran
Reserva 1994 | 11 | £10–13

Faustino V Rioja
Reserva 1996 | 12.5 | £7–10

Marqués de Murrieta
Reserva Tinto 1997 | 10 | £7–10

Marqués de Riscal Rioja
Gran Reserve 1994 | 10 | £13–20

Navasques Navarra
1999 | 16 | –£5.00

Siglo 1881 1999 | 10 | –£5.00

Valdepeñas Reserva
Aged in Oak 1995,
Safeway | 15 | –£5.00

Young Vatted
Tempranillo 1999,
Safeway | 15 | –£3.50

## SPANISH WHITE

El Velero Rosé
Valdepeñas 2000 | 12 | –£3.50

Faustino V Rioja
Crianza NV | 5 | £5–7

Marqués de Murrieta
Capellania 1996 | 12 | £7–10

## USA RED

Echelon Merlot 1998 | 15 | £7–10

Pacific Coast Ruby
Cabernet 2000 | 12 | –£5.00

Pepperwood Grove
Syrah 1999 | 13.5 | £5–7

## USA WHITE

Bonterra Muscat 1999
(half bottle) (organic) | 14 | £5–7

Pacific Coast
Chardonnay 2000 | 14 | –£5.00

Pyramid Lake Napa
Gamay Rosé NV | 8 | –£5.00

## FORTIFIED

Blandy's Duke of
Clarence Rich Madeira | 16 | £7–10

González Byass Tio
Pepe Fino Muy Sec NV | 14 | £7–10

Marsala Superiore,
Garibalde Dolce NV
(18% vol) | 16 | £5–7

Taylor's 10 Year Old
Tawny Port NV | 14 | £13–20

Taylor's LBV Port 1995 | 15 | £7–10

Vintage Character Port,
Safeway | 13 | £5–7

Warre's Optima 10
Year Old Tawny Port
NV 50cl | 13.5 | £7–10

Warre's Traditional
LBV Port 1990 | 16.5 | £13–20

Warre's Warrior Finest
Reserve Port NV | 13 | £7–10

## SPARKLING

Albert Etienne Champagne Brut Rosé NV, Safeway `10` `£13–20`

Albert Etienne Champagne Vintage 1995, Safeway `12` `£13–20`

Asti Spumante NV, Safeway `10` `–£5.00`

Baron de Moncenay Chardonnay Brut NV `12` `–£5.00`

Canard Duchêne Champagne Brut NV `14.5` `£13–20`

Chandon Argentina NV `15` `£7–10`

Chandon Australia Brut NV `13.5` `£7–10`

Conde de Caralt Cava Brut NV `16.5` `£5–7`

Freixenet Cava Rosada Brut NV `13.5` `£5–7`

Graham Beck Brut NV (South Africa) `14` `£5–7`

Lambrusco Rosé Light, Safeway (4%vol) `13.5` `–£2.50`

Le Baron de Moncenay Merlot/Gamay Brut NV `15` `–£5.00`

Le Monferrine Moscato d'Asti 1999 (5%) `13` `–£3.50`

Lindauer Brut NV (New Zealand) `14` `£7–10`

Louis Roederer Champagne Brut Premier NV `13` `£20+`

Piper-Heidsieck Champagne Vintage 1990 `10` `£20+`

Pommery Brut Royal Champagne NV `12` `£20+`

Seaview Blanc de Blancs 1996 `13` `£7–10`

Séléction XXI, Champagne, Nicolas Feuillatte NV `13` `£13–20`

**SEE STOP-PRESS SECTION AT END OF BOOK FOR LAST-MINUTE ADDITIONS OR UPDATES TO THIS RETAILER'S RANGE.**

# SAINSBURY'S

Now the measure of this retailer is in its response, considered in detail, to my probe: 'What in your opinion is the strength of your range of wines or the particular style of your way of retailing wine?' I posed this question to every retailer in this book via e-mail (with the exception of Morrisons who prefer carrier pigeons), figuring this was the quickest way. I generously offered a deadline many weeks away. Sainsbury's e-mailed reply came within a fortnight and here it is in its entirety:

*'Hi Malcolm. Apologies for the delay in getting back to you. Our paragraph from Allan Cheesman as follows:*

*Sainsbury's has a long heritage in wine retailing, starting in the early 1960s. Over the last 40 years, the own-label and exclusive ranges have remained a cornerstone of our offer with the clear objective of providing interesting, quality wines which offer excellent value. We have also set out to demystify and popularise wine, and in this respect are leading the industry. Sainsbury's is also very proud of its supplier base around the world and deals in no less than 17 countries with over 200 suppliers.*

*If you want any further information, please just let me know. With kind regards, Claire Whitehead, SAINSBURY'S.'*

The deconstruction of this message, so efficiently and proudly actioned, provides insight into the nature of the enigma this retailer will always be (often to itself). First, there is a clearly identified person, always on the ball (and in Ms Whitehead's case on the ball not only in English but also in French and Italian), to whom I can refer every query and expect a rapid and intelligent response. Second, there is not just the unusual concern that a delay of ten days might be impolite but a positive recognition that it is not the way the e-mailer, or her employer, likes to do business. Third, no one else in British supermarketing could have said what Mr Cheesman – Sainsbury's director of wine – said, and it provides us with further rich grist. Sainsbury's does have a great tradition with wine. It does have terrific own-label wines. It has tried to take the stuffiness out of the often ritualised subject of wine (in the past it published many worthy own-label wine books edited by Oz Clarke), and its suppliers are amongst the best there are.

However, all that said, Sainsbury's has suffered from a lapse in its once all-conquering fortunes, and only in the past year or so has it seemed to me to be making real inroads in sorting itself out, and is now much faster on its feet. It has had to be. The competition provides immense pressure and in the old days Sainsbury's required too much time to think; now it is beginning to react instinctively and more wisely. This, apart from anything else, must make the business a more exciting and satisfying place to work in, and indeed to shop in. In April 2001, Sainsbury's revealed that sales were up by nearly 5% – its best performance for some years.

In some ways, the turn around began with Sainsbury's announcement, in spring 2000, that the so-called naked chef, Jamie Oliver, would front its new ad campaign. Very shortly, this paid publicity dividends when the gorgeous Fat Lady, Clarissa Dickson-Wright, had a go at this campaign, on the grounds that Mr Oliver did not shop at Sainsbury's. The chef retorted that he did not shop there for ingredients for his restaurant.

However, with the opening of the first of 30 Sainsbury's flagship 'beacon' stores, based on the design of its refurbished branch on the Cromwell Road in west London (which boasts a Yo Sushi bar), the new broom heading the company, Sir Peter Davis, had something to flaunt. He remarked that the tarting up of these 'beacon' stores would take place during the coming year and also announced plans to revamp 200 stores, almost half its number, over the next year. The Cromwell Road branch, where it was said Princess Di sometimes shopped, boasted a full-time wine manager and planned to run daily in-store tastings. Sainsbury's later claimed to want to invest £500 million in developing 27 new stores in London over the next three years, creating 3,000 jobs. Other, more innovative developments followed. In one of them, Sainsbury's became the first high street chain to offer pension rights to homosexual employees' partners, also granting them access to share options, healthcare and staff discounts.

Sainsbury's new shopping trolleys also broke new ground, resulting in several customers being shocked. It was reported that 1,200 of the trolleys had to be returned to the manufacturer after they gave customers alarming tingles. It appeared that on certain types of floor the wheels allowed the build-up of static electricity.

Wine commentators, however, experienced a particular shock of their own. This was occasioned by the announcement that Sainsbury's and Oddbins were to launch a joint direct wine venture in spring 2001. 'What,' I was asked constantly by members of the trade and other wine writers, 'can this be all about?' I was able to offer no great insight. Perhaps this was exactly why Mr Cheesman was re-hired: to provide this sort of idea and the management dynamics to back it up? He had been at Sainsbury's for more than a quarter of a century when he quit a while back to help run BRL Hardy in the UK, but it was the persuasive Peter Davis who lured him back.

The first fruits of the new Destination Wine joint venture between the two retailers were seen in stores from February. Limited displays of wines offering by-the-case deals under the Taste for Wine banner went into 100 Sainsbury's and 50 Oddbins branches. Reporting this marriage in early 2001, the trade paper *Off Licence News* said that the links between the retailers were strengthened because they were effectively selling each other's own-label and exclusive label wines in their stores. *OLN* also pointed out that the launch of the joint venture had led to speculation that Sainsbury's might make a bid for Oddbins – a temptation Sainsbury's has claimed firmly to have resisted. Once the e-tailing website, *tasteforwine.co.uk*, was up and running it offered a free bottle for every case bought. Some of these free bottles represented fantastic bargains, but not all. One particular example, a Viognier, struck me as the least elegant expression of this grape that I had yet tasted but other bottles were definitely worth having.

Sainsbury's interest in Green issues was highlighted by the plan to install a commercial wind turbine at its distribution centre in Kilbride, Scotland. A spokesperson said that renewable energy was an increasingly important issue for Sainsbury's and went on to say that the turbine would provide 25% to 40% of the energy required at the 25,000 sq ft depot. This did not, however, prevent environmental protesters chaining themselves to a lorry at another Sainsbury's distribution centre in a protest against the distribution of genetically modified meat and dairy products.

Then the research group, IMRG, dubbed the Sainsbury's website, *Sainsburystoyou.com*, the worst among the major UK grocers. Sainsbury's was awarded only one star out of a possible five, with Asda and Tesco scoring much better. (If Sainsbury's website designer wants to know how to design a website, may I suggest she goes to *superplonk.com*?) On a more positive note, Sainsbury's became the first supermarket chain to become a corporate member of the Plain English Campaign which aims to tackle confusing and jargon-laden language. This presumably means that Sainsbury's wine department's habit of using quotes from wine writers to draw attention to well-regarded wines may have to be revised; when did you last read a wine writer whose language was 'jargon-free'?

Overall, then, a year of rebuilding for this retailer and no less so in its wine department – though it continues to search for new places for interesting wines. A year or so back I claimed that Sainsbury's might stock a Zimbabwean rosé but nothing came of it, but further north on the same continent there were more successful acquisitions. Sainsbury's wine buyer for North Africa, Rachel Hibbert, was reported as saying that her patch was definitely 'an area to watch' and, lo and behold, a wine from Tunisia and three from Morocco appeared on Sainsbury's shelves.

If vines were discovered on the slopes of an active Siberian volcano you can be sure that a British supermarket wine buyer would turn up there sniffing around and odds on that the buyer would be from Sainsbury's.

Sainsbury's Supermarkets Limited
33 Holborn
London
EC1N 2HT

Tel 0800 636262 Customer Careline
www.sainsburys.co.uk

## ARGENTINIAN RED

Alamos Ridge Cabernet Sauvignon 1997 — 16.5 — £5–7

Bright Brothers Barrica Cabernet Shiraz 1999 — 16 — £5–7

Finca el Retiro Bonarda 2000 — 14.5 — £5–7

La Nature Organic Barbera 2000 — 14 — −£5.00

Mendoza Cabernet Sauvignon/Malbec NV, Sainsbury's — 15.5 — −£5.00

Mendoza Country Red NV, Sainsbury's — 15 — −£3.50

Santa Julia Tempranillo 2000 — 16 — −£5.00

## ARGENTINIAN WHITE

La Nature Organic Torrontes 2000 — 14 — −£5.00

Mendoza Chardonnay, Tupungato Region NV, Sainsbury's — 15 — −£5.00

Mendoza Country White NV, Sainsbury's — 14.5 — −£3.50

## AUSTRALIAN RED

Australian Shiraz NV, Sainsbury's — 13.5 — −£5.00

Banrock Station Mataro Shiraz NV, (3 litre box) — 15 — −£5.00

Hardys Stamp Cabernet Merlot 2000 — 13.5 — −£5.00

Jacobs Creek Reserve    14    £7–10
Shiraz 1998

Nottage Hill Cabernet    16.5    £5–7
Sauvignon/Shiraz 1999

Petaluma Bridgewater    16.5    £7–10
Mill Shiraz 1998

Rosemount Estate    15.5    £7–10
Shiraz 1998

Wolf Blass Yellow    14    £7–10
Label Cabernet
Sauvignon 1999

## AUSTRALIAN WHITE

Australian Chardonnay    15.5    –£5.00
NV, Sainsbury's

Hardys Stamp of    15    –£5.00
Australia Chardonnay
Semillon (3 litre box)

Oxford Landing    16    –£5.00
Sauvignon Blanc 2000

Penfolds Botrytis    15    £5–7
Semillon 1998 (half
bottle)

Rosemount Estate GTR    15    £5–7
2000

Rosemount Estate    16    £7–10
Show Reserve
Chardonnay 1999

Stowells of Chelsea    15.5    –£3.50
Australian Chardonnay
NV (3 litre box)

## BULGARIAN RED

Blue Ridge 617 Merlot    14    –£5.00
1999

Bulgarian Cabernet    15.5    –£3.50
Sauvignon, Sainsbury's
(3 litre box)

Bulgarian Merlot NV,    15.5    –£3.50
Sainsbury's

## CHILEAN RED

Caliboro Carignan Old    14    –£5.00
Vine Reserva 2000

Chilean Cabernet    16    –£5.00
Merlot NV, Sainsbury's
(3 litre box)

Chilean Merlot NV,    16.5    –£5.00
Sainsbury's

Concha y Toro    17    –£5.00
Casillero del Diablo
Cabernet Sauvignon
2000

Cono Sur 20 Barrels    16.5    £10–13
Merlot 1999

Cono Sur Reserva    16.5    £5–7
Merlot 1999

Errázuriz Merlot 2000    16    £5–7

Errázuriz Pinot Noir    17    £7–10
Reserva 1999

Isla Negra Syrah 2000    16    £5–7

La Palmeria Merlot    18.5    £7–10
Gran Reserva 1999

MontGras Carmenère    16    £5–7
Reserva 1999

Terra Mater Zinfandel Shiraz 2000 `14` −£5.00

Valdivieso Malbec 2000 `15` −£5.00

Valdivieso Merlot 2000 `16` −£5.00

## CHILEAN WHITE

Chilean Chardonnay NV, Sainsbury's `16` −£5.00

Chilean Sauvignon Blanc NV, Sainsbury's `16.5` −£5.00

Errázuriz Wild Ferment Chardonnay, Casablanca 1999 `17` £7−10

MontGras Chardonnay Reserva 1999 `15.5` £5−7

MontGras Chardonnay Reserva 2000 `15` £5−7

Stowells Chilean Sauvignon Blanc NV (3 litre box) `15.5` −£3.50

## ENGLISH WHITE

Chapel Down Premium Medium Dry 1999 `12.5` −£5.00

Chapel Down Schonburger 1999 `11` £5−7

## FRENCH RED

Beaujolais NV, Sainsbury's `13.5` −£5.00

Beaujolais-Villages Les Roches Grillées 1999 `12` £5−7

Bourgogne Pinot Noir, Louis Max 1999 `13` £5−7

Cabernet Sauvignon d'Oc NV, Sainsbury's `16` −£3.50

Cabernet Sauvignon d'Oc NV, Sainsbury's (3 litre box) `14.5` −£3.50

Celliers des Dauphins Côtes du Rhône 2000 `14.5` −£5.00

Château Barreyres Cru Bourgeois, Haut-Médoc 1998 `14` £7−10

Château Cazal-Viel St-Chinian Larmes des Fées 1998 `13.5` £13−20

Château Coufran Cru Bourgeois, Haut-Médoc 1996 `13` £10−13

Château Fonreaud Cru Bourgeois, Listrac 1998 `13.5` £10−13

Château Gaubert, Corbières 2000 `15.5` −£5.00

Château la Tour Carnet, Haut-Médoc 1998 `16` £13−20

Château La Vieille Curé Fronsac 1997 `16.5` £10−13

Château Moulin Canon-Fronsac 1996 `16.5` £7−10

Château Semeillan Mazeau Cru Bourgeois, Listrac 1996 `14` £13−20

Château Tassin Premières Côtes de Bordeaux 1999 `15` −£5.00

Claret Cuvée Prestige, Sainsbury's `16` `−£5.00`

Claret, Sainsbury's `15` `−£3.50`

Claret, Sainsbury's (3 litre box) `15.5` `−£5.00`

Classic Selection Brouilly 1999, Sainsbury's `13` `£5–7`

Classic Selection Châteauneuf-du-Pape 1998, Sainsbury's `15` `£7–10`

Classic Selection St-Emilion 1998, Sainsbury's `15.5` `£7–10`

Côtes du Rhône NV, Sainsbury's `13.5` `−£3.50`

Côtes du Rhône NV, Sainsbury's (3 litre box) `15.5` `−£3.50`

Crozes-Hermitage Cave de Tain 1999 `16.5` `£5–7`

Crozes-Hermitage Petite Ruche 1997 `15.5` `£7–10`

Devereux Portan/ Carignan, VdP de l'Aude 2000 `14.5` `−£3.50`

Domaine de Mas Blanc Coullioure 'Les Cosprons Levant' 1997 `10` `£13–20`

Domaine des Bouziers Cabernet Franc VdP d'Oc 2000 `16.5` `−£5.00`

Domaine Ellul-Ferrières Vignes VdP d'Oc 1998 `17` `£5–7`

Eliane's Single Vineyard Corbières 'Gruissan' 2000 `16` `−£5.00`

Eliane's Single Vineyard Minervois 2000 `16` `−£5.00`

Fitou 'Les Douzes' Mont Tauch 1998 `15.5` `£5–7`

Fleurie La Madone 2000 `14` `£7–10`

French Revolution Le Rouge 1999 `16` `−£5.00`

Gevrey-Chambertin Rodet 1998 `11` `£13–20`

Hautes-Côtes de Nuits Dames Huguettes 1998 `13.5` `£7–10`

Héritage du Rhône 1999 `15` `−£5.00`

Jacques Frelin Crozes-Hermitage 1999 (organic) `13` `£7–10`

La Chasse du Pape Côtes du Rhône 1999 `14` `−£5.00`

Le Catalan Old Vine Carignan 2000 `16` `£5–7`

Le Catalan Old Vine Grenache 2000 `16.5` `£5–7`

Le Midi Cabernet Sauvignon 2000 `17` `−£5.00`

Le Midi Merlot 2000 `16.5` `−£5.00`

Le Véritable Laurent Miquel Syrah Mourvèdre VdP d'Oc 2000 `15` `−£5.00`

Les Cassagnes Merlot VdP d'Oc 2000 `15.5` `−£5.00`

Louis Bernard Côtes du Rhône-Villages 1999 `16.5` `−£5.00`

Marsannay Domaine Bertagna 1998 `15` `£7–10`

Mercurey Clos La Marche 1997 `13` `£13–20`

Merlot VdP de La Cité de Carcassonne, Caroline de Beaulieu 2000 `15.5` `−£5.00`

Minervois 2000, Sainsbury's `14.5` `−£3.50`

Old Git Grenache Syrah 1999 `15.5` `−£5.00`

Red Burgundy NV, Sainsbury's `12` `£5–7`

Regnié Duboeuf 1999 `11` `£5–7`

Réserve du Général, Margaux 1997 `15` `£13–20`

Spécial Réserve Claret, Sainsbury's `16` `−£5.00`

Stowells of Chelsea Merlot VdP d'Oc (3 litre box) `15` `−£3.50`

Syrah VdP d'Oc 2000, Sainsbury's (organic) `13` `−£5.00`

Valréas Domaine de La Grande Bellane 1999 (organic) `14.5` `£5–7`

Van Rouge, VdP de Vaucluse NV `15` `−£3.50`

Vin de Pays des Bouches du Rhône NV, Sainsbury's `14.5` `−£3.50`

Vin Rouge de France NV, Sainsbury's (3 litre box) `13` `−£3.50`

## FRENCH WHITE

Ackerman Anjou Blanc 2000 (organic) `14.5` `−£5.00`

Antonin Rodet Meursault 1998 `12` `£13–20`

Big Frank's Deep Pink 2000 `13` `−£5.00`

Bordeaux Blanc, Sainsbury's `15.5` `−£3.50`

Bourgogne Chardonnay, Louis Max 1999 `15.5` `£5–7`

Chablis Calvet 1999 `14` `£5–7`

Chablis Premier Cru Côtes de Jouan, Brocard 1999 `16` `£10–13`

Chardonnay VdP d'Oc NV, Sainsbury's (organic) `15.5` `−£5.00`

Chardonnay VdP d'Oc, Sainsbury's (3 litre box) `15.5` `−£3.50`

Château de Rully Blanc, Rodet 1998 `13` `£10–13`

Château Tassin Bordeaux Clairet 2000 `14.5` `−£5.00`

Classic Sélection Chablis Domaine Sainte Cecil 1999, Sainsbury's — 16 — £7–10

Classic Sélection Pouilly-Fumé 2000, Sainsbury's — 16 — £7–10

Classic Sélection Sancerre 2000, Sainsbury's — 15.5 — £7–10

Condrieu Guigal 1998 — 15.5 — £13–20

Cuvée Victoria Rosé de Provence 2000 — 14.5 — £5–7

Domaine de Pellehaut Côtes de Gascogne 2000 — 14 — −£5.00

Domaine de Sours Bordeaux Rosé 2000 — 14 — £5–7

Domaine Leonce Cuisset, Saussignac 1998 (50cl) — 15.5 — £5–7

Duo Rosé d'Anjou and Anjou Blanc NV (3 litre box) — 14.5 — −£3.50

French Revolution Le Blanc 1999 — 14 — −£5.00

Le MD de Bourgeois Sancerre 1999 — 15 — £10–13

Le Midi Rosé, Languedoc 2000 — 13.5 — −£5.00

Le Midi Viognier 2000 — 16 — −£5.00

Mercurey Blanc Domaine La Marche les Rochelles 1998 — 14 — £13–20

Meursault Clos de Mazeray, Domaine Jacques Prieur 1998 — 11 — £20+

Mouton Cadet Blanc 1999 — 12 — £5–7

Numero Un Bordeaux Blanc 2000 — 13.5 — −£5.00

Petit Chablis Jean Brocard NV (3 litre box) — 15.5 — −£5.00

Picpoul de Pinet 'Les Flacons' Coteaux du Languedoc 1999 — 16 — £10–13

Puilly-Fuissé Georges Duboeuf 1998 — 13.5 — £10–13

Réserve St-Marc Sauvignon Blanc, VdP d'Oc 2000 — 16.5 — −£5.00

Touraine Sauvignon Le Chalutier 2000 — 15.5 — −£5.00

Van Blanc, VdP de Vaucluse NV — 14.5 — −£3.50

Vin Blanc de France, Sainsbury's (3 litre box) — 12 — −£3.50

Vin de Pays des Côtes de Gascogne, Sainsbury's (3 litre box) — 15 — −£3.50

Vouvray La Couronne des Plantagenets 2000 — 15.5 — −£5.00

White Burgundy NV, Sainsbury's — 14 — £5–7

## GERMAN WHITE

Devil's Rock Masterpiece, St Ursula 1999 — 13 −£5.00

Dr Pauly Riesling 1999 — 13 £5–7

Hock, Sainsbury's (3 litre box) — 14.5 −£3.50

Liebfraumilch, Sainsbury's (3 litre box) — 14 −£3.50

Ockfener Bockstein Riesling Spätlese 1999 — 15.5 −£5.00

Querbach Hallgartener Schonhell Rheingau Riesling 1997 — 16 £5–7

Schloss Wallhausen Riesling Kabinett 1999 — 16 £7–10

## HUNGARIAN WHITE

Hungarian Cabernet Sauvignon Rosé NV, Sainsbury's — 11 −£3.50

## ITALIAN RED

A Mano Primitivo Puglia 2000 — 15.5 £5–7

Alario Barolo Riva 1995 — 10 £20+

Alessandra Colonna Barbera del Monferrato 1998 — 13.5 £13–20

Allora Negroamaro 2000 — 14 £5–7

Araldica Albera Barbera d'Asti Superior, Piemonte 1999 — 14 −£5.00

Barbera d'Alba Fontanelle, Ascheri 1999 — 16.5 £7–10

Barco Reale di Carmignano Capezzana 1999 — 16 £7–10

Barking Mad 15% Primitivo 2000 — 15 −£5.00

Barolo Cantine Rocca Ripalta 1995 — 15 £10–13

Chianti la Capannuccia 1999 — 14.5 −£3.50

Classic Selection Barolo 1996, Sainsbury's — 13.5 £10–13

Classic Selection Chianti Classico 1997, Sainsbury's — 15.5 £5–7

Emporio Nero d'Avola Merlot 2000 — 15 −£5.00

Inycon Syrah 2000 (Sicily) — 16 −£5.00

Morellino di Scansano Riserva 1997 — 16 £7–10

Natio Organic Chianti, Cecchi 1998 — 13.5 £5–7

Poliziano Rosso di Montepulciano 1999 — 15.5 £7–10

Promessa Rosso Salento 2000 — 15.5 −£5.00

Rosso di Provincia di Verona NV, Sainsbury's — 12 −£3.50

Sangiovese di Sicilia 2000, Sainsbury's — 13.5 −£5.00

Sicilia Red, Sainsbury's — 15 −£3.50

Teuzzo Chianti Classico 1998 — 15 £5–7

Valpolicella, Sainsbury's (3 litre box) — 12 −£3.50

## ITALIAN WHITE

Bianco di Provincia di Verona NV, Sainsbury's — 14 −£3.50

Ca'Donini Bianco di Custoza 2000 — 15.5 −£5.00

Classic Selection Pinot Grigio 2000, Sainsbury's — 15 £5–7

Figli di Augusto Pinot Bianco 2000 — 15.5 £5–7

Grecanico di Sicilia 2000, Sainsbury's — 15.5 −£5.00

Inycon Chardonnay 2000 (Sicily) — 16 −£5.00

Orvieto Classico Amabile le Cimmelle 2000 — 15 −£5.00

Pinot Grigio Veneto Borgo Paveri 2000 (organic) — 14.5 −£5.00

Sartori Organic Soave 2000 — 13.5 −£5.00

Sicilian White, Sainsbury's — 13.5 −£3.50

Soave, Sainsbury's (3 litre box) — 15 −£3.50

Villa Bianchi Verdicchio Classico dei Castelli di Jesi 2000 — 16 −£5.00

## MOROCCAN RED

Baraka Private Reserve Cabernet Merlot 1999 — 14 −£5.00

Moroccan Cabernet Sauvignon 2000, Sainsbury's — 13.5 −£5.00

Moroccan Syrah 2000, Sainsbury's — 14.5 −£5.00

## NEW ZEALAND RED

Montana East Coast Cabernet Sauvignon Merlot 1999 — 15 £5–7

## NEW ZEALAND WHITE

Nobilo Sauvignon Blanc 2000 — 14 £5–7

Shingle Peak Pinot Gris, Marlborough 2000 — 15.5 £5–7

The Sanctuary Sauvignon Blanc 2000 — 17 £5–7

## PORTUGUESE RED

Quinta de Bons-Ventos 1999 — 14 −£5.00

Quinta do Crasto 1999 — 15.5 £5–7

Segada Trincadeira Preta-Castelao 2000 — 12 −£5.00

## ROMANIAN RED

Prahova Valley Reserve Pinot Noir 1999   `13`   –£5.00

Romanian Pinot Noir NV, Sainsbury's   `13.5`   –£3.50

## ROMANIAN WHITE

Romanian Merlot Rosé NV, Sainsbury's   `14`   –£3.50

## SOUTH AFRICAN RED

Bellingham Pinotage 1999   `13`   –£5.00

Clos Malverne Cabernet Sauvignon Pinotage 1999   `13`   £5–7

Flagship Vergelegen Bordeaux Blend 1998   `14`   £13–20

Goats Do Roam Fairview, Paarl 2000   `14`   –£5.00

Graham Beck Merlot 1999   `13`   £5–7

Kumala Cabernet Sauvignon Shiraz 2000   `16`   –£5.00

Kumala Cabernet Shiraz NV (3 litre box)   `15.5`   –£5.00

Railroad Cabernet Sauvignon Shiraz 2000   `13`   –£5.00

South African Cabernet Sauvignon NV, Sainsbury's   `15.5`   –£5.00

South African Pinotage NV, Sainsbury's   `12`   –£5.00

South African Red NV, Sainsbury's   `15`   –£3.50

South African Reserve Selection Pinotage 2000, Sainsbury's   `16`   £5–7

Spice Route Andrew's Hope Cabernet Sauvignon/Merlot 1999   `16.5`   £5–7

Spice Route Pinotage 1999   `16`   £7–10

SSW Ruby Cabernet NV (1 litre)   `14`   –£5.00

Stowells of Chelsea Cinsault Pinotage Sainsbury (3 litre box)   `15.5`   –£5.00

Vergelegen Merlot 1998   `13`   £10–13

## SOUTH AFRICAN WHITE

Bellingham Chardonnay 2000   `15.5`   £5–7

Kumala Chardonnay NV (3 litre box)   `16.5`   –£5.00

Pendulum Chardonnay (3 litre box)   `15`   –£5.00

Pendulum Rosé (3 litre box)   `14`   –£5.00

Reserve Selection South African Sauvignon Blanc 2001, Sainsbury's   `15.5`   £5–7

Rhona Muscadel 1996   `16`   £5–7

South African Chardonnay 2001, Sainsbury's   `15.5`   –£5.00

South African Chenin Blanc NV, Sainsbury's — 14 −£3.50

Valencia Oak Aged NV, Sainsbury's — 13.5 −£5.00

South African Chenin Blanc NV, Sainsbury's (3 litre box) — 14.5 −£3.50

Viña Albali Gran Reserva 1993 — 15 £5–7

South African Medium White NV, Sainsbury's — 13 −£3.50

Viña Ardanza Rioja Reserva 1994 — 13.5 £10–13

SSW Chardonnay Chenin Blanc 1999 (1 litre) — 12 −£5.00

Vergelegen Chardonnay 2000 — 14 £5–7

## TUNISIAN RED

Accademia del Sole Carignan 2000 — 11 £5–7

## SPANISH RED

## URUGUAYAN RED

Alteza 600 Old Vines Garnacha NV — 16 −£5.00

Bright Brothers Merlot/Tannat 1998 — 14 −£5.00

Alteza 750 Tempranillo NV — 16 −£5.00

Don Pascual Reserve Tannat 2000 — 16 £5–7

Alteza Tempranillo Cabernet Sauvignon La Mancha 1999 — 14 −£5.00

## USA RED

Dama de Toro 1998 — 15.5 −£5.00

Blossom Hill Californian Red NV — 10 −£5.00

Epulum Rioja Crianza, Bodegas Olarra 1998 — 13.5 £5–7

Buckeye Vineyard Single Vineyard Series Cabernet Sauvignon, Kendall Jackson 1996 — 16.5 £13–20

Jumilla NV, Sainsbury's — 15.5 −£5.00

Navarra NV, Sainsbury's — 16 −£5.00

Four Vines Paso Robles Zinfandel 1997 — 11 £7–10

Ochoa Gran Reserva, Navarra 1993 — 16 £10–13

Kendall Jackson Vintners Reserve Pinot Noir 1998 — 16 £7–10

Ondarre Reserva Rioja 1996 — 15 £7–10

La Crema Pinot Noir 1998 — 16 £10–13

Stowells of Chelsea Tempranillo NV (3 litre box) — 13 −£3.50

Marc Xero Merlot 1999 — 14 −£5.00

## USA WHITE

Blossom Hill NV | 10 | −£5.00

Bonterra Muscat 1999 (half bottle) (organic) | 14 | £5–7

Fetzer Valley Oaks Rosé 2000 | 13.5 | £5–7

Kendall Jackson Single Vineyard Series Camelot Chardonnay 1998 | 13 | £10–13

Kendall Jackson Vintners Reserve Chardonnay 1998 | 15 | £7–10

Sutter Home Gewürztraminer 2000 | 14 | −£5.00

Sutter Home Sauvignon Blanc 2000 | 14 | −£5.00

## FORTIFIED

Cockburn's 10 Year Old Tawny Port (half bottle) | 13.5 | £7–10

Cockburn's Light White Port | 14.5 | £7–10

Dow's LBV Port 1995 | 14.5 | £7–10

Dow's Quinta do Bonfim Vintage Port 1987 | 16.5 | £13–20

Fino Sherry, Sainsbury's | 16 | −£5.00

Fonseca Bin No 27 Fine Reserve Port NV | 13 | £7–10

González Byass Apostoles NV (half bottle) | 16.5 | £10–13

González Byass Matusalem NV (half bottle) | 17 | £10–13

Graham's 20 Year Old Tawny Port | 14 | £20+

Graham's LBV Port 1994 | 13.5 | £10–13

Hidalgo Manzanilla la Gitana NV | 16 | £5–7

Manzanilla, Sainsbury's | 15.5 | −£5.00

Sainsbury's LBV Port 1992 | 15.5 | £7–10

Solear Manzanilla NV | 16 | £5–7

Tawny Port, Sainsbury's | 13 | £5–7

Taylor's 10 Year Old Tawny Port NV | 14 | £13–20

Taylor's 20 Year Old Tawny Port NV | 12 | £20+

Taylor's LBV Port 1995 | 15 | £7–10

Taylors Vintage Port 1985 | 16 | £20+

Ten Year Old Tawny Port, Sainsbury's | 13 | £10–13

Tio Pepe Sherry | 13.5 | £7–10

Warre's Optima 10 Year Old Tawny Port (50cl) | 13.5 | £7–10

Warre's Traditional LBV Port 1990 | 16.5 | £13–20

| | | |
|---|---|---|
| Warre's Warrior Special Reserve Port NV | 13 | £7–10 |

## SPARKLING

| | | |
|---|---|---|
| Banrock Station Sparkling Shiraz NV (Australia) | 16.5 | £7–10 |
| Blanc de Noirs Champagne NV, Sainsbury's | 16 | £10–13 |
| Canard Duchêne Champagne Brut NV | 14.5 | £13–20 |
| Cava Brut NV, Sainsbury's (Spain) | 16.5 | –£5.00 |
| Cava NV, Sainsbury's (Spain) (1.5 litres) | 16 | –£5.00 |
| Cava Rosado Brut, Sainsbury's (Spain) | 15 | –£5.00 |
| Champagne Blanc de Blancs 1997, Sainsbury's | 13 | £13–20 |
| Champagne Boizel Chardonnay NV | 16 | £13–20 |
| Champagne Charles Heidsieck Mis en Cave 1995 | 13 | £20+ |
| Champagne Demi Sec NV, Sainsbury's | 14 | £10–13 |
| Champagne Duval Leroy 1995 | 13 | £13–20 |
| Champagne E. Barnaut Blanc de Noirs NV | 15.5 | £13–20 |

| | | |
|---|---|---|
| Champagne Franck Bonville Blanc de Blancs NV | 17.5 | £13–20 |
| Champagne Lanson Black Label Brut NV | 13.5 | £13–20 |
| Champagne Laurent-Perrier NV | 13.5 | £20+ |
| Champagne Louis Roederer NV | 13 | £20+ |
| Champagne Nicolas Feuillatte Premier Cru NV | 14 | £13–20 |
| Champagne Palmer 1982 | 16 | £13–20 |
| Champagne Perrier-Jouet Belle Epoque 1995 | 13 | £20+ |
| Champagne Perrier-Jouet NV | 14 | £20+ |
| Champagne Pommery Brut Royal NV | 13 | £20+ |
| Champagne Premier Cru Extra Dry NV, Sainsbury's | 14 | £13–20 |
| Chardonnay Brut, Méthode Traditionelle, Sainsbury's (France) | 15 | £5–7 |
| Freixenet Cava Rosada NV | 13.5 | £5–7 |
| Grand Cru Millennium Champagne 1995, Sainsbury's | 13 | £13–20 |
| Green Gold Brut Organic Vin Mousseux NV (France) | 13.5 | £5–7 |

Hardys Nottage Hill Chardonnay Brut 1998 — 15 — £5–7

Hardys Stamp of Australia Chardonnay/ Pinot Noir Brut NV — 14 — £5–7

Inanda Brut NV (South Africa) — 15.5 — –£5.00

Krug Grande Cuvée NV — 10 — £20+

Millennium Vintage Cava 1997, Sainsbury's (Spain) — 13 — £5–7

Mumm Champagne Brut NV — 13 — £13–20

Piper-Heidsieck Brut NV — 15 — £13–20

Trudon Champagne Festigny Cuvée Sélection NV — 18 — £13–20

Vin Mousseux Brut, Sainsbury's (France) — 13 — –£5.00

# SOMERFIELD/KWIK SAVE

The partners in this marriage have settled down together but have kept their separate names. Early rumours that Kwik Save would cease to exist have proved groundless. It is necessary to lump them together, however, since the same wine department, headed by the quinlingual Mrs Angela Mount, runs both operations and many wines are found at both places. In the entries which follow this introduction, any distinctions necessary are clearly made. As far as I know, Mrs Mount is the only supermarket wine buyer who can swear at her suppliers in English, German, French, Italian and Spanish – small wonder she acquires bargains in all these places (excluding England where no wine bargains grow).

This retailer's answer to the question pervading this book – 'What in your opinion is the strength of your range of wines or the particular style of your way of retailing wine?' – was answered thus:

> 'Dear Malcolm,
> Sorry to have taken so long to reply – work, children, etc etc. . . . !
> I believe that the strength of our wine range and wine selection lies in the high level of quality at any given price point within the range. Our stores are in high street locations, and therefore fixture sizes are often more limited than out-of-town superstore sites. This means that we have a smaller range but, as a result, a range which needs to work harder for us – we cannot hide our basic generics behind a vast range of glitzy premium or off-the-wall wines; we have a wide selection, including both the premium and off-the-wall elements. However, the core of our business is in the under £5 market and, as you are well aware, whilst the average retail price point for wine is moving upwards, the average purchase price is still around the £3.50 mark.
>
> Therefore our mission is to put the very best product possible into each of those bottles under £5 (and indeed over £5, although the job is easier here) – we want our basic South African red and white to be the best in the market – same story with all basic generics from Claret, to Sicilian white, to Australian red. So we work closely with producers to ensure that our customers can trust our choice and rely on our selection, whatever the price point. The focus of our range and our selection criteria is always to seek the very best at each price

*point, and in each category of style/country/area, and as you know I work
closely with producers to ensure we hit exactly the right style. We want our
customers to be able to trust our selection and buy in confidence, knowing that,
whatever the price point, or whatever the promotional offer, the product will
meet, or exceed their expectations.*

*Looking forward to seeing you at our tasting next Friday. I checked out a
few restaurants close to the agency for lunch, but I suggest that once you have
finished tasting, we jump in a cab and head for a restaurant in Primrose Hill
– please let me know if you have a preference.*

*See you next week, and hope you are well, Angela.'*

And so we learn a good deal about Mrs Mount as a person (and discover
she is the dedicated mother of young children who has to juggle her life
accordingly) and as a highly focused wine buyer. We are given insight into
the ruthlessly competitive world of Somerfield and learn that Bristol-based
Somerfield has a design and PR agency in a trendy area of London. And we
are given a peek into the cushy life of the metropolitan wine critic who,
after a lazy morning spent merely exercising his cheek muscles spitting out
wine and his wrist noting down his impressions of same, is fully prepared
to have his lunch purchased for him (and tasting 125 wines in a morning
does give a chap a healthy appetite) which he will consume with a chosen
bottle from which he will deeply quaff.

You might ask this: does Mrs Mount's subsidising my wining and dining
in this way constitute a bribe or a conflict of interest? How close can a critic
get to the source of what he criticises? I have pondered these questions
regularly since becoming a wine critic and whilst I refuse all offers of
corporate hospitality I recognise that if I did not socialise in a limited way
with wine producers and wine retailers I would understand far less than I
do about the professional world I inhabit. Wine is a convivial product and its
makers and merchants convivial people. If I were a football correspondent I
would have to draw the line at lunching with the chairman of Manchester
United and I could hardly ask Mr and Mrs Beckham to dinner but I have
discovered, after 12 years of writing on wine, that I cannot draw such hard
distinctions. If you want to read my thoughts on these matters at greater
length please go to *superplonk.com* and access the 'Superplonk World of
Wine' section where I examine conflicts of interest in considerable detail.

And this was supposed to be an intro. to Somerfield that I am supposed
to be examining in detail. Well, shall we start by going back a few years?
Just as Turkey in diplomatic circles of the last century was said to be the

sick man of Europe so Somerfield, in the supermarketing sector, was said to be the sick man of supermarketing (the gender implications of both these sneers need not detain us here).

However, it has recovered. Its boss, John von Spreckelsen, told the Somerfield AGM last year that sales at both Kwik Save and Somerfield had 'stabilised' – a euphemism beloved of retailers for while it does not claim that sales are going up, it equally does not convey the grim news that sales are going down. There is something Pickwickian about such matters and I do not pretend to understand them.

I do know, though, that axing the loyalty card scheme, as Somerfield did in early 2001, claiming, like Asda and Safeway, that such schemes have lost credibility among shoppers, was an interesting move for it showed, if any further proof were necessary, that what keeps customers loyal is not cards but value for money – in the trolley. In this regard, Ms Mount's department has proved exemplary and a constant thorn in its competitors' sides with offers on wines which have defied commercial logic – until it is pointed out that selling certain bottles at less than you paid for them attracts thousands of new customers into the stores, and many of them then decide to do the weekly shop there. From my letters from *Guardian* readers, I can confidently state that this strategy works.

On the Kwik Save front, the stores received a complete revamp, more than just a fresh lick of paint, in a bid to turn around the discount chain's fortunes. A Mr Graham Maguire was appointed managing director (no reports of him being seen with a paint brush).

Sales at the revamped KS stores were reported to have increased by an average of 5% on the previous year. Out of the initial group of 200 stores, identified for the redesign, some 26 have been revamped, with completion of all 200 due by April 2001. Somerfield were said to be very optimistic about the future of KS 'as a concept' after the uplift. What will happen to the remaining 550 stores after the initial 200 have received their going over? I have no idea. Interestingly, though, in early 2001 I read a report that some Kwik Save stores, converted to the Somerfield format in the past two years, would now be returned to their original Kwik Save fascias. At the same time, the launch of a range of Kwik Save own-label products (some 250 strong) was announced. As this is a chain traditionally bothered only about selling brands rather than any own labels, this is a move with many interesting implications. Somerfield's own-label £2.99 Claret already rates highly in this book, so can we anticipate a Kwik Save own-label Claret at £2.29? It'll turn up on my doorstep one day.

As did Kwik Save staff on the doorstep of its great rival Iceland. As part of its price spat with Iceland, certain brave Kwik Save employees were persuaded to dress up in penguin suits and deploy themselves outside its rival's stores to distribute promotional leaflets. The initiative was, apparently, designed to lampoon an Iceland TV campaign in which three actors appeared dressed as penguins. Iceland condemned the Kwik Save idea as 'underhand'.

On other fronts, Somerfield joined the supermarket price war with the announcement of a major investment behind its Megadeals price promotion initiative. The Megadeals scheme, which had already undergone trials at selected stores, will be supported by a £1 million ad campaign. This sum, exceedingly modest by retail ad-spend standards (not to say parsimonious), is further proof that Somerfield has tightened its financial belt and considers every penny in its pockets.

This was the reason it was said to be quitting the rag trade only a few months after it introduced a clothing range in eight of its stores. The retailer said it wanted 'to concentrate on its core food offer'. In other words, it is sticking to what it knows best and not venturing into tricky areas. In this sense, Somerfield is a deeply conservative retailer and will, I suggest, remain so.

More evidence of this? Having announced in February that it intended to invest some £500 million in price cuts over the next 12 months, it launched a 'Buy One Get Two Free' promotion, claiming that it was the first time such an offer had been made by a high street retailer. This may well be true but this past year I can't seem to buy any little thing (eg AAA batteries for my chess computer and shampoo for my hair at Boots) without the assistant telling me, in that bored way which hints at supreme customer stupidity, that if I go back to the shelf and help myself to another one of the same product I can have both for the price of one.

By July 2001, Mr von Spreckelsen's various strategies seemed to be succeeding: he announced that like-for-like sales were growing at Somerfield for the first time in three years. Its operating profits were up. Similarly its share price (from a low of 49p at one point it had ascended to around 135p, as this book was heading to the printer).

It's been a slow grind at Somerfield, but it's beginning to pay off. In late spring, the company finally completed the conversion of its remaining 21 Gateway stores. These stores had not been updated since the acquisition of Gateway 12 years ago. Twelve years to tart up a store?

It defies belief. But then so do some of Angela's wine prices. And as far as this commentator is concerned that's all that matters.

Somerfield/Kwik Save
Somerfield House
Hawkfield Business Park
Whitchurch Lane
Bristol
BS14 0TJ

Tel 0117 935 6669 Customer Service Line
Fax 0117 935 6293
www.somerfield.co.uk

## ARGENTINIAN RED

Argentine Red 2000, Somerfield — 15 −£3.50

Argentine Sangiovese 2000, Somerfield — 16.5 −£5.00

Argentine Tempranillo 2000, Somerfield — 16 −£5.00

Argento Malbec 2000 — 17.5 −£5.00

Bright Brothers Barrica Cabernet Shiraz 1999 — 16 £5–7

Bright Brothers Barrica Shiraz 1999 — 15.5 £5–7

Bright Brothers San Juan Cabernet Sauvignon 2000 — 16 £5–7

Santa Julia Oaked Tempranillo 2000 — 16.5 −£5.00

Trivento Syrah 2000 — 16 −£5.00

## ARGENTINIAN WHITE

Argentine Chardonnay 2000, Somerfield — 15.5 −£5.00

Bright Brothers San Juan Chardonnay 2000 — 15.5 £5–7

Etchart Torrontes Chardonnay 2000 — 14 −£5.00

La Nature Organic Torrontes 2000 — 14 −£5.00

Q Chardonnay, La Agricola 1999 — 15.5 £7–10

Santa Julia Syrah Rosé 2001 — 15 −£5.00

## AUSTRALIAN RED

Australian Shiraz Cabernet 2000, Somerfield — 14 −£5.00

Banrock Station Shiraz/Mataro 2000 — 15 −£5.00

Encounter Bay Merlot 1999 — 13 £5–7

Encounter Bay Shiraz 1999 — 13.5 £5–7

297

Hardys Nottage Hill Cabernet Sauvignon/ Shiraz 1999 — 16.5 — £5–7

Hardys Tintara Cabernet Sauvignon 1998 — 15 — £7–10

Jacobs Creek Grenache Shiraz 2000 — 13.5 — –£5.00

Jacobs Creek Merlot 2000 — 13 — £5–7

Jindalee Cabernet Sauvignon 2000 — 14 — –£5.00

Lindemans Cawarra Shiraz/Cabernet 1999 — 13 — –£5.00

Masterpeace Red 2000 — 11 — –£5.00

Normans Estates Lone Gum Cabernet Merlot 2000 — 12 — –£5.00

Normans Old Vines Shiraz 1999 — 16.5 — £5–7

Omrah Plantagenet Shiraz 1999 — 14 — £7–10

Penfolds Bin 28 Kalimna Shiraz 1998 — 15 — £7–10

Penfolds Koonunga Hill Shiraz 1999 — 15 — £5–7

Rosemount Estate Shiraz/Cabernet Sauvignon 2000 — 14 — £5–7

Secession Xanadu Shiraz Cabernet 2000 — 14 — £5–7

Tortoiseshell Bay Mourvedre Shiraz 2000 — 12 — –£5.00

Wakefield Promised Land Shiraz/Cabernet Sauvignon 2000 — 12 — £5–7

## AUSTRALIAN WHITE

Banrock Station Chardonnay 2000 — 15 — –£5.00

Banrock Station Colombard Chardonnay 2001 — 14 — –£5.00

Cudgee Creek Chardonnay Colombard 2000 — 16 — –£5.00

Deakin Estate Chardonnay 2000 — 15.5 — –£5.00

Hardys Nottage Hill Chardonnay 2000 — 16 — £5–7

Hardys Stamp of Australia Riesling Gewürztraminer 2001 — 14 — –£5.00

Hardys Stamp Semillon/Chardonnay 2000 — 14.5 — –£5.00

Hardys Tintara Chardonnay 2000 — 13 — £7–10

Jacobs Creek Chardonnay 2000 — 15 — –£5.00

Jindalee Chardonnay 2000 — 16 — –£5.00

Lindemans Bin 65 Chardonnay 2000 — 16 — £5–7

Lindemans Botrytis Riesling 1998 (half bottle) — 15 — £5–7

Lindemans Cawarra Unoaked Chardonnay 2000 — 14 −£5.00

Oxford Landing Sauvignon Blanc 2000 — 16 −£5.00

Penfolds Bin 21 Rawson's Retreat Semillon/Colombard/Chardonnay 2000 — 14 −£5.00

Penfolds Koonunga Hill Chardonnay 2000 — 16 £5–7

Rosemount Chardonnay 2000 — 16 £5–7

Rosemount Semillon/Chardonnay 2000 — 15 £5–7

Shadow Ridge Chardonnay Colombard 2000 — 15.5 −£3.50

Tortoiseshell Bay Sauvignon Semillon 2000 — 13.5 −£5.00

## BULGARIAN RED

Bulgarian Cabernet Sauvignon 1999, Somerfield — 13.5 −£3.50

Bulgarian Country Red 2000, Somerfield — 13 −£3.50

## BULGARIAN WHITE

Blue Ridge Black Rosé 2000 — 13 −£5.00

Blue Ridge Chardonnay 2000 — 13.5 −£5.00

Bulgarian Chardonnay 1999, Somerfield — 16 −£3.50

Spice Trail White 2000 — 13.5 −£5.00

## CHILEAN RED

Canelo Estate Cabernet Sauvignon 2000 — 15.5 −£5.00

Canelo Estate Carmenère 2000 — 15 −£5.00

Chilean Cabernet Sauvignon Viña La Rosa 2000, Somerfield — 15.5 −£5.00

Chilean Cabernet/Merlot Viña La Rosa 2000, Somerfield — 16 −£5.00

Chilean Merlot 2000, Somerfield — 16 −£5.00

Cono Sur Cabernet Sauvignon Reserve 1998 — 16 £5–7

Cono Sur Pinot Noir 2000 — 16 −£5.00

Errázuriz Cabernet Sauvignon 2000 — 16 £5–7

Isla Negra Cabernet Sauvignon 2000 — 16 £5–7

Isla Negra Merlot 2000 — 16.5 £5–7

Santa Ines Cabernet Sauvignon Reserve 1999 — 16.5 £5–7

Tarapaca Gran Cabernet Sauvignon Reserve 1999 — 16.5 £5–7

Terrarum Merlot 2000 — 16.5 £5–7

## CHILEAN WHITE

Chilean Chardonnay 2000, Somerfield `15.5` `—£5.00`

Chilean Sauvignon Blanc 2001, Somerfield `16` `—£5.00`

Chilean Semillon Chardonnay 2000, Somerfield `16` `—£5.00`

Chilean White 2000, Somerfield `14` `—£3.50`

Cono Sur Viognier 2000 `15` `£5–7`

Errázuriz Chardonnay 2000 `16` `£5–7`

Isla Negra Chardonnay 2000 `15` `£5–7`

Terrarum Sauvignon Blanc 2000 `15` `—£5.00`

## FRENCH RED

Brouilly Les Celliers de Bellevue 2000 `14` `£5–7`

Cabernet Sauvignon d'Oc 2000, Somerfield `14` `—£3.50`

Château Blanca, Bordeaux 2000 `15.5` `—£5.00`

Château Cazal Viel, Cuvée des Fées St-Chinian 1999 `16` `£5–7`

Château Plaisance, Montagne-St-Emilion 1997 `14.5` `£7–10`

Château St-Benoit Minervois 1999 `15.5` `—£5.00`

Château Valoussière Coteaux de Languedoc 1997 `16` `—£5.00`

Châteauneuf-du-Pape Domaine La Solitude 1999 `14` `£7–10`

Claret 2000, Somerfield `15` `—£3.50`

Corbières Rouge 2000, Somerfield `13` `—£3.50`

Côte Sauvage Syrah Mourvèdre 2000 `16` `—£5.00`

Côtes du Rhône 2000, Somerfield `13` `—£3.50`

Côtes du Rhône-Villages 1999, Somerfield `14` `—£5.00`

Côtes du Roussillon 2000, Somerfield `15` `—£3.50`

Domaine de Courtilles Côte 125 Corbières 1999 `16` `£5–7`

Domaine La Tuque Bel Air, Côtes de Castillon 1998 `15.5` `£5–7`

Fitou Rocher d'Ambrée 2000, Somerfield `14` `—£5.00`

Gouts et Couleurs Syrah Mourvèdre VdP d'Oc 2000 `15.5` `—£5.00`

Hautes-Côtes de Beaune 1999 `11` `£7–10`

Médoc 2000, Somerfield `14.5` `—£5.00`

Merlot VdP l'Ardèche 2000, Somerfield `14` `—£3.50`

Oak Aged Claret 2000, Somerfield `14` `−£5.00`

Old Git Grenache Syrah 2000 `14` `−£5.00`

Organic Merlot Vin de Pays NV `15.5` `−£5.00`

Red Burgundy 1998, Somerfield `10` `£5−7`

St-Emilion 2000, Somerfield `14` `£5−7`

Stowells of Chelsea Merlot VdP d'Oc NV `12` `−£5.00`

Syrah VdP de l'Ardèche 2000, Somerfield `13` `−£3.50`

Vacqueyras, Vignerons Beaumes de Venise 2000 `16.5` `£5−7`

VdP de l'Ardèche Rouge 2000, Somerfield `13.5` `−£3.50`

Vin de Pays Hérault 2000, Somerfield `11.5` `−£3.50`

Winter Hill Rouge, VdP de l'Aude 2000 `15` `−£5.00`

## FRENCH WHITE

Anjou Blanc 2000, Somerfield `12` `−£3.50`

Bordeneuve Blanc VdP des Côtes de Gascogne 1999 `13` `−£5.00`

Chablis 1998, Somerfield `12.5` `£7−10`

Chablis Premier Cru Cottin Frères 1999 `11.5` `£10−13`

Chardonnay VdP d'Oc 2000, Somerfield `14` `−£5.00`

Côte Sauvage Chardonnay Viognier 2000 `15` `−£5.00`

Côte Sauvage Cinsault Rosé d'Oc 2000 `15` `−£5.00`

Domaine du Bois Viognier, Maurel Vedeau 1999 `15` `£5−7`

Domaine Sainte Agathe Oak Aged Chardonnay 1999, Somerfield `15` `£5−7`

Gewürztraminer d'Alsace, Turckheim 2000 `16` `£5−7`

Hautes-Côtes de Beaune Blanc, Georges Désire 1998 `13` `£7−10`

James Herrick Chardonnay VdP d'Oc 2000 `15` `−£5.00`

Kiwi Cuvée Sauvignon Blanc, VdP du Jardin de la France 2000 `14` `−£5.00`

La Baume Viognier VdP d'Oc 2000 `14.5` `−£5.00`

Laroche Chardonnay 2000 `14.5` `£5−7`

Muscadet 2000, Somerfield `13` `−£3.50`

Old Tart Terret Sauvignon 2000 `13.5` `−£5.00`

Rosé d'Anjou 2000, Somerfield `12.5` `−£3.50`

Sancerre Domaine des Grand Groux 2000, Somerfield `13` `£7–10`

VdP de l'Ardèche Blanc 2000, Somerfield `15` `–£3.50`

VdP du Comte Tolosan 2000, Somerfield `15` `–£3.50`

Vouvray 2000, Somerfield `14` `–£5.00`

White Burgundy 2000, Somerfield `13.5` `£5–7`

Winter Hill White 2000 `14` `–£5.00`

## GERMAN WHITE

Blue Nun Riesling 1999 `13.5` `–£5.00`

Hock NV, Somerfield `14.5` `–£2.50`

Kendermann Mosel Riesling 1999 `14.5` `–£5.00`

Kendermann Pinot Grigio 1999 `15` `–£5.00`

Morio Muskat 2000 `15.5` `–£3.50`

Niersteiner Gutes Domtal 1999, Somerfield `12` `–£3.50`

Niersteiner Gutes Domtal, Johannes Egberts 1999 `14` `–£5.00`

Niersteiner Spiegelberg 1999, Somerfield `14` `–£3.50`

Oppenheimer Krotenbrunner Rheinhessen Spätlese, Johannes Egberts 1999 `12` `–£5.00`

Rheingau Riesling 2000, Somerfield `15` `–£5.00`

Rheinhessen Spätlese 1999, Somerfield `13` `–£5.00`

Rudesheimer Rosengarten 2000, Somerfield `11` `–£3.50`

St Ursula Dry Riesling 2000 `14.5` `–£5.00`

## ITALIAN RED

Bardolino 2000, Somerfield `12` `–£5.00`

Bright Brothers Negroamaro Cabernet Sauvignon 1999 `14` `–£5.00`

Cabernet Sauvignon delle Venezie 2000, Somerfield `13` `–£5.00`

Chianti Serristori 2000, Somerfield `13` `–£5.00`

D'Istinto Sangiovese Merlot 1999 (Sicily) `13.5` `–£5.00`

Il Padrino Syrah di Sicilia 2000 `16` `–£5.00`

Inycon Merlot 2000 `16.5` `–£5.00`

Merlot delle Venezie 2000, Somerfield `14` `–£5.00`

Montepulciano d'Abruzzo 2000, Somerfield `14` `–£5.00`

Sicilian Red 2000, Somerfield `14` `–£3.50`

Terrale Sangiovese di Puglia 2000, Somerfield — 16.5 −£5.00

Tre Uve Ultima 1999 — 16.5 £5–7

Tre Uve VdT 2000 — 16 −£5.00

Tuscan Red 2000, Somerfield — 12 −£5.00

Valpolicella 2000, Somerfield — 12 −£3.50

## ITALIAN WHITE

Alfresco Vino da Tavola Bianco NV, Somerfield — 14 −£3.50

Alfresco Vino da Tavola Rosso NV, Somerfield — 13 −£3.50

Bright Brothers Greganico Inzolia 2000 — 14 −£5.00

Chardonnay delle Venezie 2000, Somerfield — 14.5 −£5.00

Chiaro di Luna Bianco di Custoza 2000 — 15.5 −£5.00

D'Istinto Catarratto Chardonnay 1999 — 13 −£5.00

Inycon Chardonnay 2000 (Sicily) — 16 −£5.00

La Luna Bianco di Custoza 2000 — 15.5 −£5.00

Marc Xero Chardonnay 2000 — 14 −£5.00

Pinot Grigio delle Venezie 2000, Somerfield — 14.5 −£5.00

Sicilian White 2000, Somerfield — 14 −£3.50

Soave 2000, Somerfield — 13.5 −£5.00

Trulli Chardonnay del Salento 2000 — 16 −£5.00

## MEXICAN RED

L A Cetto Petite Sirah 1999 — 15 −£5.00

## NEW ZEALAND WHITE

Montana Sauvignon Blanc 1999 — 15.5 £5–7

Nobilo White Cloud 2000 — 13 −£5.00

Villa Maria Chardonnay 1999 — 16.5 £5–7

## PORTUGUESE RED

Bright Brothers Atlantic Vines Baga 1999 — 14.5 −£5.00

Pedras do Monte 1999 — 16 −£5.00

Portada Red Estremadura 1999 — 13.5 −£5.00

Portuguese Red 2000, Somerfield — 13.5 −£3.50

## PORTUGUESE WHITE

Bright Brothers Ferñao Pires Chardonnay 1998 — 15.5 −£5.00

## ROMANIAN RED

Eagle Valley Romanian Merlot 1999 · 15 · −£5.00

## SOUTH AFRICAN RED

Andrews Hope Spice Route Cabernet Merlot 2000 · 15.5 · £5–7

Bellingham Pinotage 1999 · 13 · £5–7

Cape Soleil Organic Pinotage 2000 · 12.5 · −£5.00

Kumala Cinsault Pinotage 2000 · 13.5 · −£5.00

Kumala Reserve Cabernet Sauvignon 1998 · 15 · £7–10

South Africa Dry Red 2000, Somerfield · 12.5 · −£5.00

South African Cabernet Sauvignon 2000, Somerfield · 16 · −£5.00

South African Cinsault Ruby Cabernet 2000, Somerfield · 12 · −£5.00

South African Pinotage 2000, Somerfield · 13 · £5–7

Spice Route Pinotage 2000 · 16.5 · £7–10

Spice Route Shiraz 2000 · 16.5 · £7–10

## SOUTH AFRICAN WHITE

Arniston Bay South African Chenin Chardonnay 2001 · 14.5 · −£5.00

Bellingham Chardonnay 2000 · 15.5 · £5–7

Bellingham Sauvignon Blanc 2000 · 16.5 · −£5.00

Bush Vines Semillon 2001, Somerfield · 13.5 · −£5.00

Danie de Wet South African Chardonnay 2001 · 16 · −£5.00

Kumala Colombard Sauvignon 2001 · 14 · −£5.00

Porcupine Ridge Sauvignon Blanc 2001 · 15 · £5–7

South Africa Dry White 2001, Somerfield · 13 · −£3.50

South African Chardonnay 2001, Somerfield · 15.5 · −£5.00

South African Chenin Blanc 2001, Somerfield · 14.5 · −£5.00

South African Colombard 2001, Somerfield · 15 · −£5.00

South African Colombard Chardonnay 2001, Somerfield · 15.5 · −£5.00

Van Loveren South African Sauvignon Blanc 2001 · 15 · −£5.00

## SPANISH RED

Don Darias Red NV · 14.5 · −£3.50

Espiral Tempranillo Barrique Somontano 1999 · 15.5 · £5–7

Pergola Tempranillo 2000, Somerfield · 13 · −£5.00

Santa Elisa La Mancha Red 1999 · 10 · −£3.50

Sierra Alta Cabernet Sauvignon 1999 · 16 · −£5.00

Sierra Alta Tempranillo 1999 · 14.5 · −£5.00

Valencia Red NV, Somerfield · 13.5 · −£3.50

Viña Cana Rioja Crianza 1998, Somerfield · 14 · −£5.00

Viña Cana Rioja Reserva 1995, Somerfield · 15 · £5–7

## SPANISH WHITE

Castillo Imperial Blanco NV, Somerfield · 13.5 · −£3.50

Don Darias White NV · 14 · −£5.00

Mimbral Penedés Chardonnay 2000 · 14 · −£5.00

Moscatel de Valencia, Somerfield · 16 · −£3.50

Pergola Oaked Viura 2000, Somerfield · 15 · −£5.00

Viña Cana Rioja Blanco 2000, Somerfield · 14.5 · −£5.00

## URUGUAYAN RED

Bright Brothers Tannat Cabernet Franc 2000 · 16 · −£5.00

## URUGUAYAN WHITE

Bright Brothers Uruguayan Sauvignon/ Semillon 2000 · 15.5 · −£5.00

## USA RED

Californian Dry Red NV, Somerfield · 14 · −£5.00

Hidden Falls Carnelian Merlot 2000 · 11 · −£3.50

Laguna Canyon Zinfandel NV · 10 · −£5.00

Marc Xero Merlot 1999 · 14 · −£5.00

Talus Zinfandel 1998 · 13 · £5–7

Turning Leaf Cabernet Sauvignon 1997 · 12 · £5–7

Turning Leaf Zinfandel 1996 · 12.5 · £5–7

## USA WHITE

Fetzer Sundial Chardonnay 1999 · 14 · £5–7

Sebastiani Sonoma Chardonnay 1998 · 15.5 · £7–10

Talus Chardonnay 1998 · 16.5 · £5–7

## FORTIFIED

Amontillado Sherry, Somerfield — 15 — −£5.00

Cream Sherry, Somerfield — 13 — −£5.00

Dow's LBV Port 1995 — 14.5 — £7–10

Fino Sherry, Somerfield — 16 — −£5.00

Manzanilla Sherry, Somerfield — 16 — −£5.00

Navigators LBV Port 1995, Somerfield — 14.5 — £5–7

Navigators Ruby Port, Somerfield — 14 — −£5.00

Navigators Vintage Character Port, Somerfield — 14 — £5–7

Warre's Optima 10 Year Old Tawny Port NV50cl — 13.5 — £7–10

Warre's Warrior Special Reserve Port NV — 13 — £7–10

## SPARKLING

Asti Spumante NV, Somerfield — 11.5 — £5–7

Australian Quality Sparkling NV, Somerfield — 14 — £5–7

Australian Sparkling Chardonnay 1995, Somerfield — 14 — £7–10

Bollinger Special Cuvée NV — 13 — £20+

Cava Brut NV, Somerfield — 15 — −£5.00

Cava Rosado NV, Somerfield — 16 — −£5.00

Crémant de Bourgogne 1998, Somerfield — 14 — £7–10

De Vauzelle Champagne NV — 14 — £10–13

Freixenet Cordon Negro Brut NV — 14 — £5–7

Lindauer Brut NV (New Zealand) — 14 — £7–10

Martini Asti Spumante NV — 11 — £5–7

Moscato Fizz, Somerfield — 13 — −£2.50

Mumm Cuvée Napa Brut NV (California) — 16 — £7–10

Nicolas Feuillatte Champagne Brut NV — 14 — £13–20

Prince William Blanc de Blancs Champagne NV, Somerfield — 13 — £13–20

Prince William Blanc de Noirs Champagne NV, Somerfield — 13.5 — £10–13

Prince William Champagne Premier Cru NV, Somerfield — 14 — £13–20

Prince William Champagne Rosé NV, Somerfield — 12 — £13–20

South African Sparkling Sauvignon, Somerfield — 16 — −£5.00

Vintage Cava 1997,   16   £5–7
Somerfield

**SEE STOP-PRESS SECTION AT END OF BOOK FOR LAST-MINUTE ADDITIONS OR UPDATES TO THIS RETAILER'S RANGE.**

# SPAR

This retailer's answer to the question pervading this book – 'What in your opinion is the strength of your range of wines or the particular style of your way of retailing wine?' – was to some extent answered in autumn 2000 when Spar's managing director, Morton Middleditch (what a ringing Dickensian name! One can actually hear the reverend fellow preaching in his pulpit), said that independent licensed retailers who were looking to 'diversify their offering' should 'look to Spar'. What we have here then is a franchised retailer selling, via wholesalers, to independent store owners who may choose to buy only part of their wine range from Spar.

For Liz Aked, Spar's dogged wine buyer, the answer to the question above is more complex. She told me:

> 'The style of our retailing is every wine for every body. Only 8% of customers shop exclusively at Spar outlets – small village outfits for example where there is sense of community – and so we have to rely on passing, occasional trade, which does most of its wine buying elsewhere.' She pauses for thought. Then: 'I would like to think we provide the best retail quality at the best price.'

It is impossible, given the circumstances in which Spar operates, to guarantee things which are taken for granted with the large supermarket chains. I can't even tell you what a shop with a Spar sign outside will say if you bring back a bottle of wine on the grounds it is faulty. At retailers like Tesco and Asda, there is a clear policy of an instant, hassle-free refund or a fresh bottle. At Spar it's very much up to the philosophy of the individual who runs the store and if you are not on first name terms with the owner – like one of those small villagers – then who knows what response you'll get when returning a wine you consider unfit to drink?

Nevertheless, Spar has tried wide-ranging, ambitious initiatives. It has teamed up with neighbourhood on-line shopping service *BeepBeep.com* to provide local Internet shopping and home-delivery services. Spar International, the mother company, announced it was spreading to Russia with a store scheduled to open in Moscow in 2001, and 24 further outlets to be added during the next three years.

Spar also opened its first Express forecourt store in the Southwest, at Portishead. The Spar wholesaler concerned, Appleby Westward, is keen to open more petrol station outlets in the region. And in spring 2001, this mysterious retail force stuck its toe in the murky and expensive world of TV advertising – its first such campaign for 20 years. The £2 million campaign carried the strapline 'So near so Spar'.

Liz reckons that this year Spar will be near enough to enough drinkers for her to sell 13.5 million cases of wine, and it is a range she is working hard to improve. When I commented that I was unimpressed with many of the low priced French reds and whites, one superb Wild River Merlot from Boutinot being an exception, she was honest enough to agree. She remarked: 'Yes, I've got a lot of work to do there. Too many wines in that range are a bit hard.'

Not as hard as the job she has on her hands selling wines to all those ornery individuals who run their own little retail fiefdoms.

Spar (UK) Limited
Hygeia Building
66 College Road
Harrow
HA1 1BE

Tel 020 8426 3700
Fax 020 8426 3701
www.spar.co.uk

## ARGENTINIAN RED

Argentinian Del Sur 1999, Spar · 14 · −£5.00

## ARGENTINIAN WHITE

Argentinian Del Sur 2000, Spar · 14 · −£5.00

## AUSTRALIAN RED

De Bortoli Australian Dry Red 2000, Spar · 14 · −£5.00

De Bortoli Shiraz Cabernet 2000, Spar · 12 · −£5.00

Normans Unfiltered Grenache 1997 · 11 · £5–7

Temple Bruer Cabernet Merlot 1996 · 16 · £7–10

## AUSTRALIAN WHITE

Bleasdale Verdelho 1999 — 13.5 — £5–7

De Bortoli Australian Dry White 2000, Spar — 13 — −£5.00

De Bortoli Australian Semillon Chardonnay 1999, Spar — 13.5 — −£5.00

Lindemans Bin 65 Chardonnay 1999 — 16.5 — −£5.00

## BULGARIAN RED

Bulgarian Country Wine Cabernet Sauvignon & Merlot NV, Spar — 13 — −£3.50

Suhindol Estate Cabernet Sauvignon 2000, Spar — 12 — −£5.00

## BULGARIAN WHITE

Bulgarian Country White NV, Spar — 11 — −£3.50

Preslav Estate Bulgarian Chardonnay 2000, Spar — 12 — −£5.00

## CHILEAN RED

Canèpa Merlot 1998, Spar — 15 — −£5.00

Chilean Cabernet Sauvignon 2000, Spar — 15 — £5–7

Chilean Merlot 1999, Spar — 14 — £5–7

Tocornal Red 2000, Spar — 14 — −£5.00

## CHILEAN WHITE

Canèpa Chilean Chardonnay 1999, Spar — 15.5 — £5–7

Canèpa Chilean Sauvignon Blanc 1999, Spar — 14 — −£5.00

Tocornal Chilean White 2000, Spar — 13 — −£5.00

## FRENCH RED

Beaujolais NV, Spar — 10 — −£5.00

Claret NV, Spar — 15 — −£5.00

Coteaux du Languedoc 2000, Spar — 13 — −£5.00

Côtes du Rhône 1999, Spar — 13.5 — −£5.00

Côtes du Ventoux, Spar 1999 — 14.5 — −£5.00

Crozes-Hermitage 1999, Spar — 13 — £5–7

Fitou NV, Spar — 16 — −£5.00

French Country Red NV, Spar (1 litre) — 12 — −£3.50

Gevrey-Chambertin Les Caves des Hautes-Côtes 1994 — 12 — £13–20

Hautes-Côtes de Beaune 1995, Spar — 10 — £5–7

La Côte Syrah Merlot VdP d'Oc 1999, Spar — 13.5 −£5.00

Oaked Merlot 1999, Spar — 14 −£5.00

Salaison Shiraz/ Cabernet VdP d'Oc 1998, Spar — 16 −£5.00

Shiraz VdP d'Oc 1999, Spar — 13.5 −£5.00

Vin de Pays de l'Aude NV, Spar — 10 −£3.50

Wild River Grenache 1999 — 13 −£5.00

Wild River Merlot 1999 — 15.5 −£5.00

## FRENCH WHITE

Chablis 1998, Spar — 15 £5–7

French Country VdP de l'Hérault White NV — 13 −£5.00

La Côte Chasan Chardonnay 1999 — 14 −£5.00

Salaison Chardonnay Sauvignon 1999, Spar — 13.5 −£5.00

Unoaked Chardonnay 1999, Spar — 13 −£5.00

Vin de Pays de l'Aude NV, Spar — 14 −£3.50

White Burgundy Chardonnay 1996, Spar — 13 £5–7

Wild River Terret Sauvignon 1999 — 14 −£5.00

## GERMAN WHITE

Grans Fassian Riesling 1996 — 16 £5–7

## HUNGARIAN RED

Misty Mountain Merlot NV, Spar — 13 −£5.00

## HUNGARIAN WHITE

Misty Mountain Chardonnay NV, Spar — 13 −£5.00

## ITALIAN RED

Barolo 'Costa di Bussia' 1996 — 15 £13–20

Chianti 1999, Spar — 11 −£5.00

Chianti Classico Le Fioraie 1995 — 10 £7–10

Montepulciano d'Abruzzo 1999, Spar — 12 −£5.00

Pasta Red NV, Spar (1 litre) — 11 −£3.50

Riva Vino da Tavola NV, Spar — 10 −£3.50

Sangiovese del Rubicone Arienta NV, Spar — 11 −£5.00

Valpolicella NV, Spar — 10 −£5.00

## ITALIAN WHITE

Colli Albani NV, Spar — 14 −£5.00

Pasta White NV, Spar
(1 litre)   13   −£3.50

Riva Vino da Tavola
NV, Spar   15   −£3.50

Verdicchio dei Castelli
di Jesi 1999, Spar   14   −£5.00

## NEW ZEALAND WHITE

Saint Clair
Marlborough
Sauvignon 1996   13.5   £5–7

## SOUTH AFRICAN RED

Chiwara Cinsaut/Ruby
Cabernet 1999   14.5   −£5.00

Chiwara Pinotage 2000,
Spar   12   −£5.00

## SOUTH AFRICAN WHITE

Chiwara Colombard/
Sauvignon 1998, Spar   14   −£5.00

## SPANISH RED

Rioja Crianza 1997,
Spar   13   £5–7

Rioja NV, Spar   12   £5–7

Valencia Soft Red NV,
Spar   12.5   −£3.50

## SPANISH WHITE

Perfect for Parties
White NV, Spar (1 litre)   10   −£3.50

Valencia Dry White
NV, Spar   13.5   −£3.50

## USA RED

Fetzer Valley Oaks
Cabernet Sauvignon
1997   15.5   £5–7

Heritage Red 1999   14   −£5.00

## USA WHITE

Heritage Californian
White 1999   10   −£5.00

## FORTIFIED

Fino Sherry NV, Spar   14.5   −£5.00

Old Cellar LBV Port
1995, Spar   14   £7–10

Old Cellar Ruby Port
NV, Spar   14.5   £5–7

## SPARKLING

Asti Spumante NV,
Spar   13   −£5.00

Cava Brut NV, Spar   13   −£5.00

Marques de Prevel
Champagne NV, Spar   12   £13–20

# TESCO

This retailer's response to the question pervading this book – 'What in your opinion is the strength of your range of wines or the particular style of your way of retailing wine?' – was thus:

> 'Our key strength in the wine team is listening to our customers and understanding their needs – this underpins everything we do. We have a comprehensive range of almost 800 wines, the largest range in any mainstream supermarket, and offer something for everyone (our customer base is very diverse). We strive to offer unbeatable quality at excellent prices and respond to feedback from our customers who participate in quality assessment panels and taste our wines in store. Last year approx. 750,000 customers tasted over 150 different wines in Tesco stores.
>
> Our customers are very demanding and so we cannot stand still. Our annual Wine Festival and promotions get better and better; our organic range is booming; we have launched an own-label range of 50 top quality 'Finest' wines; we've extended our fine wine range and improved in store ambience and display; and last but not least we have launched our Tesco.com The Wine Warehouse site.'

I concur with these modestly expressed sentiments. I can confirm that Tesco's strength is its diversity and agree totally that its style is typified by a sympathy to its customers' attitudes and requirements which has duly (and truly) made this retailer closer to more drinkers than any other wine merchant on the planet. I don't know exactly how many hundreds of millions of bottles of wine it will sell this year, but I do know it will be more than anyone else.

An introduction to this company or an overview, if you will, of its activities since the last *Superplonk* came out, is very much a history not only of UK retailing during this period but also of many of the social and economic issues preoccupying us. In July 2000, for example, Tesco reverted to selling produce in pounds and ounces following frustration from its customers who felt that the metric system was being imposed on them (it was later taken to court by Edinburgh Trading Standards for this backsliding to Imperial measurements). The fact that this was first reported in the *Sun* newspaper, and that this Murdoch mouthpiece felt it important to make it known, tells us a good deal about the state of Britain in the new Millennium. If you require further proof of this, then you have only to consider that Tesco said, in 2000, that it would open 10 Internet cafes in its stores following a successful trial at its Kensington store. It opened a dog crèche at one store and began to flog travel insurance in others and, in a move to send shivers down the spine of the average car dealer, it was also reported that Tesco intended to flog cars on-line at Tesco.com from early 2001. In the summer, it appointed John Hoerner (who once ran the Arcadia fashion shops) as boss of its clothing side.

Tesco later received a government grant of £1 million to open those Internet cafes. Tesco announced six months after this that it wanted to double the turnover of its on-line business in the next three years from its 2001 level of £250 million a year. Interestingly, the average sum Tesco shoppers spend on-line is between £80 and £90, four times the in-store average. (Reports that wealthier Tesco customers get their Internet groceries delivered in Harrods-green, but otherwise unmarked Range Rovers, I put down to an April fool joke. Later, I discovered it was true.)

The *Sun's* sister rag, *The Times*, revealed that Tesco now had the first all-female wine buying team of any UK supermarket and reported at length on this, linking it to the publication of a survey, which revealed that it was women more than men who chose most of the wine purchased in the country.

It is not true that Tesco's wine department is all-women, however, since it is very definitely a male who co-ordinates their buying operations in Australia and I have surely seen hairy beasts in dark suits at Tesco wine tastings. Ancillary to this, Tesco denied that it was dumbing down its wine range despite the fact that it has, according to a report in the *Off Licence News*, cut down on label detail and is moving towards lighter, fruitier wines. The retailer said that it was responding to demands from female shoppers who were tired of heavy wine styles and too much technical information on labels. 'There's no danger of dumbing down,' said a spokeswoman. 'The idea is to make the labels clearer.' Amen to that.

National concerns thus matter to Tesco as much as international ones. Its first store in Taiwan opened in December and a score more are promised over the next five years. The retailer already has stores in Thailand (24 branches as of August 2000) and seven in South Korea. It was also reported to be stepping up its plans to move into Japan, having sent a research team to the country to sniff out potential deals. Tesco reported at this time interim profits of £415 million on a turnover of £10 billion and forecasted that 45% of the company's retail space would be outside the UK by 2002.

Back in Britain, a shop-by-bike scheme was launched at two Tesco stores. For an £8 fee the customer buys a tow hook for her bike, to which is affixed a trailer packed at the checkout with the purchased groceries. Customers are expected to return the trailers within three days if they don't return for more groceries – and on the return journey the trailer can be filled with recyclable materials like glass and paper for deposit in the appropriate banks in the Tesco car park. I have yet to investigate this phenomenon. I do all my own supermarket shopping by bike, and a trailer would come in useful when I'm doing a lot of entertaining over a weekend. I am, though, many miles from the nearest Tesco but, hint hint, if a trailer scheme was in place there I'd certainly give it a go.

Tesco also tested out a new-style trolley with a built-in seat at its Eastbourne store. The trolley is designed for use by pensioners who make up more than 50% of the customers who shop at the seaside branch. What I haven't been able to find out is what method of locomotion is required to propel the trolley once the customer is seated in it. I suspect, however, that the seat is merely to allow the shopper to take the weight off her feet; the concept of crazed wrinklies zooming around a supermarket on motorised trolleys doesn't bear thinking about.

Nor does a report (originally in the *Daily Mail*) that Tesco was sending new recruits on courses to learn basic maths and spelling. A £100,000 pilot programme was being run in Leeds. Since the educational system seems to have failed these new recruits, and Tesco is rescuing them, I am surprised that the Blair government doesn't learn a lesson itself from this and simply hand over the whole of British primary education to Tesco. Isn't the overriding theme of the Blair administration one of the private sector and public sector working hand in hand?

One reason why Tesco require numerate employees is because they are required to count large sums of money. Tesco employees, some 33,000 of them, received a £123 million windfall as part of the company's SAYE scheme in 2000. This figure represented a return on their investment of some 200%. It pays to work at Tesco and it helps if you can count.

Less literacy is required from its customers. Anyone can understand when a brand is cheaper in one store than its rival down the road. Hence Tesco cut £70 million from the prices of key shopping items in the hope of luring customers from Sainsbury's and Safeway (so it said). This inspired widespread comment that a new supermarket price war was about to begin. Many shoppers were unaware, me included, that any cessation in hostilities had previously been declared.

Tesco came in for criticism from the civil rights group, Liberty, regarding its plans to sell information on 14 million Tesco Clubcard holders. No one, however, complained about the civil rights violation of Mancunians aged between 11 and 18 banned from the branch in Didsbury (Manchester), during certain hours, after complaints about gangs of teenagers roaming the aisles. In a contrary and unconnected move, Mr Terry Leahy, Tesco chief exec., was awarded the freedom of his home city of Liverpool.

Tesco then announced a £250 million investment programme for London, aiming to create 5,000 jobs over the next two years. The plans include job training for the long-term unemployed and it was also said Tesco was considering building housing near its stores aimed at its lower and middle income employees. This must provide further thought for New Labour strategists – having handed primary education over to Tesco why not ask the retailer to run all the nation's council estates?

Hard on the heels of the announcement above came news that Tesco planned to double the number of its so-called Extra hypermarkets in the UK over the next two years in order to reach £5 billion in non-food turnover by the end of 2002. Currently there are 23 Extra hypermarkets, in which some 50% of the selling area is devoted to non-food products. This was closely followed by the report of Tesco profits: over £1 billion for the first time.

Tesco was now said to be building the largest foodstore in London on the site of the former gasworks in Beckton. The £20 million project will create 400 jobs when it opens in 2002, though no mention was made of any local Tesco primary schools or Leahy housing estates.

Nor indeed have we yet received news of the first Tesco employee millionaire. This, however, is surely on the loyalty cards. At the last divi-up in 2001, more than 70,000 Tesco staff split £38 million worth of shares between them – shares which had risen in value by 31% over three years.

I leave it to a certain *Guardian* reader (how are you, Ron?) to write and tell me how long it will take a thrifty Tesco employee with an average shareholding, on the basis of those figures and assuming a constant rate of the same growth, to reach millionairedom. I would guess about the same length of time as it will take before Spurs win the premiership title again.

Tesco
Tesco House
PO Box 18 Delamare Road
Cheshunt
EN8 9SL

Tel 0800 505555 Customer Careline
www.tesco.co.uk

## ARGENTINIAN RED

| | | |
|---|---|---|
| Argento Malbec 2000 | 17.5 | −£5.00 |
| Bright Brothers Barrica Reserve Cabernet Sauvignon/Shiraz 1998 | 15 | £5–7 |
| Catena Cabernet Sauvignon 1996 | 17 | £7–10 |
| Deep Purple Shiraz 2000 | 14 | −£5.00 |
| Monster Spicy Red Syrah NV, Tesco | 16 | −£5.00 |
| Picajuan Peak Bonarda 2000 | 15.5 | −£5.00 |
| Picajuan Peak Malbec 2000, Tesco | 15 | −£5.00 |
| Picajuan Peak Sangiovese 2000, Tesco | 14.5 | −£5.00 |
| Q Tempranillo 1998 | 16.5 | £7–10 |
| Santa Julia Bonarda/ Sangiovese Reserva 1999 | 15 | £5–7 |
| Santa Julia Merlot Oak Aged 2000 | 15.5 | −£5.00 |
| Santa Julia Oaked Tempranillo 2000 | 16.5 | −£5.00 |

## ARGENTINIAN WHITE

| | | |
|---|---|---|
| Argentinian Torrontes 1999, Tesco | 13 | −£3.50 |
| Argento Chardonnay 2000 | 17 | −£5.00 |
| La Nature Organic Torrontes 2000 | 14 | −£5.00 |
| Picajuan Peak Chardonnay 2000, Tesco | 15.5 | −£5.00 |
| Seriously Fruity Rosé NV, Tesco | 14.5 | −£5.00 |

## AUSTRALIAN RED

| | | |
|---|---|---|
| Angove's Lock 9 Carignan/Mataro/ Shiraz 2000 | 10 | −£5.00 |
| Angove's Stonegate Barbera 2000 | 14 | −£5.00 |
| Australian Cabernet/ Merlot NV, Tesco | 15.5 | −£3.50 |
| Australian Red NV, Tesco | 15 | −£3.50 |
| Australian Shiraz NV, Tesco | 14 | −£3.50 |

Banrock Station Shiraz 2000 — 14.5 −£5.00

Banrock Station Shiraz/Mataro 2000 — 15 −£5.00

Barramundi Shiraz/Merlot NV — 15.5 −£5.00

Blue Pyrenees Estate Red 1996 — 14 £10–13

Buckleys Grenache/Shiraz/Mourvèdre 1998 — 14 £7–10

Casella Carramar Estate Merlot 2000 — 14 −£5.00

Chapel Hill Cabernet Sauvignon 1997 — 14 £7–10

Coonawarra Cabernet Sauvignon 1997, Tesco — 16 £5–7

Hardys Stamp Shiraz/Cabernet 2000 — 13 −£5.00

Image Cabernet/Merlot 2000 — 13.5 −£5.00

Lindemans Bin 50 Shiraz 1999 — 16 £5–7

McLaren Vale Grenache 1999, Tesco — 13.5 £5–7

McLaren Vale Shiraz 1999, Tesco — 14.5 £5–7

Miranda Rovalley Ridge Petit Verdot 2000 — 14 £5–7

Oxford Landing Cabernet Sauvignon Shiraz 1999 — 15.5 £5–7

Oxford Landing Merlot 2000 — 15 £5–7

Penfolds Bin 128 Coonawarra Shiraz 1998 — 15.5 £7–10

Penfolds Bin 28 Kalimna Shiraz 1998 — 15 £7–10

Penfolds Bin 35 Rawsons Retreat Shiraz/Cabernet 1999 — 16 £5–7

Rosemount Estate Cabernet/Merlot 2000 — 14 £5–7

Rosemount Estate Grenache/Shiraz 2000 — 13 £5–7

Rosemount Estate Merlot 1999 — 15 £7–10

Smithbrook Cabernet Sauvignon/Cabernet Franc/Petit Verdot 1998 — 16 £7–10

St Hallett Faith Barossa Shiraz 1999 — 15 £7–10

Sunstone Fresh Spicy Red NV — 12 −£5.00

Tim Adams Shiraz 1999 — 17 £7–10

Wilkie Estate Organic Cabernet Merlot 2000 — 13 £7–10

Wolf Blass Green Label Shiraz 1999 — 16 £5–7

Wolf Blass Yellow Label Cabernet Sauvignon 1999 — 15.5 £7–10

Woolpunda Cabernet Sauvignon 1998 — 15 −£5.00

Woolpunda Merlot 1999 — 14.5 −£5.00

Woolpunda Shiraz 1998 — 16 −£5.00

## AUSTRALIAN WHITE

Australian Chardonnay, Tesco — `16` `−£3.50`

Australian White NV, Tesco — `15.5` `−£3.50`

Banrock Colombard Chardonnay 2000 — `15` `−£5.00`

Banrock Station Chardonnay 2000 — `15` `−£5.00`

Barramundi Semillon/ Chardonnay NV — `16` `−£5.00`

Blue Pyrenees Estate Chardonnay 1997 — `16.5` `£10–13`

Bonic Estate Chardonnay 2000 — `15` `−£5.00`

Brown Brothers Dry Muscat 2000 — `14` `−£5.00`

Great Southern Riesling 2000, Tesco — `16.5` `£5–7`

Hardys Stamp of Australia Chardonnay Semillon 2000 — `15` `−£5.00`

Hunter Valley Semillon 2000, Tesco — `16` `£5–7`

Image Chardonnay 2000 — `13` `−£5.00`

Jacobs Creek Chardonnay 2000 — `15` `−£5.00`

Jacobs Creek Dry Riesling 2000 — `15` `−£5.00`

Langhorne Creek Verdelho 2000, Tesco — `15` `£5–7`

Lindemans Bin 65 Chardonnay 2000 — `16` `−£5.00`

Lindemans Cawarra Chardonnay 2000 — `15.5` `−£5.00`

Miranda White Pointer 2000 — `13.5` `−£5.00`

Mount Pleasant Elizabeth Semillon 1994 — `15.5` `£7–10`

Normans Unwooded Chardonnay 2000 — `16.5` `−£5.00`

Overtly Aromatic White NV, Tesco — `15` `−£5.00`

Oxford Landing Chardonnay 2000 — `15.5` `−£5.00`

Oxford Landing Sauvignon Blanc 2000 — `16` `−£5.00`

Padthaway Chardonnay 2000, Tesco — `16` `£5–7`

Rosemount Chardonnay 2000 — `16` `£5–7`

Rosemount Sauvignon Blanc 2000 — `15` `£5–7`

Rosemount Semillon/ Chardonnay 2000 — `15` `£5–7`

Rosemount Semillon/ Sauvignon 2000 — `15` `£5–7`

Smithbrook Chardonnay 1998 — `15` `£7–10`

Smooth Voluptuous White NV, Tesco — `15` `−£5.00`

Tim Adams Riesling 2000 — `16` `£7–10`

Tim Adams Semillon 1998 — `16.5` `£7–10`

Woolpunda Blue Block Chardonnay 1998 — 15.5 −£5.00

Yendah Vale Chardonnay/Merlot Rosé 2000 — 12 −£5.00

## AUSTRIAN RED

Blauer Zweigelt Lenz Moser 1997 — 14.5 −£5.00

## BULGARIAN RED

Reka Valley Bulgarian Cabernet Sauvignon NV, Tesco — 14.5 −£3.50

## CHILEAN RED

Caliterra Syrah 1999 — 16 £5–7

Chilean Cabernet Sauvignon NV, Tesco — 16 −£5.00

Chilean Cabernet Sauvignon Reserve 2000, Tesco — 15.5 −£5.00

Chilean Malbec NV, Tesco — 16.5 −£5.00

Chilean Merlot NV, Tesco — 16 −£5.00

Chilean Merlot Reserve 2000, Tesco — 15.5 −£5.00

Chilean Red NV, Tesco — 15 −£3.50

Cono Sur Pinot Noir 2000 — 16 −£5.00

Cono Sur Pinot Noir Reserve 1999 — 16.5 £5–7

Errázuriz Cabernet Sauvignon Reserva 1998 — 16.5 £7–10

Errázuriz Don Maximiano 1998 — 16 £13–20

Errázuriz Merlot 2000 — 16 £5–7

Errázuriz Syrah Reserva 1998 — 16 £7–10

Isla Negra Cabernet Sauvignon, Rapel 1999 — 16 −£5.00

Isla Negra Merlot 2000 — 16.5 £5–7

Luis Felipe Edwards Cabernet Sauvignon Reserva 1999 — 15.5 £5–7

Salsa Cabernet Sauvignon 2000 — 14 −£5.00

Santa Ines Cabernet/ Merlot 2000 — 17 −£5.00

Stowells Chilean Cabernet/Merlot NV — 14.5 −£5.00

Terra Mater Cabernet Sauvignon 2000 — 15 −£5.00

Two Tribes Red NV — 14.5 −£5.00

Valdivieso Cabernet Franc Reserve 1999 — 17 £7–10

Valdivieso Cabernet Sauvignon Reserve 1998 — 17 £5–7

Valdivieso Carignan 1999 — 16 −£5.00

Valdivieso Malbec Reserve 1997 — 16.5 £7–10

Vision Merlot Reserve 2000 — 16.5 £7–10

## CHILEAN WHITE

| | | |
|---|---|---|
| Chilean Chardonnay Reserve 2000, Tesco | 16 | −£5.00 |
| Chilean Chardonnay, Tesco | 14 | −£5.00 |
| Chilean Sauvignon Blanc NV, Tesco | 14.5 | −£5.00 |
| Chilean White NV, Tesco | 14.5 | −£3.50 |
| Errázuriz Chardonnay 1999 | 16 | £5–7 |
| Errázuriz Chardonnay Reserva 1997 | 17 | £7–10 |
| Isla Negra Chardonnay 2000 | 15 | −£5.00 |
| Luis Felipe Edwards Chardonnay 1999 | 16.5 | −£5.00 |
| Santa Ines Sauvignon Blanc 2000 | 16 | −£5.00 |
| Stowells Chilean Sauvignon Blanc NV | 12 | −£5.00 |
| Terra Mater Chardonnay 2000 | 14.5 | −£5.00 |
| Two Tribes White NV | 14 | −£5.00 |
| Valdivieso Malbec Rosé 2000 | 16.5 | −£5.00 |

## FRENCH RED

| | | |
|---|---|---|
| Beaujolais NV, Tesco | 11 | −£3.50 |
| Beaujolais-Villages 2000, Tesco | 12 | −£5.00 |
| Bordeaux Réserve Calvet 1998 | 14.5 | £5–7 |
| Cabernet Sauvignon Prestige VdP d'Oc NV, Tesco | 15.5 | −£5.00 |
| Cabernet Sauvignon Réserve 1998, Tesco | 15.5 | −£5.00 |
| Cabernet Sauvignon VdP d'Oc NV, Tesco | 14 | −£3.50 |
| Château Clement Pichon, Cru Bourgeois Haut-Médoc 1996 | 13 | £13–20 |
| Château de Côte de Montpezat, Côtes de Castillon 1998 | 16 | £5–7 |
| Château la Fleur Bellevue Premières Côtes de Blaye 1998 | 14 | −£5.00 |
| Château la Tour de Mons Bordeaux 1996 | 13.5 | £13–20 |
| Château Lafarque Pessac Léognan 1996 | 12 | £10–13 |
| Château Liliane-Ladouys Cru Bourgeois Supérieur Saint-Estephe 1996 | 12 | £13–20 |
| Chinon Baronnie Madeleine, Couly Dutheil 1999 | 16.5 | £5–7 |
| Claret, Tesco | 12.5 | −£3.50 |
| Clarity Bordeaux Rouge 1998 | 14 | −£5.00 |
| Corbières NV, Tesco | 13.5 | −£3.50 |
| Corbières Réserve La Sansoure 2000, Tesco | 13.5 | −£5.00 |
| Côtes du Rhône NV, Tesco | 13.5 | −£3.50 |

Côtes du Rhône-Villages 2000, Tesco `16` −£5.00

Côtes du Rhône-Villages Réserve Domaine de la Grande Retour 2000, Tesco `15` −£5.00

Crozes-Hermitage Cave de Tain 1999 `16.5` £5–7

Domaine du Soleil Syrah/Malbec VdP d'Oc NV `14.5` −£5.00

Domaine Richeaume Organic Syrah Côtes de Provence 1999 `16.5` £13–20

Dorgan VdP de l'Aude NV `14` −£3.50

Fitou NV, Tesco `14.5` −£3.50

Fitou Réserve Baron de la Tour 1999, Tesco `16` −£5.00

Fleurie Louis Josse 1999 `11` £5–7

French Cabernet Sauvignon Réserve, VdP d'Oc 1998 `16` −£5.00

French Merlot VdP d'Oc NV, Tesco `14.5` −£3.50

Gamay NV, Tesco `10` −£3.50

Gevrey-Chambertin Jean-Philippe Marchand 1998 `12` £13–20

Grenache Prestige VdP d'Oc NV, Tesco `13` −£5.00

Grenache VdP d'Oc NV, Tesco `14.5` −£3.50

Hautes-Côtes de Beaune Les Caves des Hautes-Côtes 1998 `13` £5–7

Hautes-Côtes de Nuits Louis Josse 1998 `12` £5–7

Juliénas Georges Duboeuf 1999 `13` £5–7

Le Monstre Grenache Noir 2000 `15` −£5.00

Les Etoiles French Organic Red Wine NV `13` −£5.00

Louis Jadot Beaujolais-Villages 2000 `14` £5–7

Margaux 1998, Tesco `14` £10–13

Médoc 1998, Tesco `16` £5–7

Merlot Prestige VdP d'Oc NV, Tesco `15` −£5.00

Minervois NV, Tesco `14` −£3.50

Oak Aged Red Burgundy 1998, Tesco `13.5` £5–7

Oaked Côtes du Rhône NV `13.5` −£5.00

Perrin Vacqueyras 1998 `14` £7–10

St-Emilion 1999, Tesco `16` £7–10

Valréas Domaine de La Grande Bellane 1999 (organic) `14.5` £5–7

Vintage Claret 1998 `14` −£5.00

Yvecourt Claret Bordeaux 1999 `13.5` −£5.00

## FRENCH WHITE

Alsace Gewürztraminer 1999, Tesco — 17 — £5–7

Alsace Riesling 1999, Tesco — 14.5 — £5–7

Anjou Blanc NV, Tesco — 13 — −£3.50

Bergerac Blanc NV, Tesco — 14.5 — −£3.50

Cabernet de Saumur Rosé NV, Tesco — 14.5 — −£5.00

Celsius Cabernet Sauvignon Rosé, VdP d'Oc 2000 — 14 — −£5.00

Celsius Medium Chardonnay, VdP d'Oc 2000 — 13.5 — −£5.00

Chablis 2000, Tesco — 15 — £5–7

Chablis Premier Cru 1998, Tesco — 16 — £10–13

Chardonnay Barrel-aged Reserve, VdP d'Oc 1999 — 15 — −£5.00

Chardonnay Réserve 1999, Tesco — 14 — −£5.00

Château Baratet Blanc 1999 (organic) — 14 — −£5.00

Château Talmont 2000 — 16 — −£5.00

Côtes du Rhône Blanc NV, Tesco — 15 — −£3.50

Côtes du Rhône Rosé, AC Côtes du Rhônes 2000 — 14 — −£5.00

Domaine Cazal Viel Viognier 1999 — 16 — £5–7

Domaine du Soleil Chardonnay VdP d'Oc NV — 14 — −£5.00

Domaine du Soleil Sauvignon/ Chardonnay VdP d'Oc NV — 14 — −£5.00

Entre-Deux-Mers NV, Tesco — 13.5 — −£5.00

French Chardonnay NV, Tesco — 13.5 — −£3.50

French Chenin Blanc NV, Tesco — 14.5 — −£3.50

French Viognier VdP d'Oc 2000, Tesco — 16 — −£5.00

Kiwi Cuvée Sauvignon Blanc, VdP du Jardin de la France 2000 — 14 — −£5.00

Les Estoiles Organic Chardonnay/Chenin VdP d'Oc NV — 13.5 — −£5.00

Les Quatre Clochers Chardonnay 1998 — 15.5 — £5–7

Mâcon Villages-Blanc 2000, Tesco — 15 — −£5.00

Muscadet NV, Tesco — 14.5 — −£3.50

Muscadet sur Lie 2000, Tesco — 14 — −£5.00

Oak Aged Bordeaux NV, Tesco — 13 — −£5.00

Oak Aged White Burgundy 1999, Tesco — 13 — £5–7

Petit Chablis 1999, Tesco — 15 — £5–7

Pouilly-Fuissé Louis Jadot 1998 `11` £13–20

Pouilly-Fumé Cuvée Jules 1999 `13` £7–10

Sancerre 2000, Tesco `16` £5–7

Vouvray, Tesco `12` −£5.00

## GERMAN RED

Fire Mountain Pinot Noir 1999 `10` −£5.00

## GERMAN WHITE

Bernkasteler Graben Riesling Kabinett 1999 `15` £5–7

Carl Erhard Rheingau Riesling 1999 `14` −£5.00

Fire Mountain Riesling 1999 `14` −£5.00

Grans Fassian Riesling 1999 `14.5` £5–7

Steinweiler Kloster Liebfrauenberg Kabinett, Tesco `14` −£5.00

Steinweiler Kloster Liebfrauenberg Spätlese, Tesco `13` −£5.00

## GREEK RED

Grande Reserve Naoussa 1996 `14` £5–7

## GREEK WHITE

Santorini 1999 `16` −£5.00

## HUNGARIAN RED

Reka Valley Hungarian Merlot, Tesco `13` −£3.50

Riverview Kékfrancos/ Merlot 2000 `13.5` −£5.00

## HUNGARIAN WHITE

Emerald Hungarian Sauvignon Blanc 2000 `15.5` −£5.00

Nagyrede Estate Barrel Aged Pinot Grigio/ Zenit 1998 `16` −£5.00

Reka Valley Chardonnay NV, Tesco `12` −£3.50

Riverview Chardonnay/Pinot Grigio 2000 `15` −£5.00

## ITALIAN RED

Badia a Coltibuono Chianti Classico 1998 `14` £7–10

Barbera d'Asti Calissano 1999 `14` −£5.00

Chianti 1999, Tesco `12` −£3.50

Chianti Classico Riserva 1998, Tesco `16.5` £5–7

Chianti Rufina 1999, Tesco `15.5` −£5.00

Inycon Merlot 1999 (Sicily)　15.5　−£5.00

Inycon Syrah 2000 (Sicily)　16　−£5.00

La Gioiosa Merlot 2000　15.5　−£5.00

Merlot del Piave NV, Tesco　11　−£5.00

Monte d'Abro Montepulciano Abruzzo NV　15　−£5.00

Pendulum Zinfandel 1999　15.5　−£5.00

Pinot Noir del Veneto NV, Tesco　11　−£5.00

Sicilian Red NV, Tesco　14　−£3.50

Terra Viva Organic Red 2000　14　−£5.00

Terre Dego 2000　15.5　−£5.00

Tre Uve Ultima 1998　16　£5–7

Trulli Primitivo Salento 1999　14.5　−£5.00

Valpolicella Classico 1999, Tesco　13　−£5.00

Villa Pigna Rosso Piceno 1998　14　−£5.00

## ITALIAN WHITE

Antinori Orvieto Classico Secco 1999　13　−£5.00

Asti NV, Tesco　13　−£5.00

Cataratto Chardonnay Sicilia NV, Tesco　15.5　−£5.00

'I Portali' Basilicata Greco 1999　16　−£5.00

Inycon Chardonnay 2000 (Sicily)　16　−£5.00

Italia Pinot Grigio 2000　12.5　−£5.00

La Gioiosa Pinot Grigio 2000　15　−£5.00

Lamberti Pinot Grigio 2000　16　−£5.00

Terra Viva Organic Soave Superiore 2000　14　−£5.00

Terra Viva Organic White 2000　15.5　−£5.00

Trulli Dry Muscat 2000　15　−£5.00

Verdicchio Classico dei Castelli di Jesi 2000, Tesco　14.5　−£5.00

Viña Clara Frascati Classico Superiore 2000　14.5　−£5.00

## MEXICAN RED

Mexican Cabernet Sauvignon 1999, Tesco　13　−£5.00

## MEXICAN WHITE

Mexican Chardonnay 1999, Tesco　15　−£5.00

## NEW ZEALAND RED

Babich Cabernet Franc/Pinotage 1999　13.5　£5–7

Babich Winemaker's  15  £7–10
Reserve Syrah 1998

Montana Cabernet  14  £5–7
Sauvignon/Merlot 2000

Montana Pinotage 2000  14  £5–7

Montana Reserve  15  £7–10
Merlot 1999

## NEW ZEALAND WHITE

Azure Bay  13.5  –£5.00
Chardonnay/Semillon
2000

Jackson Estate  16.5  £7–10
Sauvignon Blanc 2000

Lawsons Dry Hills  17  £7–10
Sauvignon Blanc 2000

Marlborough  16  £5–7
Sauvignon Blanc 2000,
Tesco

Montana Reserve  17  £7–10
Chardonnay 1999

Montana Reserve  16.5  £7–10
Sauvignon Blanc,
Marlborough 2000

Montana Unoaked  16  £5–7
Chardonnay 2000

New Zealand Dry  13.5  –£5.00
White, Tesco

Nobilo White Cloud  15  –£5.00
1999

Villa Maria Private Bin  15  £5–7
Sauvignon Blanc 2000

## PORTUGUESE RED

Dão, Tesco 1999  14.5  –£5.00

Portuguese Red NV,  14.5  –£3.50
Tesco

## PORTUGUESE WHITE

Dry Vinho Verde,  13.5  –£5.00
Tesco

## ROMANIAN RED

Reka Valley Romanian  15.5  –£3.50
Pinot Noir, Tesco

## ROMANIAN WHITE

Shaw & Smith  16  £7–10
Unoaked Chardonnay
1999

## SOUTH AFRICAN RED

African Legend  13  –£5.00
Pinotage 1999

Apostles Falls Cabernet  15  £5–7
Sauvignon 1999

Apostles Falls Merlot  15.5  £5–7
1999

Beyers Truter Pinotage  16  –£5.00
NV, Tesco

Cape Cinsault NV,  13.5  –£5.00
Tesco

Cape Cinsault/  15  –£5.00
Pinotage NV, Tesco

Fairview Shiraz 1999  16.5  £5–7

Goats Do Roam `14` `−£5.00`
Fairview, Paarl 2000

Goiya Glaan 2000 `15` `−£5.00`

Kumala Cabernet `15` `−£5.00`
Sauvignon Shiraz 2000

Kumala Cinsault/ `14` `−£5.00`
Cabernet Sauvignon
2000

Kumala Reserve `15` `£7–10`
Cabernet Sauvignon
1999

Landskroon Premier `14` `£5–7`
Reserve Cabernet
Sauvignon 1998

Oak Village Vintage `15` `−£5.00`
Reserve 2000

Rylands Grove `16.5` `−£5.00`
Cabernet/Merlot 2000

Rylands Grove `13` `−£5.00`
Cinsaut/Tinta Barocca
2000

South African Red NV, `11` `−£3.50`
Tesco

South African Reserve `12` `−£5.00`
Cabernet NV, Tesco

Winds of Change `14.5` `−£5.00`
Cabernet Sauvignon/
Pinotage 2000

## SOUTH AFRICAN WHITE

African Legend `14` `−£5.00`
Colombard 2000

Apostles Falls `13` `£5–7`
Chardonnay 2000

Arniston Bay Rosé 2000 `13` `−£5.00`

Cape Chenin Blanc NV, `15` `−£3.50`
Tesco

Fairview Chardonnay `16` `£5–7`
2000

Fairview Goats do `16` `−£5.00`
Roam Rosé 2000

Fire Finch Sauvignon `15.5` `−£5.00`
Blanc 2000

Goiya Kgeisje 2001 `15` `−£5.00`

Oak Village Sauvignon `14` `−£5.00`
Blanc 2000

Rylands Grove Barrel `15.5` `−£5.00`
Fermented Chenin
Blanc 2000

Rylands Grove Dry `15` `−£5.00`
Muscat 2000

Rylands Grove `14.5` `−£5.00`
Sauvignon Blanc 2000

South African `15` `−£5.00`
Chardonnay 2000,
Tesco

South African `14` `−£5.00`
Chardonnay/
Colombard NV, Tesco

South African Medium `13` `−£3.50`
Sweet White NV,
Tesco

Third Millennium `14` `−£5.00`
Chenin Chardonnay
2001

Van Loveren Blanc de `14` `−£3.50`
Noir Red Muscadel
Rosé 2000

| | | |
|---|---|---|
| Winds of Change Chardonnay 2000 | 13 | −£5.00 |

## SPANISH RED

| | | |
|---|---|---|
| Campillo Reserva Rioja 1995 | 13 | £10–13 |
| Campo Viejo Crianza 1997 | 13 | £5–7 |
| Don Darias NV | 15.5 | −£5.00 |
| Huge Juicy Red NV, Tesco | 15.5 | −£5.00 |
| Las Postas Rioja 2000 | 14 | −£3.50 |
| Marqués de Chive Reserva 1995, Tesco | 14.5 | −£5.00 |
| Marqués de Chive Tempranillo NV, Tesco | 15 | −£3.50 |
| Marqués de Griñon Rioja 1999 | 16 | £5–7 |
| Orobio Tempranillo Rioja 1999 | 16 | −£5.00 |
| Señorio de los Llanos Valdepeñas Gran Reserva 1994 | 14 | −£5.00 |
| Señorio de los Llanos Valdepeñas Reserva 1996 | 14 | −£5.00 |
| Simply Garnacha 1999, Tesco | 14 | −£3.50 |
| Tempranillo 1999, Tesco | 15 | −£5.00 |
| Torres Coronas Tempranillo 1999 | 16 | £5–7 |

| | | |
|---|---|---|
| Torres Sangre de Toro 1999 | 14 | £5–7 |
| Viña Mara Gran Reserva Rioja 1994 | 13 | £7–10 |
| Viña Mara Rioja Reserva 1996, Tesco | 15.5 | £7–10 |
| Viña Mara Rioja, Tesco | 14 | −£5.00 |
| Viña Montana Monastrell/Merlot 1998 | 16 | −£5.00 |
| Zorro Tempranillo/ Monastrell 2000 | 14 | −£5.00 |

## SPANISH WHITE

| | | |
|---|---|---|
| Moscatel de Valencia, Tesco | 16 | −£3.50 |
| Torres Viña Sol 2000 | 15.5 | −£5.00 |

## USA RED

| | | |
|---|---|---|
| Fetzer Barrel Select Pinot Noir 1997 | 15 | £7–10 |
| Fetzer Barrel Select Zinfandel 1997 | 15.5 | £7–10 |
| Fetzer Syrah 1997 | 12 | £5–7 |
| Gallo Turning Leaf Zinfandel 1998 | 12 | £5–7 |
| West Coast California Cabernet/Shiraz 2000, Tesco | 12 | −£5.00 |
| West Coast Merlot Reserve 1999, Tesco | 14.5 | £5–7 |
| West Coast Ruby Cabernet/Merlot 1999, Tesco | 15 | −£5.00 |

West Coast Zinfandel Reserve 1999, Tesco — 13 £5–7

## USA WHITE

Fetzer Barrel Select Chardonnay 1997 — 15 £7–10

Fetzer Valley Oaks Rosé 2000 — 13.5 £5–7

Gallo Turning Leaf Chardonnay 1999 — 13 £5–7

West Coast California Chardonnay 1999, Tesco — 14.5 −£5.00

## FORTIFIED

10 Year Old Tawny Port, Tesco — 14 £10–13

Dow's LBV Port 1995 — 14.5 £7–10

Dow's Quinta do Bonfim Vintage Port 1986 — 13 £13–20

Superior Oloroso Seco, Tesco — 16 −£3.50

Superior Palo Cortado, Tesco — 16 −£5.00

Warre's Otima 10 Year Old Tawny Port NV 50cl — 13.5 £7–10

## SPARKLING

Australian Sparkling Wine NV, Tesco — 13 −£5.00

Banrock Station Sparkling Shiraz NV (Australia) — 16.5 £7–10

Blanc de Blancs Champagne NV, Tesco — 15 £13–20

Blanc de Noirs Champagne NV, Tesco — 17 £10–13

Cava NV, Tesco — 15 −£5.00

Champagne Perrier-Jouet Belle Epoque 1995 — 13 £20+

Cockatoo Ridge Black Sparkling Red NV — 16.5 £7–10

Demi Sec Cava NV, Tesco — 13 −£5.00

Demi Sec Champagne NV, Tesco — 13.5 £10–13

Hardys Stamp of Australia Chardonnay/ Pinot Noir Sparkling NV — 14 £5–7

Heidsieck Dry Monopole Blue Top Champagne NV — 13 £13–20

Hungarian Sparkling Chardonnay NV, Tesco — 13.5 −£5.00

Jacob's Creek Sparkling Chardonnay/Pinot Noir NV (Australia) — 15 £5–7

Laurent-Perrier Cuvée Rosé Brut NV — 11 £20+

Laurent-Perrier Vintage 1990 — 13 £20+

Les Etoiles Organic Sparkling Wine NV — 12 £5–7

329

Lindauer Brut NV `14` `£7–10`
(New Zealand)

Lindauer Brut Rosé NV `14` `£7–10`
(New Zealand)

Lindauer Special `16` `£7–10`
Reserve NV (New
Zealand)

Organic Champagne `13.5` `£13–20`
Jose Ardinat NV

Premier Cru `15` `£10–13`
Champagne NV, Tesco

Rosé Cava NV, Tesco `15.5` `–£5.00`

Rosé Champagne Brut `14` `£13–20`
NV, Tesco

South African Sparkling `12` `–£5.00`
Sauvignon 2000, Tesco

Taittinger Champagne `12` `£20+`
Brut NV

Vintage Cava 1997, `15` `£5–7`
Tesco

Vintage Champagne `14.5` `£13–20`
1995, Tesco

**SEE STOP-PRESS SECTION AT END OF BOOK FOR LAST-MINUTE
ADDITIONS OR UPDATES TO THIS RETAILER'S RANGE.**

# WAITROSE

No keeping journalists waiting here. The answer to the question I asked everyone else in this book – 'What in your opinion is the strength of your range of wines or the particular style of your way of retailing wine?' – came whizzing back by e-mail in no time. It was written by Julian Brind, the head of Waitrose's wine buying department. Mr Brind advised me:

'Waitrose aims to inspire and delight its customers with its offer of a wide choice of the best quality and best value for money wines at all price levels ranging from well-known classics to the latest wine styles to be found anywhere in the world.'

This is substantially true. It obscures the hard work this wine department puts in living up to those ambitions and conceals obvious weirdities (like the dreadful Canadian wines, acquired and put on shelf for no reason that I can divine except that it would, and indeed does, make Waitrose unique). No hint in Mr Brind's response is given, either, of Waitrose's breadth as well as depth, and I speak here of its food operations as much as its wine range.

Last year, for example, the company expanded its *Waitrose@work* intranet office shopping scheme, signing up a further 24 companies. This service permits employees of Waitrose to do their Waitrose food shopping on-line. It was a very savvy business move this one and demonstrates Waitrose's quiet, unobtrusive yet dogged approach to ideas, which the bigger retailers miss by thinking so large. Another good move was the store's strengthening of its position in the organic market with the addition of several organic wines to its range. It also expanded its Internet services where the retailer's full range is to be offered on-line when the Waitrose Deliver home-shopping service is launched. It was said that Waitrose hoped to generate 5% of its total sales from the Internet by 2005.

That represents a lot of money. Consider: Waitrose announced a turn-over in the financial year to end of January 2001 of £1.85 billion.

Other initiatives included making available its Waitrose Deliver scheme in 20% of the company's stores by May 2001. It was already running in four stores but was only available to John Lewis account card holders. The scheme was extended to all customers in four test stores in February 2001 and to as many as 25 to 30 stores by May.

Around this time it was reported in the magazine *Retail Week* that Waitrose was to be very daring and trying its hand at TV advertising. A £2.5 million campaign was due to go live in early May in the London and Southeast region though not having a TV I failed to see it. What did I miss? If the slogan – 'Quality food, honestly priced' – is anything to go by not much, though I have no doubt, knowing ad agencies and the way they handle retail clients, that the food shots were mouthwateringly art directed. 'The campaign,' said managing director David Felwick, 'is designed to underline the authority, care, quality and passion that set Waitrose apart.'

Waitrose echoes the ambitions of the National Health service under New Labour. Well, in a way Waitrose is more like a social service than a hard-nosed business.

It doesn't have employees; the staff are all 'partners'. For Waitrose is a division of the John Lewis Partnership and the high ideals, which motivated the forming of that business, permeate Waitrose, giving it an old-fashioned charm and meticulous sense of propriety which is not so richly evident in any other retailer I deal with.

Waitrose Limited
Customer Service Department
Southern Industrial Area
Bracknell
Berkshire
RG12 8YA

Tel 0800 188884 Customer Service Line
Tel 0800 188881 Waitrose Direct mail order
www.waitrose.com

## ARGENTINIAN RED

Balbi Malbec Reserva, 14 £5–7
Mendoza 1999

Familia Zuccardi Q 16 £7–10
Merlot 1998

Finca el Retiro Malbec, 16.5 £5–7
Mendoza 2000

Santa Julia Bonarda/ 17 −£5.00
Sangiovese 2000

Trivento Sangiovese, 14 −£5.00
Mendoza 2000

## ARGENTINIAN WHITE

| | | |
|---|---|---|
| Bodega Lurton Pinot Gris, Mendoza 2000 | 15 | −£5.00 |
| Catena Agrelo Vineyards Chardonnay 1999 | 15 | £7–10 |
| Chenin Blanc/ Torrontes, Mendoza 2000, Waitrose | 14 | −£5.00 |
| Santa Julia Viognier Reserve 2000 | 16 | £5–7 |
| Trivento Chardonnay 2000 | 14 | −£5.00 |

## AUSTRALIAN RED

| | | |
|---|---|---|
| Brown Brothers Nebbiolo 1996 | 13 | £7–10 |
| Brown Brothers Tarrango 2000 | 13 | £5–7 |
| Charleston Pinot Noir 1998 | 11 | £7–10 |
| Church Block Cabernet Shiraz Merlot, Wirra Wirra Vineyards 1998 | 15.5 | £7–10 |
| Clancy's Red 1998 | 15.5 | £7–10 |
| Deakin Estate Merlot, Victoria 2000 | 15.5 | £5–7 |
| Eileen Hardy Shiraz 1997 | 14 | £20+ |
| Fishermans Bend Cabernet Sauvignon 1999 | 13 | −£5.00 |
| Garry Crittenden Barbera 'i' 1999 | 14 | £7–10 |

| | | |
|---|---|---|
| Greg Norman Shiraz 1999 | 13 | £7–10 |
| Jindalee Shiraz 2000 | 13 | −£5.00 |
| Katnook Cabernet Sauvignon 1998 | 15.5 | £10–13 |
| Ninth Island Pinot Noir, Tasmania 2000 | 12 | £7–10 |
| Penfolds Clare Valley Cabernet Sauvignon/ Shiraz 1999 (organic) | 14 | £7–10 |
| Penfolds Grange South Australia Shiraz 1995 | 14 | £20+ |
| Peter Lehmann The Barossa Shiraz 1999 | 16 | £7–10 |
| Rosemount 'Hill of Gold' Cabernet Sauvignon, Mudgee 1998 | 17.5 | £7–10 |
| Settler's Station Tempranillo 2000 | 14 | £5–7 |
| Tatachilla Cabernet Sauvignon/Merlot, McLaren Vale 1998 | 14 | £7–10 |
| Tatachilla Foundation Shiraz 1998 | 13.5 | £13–20 |
| Tatachilla Growers Grenache Mataro 1999 | 14 | −£5.00 |
| Tea Tree Malbec/Ruby Cabernet 2000 | 13 | −£5.00 |
| The Angelus Cabernet Sauvignon, Wirra Wirra 1998 | 16 | £13–20 |
| Yaldara Grenache Reserve, Barossa 1999 | 3 | £5–7 |
| Yellowtail Merlot 2000 | 12 | −£5.00 |

## AUSTRALIAN WHITE

| | | |
|---|---|---|
| Brown Brothers Late Harvested Orange Muscat & Flora 1999 (half bottle) | 16.5 | £5–7 |
| Bushmans Crossing Semillon/Chardonnay 2000 | 13 | –£5.00 |
| Cape Mentelle Semillon/Sauvignon 2000 | 17 | £7–10 |
| Chapel Hill Verdelho 1999 | 16.5 | £7–10 |
| Charleston Pinot Gris 2000 | 15 | £5–7 |
| Château Tahbilk Marsanne 1998 | 17 | £5–7 |
| Currawong Creek Chardonnay 2000 | 13 | –£5.00 |
| De Bortoli Yarra Valley Chardonnay 1999 | 14 | £10–13 |
| Glenara Organic Dry Riesling 1996 | 16.5 | £7–10 |
| Greg Norman Estates Yarra Valley Chardonnay 2000 | 13 | £7–10 |
| Hardys Stamp of Australia Grenache Shiraz Rosé 1999 | 13.5 | –£5.00 |
| Houghton Classic Dry White 1998 | 15.5 | £5–7 |
| Jindalee Chardonnay 2000 | 16 | –£5.00 |
| Nepenthe Lenswood Riesling 2000 | 16 | £7–10 |
| Nepenthe Vineyards Lenswood Semillon 1998 | 16.5 | £7–10 |
| Nepenthe Vineyards Sauvignon Blanc 2000 | 16 | £7–10 |
| Oxford Landing Limited Release Viognier 2000 | 17 | £5–7 |
| Oxford Landing Sauvignon Blanc 2000 | 16 | –£5.00 |
| Penfolds Bin 95a Chardonnay | 13.5 | £13–20 |
| Penfolds Old Vine Semillon, Barossa 1998 | 16 | £5–7 |
| Penfolds Rawson's Retreat Bin 202 Riesling 2000 | 14 | –£5.00 |
| Rosemount Estate Show Reserve Chardonnay 1999 | 16 | £7–10 |
| Roxburgh Chardonnay 1997 | 13.5 | £20+ |
| Tea Tree Estate Chardonnay/ Sauvignon Blanc 2000 | 13.5 | –£5.00 |
| Voyager Estate Chardonnay 1999 | 13 | £10–13 |
| Wirra Wirra Oaked Chardonnay 1998 | 17 | £7–10 |
| Yalumba Eden Valley Viognier 1999 | 17.5 | £7–10 |

## AUSTRIAN WHITE

Münzenrieder 1997   `13`   `£5–7`
(half bottle)

## BULGARIAN RED

Blue Ridge American   `14.5`   `–£5.00`
Barrel Merlot 1999

Domaine Boyar   `15`   `–£3.50`
Merlot/Gamza, Iambol
1999

## CANADIAN WHITE

Mission Hill Private   `11`   `£5–7`
Reserve Pinot Blanc
1999

Peller Estates Founders   `10`   `–£5.00`
Series Vidal 1999

## CHILEAN RED

Caballo Loco No 4 NV   `16.5`   `£13–20`

Concha y Toro Merlot   `14`   `–£5.00`
2000

Cono Sur Cabernet   `17`   `–£5.00`
Sauvignon, Rapel
Valley 2000

Errázuriz Cabernet   `15.5`   `£5–7`
Sauvignon 1999

Errázuriz Merlot 1999   `16`   `£5–7`

Isla Negra Cabernet   `16`   `£5–7`
Sauvignon, Rapel 1999

Mont Gras Carmenère   `15.5`   `£5–7`
Reserva 2000

Valdivieso Barrel   `16.5`   `£5–7`
Selection Cabernet/
Merlot 1997

Valdivieso Cabernet   `17.5`   `£7–10`
Franc Reserve 1998

Valdivieso Pinot Noir   `16`   `£5–7`
Reserve 1997

## CHILEAN WHITE

35 South Sauvignon   `14.5`   `–£5.00`
Blanc 2000

Caliterra Chardonnay   `15.5`   `–£5.00`
2000

Canèpa Sémillon 2000   `14.5`   `–£5.00`

Gracia Temporal   `15`   `£7–10`
Reserva Superior
Chardonnay 1997

## ENGLISH WHITE

Chapel Down   `15`   `–£5.00`
Downland Oak NV

Chapel Down Flint Dry   `13.5`   `–£5.00`
1998

## FRENCH RED

Abbotts Ammonite   `14`   `–£5.00`
Côte du Roussillon
1999

Beauchatel Claret,   `12`   `–£5.00`
Bordeaux 1999

Bistro Rouge VdP d'Oc   `14.5`   `–£5.00`
2000

Boulder Creek Red VdP du Vaucluse 2000 `13` `−£3.50`

Cahors 1999 `15` `−£5.00`

Château Beauchêne Châteauneuf-du-Pape 1999 `13` `£7–10`

Château Calon-Segur Bordeaux 1997 `14` `£13–20`

Château Cazal Viel, Cuvée des Fées St-Chinian 1999 `16` `£5–7`

Château d'Aiguilhe Côtes de Castillon 1997 `15` `£7–10`

Château de Caraguilhes Corbières 1998 (organic) `13.5` `£5–7`

Château de Castres Graves 1998 `15` `£7–10`

Château de Targé, Saumur 1999 `15.5` `£5–7`

Château des Jacques, Moulin-à-Vent 1999 `13` `£7–10`

Château du Glana Cry Bourgeois St-Julien 1997 `14` `£10–13`

Château Haut d'Allard Côtes de Bourg 1998 `15` `£5–7`

Château Haut-Nouchet Pessac-Léognan 1998 (organic) `15.5` `£10–13`

Château l'Evangile, Pomerol 1997 `16` `£20+`

Château Leoville-Barton 2ème Cru Classé, St-Julien 1997 `15.5` `£20+`

Château Leoville Las-Cases 2ème Cru Classé, St-Julien 1994 `16` `£20+`

Château Pavie-Macquin St-Emilion Grand Cru Classé 1996 `12` `£20+`

Château Pech-Latt, Corbières 1999 `15` `£5–7`

Château Rauzan-Segla 2ème Cru Classé, Margaux 1997 `13.5` `£20+`

Château Tayac Cru Bourgeois, Margaux 1995 `13` `£13–20`

Châteauneuf-du-Pape Clos St-Michel 1999 `16` `£7–10`

Chinon Les Petites Roches 2000 `13.5` `£5–7`

Chorey-les-Beaune Domaine Maillard 1998 `14.5` `£7–10`

Côtes du Rhône 2000, Waitrose `13` `−£5.00`

Côtes du Ventoux 2000 `13.5` `−£5.00`

Crozes-Hermitage Domaine de Thalabert 1998 `13` `£10–13`

Domaine de Courtille Corbières 1999 `15` `£7–10`

Ermitage du Pic Saint-Loup Coteaux du Languedoc 1999 `16.5` `£5–7`

Fleurie Montreynaud 2000 `12` `£7–10`

Fortant Grenache VdP d'Oc 2000 `16` `−£5.00`

Gevrey-Chambertin Domaine Heresztyn 1999 — 13 — £13–20

Good Ordinary Claret Bordeaux NV, Waitrose — 13 — –£5.00

Hermitage Le Pied de la Côte, Paul Jaboulet Aine 1998 — 12 — £13–20

La Colombe Côtes du Rhône 1999 (organic) — 14 — –£5.00

La Cuvée Mythique VdP d'Oc 1998 — 16 — £5–7

La Nature Oaked Merlot VdP d'Oc 2000 — 14.5 — –£5.00

Les Quarterons St-Nicolas de Bourgueil 2000 — 15.5 — £5–7

Maury, Les Vignerons du Val d'Orbieu NV — 16 — –£5.00

Maury Vin Doux Naturel NV (half bottle) — 16 — –£5.00

Mercurery Rouge Premier Cru 'Les Puillets', Château Le Hardi 1998 — 13 — £10–13

Merlot/Cabernet Sauvignon VdP d'Aigues 2000 — 16 — –£3.50

Oaked Merlot VdP d'Oc 1999 — 14 — –£5.00

Parallele 45 Côtes du Rhône, Paul Jaboulet 1998 — 16 — £5–7

Pommard Premier Cru Les Boucherottes 1999 — 12.5 — £13–20

Prieurs de Foncaire, Buzet Grande Réserve 1998 — 15.5 — –£5.00

Saint Roche VdP du Gard 1999 (organic) — 13.5 — –£5.00

Savigny-les-Beaune Caves des Hautes-Côtes 1999 — 13 — £7–10

Seigneurs d'Aiguilhe Côtes de Castillon 1998 — 13 — £7–10

Special Reserve Claret Bordeaux 1999, Waitrose — 13 — –£5.00

Special Reserve Claret, Côtes de Castillon Limited Edition Millennium Magnum 1996 (magnum) — 16 — –£5.00

St-Emilion Yvon Mau NV — 13 — £5–7

Volnay Premier Cru Les Caillerets, Clos des 60 Ouvrées, Domaine de la Passe d'Or 1996 — 10 — £20+

Volnay Premier Cru Les Chevrets 1999 — 13.5 — £20+

Winter Hill Shiraz, VdP d'Oc 2000 — 14 — –£5.00

## FRENCH WHITE

Alsace Gewürztraminer 1999, Waitrose — 16 — £5–7

Alsace Pinot Blanc, Paul Blanck 1999 — 14 −£5.00

Anjou Blanc Ackerman 1999 — 13 −£3.50

Bordeaux Blanc Medium Dry, Yvon Mau NV — 12 −£3.50

Bordeaux Sémillon 2000 — 15.5 −£5.00

Boulder Creek White 2000 — 13 −£3.50

Chablis Gaec des Reugnis 1998 — 14.5 £7–10

Chablis Grand Cru Vaudésir 1998 — 11 £13–20

Chablis, William Fèvre 1999 — 13 £7–10

Chardonnay VdP du Jardin de la France 2000, Waitrose — 13.5 −£5.00

Chassagne-Montrachet Bouchard Père 1999 — 13 £20+

Château Carsin Cuvée Prestige 1998 — 15 £7–10

Château Climens Barsac 1996 (half bottle) — 13 £13–20

Château de Caraghuiles Organic Rosé 2000 — 14 £5–7

Château La Garenne Sauternes 1997 — 13.5 £13–20

Château Liot Sauternes 1997 (half bottle) — 14 £7–10

Château Petit Roubie, Picpoul du Pinet 2000 (organic) — 15.5 −£5.00

Château Rieussec, Sauternes 1996 (half bottle) — 15 £13–20

Château Saint-Jean-des-Graves, Graves 2000 — 10 £5–7

Château Thieuley, Bordeaux 2000 — 15 £5–7

Château Vignal Labrie, Monbazillac 1997 — 16 £7–10

Coteaux du Giennois Blanc 1999 — 14.5 £5–7

Fortant 'F' Limited Release Chardonnay, VdP d'Oc 1998 — 13 £7–10

Huet Clos de Bourg Demisec, Vouvray 1999 — 17.5 £7–10

La Baume Viognier VdP d'Oc 2000 — 14.5 −£5.00

La Cité Chardonnay, VdP d'Oc 2000 — 13 −£5.00

Mâcon-Villages Chardonnay, Cave de Lugny 2000 — 14 −£5.00

Mercurey Blanc Château le Hardi 1999 — 12 £10–13

Montagny Premier Cru Bouchard Père 1998 — 10 £7–10

Muscadet sur Lie 'Fief Guerin' 1999 — 14 −£5.00

Muscat Sec Domaine de Provenquiere, VdP d'Oc 2000 — 16 −£5.00

| | | |
|---|---|---|
| Muscat de Beaumes-de-Venise NV (half bottle) | 15.5 | −£5.00 |
| Pinot Gris Grand Cru Rangen de Thann Clos St Urbain, Domaine Zind Humbrecht 1996 | 18.5 | £20+ |
| Pouilly-Fuissé Château Vitallis 2000 | 11 | £10–13 |
| Pouilly-Fumé Masson Blondelet 1999 | 14.5 | £7–10 |
| Puligny-Montrachet Premier Cru Champs Gains 1997 | 13 | £20+ |
| Quincy La Boissière 1999 | 13 | £5–7 |
| Rosé d'Anjou 2000, Waitrose | 11 | −£5.00 |
| Saumur Blanc 'Les Andides' Saint Cyr-en-Bourg 1999 | 14 | −£5.00 |
| Tokay Pinot Gris Heimbourg, Domaine Zind Humbrecht 1998 | 17 | £20+ |
| Top 40 Chardonnay VdP d'Oc 1999 | 17 | £5–7 |
| Touraine Sauvignon Blanc 2000, Waitrose | 12 | −£5.00 |
| Vin Blanc Sec VdT Francais NV, Waitrose | 12 | −£3.50 |
| Winter Hill Syrah Rosé, VdP d'Oc 2000 | 13 | −£5.00 |
| Winter Hill VdP d'Oc 1999 | 15 | −£3.50 |

## GERMAN RED

| | | |
|---|---|---|
| Dornfelder Pfalz Lergenmüller 1999 | 16 | £5–7 |

## GERMAN WHITE

| | | |
|---|---|---|
| Bernkasteler Badstube Spätlese Dr Thanisch 1997 | 14 | £7–10 |
| Devil's Rock Masterpiece, St Ursula 1999 | 13 | −£5.00 |
| Dr Loosen Wehlener Sonnenuhr Riesling Spätlese 1995 | 15 | £10–13 |
| Dr Wagner Ockfener Bockstein Riesling 2000 | 15 | £5–7 |
| Erdener Treppchen Riesling Auslese 1990 | 15.5 | £7–10 |
| Erdener Treppchen Riesling Spätlese 1997 | 16.5 | £5–7 |
| Hedgerow Rheinhessen 2000 | 13 | −£5.00 |
| Kendermann Vineyard Selection Dry Riesling 1998 | 13.5 | −£5.00 |
| Riesling Bassermann Jordan, Pfalz 2000 | 13 | £5–7 |
| Scharzhofberger Riesling Auslese, Egon Müller 1999 | 10 | £20+ |
| Scharzhofberger Riesling Kabinett, Egon Müller 1999 | 13 | £13–20 |

Villa Wolf Pinot Gris 1999 — 14 — £5–7

Wehlener Sonnenuhr Riesling Auslese 1990 — 17 — £13–20

Wehlener Sonnenuhr Riesling Spätlese, JJ Prum 1994 — 15 — £13–20

## GREEK RED

Pathos Xinomavrou, Tsantali 1999 — 15 — –£5.00

## HUNGARIAN WHITE

Deer Leap Gewürztraminer, Zemplen 2000 — 16.5 — –£5.00

Deer Leap Sauvignon Blanc 2000 — 16 — –£5.00

Matra Springs 2000 — 14 — –£3.50

Nagyrede Cabernet Sauvignon Rosé 2000 — 14 — –£3.50

Riverview Chardonnay/Pinot Grigio 2000 — 15 — –£5.00

## ITALIAN RED

Amarone della Valpolicella Classico Riserva, Zenato 1993 — 15 — £20+

Amativo Negroamaro Primitivo 1999 — 15.5 — £5–7

Araldica Albera Barbera d'Asti Superior, Piemonte 1999 — 14 — –£5.00

Arcano Chianti Colli Senesi, Cecchi 1999 (organic) — 15.5 — £5–7

Barolo Terre da Vino 1997 — 13.5 — £10–13

Bonarda Sentito, Oltrepo Pavese 1999 — 15.5 — –£5.00

Buonasera, Argiolas NV (Sardegna) — 15 — –£5.00

Capitel dei Nicola Valpolicella Classico Superiore 1997 — 15.5 — £5–7

Castello di Fonterutoli Chianti Classico Riserva 1997 — 14 — £20+

Chianti 1999, Waitrose — 13.5 — –£5.00

Chianti Classico Fattoria di Capraia, Rocca di Castagnoli 1998 — 13.5 — £7–10

Emporio Barrel Aged Syrah 1998 (Sicilia) — 15 — £5–7

Il Padrino Sangiovese 2000 (Sicilia) — 15.5 — –£5.00

La Rena Salice Salento Leone de Castris 1998 — 16 — £5–7

Mezzomondo Negroamaro 1999 — 16 — –£5.00

Natural State Montepulciano d'Abruzzo 1999 (organic) — 16.5 — –£5.00

Nero d'Avola Syrah, Firriato 2000 (Sicilia) — 14.5 — –£5.00

Pendulum Zinfandel 1999 — 15.5 −£5.00

Planeta Cabernet Sauvignon 1998 — 17 £13–20

Sangiovese Marche, Waitrose — 13 −£3.50

Tenute Marchese Antinori Chianti Classico Riserva 1997 — 16 £10–13

Terra Viva Merlot del Veneto 2000 (organic) — 14 −£5.00

Tignanello 1997 — 13 £20+

Valpolicella 2000, Waitrose — 13 −£3.50

Vigna Alta Merlot/ Cabernet Venosa, Basilicata 2000 — 16.5 −£5.00

## ITALIAN WHITE

Buongiorno Argiolas Sardegna NV — 16 −£5.00

Inycon Chardonnay 2000 (Sicily) — 16 −£5.00

Lugana Villa Flora 2000 — 16 £5–7

Mezzo Mondo Chardonnay 2000 — 15 −£5.00

Orvieto Classico Cardeto 2000 — 15.5 −£5.00

Pinot Grigio Alto Adige San Michele-Appiano 2000 — 15.5 £5–7

Planeta Chardonnay 1999 — 18 £13–20

Sauvignon Friuli, San Simone 2000 — 15.5 −£5.00

Soave Classico Vigneto Colombara 2000 — 16.5 −£5.00

Verdicchio dei Castelli Jesi, Moncaro 2000 — 14 −£5.00

Zagara Catarratto Chardonnay Firriato 2000 (Sicily) — 16.5 −£5.00

## MEXICAN RED

L A Cetto Petite Sirah 1998 — 16 −£5.00

## NEW ZEALAND RED

Church Road Cabernet Sauvignon/Merlot 1998 — 15.5 £7–10

Montana Cabernet Merlot 1999 — 15 £5–7

Montana Reserve Pinot Noir 1999 — 13.5 £7–10

Unison Selection, Hawkes Bay 1998 — 12 £13–20

Wither Hills Pinot Noir 1999 — 13 £10–13

## NEW ZEALAND WHITE

Azure Bay Chardonnay/Semillon 2000 — 13.5 −£5.00

Craggy Range Old Renwick Vineyard Sauvignon Blanc 2000 — 14.5 £7–10

Craggy Range Winery Chardonnay, Hawkes Bay 1999 — 16 — £10–13

Jackson Estate Sauvignon Blanc 2000 — 16.5 — £7–10

Montana Reserve Barrique Fermented Chardonnay 1999 — 16.5 — £7–10

Montana Riesling 2000 — 14 — −£5.00

Oyster Bay Marlborough Chardonnay 2000 — 15.5 — £5–7

Oyster Bay Sauvignon Blanc 2000 — 16 — £5–7

Stoneleigh Vineyard Sauvignon Blanc 2000 — 15 — £5–7

Tiki Ridge Dry White 2000 — 13 — −£5.00

Villa Maria Private Bin Riesling 2000 — 16 — £5–7

Wither Hills Sauvignon Blanc 2000 — 15 — £7–10

## PORTUGUESE RED

Altano 1999 — 14 — £5–7

Terra de Lobos, Quinta do Casal Branco 2000 — 14 — −£5.00

Trincadeira Joao Portugal Ramos 1999 — 14 — £7–10

Vila Santa Alentejano 1999 — 15 — £7–10

Vinho do Monte, Alentejo 1999 — 15 — −£5.00

## PORTUGUESE WHITE

Terras do Rio Quinta de Abrigada 1998 — 15 — −£3.50

## ROMANIAN RED

Willow Ridge Pinot Noir/Merlot 1999 — 15.5 — −£5.00

## ROMANIAN WHITE

Willow Ridge Sauvignon Blanc/ Feteasca 2000 — 15 — −£3.50

## SOUTH AFRICAN RED

Andrew's Hope Spice Route Pinotage 2000 — 15.5 — £5–7

Clos Malverne Basket Pressed Pinotage, Stellenbosch 1999 — 16 — £5–7

Culemborg Cape Red 2000 — 12 — −£5.00

Goats Do Roam Fairview, Paarl 2000 — 14 — −£5.00

Graham Beck The Ridge Shiraz 1999 — 15 — £7–10

Natural State Shiraz 1999 (organic) — 14.5 — £5–7

Spice Route Cabernet Sauvignon/Merlot 1998 — 16.5 — £7–10

Spice Route Flagship Merlot 1998 — 17 — £13–20

Villiera Merlot, Paarl 1998 — 14.5 — £7–10

## SOUTH AFRICAN WHITE

Colombard Chardonnay 2000, Waitrose — 14.5 −£5.00

Culemborg Cape White 2000 — 13 −£3.50

Culemborg Unwooded Chardonnay, Western Cape 2000 — 12.5 −£5.00

Diamond Hills Chenin Blanc/Chardonnay 2000 — 12 −£5.00

Excelsior Estate Sauvignon Blanc 2000 — 15 −£5.00

Fairview Viognier, Paarl 2000 — 16.5 £7–10

Jordan Chardonnay 2000 — 15.5 £7–10

Kumala Colombard/Chardonnay 2000 — 14 −£5.00

Spice Route Abbotsdale Colombard/Chenin Blanc 1999 — 15 £7–10

Springfield Sauvignon Blanc Special Cuvée 2000 — 14.5 £5–7

Steenberg Sauvignon Blanc 2000 — 13.5 £7–10

Steenberg Semillon 1999 — 16 £7–10

Warwick Estate Chardonnay, Stellenbosch 2000 — 16 £5–7

## SPANISH RED

Chivite Coleccion 125 Reserva 1996 — 16 £13–20

Cosme Palacio Rioja 1998 — 15 £5–7

Espiral Oaked Tempranillo 1998 — 15 £5–7

Espiral Tempranillo/Cabernet Sauvignon 1998 — 16 −£5.00

Marqués de Griñon Dominio de Valdepusa Syrah 1998 — 17 £10–13

Palacio de Otazu Reserva, Navarra 1996 — 16 £7–10

Torneo Reserva, Valdepeñas 1996 — 14 −£5.00

Torres Gran Sangre de Toro Reserva 1996 — 16 £5–7

Totally Tinto Tempranillo NV — 14 −£5.00

Totally Two Thousand Tempranillo NV (magnum) — 15.5 −£3.50

Viña Fuerte Garnacha, Calatayud 2000 — 15.5 −£5.00

Viña Herminia Graciano Reserva Rioja 1995 — 14 £7–10

Viña Herminia Rioja Crianza 1996 — 14 £5–7

Viña Lanciano Reserva 1995 — 13 £13–20

## SPANISH WHITE

Albarino Pazo de Seoane, Rias Baixas 2000 — 12 — £7–10

Cune Monopole Rioja Blanco 1998 — 14 — £5–7

Lustau Moscatel de Chipiona NV — 16 — −£5.00

Palacio de Bornos Rueda 2000 — 15 — −£5.00

Torres Viña Sol 2000 — 15.5 — −£5.00

## URUGUAYAN RED

Pisano Family Reserve Tannat 1999 — 13 — £7–10

## USA RED

Bonterra Vineyards Merlot 1997 (organic) — 16.5 — £7–10

Fetzer Valley Oaks Cabernet Sauvignon 1998 — 14.5 — £5–7

Hedges Three Vineyards Columbia Valley 1998 — 13 — £13–20

Ironstone Vineyards Zinfandel 1998 — 10 — £5–7

Yorkville Cellars Cabernet Franc 1997 (organic) — 14 — £7–10

Yorkville Petit Verdot 1997 — 16 — £7–10

## USA WHITE

Bonterra Muscat 1999 (half bottle) (organic) — 14 — £5–7

Fetzer Echo Ridge Viognier 2000 — 15.5 — £5–7

Mandolin Californian Chardonnay 1999 — 11 — £5–7

## FORTIFIED

10 Year Old Tawny Port, Waitrose — 14 — £10–13

Apostoles Palo Cortado Muy Viejo (half bottle) — 18.5 — £10–13

Dow's LBV Port 1995 — 14.5 — £7–10

Fino Sherry, Waitrose — 15.5 — −£5.00

Graham's LBV Port 1994 — 13.5 — £10–13

Matusalem Oloroso Dulce Muy Viejo (half bottle) — 16.5 — £10–13

Quinta da Noval 10 Year Old Tawny Port NV — 15 — £13–20

Solera Jerezana Dry Amontillado, Waitrose — 16 — £5–7

Solera Jerezana Old Oloroso, Waitrose — 16.5 — £5–7

Vintage Warre Quinta da Cavadinha Port 1987 — 17.5 — £13–20

Warre's Optima 10 Year Old Tawny Port NV 50cl — 13.5 — £7–10

Warre's Traditional LBV Port 1990 — 16.5 £13–20

Warre's Warrior Special Reserve Port NV — 13 £7–10

## SPARKLING

Alexandre Bonnet Brut Rosé NV (France) — 14 £13–20

Banrock Station Sparkling Shiraz NV (Australia) — 16.5 £7–10

Brut Vintage 1996, Waitrose — 14 £13–20

Cava Brut NV, Waitrose (Spain) — 15 −£5.00

Champagne Blanc de Blancs NV, Waitrose — 14 £13–20

Champagne Blanc de Noirs NV, Waitrose — 15 £10–13

Champagne Blanc de Noirs NV, Waitrose — 16 £10–13

Champagne Bredon Brut NV — 12 £7–10

Champagne Brut NV, Waitrose — 14 £13–20

Champagne Fleury Brut 1993 — 13 £20+

Champagne Fleury Brut NV — 13 £13–20

Champagne Lanson Noble Cuvée 1988 — 12 £20+

Champagne Moët et Chandon Brut Imperial Vintage 1992 — 13.5 £20+

Chandon Argentina Brut Fresco NV — 13.5 £7–10

Chandon Australia Brut NV — 13.5 £7–10

Chapel Hill Pinot Noir/ Chardonnay NV — 15 −£5.00

Chapel Hill Sparkling Chardonnay/Pinot Noir NV (Hungary) — 12 −£5.00

Charles Heidsieck Champagne Blanc de Blancs 1982 — 20 £20+

Charles Heidsieck Reserve Mise en Cave 1996 (France) — 16 £20+

Clairette de Die Jadissane NV (organic) — 11 £5–7

Crémant de Bourgogne Rosé NV (France) — 14 £7–10

Cuvée Royale Blanquette de Limoux NV — 13.5 £5–7

Deutz Marlborough Cuvée NV — 13 £10–13

Duc de Marre Spécial Cuvée Champagne Brut Non Vintage — 13.5 £13–20

Jacob's Creek Sparkling Chardonnay/Pinot Noir NV (Australia) — 15 £5–7

Lanson Vintage Gold Label 1994 — 13 £20+

## WAITROSE

Le Mesnil Blanc de Blancs Grand Cru Champagne Brut Non Vintage — `13` `£13–20`

Lindauer Brut NV (New Zealand) — `14` `£7–10`

Moët et Chandon L-D Champagne 1992 — `14` `£20+`

Saumur Brut NV, Waitrose — `16` `£5–7`

Seaview Brut NV (Australia) — `14` `£5–7`

Seaview Brut Rosé NV (Australia) — `13.5` `£5–7`

Sparkling Burgundy NV — `12` `£7–10`

Taittinger Comtes de Champagne Blanc de Blancs 1990 — `13` `£20+`

**SEE STOP-PRESS SECTION AT END OF BOOK FOR LAST-MINUTE ADDITIONS OR UPDATES TO THIS RETAILER'S RANGE.**

# PART 5

# STOP PRESS

## MARKS & SPENCER

**Torre Scalza**  17.0  £6.99
**Montepulciano
d'Abruzzo 2000, Italian
Red**
Superb vibrancy and tonal
complexity here with baked
berries, spicy tannins, chocolate
and an overall textured charm,
which is both benchmark
Montepulciano yet also
something more modern and
vivid.

**Aramonte Catarratto**  16.5  £4.99
**Barrique 2000 (Sicily),
Italian White**
Delicious plump fruits (hard and
soft and nutty) with a superb
enveloping oiliness that gives the
whole structure class and real
style. A purposeful, poised,
polished white wine of huge
charm.

**Rustica Primitivo**  16.0  £4.49
**Salento 2000, Italian
Red**
Amazing level of svelte elegance
from this beautifully textured
wine. Has richness yet subtlety,
power yet delicacy, finesse yet
loads of flavour.

**Clos Roque D'Aspes**  17.0  £6.50
**Faugères 1998, French
Red**
Chocolate, coffee, berries, herbs,
tannins. This glittering recipe
coalesces into something truly
gripping and deep. A terrific red.

**Sierra Los Andes**  16.0  £4.99
**Chardonnay 1999,
Chilean White**
Baked melon richness is not OTT
but fresh and fine and the finish is
very elegant.

**Villa di Rovo Insolia**  16.0  £4.99
**2000, Italian White**
Evolves slowly but deliberately
from fresh citrus-tinged richness
to a nutty melonosity and even a
touch of raspberry. A delightful
wine of charm and individuality.

**Dolce Vita Dolcetta**  16.5  £4.99
**d'Alba 2000, Italian Red**
Very posh bottle with a brilliant
label, this is obviously a proud
production – even before we get
to the fruit. And this is indeed a
marvel, offering plums and
cherries in controlled profusion
plus delightful tannins. A
remarkably couth performer for a
strikingly modest sum.

**Vibra Monastrell/** 16.0 £3.99
**Garnacha 2000, Spanish**
**Red**
Encroaches delightfully slowly on
the taste buds offering spicy
plums, then cherries and
raspberries – plus fine tannins.

**Amoskuil Sauvignon** 16.0 £5.99
**Blanc 2001, South**
**African White**
Very classic Sauvignon with dry
gooseberry, nuts and a touch of
pear and pineapple. A very
elegant, textured, well-structured
wine.

**Campo Fiorito Nero** 16.0 £8.99
**d'Avola 2000, Italian**
**Red**
Places the Nero d'Avola grape in
the same league as Shiraz, if not
Merlot. The wine here is boldly
complexioned yet not ruddy,
strongly jawed yet not
pugnacious, and feisty yet not
flashy. A finely knitted set of
tannins give the whole structure
decisive charm.

**Château de L'Ille 1998,** 16.5 £6.99
**French Red**
Brilliant throaty richness here,
where herby berries meld with
tannins of depth and decisiveness.

**Las Mulas Verdejo** 16.0 £4.99
**Rueda 2000, Spanish**
**White**
Very elegant, warm, soft-yet-fresh
fruited white wine with real
individuality and charm – and it
makes a refreshing change from
Chardonnay.

**Padronale Syrah Sicilia** 16.5 £4.99.
**2000, Italian Red**
Superbly spicy and sunny fruit
with hints of coffee and nuts to its
wide-ranging berries. Lovely
tannins enrich the bass notes of
the wine, which gives character
and depth.

**Flor de Maig Tarragona** 16.0 £6.49
**1999, Spanish Red**
Interesting, characterful blend of
local grapes plus 15 per cent
Cabernet. Has texture, tension,
tautness and terrific pace. Finely
arranged and well played by its
trio of winemakers (which
includes a Wagner).

**Château Plo du Roy Le** 17.5 £7.50
**Balcon du Diable 1998,**
**French Red**
Massive, mouth-filling boulders of
bold berries marching in unison
over the taste buds, providing a
really vivid performance. There
are craggy tannins too, and so the
balance is high class, the texture
tremendous, and the finish
lingering and richly memorable.

**Rasteau Rhône Valley** 16.0 £7.99
**2000, French Red**
Delicious coffee-edged, cassis-
minded richness with raspberry-
tinged tannins. A good energetic
mouthful of weight and wit.

**Château Bel Air** 16.5 £23.00
**Lagrave 1990, French**
**Red**

At its peak of durability with its tannins holding up well against the toffee-edged berries and herbs. A finely mature claret, at a high price but has an elegance and well-tailored cut of great class. 25 stores only.

**Castillo de Madax** 16.0 £5.99
**Cabernet Sauvignon/
Monastrell 2000,
Spanish Red**
Rich, invigorating berries with very lingering, cocoa-edged tannins. A well-textured, very well-priced wine of depth and deliciousness.

**Château Franc-Maillet,** 17.5 £17.99
**Pomerol 1999, French
Red**
Now here is evidence that claret, at admittedly a high price, can be justifiably brilliant, complex, vibrant, fruity and ineffably excitingly tannic. Has great smoothness in the face of the rippling tannins (I nearly wrote ripping talons).

**Vacqueyras, Cuvée des** 17.5 £8.99
**Vieilles Vignes 1998,
French Red**
Deeply serious, richly romantic, highly developed berries of great class and clout. Terrific tannins put in a ripe supporting role and the overall texture is brilliant. This is a complex, complete, very accomplished performer.

**Amoskuil Red 1999,** 16 £8.99
**South African Red**
Very juicy but judiciously so. Has an enticing perfume and well-realised rich berries and tannins to back it up.

**Weandre Stream** 16.5 £4.99
**Chardonnay 2000,
Australian White**
Fantastic complexity and boldness for a fiver. Has lovely creaminess, and vegetal richness, freshness, texture, flavour and real class as it finishes.

**Sierra Los Andes** 16 £5.50
**Gewürztraminer 2001,
Chilean White**
Gewürz in its subtle, aperitif-style manifestation. Has lovely dry, would-be-rich fruit that recalls spicy melon and pineapple rather than upfront lychee. A very elegant, subtly spicy wine of great charm.

**Casa Leona Cabernet** 17 £6.50
**Sauvignon Reserve
2000, Chilean Red**
Superb layers of berries, plums, cherries and tannins that sweep all before them as they proceed, aromatically, from nose to throat. The texture is high class, the finish exciting.

**Freedom Ridge** 16 £5.99
**Viognier 2000, USA
White**
Superb texture – polished and warm – offering nuts, apricots and gooseberry all wrapped in a charming dry coat of good acidity. A most elegant performer.

**Gordon Brothers**  `16`  `£14.00`
**Merlot 1998, USA Red**
Very superior, richly-textured
fruit of high-class and
consummate clout. A most stylish
Merlot of considerable verve,
vibrancy and great wit.

**15 Year Old Solera**  `16`  `£7.99`
**Especial Oloroso (Half
Bottle), Spanish
Fortified**
Develops by degrees from tarry
berries to molasses as it proceeds
to the throat. A wonderful wine
for cake, biscuits, or even ice-
cream.

**12 Year Old Solera**  `17`  `£6.99`
**Especial Amontillado
(Half Bottle), Spanish
Fortified**
A wonderfully oily, intense, dry,
rich, tarry sherry of complexity
and beautifully-textured elegance.
It keeps its texture all the way and
doesn't lose its grip, go too saline
or austere, or become deflected
from its rich, smooth course.

## SAFEWAY

**Villa Maria Private Bin**  `17.0`  `£7.99`
**Sauvignon Blanc 2001,
New Zealand White**
I see no reason not to clone this
wine – one of the most complete
Sauvignons I've tasted from the
2001 vintage.

**Ravenswood Lane**  `16.5`  `£13.99`
**'Beginning'
Chardonnay 1999,
Australian White**
Expensive, hugely elegant, superb
wood/fruit integration and the
creamy vegetality is outstandingly
controlled. A finely-textured, very
fine wine.

**Errázuriz Chardonnay,**  `16.5`  `£5.99`
**La Escultura Estate
Casablanca Valley 2000,
Chilean White**
The standard bearer for dry, full-
of-finesse-yet-rich Chardonnays
worldwide.

**Trulli Chardonnay del**  `16.0`  `£4.49`
**Salento 2000, Italian
White**
Deliciously elegant and easy-
going. Homophonically a 100 per
cent Chardonnay? And so in fact.
Lovely ripe melons controlled by
citrus acids. Regulation recipe but
exemplary for the money.

**Montana Sauvignon**  `16.0`  `£5.99`
**Blanc 2001, New
Zealand White**
Can subtlety have great impact?
Well it does here. Brilliantly
delicate yet emphatically
Sauvignon.

**Tinta da Anfora 1999,**  `16.5`  `£5.99`
**Portuguese Red**
A marriage of Trincadeira Preta,
Periquita Aragonez and Moreta
grapes, that startles with its svelte
texture and deep berries. A very

full, deep wine of class and precision.

**Black River Merlot/** `16.0` `£4.99`
**Pinot Noir 2000,**
**Argentinian Red**
Lovely bush fruit with highly active, chewy tannins. A very deep wine of great flavour.

**Simon Gilbert** `17.5` `£5.99`
**Chardonnay 1999,**
**Australian White**
Has an interesting aroma of bread in its doughy stage and this leads to really excitingly-textured fruit of individuality and most committed subtle richness. This is an outstanding, modern classic Chardonnay. Has complex fruit of huge class. One of the most original Aussie Chardonnays in years.

**Oyster Bay Sauvignon** `16.5` `£6.99`
**Blanc 2001, New**
**Zealand White**
Has beautiful pebbly and minerally acids allied to elongated gooseberry and lemon fruit.

**Moscatel de Valencia** `16.5` `£3.99`
**2000, Safeway, Italian**
**White**
Classic sweet wine with touches of Muscat spice and mild marmalade. Brilliantly effective with ice-cream and other rampant desserts.

**L'Enclos des Cigales** `16.5` `3.99`
**Syrah VdP d'Oc 2000,**
**French Red**
Magnificent value for money and

hugely competitive with Aussie Shirazes at three times the price. Has bustling fruit, great deep tannins and oomph on the finish.

**Domaine des Lauriers,** `16.5` `5.99`
**Faugères 1998, French**
**Red**
No nods to the New World here, and what a triumph of plummy richness, spice, herbs and lovely polished, textured tightness it is. A delightfully daring wine. Selected stores.

**Danie de Wet** `16.5` `£3.99`
**Chardonnay Sur Lie**
**2001, South African**
**White**
One of the most elegant Chardonnays in the world – for the money. It's simply gob-smacking.

**Domaine La Tour du** `16.0` `£4.99`
**Maréchal Chardonnay,**
**VdP de l'Hérault 2000**
**(Organic), French**
**White**
An intensely dry specimen of Chardonnay but very crisp. Great food wine. Selected stores.

**Concha y Toro** `16.0` `£4.99`
**Castillero de Diablo**
**Cabernet Sauvignon**
**2000, Chilean Red**
With fish risotto this turned in a triumphant performance: gently spicy, rich, well-textured and classy.

**St Nikolaus Wehlener**  `16.0`  `£5.99`
**Sonnenuhr Riesling**
**Spätlese 1997, German**
**White**
Great drinking now with its
honeyed gooseberry and
raspberry fruit, insistent acids and
stealthy, wealthy finish.

**KJ Collage Semillon/**  `16.0`  `£6.99`
**Chardonnay 1999, USA**
**White**
Another fine blend of grapes. Is
Safeway making a speciality of
this? If so, I applaud them.

**Michel Torino**  `16.0`  `£5.99`
**Coleccion Merlot 2000,**
**Argentinian Red**
Vibrates with raspberries,
blackberries, plums and a very
vague spiciness. Superb texture
and finish.

**Starve Dog Lane**  `16.0`  `£8.99`
**Sauvignon Blanc 2001,**
**Australian White**
Very pure, unfussy fruit of great
elegance and delicacy. Has a
suppressed richness (melon and
lemons) and a very fine, crisp
finish.

**Errázuriz Syrah 2000,**  `16.5`  `£7.99`
**Chilean Red**
A delightfully serious yet
provocative Syrah (with one per
cent Cabernet) which has
individuality, poise, texture,
superb tannins and remarkably
couth richness.

**Pencil Pine Cabernet/**  `16.0`  `£6.99`
**Merlot 2000, Australian**
**Red**
Here the jamminess is in good
balance with the tannins, and the
resultant texture is plummy, ripe
and classy.

**Chilean Sauvignon/**  `16.0`  `£3.69`
**Chardonnay 2001,**
**Chilean White**
A most original blend of
gooseberry, melon, raspberry and
good firm acids.

**Versus 2001 (1 litre),**  `16.0`  `£5.49`
**South African White**
Brilliant marriage of soft Chenin
and crisp, suave Sauvignon.

**Castillo de Molina**  `17.0`  `£5.99`
**Cabernet Sauvignon**
**2000, Chilean Red**
Frighteningly good. Has very rich
berries, complex and complete,
superb tannins and tantalisingly
tasty acids, which combine with
power and pace. A lovely wine of
consummate class and
drinkability.

**Booarra Chardonnay/**  `16.0`  `£6.99`
**Viognier 2001,**
**Australian White**
Terrific marriage of hope over
expectation (I speak of the two
grape varieties in the blend).
Melons and apricots perfectly
suited and deliriously happy.

**Accademia de Sole**  `16.5`  `£4.99`
**Vioca Familia Plaia**
**2000, Italian White**
Gorgeous dry nuttiness, very

subtle and that hint of oily richness as it finishes – all terrific.

**Dow's 20 Year Old Tawny Special Reserve Port, Portuguese Fortified**   `17.0`   `£23.59`
Combines piles of sweet flavour: honey, crème caramel, custard and strawberries. To be drunk by a roaring fire for the sheer hell of its richness.

**Douglas Green Sauvignon 2001, South African White**   `16.0`   `£4.49`
Amazing price for such classy fruit: dry, crisp, stylish.

**Ca Bianca Gavi 2000, Italian White**   `16.0`   `£5.99`
The essence of crisp nuttiness. Delicious dry fruit.

**Pencil Pine Chardonnay 2000, Australian White**   `17.0`   `£6.99`
Wonderfully oily richness here. Subdued vegetality, lovely firm acids and complex layers of lemon on the finish. An outstanding Chardonnay of relaxed classiness.

**Errázuriz Cabernet Sauvignon 2000, Chilean Red**   `16.5`   `£6.49`
Dark, charcoal richness; soft tannins; lovely berries in layered profusion and a soft finish of pace and power.

**Fetzer Zinfandel/Shiraz 2000, USA Red**   `16.5`   `£5.99`
Superbly cheeky blend of chutzpah and cheerful cherries, plums, raspberries, ripe tannins, spice and a very lingering soft finish. A very energetic wine of great food compatibility.

## SOMERFIELD

**Argentine Chardonnay Penaflor NV, Somerfield, Argentinian White**   `16.0`   `£4.49`
Elegant, ripe, very ready.

**Trulli Chardonnay del Salento 2000, Italian White**   `16.0`   `£4.79`
Deliciously elegant and easy-going. Homophonically a 100 per cent Chardonnay? And so in fact. Lovely ripe melons controlled by citrus acids. Regulation recipe but exemplary for the money.

**Chilean Sauvignon Blanc Jose Canepa 2001, Somerfield, Chilean White**   `16.0`   `£3.99`
On the richer side but balanced by melon fruit and ripe lemon acids.

**Normans Old Vine Shiraz 1999, Australian Red**   `16.0`   `£5.99`
A brilliant spicy food wine with its baked berry fruit, subtle tannins (which do linger on the finish and don't quit early as many Aussie tannins do). Overall it is deep and engaging.

**Terrarum Reserve** `16.0` `£5.99`
**Morrande Merlot 2000,**
**Chilean Red**
Has an acquired grassiness that
melts to provide vivid, clear and
ripe fresh fruit.

**Penfolds 'The Valleys'** `16.5` `£5.99`
**Chardonnay 1998,**
**Australian White**
Big and full, but has a very
graceful finishing thrust of
creamy nuttiness (from the
wood).

**Australian Cabernet** `16.0` `£4.99`
**Sauvignon NV,**
**Somerfield, Australian**
**Red**
Delightfully uncluttered fruit of
blackberries and plums, brilliantly
soft and textured without being
gooey, and very firm tannins.

## TESCO

**Valdivieso Barrel** `16.5` `£5.99`
**Selection Syrah 2000,**
**Chilean Red**
Very berried, bustling richness,
superbly classy tannins and a
lovely lingering spiciness. A
superb Syrah/Shiraz for the
money.

**Australian Reserve** `16.0` `£4.99`
**Chardonnay, Tesco**
**2000, Australian White**
Superb example of Aussie
Chardonnay under a fiver: rich
textured, complex, plump yet

lithe, beautifully polished. Part of
Tesco's so-called 'Finest' range.

**Great with Chicken,** `16.5` `£3.99`
**Tesco 2000, French**
**White**
A superbly oily cultured wine of
deep fruit, slightly toffeed and
melony, and it has a superb
texture. And it would be great
with roast chicken.

**Chianti Classico,** `16.0` `£22.99`
**Castello di Fonterutoli**
**1998, Italian Red**
Delicious Chianti, remarkably
couth and hugely and devilishly
tannic. Laying it down for three
to four years will mitigate the
latter, but will the fruit still show
such vibrancy? I think so. One of
the finest Chiantis – 15 per cent of
the blend is Cabernet (plus 85 per
cent Sangiovese).

**Valdivieso Cabernet** `16.0` `£4.99`
**Sauvignon 2001,**
**Chilean Red**
Delicious chewy tannins, savoury
and rich, cling to the fruit for a
thrilling conclusion.

**Frescobaldi Pomino** `16.5` `£11.99`
**Benefizio 1998, Italian**
**White**
One of Italy's most compelling
white wines to compare, mutatis
mutandis, with fine Meursault. It
has beautiful texture, lovely
lingering creamy vegetality and
great elegance. 100 stores.

**Great with Pizza and** 16.0 £3.99
**Pasta Red, Tesco 2000,**
**Italian Red**
Soft and spicy, it lives up
effortlessly to its billing.

**Marlborough** 16.5 £6.49
**Sauvignon Blanc, Tesco**
**2001, New Zealand**
**White**
Starts crisp and clean then
develops a lovely, lifting
gooseberry richness. An elegant
white of great charm. Part of
Tesco's so-called 'Finest' range.

**Minervois, Tesco 2000,** 16.5 £4.99
**French Red**
Such insouciant richness and
tempered tannicity. Depth,
delicacy, daring and sheer velvet
class here. Part of Tesco's so-
called 'Finest' range.

**Fetzer Zinfandel/** 16.5 £5.99
**Shiraz 2000, USA Red**
Superbly cheeky blend of
chutzpah and cheerful cherries,
plums, raspberries, ripe tannins,
spice and a very lingering soft
finish. A very energetic wine of
great food compatibility.

**Great with Pizza and** 16.5 £3.99
**Pasta White, Tesco**
**2000, French White**
Yes, it's terrific, superb,
marvellous – and it speaks truly.
Has bright, rich, nutty fruit, is dry
and incisive and has a lovely crisp
finish.

**Thelema Mountain** 17.5 £9.99
**Chardonnay 1999,**
**South African White**
One of the Cape's greatest
Chardonnays in its subtle,
smokey richness and complex
vegetality. Brilliant balance and
elegance, and makes Le
Montrachet look distinctly dodgy
at five times the price. Wine
advisor stores only.

**Charles Heidsieck** 16.0 £23.49
**Réserve Mise en Cave**
**1996, French Sparkling**
**Wine/Champagne**
Compelling dryness and delicacy.
A bubbly to make the heart sing.
To be served to old soldiers on
their deathbeds.

**Luis Felipe Edwards** 16.5 £5.99
**Carmenère 2000,**
**Chilean Red**
Quite the perfect balance of
berries, tannins and acids, which
swing well together in textured
collusion. A memorably aromatic,
very modern carmenère of
scrumptiousness and stealth.

**Lawsons Dry Hills** 16.5 £7.99
**Sauvignon Blanc 2001,**
**New Zealand White**
Now screwcapped and all the
better for it. It'll keep its gorgeous
subtle freshness and flavour in
much better condition than any
cork. This is a beautifully subtle,
elegant Sauvignon.

**Valdivieso Merlot 2000,** 16.0 £4.99
**Chilean Red**
Soft as a Gucci loafer, half as

357

aromatic, twice as delicious and fifty times better value.

**Great with Curry, Tesco 2000, French White**  `16.0`  `£3.99`
A terrific, modern, warm-yet-crisp Sauvignon of zip yet melonosity. A lovely quaffing bottle. Does it suit curry? The milder sort, I guess, but it would not be my first choice – though Thai fish cakes would be excellent.

**Zorro Tempranillo/ Monastrell 2000, Spanish Red**  `16.0`  `£4.49`
Ripe, dry and hugely curry-friendly. Hugely entertaining richness and spicy tannicity. A lovely forward wine of brilliant unpretentious and fruity charm.

**Bordeaux Sauvignon Blanc, Tesco 2000, French White**  `16.0`  `£4.99`
A classy white wine of classic Bordeaux blanc proportions: clean, minerally, crisp and dry. Part of Tesco's so-called 'Finest' range.

**Concha y Toro Casillero del Diablo Cabernet Sauvignon 2000, Chilean Red**  `16.5`  `£3.99`
Berried up to its neck in hedgerow pickings, which present beautifully structured interplay between the tannins, the texture and the classy, complex finish.

## WAITROSE

**Cape Mentelle Cabernet/Merlot 1999, Australian Red**  `16.0`  `£10.49`
A Bordeaux blend-alike but far from taste-alike: this offers tar, tannins, nuts, liquorice, hedgerows and baked spices.

**L A Cetto Petite Sirah 1999, Mexican Red**  `16.0`  `£4.99`
Superb value. Has brilliant creamy, spicy berries and plump, rich tannins.

**Charles Heidsieck Réserve Mise en Cave 1996, French Sparkling Wine/Champagne**  `16.0`  `£27.49`
Compelling dryness and delicacy. A bubbly to make the heart sing. To be served to old soldiers on their deathbeds.

**Wither Hills Sauvignon Blanc 2001, New Zealand White**  `17.0`  `£7.99`
Has multi-layered lushness that retains a surprising complexity of fruits (including pineapple, pear and peach) and a rich finish.

**La Cetate Merlot 1999, Romanian Red**  `16.5`  `£4.99`
Magnificently assertive berries and fine tannins, great leathery texture and a rousing finish.

**Yellow Tail Merlot 2000, Australian Red**  `16.0`  `£4.99`
Different approach here. Has a crunchy leatheriness, spiced cherries and very good tannins.

**Errázuriz Syrah 2000,** 16.5 £7.99
**Chilean Red**
A delightfully serious yet
provocative Syrah (with one per
cent Cabernet) which has
individuality, poise, texture,
superb tannins and remarkably
couth richness.

**Bacchus English Table** 16.0 £7.99
**Wine 2000, English
White**
Certainly England's most
adventurous and stylish bottle –
and not only if we restrict
ourselves to the label. This is the
best 2000 vintage English
(Suffolk) white wine I've tasted.
Has lovely crisp, fresh fruit of
elegance and style.

**Amativo Salento 2000,** 16.0 £5.99
**Italian Red**
This has such rich exuberance
that it startles the palate with its
berried treasures just as the
tongue reels from the delicious
tannins.

**Pietracalda Fiano di** 17.5 £12.99
**Avellino 2000, Italian
White**
Has quite wonderful textured
fruit of highly tempered richness
without paranoia. Offers cashews,
milk chocolate, raspberry,
pineapple and, crucially, great
unmeshed acids. A wine to drink
in preference to much more
expensive Chardonnays. Available
at only 13 branches.

**Bodegas Lurton Pinot** 16.0 £4.49
**Gris 2000, Chilean
White**
Fantastic apricot dryness and crisp
nuttiness. A lithe, dry, classy
Pinot Gris of class and style.

**French Connection** 16.5 £4.99
**Réserve Viognier VdP
d'Oc 2000, French
White**
Has remarkably smooth, crisp
peach, apricot, lemon and
gooseberry with a touch of
macadamia on the finish.

**Basedow Barossa** 16.5 £5.99
**Valley Semillon 2000,
Australian White**
Superb texture, oily and free-
running. Terrific balance of acids
of ripe fruit – pineapple,
strawberry and melon.

**Gracia Chardonnay** 16.5 £5.99
**Reserva Superior 1999,
Chilean White**
Gently dry, delicately woody,
decidedly stylish and individual.
Lingering creaminess and subtle
vegetality combine on a finish of
considerable impact.

**Wither Hills** 18.0 £8.99
**Chardonnay 2000, New
Zealand White**
To be compared with the world's
finest Chardonnays. This slow-to-
evolve, creamy, vegetal, rich,
classic specimen has new world
chutzpah and old world subtlety.

**Kendermanns Cellar**    16.0    £5.99
**Selection Late Harvest**
**1999, Rheinhessen,**
**German White**
A delicious, sweet but far from
cloying wine to sip at the end of a
meal.

**Fairview Viognier 2001,**    16.0    £8.99
**South African White**
Pure apricot richness of
impressive finesse.

**Vouvray Pierre Brevin**    16.0    £5.75
**2000, Demi Sec, French**
**White**
What a lovely tangy richness.
Terrific, different, finely blended
minerals, acids and fruit.

**W2 Chardonnay 2000,**    16.0    £5.99
**Australian White**
Classy ripeness yet fresh nutty
edge to the acids, which confine,
deliciously, the characteristic
melon richness.

**Fairview Barrel**    16.0    £4.99
**Fermented Chenin**
**Blanc 2001, South**
**African White**
Very dry, surprisingly so for
Fairview, but the crispness of the
nuts and apricots, though very
subtle, is telling.

**Mehringer Zellerberg**    16.0    £5.99
**Riesling Kabinett 1993,**
**German White**
Delightful mineral tang to the
dry, rich fruit of great elegance.

**Castello di Arcano**    16.0    £6.99
**Superiore Pinot Grigio**
**2000 (Organic), Italian**
**White**
A beautifully dry, apricoty Pinot
Grigio with delicious, chewy,
nutty elegance.

**Wild Cat Catarratto**    17.0    £4.49
**2000 (Organic), Italian**
**White**
Beautifully oily, crunchy fruit
with raspberry, olives, melon and
a touch of chive. Remarkable
texture, highly individual and
classy.

**Château Terres Douces**    16.0    £5.69
**Cuvée Prestige 1999,**
**French White**
Startlingly original – lovely wood
integration – yet stays pertly fresh
and keen. Very classy and elegant.

**French Connection**    16.0    £4.99
**Réserve Marsanne/**
**Rousanne VdP d'Oc**
**2000, French White**
Slightly oily peach fruit with
gently citrusy surging acids to
provide balance. Superb value for
money.

**Bidoli Cabernet, Fruili**    16.0    £5.99
**2000, Italian Red**
Dry, peppery richness with
energetic blackberries and
gripping tannins.

**Château Segonzac,**    16.5    £6.99
**Premières Côtes de**
**Blaye 1999, French Red**
Superb claret for the money.
Spicy plums, blackberries,

cherries, herbs and meaty tannins all coalesce on the finish for a memorable climax.

**Santa Julia Bonarda/** 16.0 £4.49
**Sangiovese 2001,**
**Argentinian Red**
Superb texture, plummy, plump and ripe, with brilliant tannins backing rich, complex, warm, steady berries.

**Canepa Semillon 2001,** 16.0 £3.99
**Chilean White**
Deliciously chewy and under-ripe fruit with a hint of cob nut, melon and lime.

**Saumur Rouge 2000,** 16.0 £4.25
**Les Nivières, French**
**Red**
Gloriously minerally edge, slatey berries (black and rasp) and fine, lush tannins.

**Domaine Zind** 16.0 £3.99
**Humbrecht Riesling**
**Herrenweg 1999,**
**French White**
Delicious, dry peachy richness with nuts, minerals and a touch of honey.

**La Rena Salice** 16.0 £5.99
**Salentino Riserva 1998,**
**Puglia, Italian Red**
Remarkably warmly textured and chewy. The berries are ripe but not over-insistent and the tannins are finely spread.

**MontGras Cabernet/** 17.0 £6.99
**Syrah Reserva 2000,**
**Chilean Red**
Awesome texture here, where

layers of berries descend in order of sweetness to meet chocolate, cream, toffee and savoury tannins and then explode with quality and power in the throat.

**Hilltop Riverview** 16.0 3.99
**Chardonnay/Pinot**
**Grigio 2000, Hungarian**
**White**
A lovely rich, warm, spicy food wine that has sufficient heft to go with oriental cuisine.

**Abbotts Ammonite** 16.0 £4.99
**Côtes du Roussillon**
**2000, French Red**
An impressively cohesive blend of grapes. Smooth yet characterful, herby, rich, with good tannins and acids.

**Château Saint-Maurice,** 16.0 £4.49
**Côtes du Rhône 2000,**
**French Red**
A lovely jammy opening that provides herbs, then toffee, then berries – and only then do the tannins cruise in.

**Coteaux du Giennois** 16.0 £5.49
**2000, French White**
An individual, fresh (and very refreshing approach to) Sauvignon: crisp and clean as a whistle.

**Oyster Bay Sauvignon** 16.5 £6.99
**Blanc 2001, New**
**Zealand White**
Has beautiful pebbly and minerally acids allied to elongated gooseberry and lemon fruit.

**Huet Clos de Bourg**  `17.0`  `£9.95`
**Vouvray 1999, Demi
Sec, French White**
Gloriously individual, dry,
honeyed fruit and baked nuts. A
magnificent conversation piece.

**La Cite Cabernet**  `16.5`  `£3.99`
**Sauvignon VdP d'Oc
2000, French Red**
Superbly textured, complex and
charmingly fruity. Uniting berries,
acids, herbs, liquorice and tannins
in outstanding harmony.

**Cape Mentelle**  `17.0`  `£9.99`
**Semillon/Sauvignon
Blanc 2001, Australian
White**
Always one of Western
Australia's greatest whites, this
has tangy fruits and lovely acids
but will improve even further
over the next year.

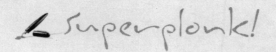
*Superplonk!*

**This book may end here, but *Superplonk* doesn't ...**

Visit ***www.superplonk.com*** for the latest wine news and up-to-date ratings and recommendations on thousands of wines.

With reviews of well over 6,000 wines ***www.superplonk.com*** is the definitive online guide to buying supermarket and high street wine. Updated daily to include new lines, the latest vintages and those special one-off superplonking bargains as they arrive on the shelves, the site has quickly become an indispensable adjunct to this book.

***Plus*:**

- Quickly find the wines you want using the powerful search capabilities
- Select and save your favourite wines in your own virtual cellar
- Print off a shopping list to take with you on your next shopping trip
- Become a critic yourself by adding your own comments and ratings to my reviews
- Grow your knowledge by browsing the articles in the *Superplonk World of Wine*
- Email your wine questions to me at *Ask Malcolm*
- And even take *superplonk.com* with you on your Palm pilot or Pocket PC.

All registered users get my weekly feature-packed newsletter full of all the last-minute wine deals which appear too late to make the book or even my *Guardian* column.

**So get online and sign up today for free at *www.superplonk.com* to get the lowdown on the best-value wines before everyone else does.**